ACT now.

Since getting into college is in the forefront of your thoughts, here's something that will help ease your mind.

The Princeton Review is giving away a free ACT, SAT, GMAT, GRE, LSAT, or MCAT course every other month.

Interested? Simply fill out the card on the right and mail it back to us. Every other month, in a random drawing, we'll choose one lucky winner who will be entitled to a free course.

So send in this card for a chance to take The Princeton Review on us.

For more information, call **(800) REVIEW-6**.

Entries must be received by August 14, 1995. You don't need to buy this book to enter. See official rules on reverse side.

WHOCARES

In a world of homelessness, AIDS, pollution, and poverty — why should you care?
(If you care, turn the page.)

"One of the Ten Best New Magazines of 1993."
— The Utne Reader and Library Journal.

I CARE!

Please enter my **charter** subscription at the special rate of only $15.00 for a year (4 issues) - a great savings off the newsstand rate.

Name: _____

Address: _____

City: _____ State: _____ Zip: _____

Payment Method

❑ Check enclosed

❑ AMEX ❑ VISA ❑ MasterCard (use envelope)

❑ Bill me (Institutions only)

Account No._____ Exp. Date_____

Signature _____

If you don't love *Who Cares*, you may cancel your subscription at any time and receive a full refund on all unreserved issues. Allow 4-6 weeks for delivery of your first issue.

Call 1-800-628-1692 to charge your order by phone, for you or a friend. A subscription to *Who Cares* makes a great gift! *Who Cares* is a nonprofit organization.

3PR1

THE PRINCETON REVIEW
2315 BROADWAY
THIRD FLOOR
NEW YORK NY 10024-4332

THE
PRINCETON
REVIEW

We Score More

WH◉CARES
30 Broad Street
Denville, NJ 07834

Who Cares: *A Journal of Service and Action* is a new magazine covering community service nationwide.

Nicole Kelly,
MBA, University of Michigan and founder of Hands On Greenville, a program that engages professionals in direct community service projects in South Carolina.

"It wasn't until after graduate school that I got involved in service," says Kelly, who first started volunteer tutoring through New York Cares, a program that provided the flexibility that she needed as an executive with Elizabeth Arden.

Henry Fernandez, J.D.,
Yale Law School and founder of the Leadership, Education, and Athletics in Partnership (L.E.A.P.) program in New Haven, CT.

"I like the camaraderie of people engaged in the struggle to make our neighborhood a better place for children and families." Fernandez founded L.E.A.P. to recruit college students as mentors and counselors for children in public housing developments and low income neighborhoods.

Created to inspire, challenge, and educate people who want to make a difference, *Who Cares* is about what works—and what doesn't— in community service and advocacy.
A resource for innovative ideas, a tool for turning visions into reality, and an ongoing source of constructive debate about solutions to society's most pressing problems, *Who Cares* has the edge.

**Call 1•800•628•1692 to subscribe now!
Satisfaction Guaranteed. Only $15.00/year**

***Who Cares*—the magazine for people who do**

THE PRINCETON
REVIEW

CRACKING THE ACT

1995-96 EDITION

THE PRINCETON REVIEW

Cracking the ACT

GEOFF MARTZ, KIM MAGLOIRE, AND
THEODORE SILVER, M.D.
EDITED BY ALICIA ERNST

1995-96 EDITION

NEW YORK 1995

Permission has been granted to reprint portions of the following:
The Unbearable Lightness of Being by Milan Kundera, Harper and
Row, New York, 1984, pp. 74–75
Far as the Human Eye Could See by Isaac Asimov, Doubleday and
Co., Garden City, 1986, pp. 60–61
Myth of the Robber Barons by Burtow W. Folsom Jr., Young Ameri-
cans Foundation, 1987, pp. 2–3
The Story of Art by E.H. Gombrich, Prentice Hall, 12th edition, 1972,
pp. 447–49

ISSN 1059-101X
ISBN 0-679-75912-3

ACT and American College Test are registered trademarks of the
American College Testing Program.

Manufactured in the United States of America

9 8 7 6 5 4 3 2

1995-96 Edition

FOREWORD

If you were a college admissions officer, what would you look for in a potential student?

That's an easy question. We've asked hundreds of admissions folks, and their answers are always the same. They want students who can handle the workload, who have a curiosity and desire to learn, and who will add something to the campus—impressive math or science skills, athletic or artistic ability, or just great personalities. Because most good schools want a diverse student body, they will look for students with unusual backgrounds or skills.

Here's a tougher question. Let's say you already had a record of each applicant's school performance over the past four years. *And* you had some essays he/she had written. *And* you had letters of recommendation from two of his/her teachers and from the school counselor. *And* you had met with the applicant for an hour to talk about his/her goals and record. What would you need, in addition to all of that, to see if that student was right for your college?

A. A measure of the student's raw intelligence

B. A measure of the student's reasoning ability

C. A national standard to check his/her grades in school

D. A rough prediction of his/her freshman year grades in college

E. His/her parents' bank account balances

Most admissions officers answer (C). Every school has a different way of grading students, and a different curriculum. Every school has teachers who are terrific, but who are very tough graders. Colleges need some common measure against which they can judge students from hundreds of high schools. The ACT was originally designed to give colleges a rough idea of how much you'd learned in math, English, science, and history.

The SAT, on the other hand, supposedly measures intelligence. (Actually, it doesn't measure much of anything). Even though we've rarely met a director of admissions who answered (A) or (B), most colleges require students to take the SAT. Between the actual test and preparation for it, the U.S. spends over $100 million every year on the SAT.

Which is why the ACT was changed a few years ago to test reasoning and intelligence—because testing intelligence is sexier than testing math skills, even though your ability to reason is evident in your essays, interviews, recommendations, and grades, *and even though there has never been a single study to suggest that the ACT and SAT actually measure intelligence.* Although the ACT measures less than it once did, it is now accepted at almost every college in the country.

Despite its shifting emphasis, the ACT remains a better test than the SAT (neither test, by the way, predicts college grades with any accuracy), especially if you're the kind of student who understands the material but doesn't perform well on tests. The ACT staff is friendly and helpful, and you should feel free to call them if you're confused about the testing process or about a specific question on the test.

And if they can't help you, feel free to call us.

—John Katzman
President
The Princeton Review

P.S. If you are paying attention to the problems colleges are having today, you might have answered (E) on that multiple choice question. College has become very expensive. Don't let that discourage you, though. A college diploma will more than pay for itself in the job market, and with some good advice (speak to the financial aid people at the schools to which you're apply-ing), grants, work, and some debt, almost everyone can still afford college.

ACKNOWLEDGMENTS

A test preparation course is much more than clever techniques and powerful computer score reports; the reason our results are so great is that our teachers care so much. Five years ago a small group of Princeton Review instructors enthusiastically created a program to prepare students for the previous version of the ACT. We would like to thank John Cauman, Judy Moreland, and Jim Reynolds for their commitment to the original ACT and PRA projects.

The completion of this book would not have been possible without the help and dedication of several individuals. We would like to thank Mike Freedman for his revision of the PRA, Linda Tarleton for her work on the reading chapter, Andrea Paykin and Julian Ham for making our words look so good, and Rob Zopf for his patience. We would also like to thank Adam Robinson and David Owen for giving us a fine launch, and John Katzman for his unceasing faith in our work.

CONTENTS

PART I

Orientation

We at The Princeton Review have a reputation for test bashing that is pretty richly deserved. In general, we don't have many nice things to say about the tests we tackle or the organizations that write them. So it's a pleasure this time to take on what we feel is essentially a fair and good-hearted test, written by intelligent people who do not have a mean bone in their collective body.

The ACT measures what it says it does: academic achievement. It doesn't pretend to measure your ability or your intelligence. The people at ACT admit that you can increase your score by preparing for the test. They even put out their own coaching book.

So if we ever seem to be poking fun at the test, or the people who write it, we want you to remember that it does not lessen our underlying affection and respect.

If there is any flaw in the ACT, it is that in its attempt to be fair, it has become a little, well, predictable. Of course, when we say that the ACT is a completely predictable test, we mean it in the nicest possible way. We *like* predictable tests.

THE ACT IS A ~~STANDARDIZED~~ PREDICTABLE TEST

From now on, whenever you see the word "standardized," think "predictable" instead. The ACT tests the same information the same way, year after year. For example, there are always 14 plane geometry questions on the ACT. Not 13, not 15. Exactly 14. There are exactly 10 questions on punctuation. You can count on it. Even the way they ask the questions is predictable, based on the need for a standardized product.

The review you will find in this book is based on the very specific knowledge you need to do well on this test. The test-taking strategies we have developed are designed to take advantage of the ACT's predictability.

I HAVE GOOD GRADES IN SCHOOL.
DO I NEED TO PREPARE?

Let's take the hypothetical case of Sid. Sid is valedictorian of his class, editor of the school paper, and the only teenager ever to win the Nobel Prize. To support his widowed mother, he sold more seeds from the back of comic books than any other person in recorded history. He speaks eight languages in addition to being able to communicate with dolphins and wolves. He has recommendations from General Schwarzkopf *and* Mother Teresa. So if Sid had a bad day when he took the ACT (the plane bringing him back from his medal of freedom award presentation was late) we are pretty sure that he is going to be just fine anyway.

But Sid wants to make sure that when his colleges look at his ACT score, they see the same high-calibre student they see when they look at the rest of his application.

I HAVE LOUSY GRADES IN SCHOOL. IS THERE ANY HOPE?

Let's take the case of Tom. Tom didn't do outstandingly well in high school. In fact, he has been on academic probation since kindergarten. He has caused four of his teachers to give up teaching as a profession, and prides himself on his perfect homework record: he's never done any. Not ever. But if Tom aces his ACT, a college might decide that he is actually a misunderstood genius, and give him a full scholarship.

Most of us, of course, fall between these two extremes. So is it important to prepare for the ACT?

If you were to look in the information bulletin of any of the colleges in which you are interested, we can pretty much guarantee that somewhere you would find the following paragraph:

> "Many factors go into the acceptance of a student by a college. Test scores are *only one* of these factors—grades in high school, extracurricular activities, essays, and recommendations are also important, and may in some cases outweigh test scores."

(1995 University of Anywhere Bulletin)

Truer words were never spoken. In our opinion, just about *every* other element in your application "package" is more important than your test scores. The Princeton Review (among other organizations) has been telling colleges for years that scores on the ACT or the SAT are pretty incomplete measures of a student's overall abilities. Some colleges have stopped looking at test scores entirely, and others are downplaying their importance.

SO WHY, IF ALL THIS IS TRUE, SHOULD YOU SPEND ANY TIME AT ALL PREPARING FOR THE ACT?

Because, out of all the elements in your application "package," your ACT score is the easiest to *change*. The grades you've received up to now are written in stone. You aren't going to become captain of the football team or editor of the school paper overnight. Your essays will only be as good as you can write them, and recommendations are only as good as your teachers' memories of you.

On the other hand, in a few weeks you can radically change your score on the ACT (and the way colleges will look at your application). The test does not pretend to measure ability or intelligence. It measures your knowledge of specific skills like grammar, algebra, and reading comprehension.

WHEN IT COMES TO THE ACT, *NOTHING* IS WRITTEN IN STONE

It doesn't matter how well you've done in school up to now. Good grades are not a guarantee that you will do well on the ACT. It doesn't matter if you've always been bad at taking standardized tests before. Colleges aren't going to see any of your scores from earlier standardized tests (not even scores from previous ACTs). It doesn't matter if you hate math in general or English in general or science in general. The ACT doesn't measure math in general. It measures the math that is on the ACT.

By reviewing the very specific knowledge that the people who write the ACT think is important, and by learning good test-taking strategy, it should be possible to increase your ACT score significantly. This is not just our opinion. Even the people who write the test agree.

WHAT IS THE ACT?

The ACT is a multiple-choice standardized test which is supposed to measure your knowledge of some of the subjects taught in high school. With breaks, the test takes about three and a half hours. It is divided into four sections which are always given in the same order.

1. English (45 minutes—75 questions)

In this section you will see short reading passages on the left side of the page. Some words or phrases will be underlined. On the right side of the page, you will be asked whether the underlined portion is correct as written or whether one of the three alternatives listed would be better. This is a test of grammar, punctuation, sentence structure, and rhetorical skills. At the end of each passage there will be a few questions about overall organization and style, or perhaps about how the writing could be revised or strengthened.

2. Math (60 minutes—60 questions)

These are the regular multiple-choice math questions you've been doing all your life. The easier questions *tend* to come first—they test basic math proficiency. A good third of the test covers pre-algebra and elementary algebra. Slightly less than a third will cover intermediate algebra and coordinate geometry (graphing). Regular geometry accounts for less than a quarter of the questions, and there will be a few questions (toward the end) about trigonometry.

3. Reading (35 minutes—40 questions)

In this section there will be four reading passages of about 750 words each—the average length of a *People* magazine article, although maybe not as interesting. There is always one fiction passage, one science passage, one "humanities" passage, and one social science passage, but they are not always in the same order from test to test. After each passage you will be asked ten questions.

4. Science (35 minutes—40 questions)

No specific scientific knowledge is necessary for the science test. You won't need to know the chemical makeup of hydrochloric acid or any formulas. Instead, you will be asked to understand seven sets of scientific information presented in graphs, charts, tables, research summaries, or conflicting viewpoints.

There may be one additional section on the ACT that you take. It will look just like one of the other sections, but it won't count toward your score. During this section, you will pay for the privilege of being a guinea pig while the test writers at ACT try out some experimental questions on you.

WHERE DOES THE ACT COME FROM?

The ACT is written by a company called American College Testing. The company's main offices are in Iowa City, Iowa. The people at ACT have been writing a version of this test since 1959. Even if you aren't looking forward to taking the ACT this year, you would probably prefer it to the version they used to give. In the old days the test included detailed questions about topics like the Constitution of the United States, electrostatic forces, and planets in the solar system.

The people at ACT also write a number of other tests, including the medical school admission test (MCAT), a test for professional golfers, and a test for dieticians. About a million high school students take the ACT every year.

HOW IS THE ACT SCORED?

Between four and seven weeks after you take the ACT, you and the colleges you have selected, if any, will receive your ACT scores in the mail. Unfortunately, ACT won't give anyone permission to reprint its score report, but since its score report provides very limited information—basically, scores and percentile ranking—it is easy to describe.

Scores in each of the four sections of the test are reported on a scale of 1 to 36 (36 being the highest score possible). Next to each scaled score is a percentile ranking. Percentile ranking refers to the percentage of people who performed better or worse than you did on the test. For instance, a percentile ranking of 87 indicates that 87% of the people who took the test scored lower than you did, and 13% scored higher.

Some of the sections have subheadings as well. English is broken down into Usage/Mechanics and Rhetorical Skills. The subcategories may be of some marginal use to colleges; they are much more useful to you if you decide to take the test again, as a way to pinpoint your strengths and weaknesses. In these subheadings, scores are reported on a scale of 1 to 18 (18 being the highest score possible). They are also reported as percentiles. Finally, at the bottom of the page, you will find a composite score. This is an average of what you received on the four main sections.

WHEN SHOULD YOU TAKE THE ACT?

The test is given five times each year, usually at 8 A.M. on a Saturday morning. Most students take the ACT in the spring of junior year or in the fall of senior year. A good case can be made for taking it at the earlier date. For one thing, you'll have a better idea of where you stand. If your score is about what you want, you can spend the summer visiting the colleges in which you are interested, or getting started on your applications. If your score is lower than you want, you can use the summer to prepare to take the test again in the fall.

You can obtain a registration packet at your high school guidance office, or by writing or calling ACT at:

ACT Registration Department
P.O. Box 414
Iowa City, IA 52243
Tel #: 319/337-1270

But before you decide on a test date, there is something you should know....

Some ACT Test Dates are Better than Others

On certain dates, the ACT offers what it calls "Test Information Release." If you take the ACT on one of these dates, you can, for a small fee, receive a copy of the test that you took, and for a small additional fee, a photocopy of your actual answer sheet. We strongly advise that you take the test on one of these dates. It is not unheard of for ACT to make a mistake in scoring. You certainly won't find out about this unless you can see the test you took and your own answers. For example, it is possible to fill in an oval on the answer sheet darkly enough for the human eye to see, but not darkly enough for the scantron machine that scores the test to read. In this case, if you point it out to them, for another small additional fee, ACT will hand-score your test, and change your grade if they made a mistake.

This year three of the five test dates will have test information release. Check your registration booklet for exact dates.

WHAT IF I'VE ALREADY TAKEN THE ACT ONCE BEFORE?

The nice folks at ACT allow you to decide which of your ACT scores they report to the colleges. If you want to have full control over this, it is a good idea *not* to take advantage of the three, free score reports ACT will send to colleges directly after the test. Why send colleges scores you might not want them to see? While it costs a few extra dollars to get ACT to send scores to schools later, it is well worth being able to send the colleges your best results.

HOW TO PREPARE FOR THE ACT

The Princeton Review review materials and test-taking techniques contained in this book should give you all the information you'll need to improve your score on the ACT. However, you will also need to practice our techniques and reinforce your review of math and verbal skills by taking some practice tests.

Some popular coaching books contain several complete practice ACT tests. We would strongly advise you *not* to waste your time taking these tests. Unfortunately, the questions in these books are not real ACT questions. Some of the questions in these books cover material that is not even on the real ACT. Others give the impression that the ACT is much easier or more difficult than it really is. In some cases, taking the practice tests offered in these books could actually hurt your score.

One reason these coaching books do not use real ACT questions is that the folks at ACT won't let them. The American College Testing company has refused to let anyone (including us) license actual questions from old tests.

Cynics might suggest that this is because the American College Testing company has its *own* review book, which it sells for $12.95, called *The Official Guide to the ACT Assessment*. Although *The Official Guide* doesn't contain a very full review section and its test-taking strategies are a little gentle (after all, it is hard to burgle your own house), we think their book is worth the price just for the three real tests it contains. We recommend that you either buy their book or ask your high school to send away to ACT for back copies of old tests.

WHAT IS THE PRINCETON REVIEW?

The Princeton Review is a coaching school based in New York City. It has offices in over forty cities across the country and several branches abroad. The Princeton Review's test-taking techniques and review strategies are unique and powerful. We developed them after studying all the real ACT tests we could get our hands on, and analyzing them with sophisticated computer programs.

A FINAL THOUGHT BEFORE YOU BEGIN

The ACT does not measure intelligence and it does not predict your ultimate success or failure as a human being. No matter how high or how low you score on this test initially—and no matter how much you may increase your score through preparation—you should *never* consider the score you receive on this or any other test a final judgment of your abilities.

CHAPTER 1

Triage

WOULDN'T IT BE GREAT IF...

Wouldn't it be great if all the questions on the ACT were arranged in order of difficulty? Then you could do the easiest question first, and then the next easiest, and so on. That way you wouldn't waste a lot of time trying to answer difficult questions before you had answered all the easy questions, which count for the same number of points anyway.

Unfortunately, the ACT is not really organized that way.

According to the ACT test writers we interviewed, the English section of the test is not in any order of difficulty. In the math section, according to ACT literature, "most people find the first questions on the test easier... than the ones that come later" but these are only very rough guidelines. Many Princeton Review students find that some questions toward the end of the test are easier than most of the questions that preceded them.

OH. BUT WHAT IF...

But what if, in the science and reading sections, the *passages* were arranged in order of difficulty? Some of the test preparation books you can buy in bookstores maintain that the passages in the reading section and the science section are in order of difficulty. According to one ACT test writer, this is true, "... only in an average sense. We believe in the *philosophy* that if students are running out of time, the questions they don't get to should be ones they would have difficulty with anyway. But students will find plenty of exceptions."

OH. BUT...

It's no use. On the ACT, if you want to do the easy questions first, you're going to have to find them for yourself. We have a good way to think about this. We call it "Triage."

TRIAGE

This is a medical term that describes a technique used by emergency room doctors when they have several emergencies at the same time. In order to save lives, the doctors treat the patients with the worst wounds or illness first, then progress downward in severity, until they finally get around to the patient with the scratch on his nose.

In ACT triage, we want you to learn to do exactly the same thing—*in reverse*. See that really tough algebra problem lying over there? Forget it, it's a goner. Send for the chaplain. Now this easy addition problem, on the other hand—this is one to do right now.

See that tough, horrible passage about European author-itarianism during the nineteenth century? Let's see if it's still breathing after we finish the one about Jimmy Carter's election in 1976.

JUST ONE MORE MINUTE...

The temptation to get stubborn and stay with a particular problem can be very strong, especially when it is an early one. We've all had the experience of *thinking* we were on the verge of an answer. But if it takes you four minutes to solve question number five, that might mean you will never get a chance to look at several other questions later in the test that you would have found easy.

"Oh Yeah!"

We've also all had the experience of riding home in the car, and suddenly clapping our hand to our forehead as we finally realized exactly how to do question number five. By using triage, you can sometimes have this burst of revelation *before* the test is over, when you can still do something about it. So how does triage work exactly?

NOW, LATER, MUCH LATER

Do you want to do the problem NOW? That is the question you should constantly be asking yourself during the exam. If you finish reading a problem and immediately know how to solve it, then of course you should do it right away.

But what if you finish reading a problem and you aren't really certain how to begin? Put a circle around it and move on. This might seem hard to do at first, but it is one of the central tenets of good test taking, and it gets easier with practice. You aren't skipping the problem forever. You're just putting it at the back of the line.

TWO PASSES

We want you to do each section in two passes. During the **first pass**, the object is to nail every single question that already has your name on it. By answering all the questions you're sure of, you will never have to hear the words, "O.K., pencils down," and know that there were several more questions you could have done if only there had been more time. You will already have done them.

WHAT HAPPENS IF I THINK I KNOW HOW TO DO IT, BUT THEN I REALIZE I WAS WRONG?

Nobody's right all the time. As soon as you realize you're stuck, you should put a big circle around the question and move on. This is the time when people tend to get stubborn. They think, "But I've already spent so much time on this question. It would be a waste to skip it now."

YOU HAVEN'T WASTED THE TIME; YOU'VE INVESTED IT

When you come back to this question on the second pass, you won't be starting from scratch. You'll already have read the question once. You might have made some notes in the margin. Perhaps reading it again will make you realize an important point you missed the first time. If not, throw it to the back of the list, and count your blessings: you could still be back there working on question number five!

THE SECOND PASS

Now, with about ten minutes left in the section, come back to the questions you circled for a **second pass**. Again, think ACT triage. Most of the "patients" in your emergency room have now been handled. Look over the remaining problems and ask yourself the same question: Which one do I want to do NOW? Obviously, none of them struck you as *easy* the first time or you would have done them on the first pass. On the other hand, among the remaining problems, some are probably more likely bets than others.

Sometimes when you read a question again, you suddenly realize what the point of the question really is. This will save you from having that "Oh yeah!" revelation riding home in the car. Sometimes when you reread a question, you suddenly realize that you will hate this question for the rest of your life and you never, ever want to see it again. Fine. Throw it to the back of the list, and keep looking.

Sometimes you rejected a question initially because you thought it would take too much time. Well, now you have time. You've already locked in all the sure points, so maybe this is the question to do now.

O.K., I'VE DONE ALL THE QUESTIONS I KNOW HOW TO DO, AND ALL THE QUESTIONS I THINK I KNOW HOW TO DO. NOW WHAT?

You guess. Guessing on the ACT is so important that we've given it its own chapter.

CHAPTER 2

Guessing and POE

Imagine for a moment that you are a contestant on *Let's Make a Deal*. It's the final, big deal of the day. Monty Hall asks you, "Do you want curtain number one, curtain number two, or curtain number three?" As you carefully weigh your options, the members of the audience are screaming out their suggestions. But you can bet that there is one suggestion no one in the audience is going to shout to you:

"Skip the question!"

It wouldn't make sense. You have a one in three shot of winning, and there is no penalty for guessing wrong. (O.K., you might have to cart home a lifetime supply of toilet paper.)

On the ACT, you don't even have to worry about the toilet paper, because there is no guessing penalty at all.

YOU MUST ANSWER EVERY SINGLE QUESTION ON THE ACT

There are 255 questions on the ACT. If you went in to the test room, filled out your name and then went to sleep for three and a half hours, your composite score would be just about what you might expect: 0.

However, if you went into the test room, filled out our name, went to sleep for 3 and a *quarter* hours, and then picked answer choice "B" 255 times, guess what your composite score would be? 12!

We would not recommend random guessing as an *overall* strategy (unless all you need is a 12), but you can see that it is in your interest to guess on every question.

Ah, but there's guessing and then there's guessing.

HOW TO SCORE HIGHER ON THE ACT

Try the following question:

What is the French word for "eggplant"?

What? You don't know? Well then, you'd better guess at random. (By the way, there are no questions about vegetables, French or otherwise, on the ACT. We're just using this question to make a point.)

If you really don't know the answer to a question, of course, you should always guess. But before you choose an answer at random, take a look at the problem the way you would see it on the ACT:

1. What is the French word for eggplant?

    A. のみもの
    B. すきやき
    C. aubergine
    D. デザート

Suddenly the question looks a lot easier, doesn't it? You may not have known the correct answer to this question, but you certainly knew three answers that were incorrect.

POE

The Process of Elimination (POE for short) will enable you to make your guesses really count. Incorrect answer choices are often easier to spot than correct ones. Sometimes they are logically absurd; sometimes they just sound wrong. While you will rarely be able to eliminate *all* the incorrect answer choices, it is often possible to eliminate one or two. And each time you can eliminate an answer choice, your odds of guessing correctly get better.

Try another question:

1. What is the Sioux Indian word for "beautiful"?

    A. hopa
    B. のみもの
    C. hunhe
    D. デザート

This time you could probably only eliminate two of the answer choices. However, that meant you were down to a fifty-fifty guess—much better than random guessing.

The Process of Elimination is a tremendously powerful tool. We will refer to it in every single chapter of this book.

THE ACT vs. THE SAT

You may have to take the ACT anyway, but many of the schools you're interested in will also accept the SAT. We think the SAT is nowhere near as good a test as the ACT. Whereas the ACT says it measures "achievement" (which we believe *can* be measured), the SAT says it measures "ability" (which we don't think can be measured at all; and if it can, the SAT sure isn't doing it).

While we are obviously not tremendously fond of the SAT, you should know that some students end up scoring substantially higher on the SAT than they do on the ACT.

WHAT, EXACTLY, ARE THE DIFFERENCES?

The verbal sections of the SAT are designed primarily to test vocabulary. If you have a strong vocabulary but are weak on usage, it could be to your advantage to take the SAT.

The math sections on the SAT are trick oriented, with a heavier emphasis on arithmetic. However, there is no trigonometry and virtually no coordinate geometry. If your strengths lie in arithmetic, the SAT might get you a higher score.

To find out which test might be better for you, we have devised the PRA (Princeton Review Assessment) which appears at the back of this book.

WHAT IS THE PRA?

The Princeton Review Assessment is a test that is used to predict your scores on both the ACT and the SAT. The test allows you to see whether it would be in your interest to take the SAT instead of (or as well as) the ACT. An answer key and score charts are provided on the pages right after the test. By following the step-by-step directions you can get approximate scores for both tests, and compare them using the conversion chart used by many colleges. In addition, the answer key tells you which types of question come from which test, so you can assess your performance on each directly.

Because it is brief, the PRA will only give you a possible range of scores. If there is only a slight discrepancy between your projected ACT and SAT scores, it certainly isn't worth taking both. However, if there's a big difference in favor of the SAT, you should consider taking the SAT as well.

Taking the ACT

The best way to prepare for any test is to find out exactly what is going to be on it. This book will provide you with just that information. In the following chapters you will find a comprehensive review of all the question types on the ACT, complete information on all the subjects covered by the ACT, and some powerful test-taking strategies developed specifically for the ACT.

To take full advantage of the review and the techniques, it's important that you practice on real ACT questions. We've already told you in the first chapter how to obtain copies of real ACT tests.

Periodically, as you work through this book, you should take a real ACT practice test. This will allow you to chart your progress, give you confidence in our techniques, and develop your stamina. Don't bother to take the practice tests in other coaching books. No matter how carefully they were written, they will never be real ACT questions. We've found that some of the exams in these books cover information that is not tested on the ACT at all. Other books inadvertently gloss over important subjects.

THE NIGHT BEFORE THE TEST

Unless you are the kind of person who remains calm only by staying up all night to do last-minute studying, we recommend that you take the evening off. Go see a movie, or read a good book, and make sure you get to bed at a normal hour. No final frantic math formula or grammatical rule is going to make or break your score. A positive mental attitude comes from treating yourself decently. If you've prepared over the last several weeks or months, then you're ready.

If you haven't really prepared, there will be other opportunities to take the test, so get some rest and do the best you can. Remember, the colleges will only see the score you choose to let them see. No *one* ACT is going to be crucial. We don't think night-before-the-test cramming is very effective. For example, we would not recommend that you try going through this book in one night.

ON THE DAY OF THE TEST

It's important that you eat a real breakfast, even if you normally don't. We find that about two thirds of the way through the test, people who didn't eat something beforehand suddenly lose the will to live. Equally important, bring a snack to the test center. You will get several breaks, during which food is allowed. Some people spend the breaks out in the hallways comparing answers and getting upset when their answers don't match. Ignore the people around you, and eat your snack. Why assume they know any more than you do?

WARMING UP

While you're having breakfast, do a couple of questions from an ACT you've already seen before to get your mind working. You don't want to use the first section of the real test to warm up.

At the test center, you'll be asked to show some form of picture I.D. or provide a note from your school, on school stationary, describing what you look like. The time is NOT announced during the test sections, so you should also bring a reliable watch—not the beeping kind—and, of course, several number two pencils and an eraser.

When you get into the actual room where you'll be taking the test, make sure you're comfortable. Is there enough light? Is your desk sturdy? Don't be afraid to speak up; you're going to be spending three and a half hours at that desk.

ZEN AND THE ART OF TEST-TAKING

Once the test begins, tune out the rest of the world. That person with the annoying cough in the next row? You don't hear her. The person who is fidgeting in the seat ahead of you? You don't see him. It's just you and the test. Everything else should be a blur.

As soon as one section ends, erase it completely from your mind. It no longer exists. The only section that counts is the one you are taking right now. Even if you are upset about a particular section, erase it from your mind. Most people in the middle of taking the ACT are not great at assessing how a particular section went anyway. We once asked a group of students who were taking a practice test to write down at the end of each section how they thought they were doing compared to past tests. There was practically no correlation at all.

KEEP YOUR ANSWERS TO YOURSELF

Please don't let anyone cheat off you. Test companies have developed sophisticated anti-cheating measures that go way beyond having a proctor walk around the room. We know of one test company that gets seating charts of each testing room. Their computers scan the score sheets of people sitting in an immediate vicinity for correlations of wrong answer choices. Innocent and guilty are invited to take the test over again, and their scores from the first are invalidated.

MISBUBBLING YOUR ANSWER SHEET

Probably the most painful kind of mistake you can make on the ACT is to bubble in A with your number two pencil when you really meant B. The proctor isn't allowed to let you change your answers after a section is over, so it is fairly important that you either catch yourself before the section ends, or—even better—that you don't make a mistake in the first place.

We suggest to our students that they write down their answers in their test booklet. This way, whenever they finish a page of questions in the test booklet, they can transfer all their answers from that page in a group. We find this cuts down the possibility of misnumbering, and saves time as well. Of course, as you get near the end of a section, you should go back to bubbling question by question.

If you get back your scores from ACT and they seem completely out of line, you can ask the ACT examiners to look over your answer sheet for what are called "gridding errors." If you want to, you can even be there while they look. If it is clear that there has been an error, ACT will change your score. An example of a clear gridding error would be a section in which, if you moved all the responses over by one, they would suddenly all be correct.

SHOULD I EVER CANCEL MY SCORE AT THE TEST CENTER?

No. ACT allows you to cancel your score at *any* time, even after they have graded your test and sent it back to you. If you did badly, wouldn't it make sense to find out how badly, and learn on which areas you need to work?

If you have already requested that this test date's scores be sent to colleges, you may ultimately decide to cancel, but you should still go home and think about it for a day. There's no need to make a hasty decision.

PART II

How to Beat the ACT English Test

THERE'S AN ABSENCE OF SOLAR WARMTH WHEN SHE'S AWAY FROM THE PREMISES

Deciding what constitutes good writing is difficult. So much depends on the context, on what the writer is trying to accomplish—and on who is doing the deciding.

CALL US IGNORANT, CALL US SENTIMENTAL, BUT WE PREFER "AIN'T NO SUNSHINE WHEN SHE'S GONE"

These days, there are even computer programs that are supposed to fix our writing. Mike Royko, the national columnist, recently decided to try out one of these computer programs on Abraham Lincoln's Gettysburg Address, with predictably humorous results. "Four-score and seven years ago" became "eighty seven years ago" and it went downhill from there, turning a moving document of history into trite, conventional, standard written English.

WHAT THE ENGLISH ACT TEST TESTS

The English section of this test measures how well you understand "the conventions of standard written English." There are five passages to read. Portions of the passages will be underlined, and you must decide whether these portions are correct as they stand, or whether one of the other answer choices is better.

These questions are designed to measure punctuation (10 questions), grammar (12 questions), and sentence structure (18 questions). Other questions are designed to see how you might revise and strengthen a passage (11 questions), whether you would change particular words for style or clarity (12 questions), or how you might "explain or support a point of view [more] clearly and effectively" (12 questions). There are a total of 75 questions to answer in 45 minutes.

WHAT YOUR SCORE MEANS

Good writing is, to some extent, a matter of opinion. No matter how well or how badly you do on the English portion of this test, you should not feel that your ACT score truly represents your ability to write. A good score does not make you the next Jane Austen; a bad score does not make you the next Bart Simpson.

We don't mean to imply that ACT is doing a bad job. It's tough to measure English skills, and we think the test writers have constructed a fine test. In the end, however, what the ACT English test is measuring is how well you take the ACT English test.

REMEMBER, THIS IS A STANDARDIZED TEST

PREDICTABLE

Every time the ACT is given, it tests the same things, the same way. You don't need to be a strong writer to do well on this test. You *do* need to know what types of errors crop up again and again.

We are going to review all the punctuation, grammar, sentence structure, and rhetorical skills that are tested on this exam.

WHAT DO THE PASSAGES LOOK LIKE?

Here is part of a sample passage:

When studying a foreign language, <u>its</u>
₁

1. **A.** NO CHANGE
   B. its'
   C. it's
   D. it, is

helpful to have a grasp <u>with</u> other
₂

2. **F.** NO CHANGE
   G. of
   H. to
   J. OMIT the underlined portion

foreign <u>languages, if only</u>
₃
because one has already learned what
things are most important to know how
to say first.

3. **A.** NO CHANGE
   B. languages. Only
   C. languages, only if
   D. language: only if

I am proud to tell you that I can ask,
"Where is the bathroom?" in four
different languages, but this pales
beside the accomplishments of my
clumsy friend, Al. He can <u>says</u> he is
₄
sorry in fourteen different languages.

4. **F.** NO CHANGE
   G. say
   H. said
   J. says that

5. Considering the subject matter and tone of the passage, is the writer's use of the pronoun "I" appropriate?

   A. No, because the writer is speaking about the general experience of learning a language.
   B. No, because the writer is not just discussing her own experiences but also those of her friend.
   C. Yes, because this is an informal narrative which needs a personal feel.
   D. Yes, because there is no way for the author to get across her thoughts without the personal pronoun.
   (answers: 1C, 2G, 3A, 4G, 5C)

TRIAGE

In Chapter One, we introduced you to the concept of triage, and told you that it would be useful on every section of this test. In this section, the ACT test writers have concocted their own brand of triage by organizing the questions so that the easier specific questions (on subjects like punctuation and grammar and sentence structure) tend to come first. At the end of each passage, there will be a couple of tougher rhetoric questions based on the passage as a whole.

However, some rhetoric questions are sprinkled throughout the questions — and just because a question is at the beginning of a passage or because it only deals with a small mistake in grammar doesn't mean that you will necessarily spot the correct answer right away. If you are not sure what point of grammar, or punctuation, or sentence structure is being tested, you might want to circle the question and move on.

In our students' experience, the format of this section — passages side by side with the questions — tends to make them want to guess too quickly. The impulse to pick the first answer that sounds good is sometimes very strong. After all, this *is* English, which for many of us is our first language.

The problem, of course, is that it is *not* English exactly — at least not the English we speak every day.

ACT ISLAND

Imagine that a bunch of ACT test writers were shipwrecked on a desert island about twenty years ago. Not having much to do, they go on writing tests, which they slip into empty bottles and cast into the sea. The tests regularly wash up on the coast of Iowa (yes, we know that Iowa is land-locked), where the national headquarters for the American College Testing company is located. The company is grateful, and uses the tests regularly.

The only problem is that, after twenty years, the test writers' English is getting a little old-fashioned and stilted. Still, the company feels a lot of loyalty to these shipwrecked mariners, and wouldn't dream of changing their tests.

If you make a lot of mistakes in this section it is probably because you are relying on your ear—which is used to hearing a less formal English than is spoken on the ACT. A much better way to approach this section is to look for the specific errors that appear on the test all the time. By looking for these errors, you can take the guesswork out of your approach to the English ACT test.

LOOKING FOR CLUES

One of the best ways to look for errors is to search the answer choices for clues. The underlined portions are very short, usually only a few words, so it's easy to see how each choice is different from the others. These differences offer a strong indication of what is on the minds of the ACT test writers. Look at the following example:

27. **A.** NO CHANGE
    B. one goes
    C. you go
    D. he goes

Clearly, this question is about pronouns. Even if you had not spotted something wrong with the underlined portion of the passage as you read it, the answer choices are telling you to check to see which of these pronouns agrees with the noun referred to in the passage. (Don't worry if you are rusty on pronouns—we'll cover them in detail later in this section.)

In the sections that follow we will show you the key elements to look for in the passages *and in the answer choices*.

WHAT IF THERE IS MORE THAN ONE THING WRONG?

There is often more than one error in the underlined portion of a sentence. However, the best way to approach these questions is not to try to see everything at once. Find *one* error. Eliminate the answer choices that contain the same error. Then look among the remaining answer choices for the one you like best.

NO CHANGE

Many of the questions in this section have NO CHANGE as the first of the answer choices. This turns out to be the correct answer a bit less than a quarter of the time when the choice is offered.

OMIT THE UNDERLINED PORTION

A few of the questions in this section will have "OMIT the underlined portion" as the last of the four answer choices. When this choice is offered it has a high probability of being correct—better than half the time on the tests we have been able to look at.

While this may change (perhaps when this book comes out) it is worth noting that when you do see the OMIT option, you should examine it very carefully indeed.

A WARNING

To forestall the objections of the expert grammarians out there, let us say at the outset that this discussion is not designed to be an all-inclusive discussion of English grammar and usage. You are reading this chapter to do well on the English section of the ACT. Thus, if we seem to oversimplify a point, or ignore an arcane exception to a rule, it's because we do not feel that any more detail is warranted.

BEFORE WE BEGIN, SOME TERMINOLOGY

The ACT is not going to ask you to identify parts of speech, or diagram a sentence, but it will be helpful for the discussion that follows if you know some basic definitions.

Here's a simple sentence:

Tom broke the vase.

This sentence is made up of two nouns, a verb and an article.

- A **noun** is a word used to name a person, place, thing, or idea.

- A **verb** is a word that expresses action.

- An **article** is a word that modifies or limits a noun.

In the sentence above, *Tom* and *vase* are both nouns. *The* is an article. *Broke* is a **verb**. *Tom* is the **subject** of the sentence because it is the person, place, or thing about which something is being said. *Vase* is the **object** of the sentence because it receives the action of the verb.

Here's a more complicated version of the same sentence:

Tom accidentally broke the big vase of flowers.

We've added an adverb, an adjective, and a prepositional phrase to the original sentence.

- An **adverb** is a word that modifies a verb.

- An **adjective** is a word that modifies a noun.

- A **preposition** is a word that notes the relation of a noun to an action or a thing.

- A **phrase** is a group of words that acts as a single part of speech. A phrase is missing either a subject or a verb or both.

- A **prepositional phrase** is a group of words beginning with a preposition.

In the sentence above, *accidentally* is an adverb modifying the verb *broke*. *Big* is an adjective modifying the noun *vase*. *Of* is a preposition because it shows a relationship between *vase* and *flowers*. *Of flowers* is a prepositional phrase that acts like an adjective by modifying *vase*.

Here's an even more complicated version of the same sentence:

> *As he ran across the room, Tom accidentally broke the big vase of flowers.*

Now, we've added a secondary clause containing a pronoun to the original sentence.

- A **pronoun** is a word that takes the place of a noun.

- A **clause** is a group of words containing a subject and a verb.

Tom accidentally broke the big vase of flowers is considered the independent clause in this sentence, because it contains the main idea of the sentence and could stand by itself. *As he ran across the room* is also a clause (it contains a subject and a verb) but because it is not a complete thought, it is called a dependent clause. This particular dependent clause is also known as an adverbial clause because it tells us something *about* the action that took place. *He* is a pronoun taking the place of *Tom*.

Now let's begin our sentence stucture review.

C H A P T E R 4

Sentence Structure

Good sentence structure is about putting clauses and phrases—the essential building blocks of sentences—together in logical ways. Before we talk about the *errors* of sentence structure, let's spend a moment talking about correct structure. Here is that first example again:

As he ran across the room, Tom broke the vase.

We said before that this sentence consists of two clauses. Each clause has a subject and a verb. The second clause ("Tom broke the vase") is considered the main clause and **independent**, because it can stand alone. The first clause ("As he ran across the room,") is called **dependent** because it can't.

You can easily change a dependent clause into an independent clause and vice versa. Often, all it takes is a single word:

He ran across the room.

By removing "as" from the dependent clause, we suddenly have a sentence that can stand on its own. By adding an "as" to the second clause, we can instantly change it into a dependent clause:

As Tom broke the vase, . . .

If we stuck these two new clauses together now, the meaning of the sentence would be very different. Could we have kept the meaning more or less the same and still made the first clause independent? Sure. Try this:

Tom ran across the room, breaking the vase.

Now the first half of the sentence contains the main independent clause. We had to change "he" to "Tom" so the reader would know who the sentence was talking about. We also had to change the second half of the sentence from a clause into a modifying phrase. While a clause has a subject and a verb, a phrase generally has no subject.

PUTTING THE PIECES TOGETHER

Proficient writers use a mixture of dependent clauses, independent clauses, and phrases to add variety to their writing and to create emphasis. By combining these building blocks in different ways, writers show the reader which thoughts are most important, and create a rhythm.

Here are the most often used structures:

- Independent clause (period) New independent clause (period)

    Jane lit the campfire. Frank set up the tent.

- Independent clause (comma) AND independent clause (period)

  Jane lit the campfire, and Frank set up the tent.

- Independent clause (semicolon) independent clause (period)

  Jane lit the campfire; Frank set up the tent.

- Independent clause (comma) dependent clause (period)

  Jane lit the campfire, while Frank set up the tent.

- Dependent clause (comma) independent clause (period)

  As Jane lit the campfire, Frank set up the tent.

All of these sentences are correct. A writer might choose one over another to emphasize one thought over another. For example, in the last sentence, the writer is choosing to make "setting up the tent" the focus of the sentence. Perhaps in the next sentence the tent is going to collapse with Frank inside it.

There are four main types of errors in sentence structure:

- Sentence fragments

- Run-ons and comma splices

- Misplaced modifiers

- Parallel construction

All of these errors are a result of incorrect placement of the building blocks which make up sentences. Sentence structure on the ACT is closely tied to punctuation. The two are related because sentence structure errors can often be fixed through proper punctuation. In fact, you will find that by using punctuation clues from the answer choices, you will often be able to zero in on sentence structure errors in the passages.

SENTENCE FRAGMENTS

A complete sentence must have a subject and a verb, and stand alone. In other words it must be, or contain, an **independent clause**. Remember the very first example in this chapter?

Tom broke the vase.

This is an independent clause. We can change it into a **dependent clause** by adding just one word:

When Tom broke the vase, ...

Even though it still has a subject and a verb, this clause can no longer stand alone. It is now waiting for an independent clause to finish the sentence.

When Tom broke the vase, Sid ran to tell his Aunt Sally.

You can turn any independent clause into a dependent clause by *adding* one of these words to the beginning of it:

> when, where, why, how, if, as, because,
> although, while, despite, that, who, what

(You may see these words referred to in *The Official Guide* or in grammar books as subordinating conjunctions, relative pronouns, or prepositions, but the names of these terms are not important.)

By the same token, you can turn most dependent clauses into independent clauses by *taking away* the subordinating conjunction or relative pronoun.

The First Sentence Fragment Type

There are two kinds of sentence fragment. The first is just a dependent clause waiting for a second half that isn't there. Here's an example:

The bride and groom drove away in their car. <u>As the</u> children ran behind, shouting and laughing.

1. **A.** NO Change
   B. While the
   C. During which the
   D. The

Here's how to crack it:

The second "sentence" in the example isn't a sentence at all; it is a dependent clause, beginning with one of those words we told you to be on the lookout for— "as." Answer choices B and C repeat the same error by using other words from the same list. The only answer which makes the clause independent is answer choice **D**.

Could we have combined the second "sentence" with the first to make a correct sentence? Yes, but in this case, ACT didn't give us that option: the period at the end of the *first* sentence wasn't underlined, so we couldn't change it.

The Second Sentence Fragment Type

In the second type of sentence fragment question, the ACT writers ask you to *incorporate* the sentence fragment into the complete sentence that comes immediately before or after the fragment. In the example that follows, notice that the underlining extends from the end of one sentence through the beginning of the next sentence, and includes the punctuation as well:

Although it will always be associated with Shakespeare's famous literary character. The castle at Elsinore was never home to Hamlet.

2. F. NO CHANGE
    G. character, the
    H. character; the
    J. character. A

Here's how to crack it:

The underlined portion of this passage includes pieces of two sentences and the punctuation in between. We have to check both "sentences" to make sure that they are complete. Let's check the first "sentence" first. Can it stand on its own? No. It's a dependent clause. Aha! This is the error. Could we have removed the "Although" at the beginning to create an independent clause? Sure, but in this case, that isn't an option because "Although" isn't underlined.

This time, the only way to fix the passage is to combine the dependent clause with the independent clause to form one big sentence. As we will discuss further in the punctuation review, you need a comma between a dependent and an independent clause. The only answer choice that contains a comma is choice **G**. This must be the correct answer.

How Do You Spot a Sentence Fragment?

You will often be able to spot this type of error as you read the passage itself, now that you know to look for a dependent clause all by itself. However, if you don't see the error as you read the passage the first time, don't despair. There are four terrific clues waiting for you.

The Answer Choices Contain Valuable Clues

If you're having trouble deciding whether a passage has a sentence construction error, it helps to look at the answer choices. They often contain great clues as to what is going on in the test writers' minds. For example, in the last question it might have helped to look at the differences in *punctuation* among the answer choices. Some of the choices break the two clauses into two sentences. Others combine them. This might make you ask, "Why would ACT be giving me this choice? Maybe this question is about sentence construction. Would it be better to combine the two clauses? Hmm. Let me check for sentence fragments."

Sometimes, of course, there will be no need to change the sentence at all. Remember, the answer NO CHANGE is right slightly less than a quarter of the time. However, the flip side of this is that NO CHANGE is wrong more than three quarters of the time.

COMMA SPLICES AND RUN-ONS

In a **comma splice**, two independent clauses are jammed together into one sentence, usually with only a comma to try to hold them together:

Aunt Sally ran into the room, Tom was already gone.

There are several ways to fix this sentence. The easiest way would be to break it up into two sentences:

Aunt Sally ran into the room. Tom was already gone.

If there is a clear reason why one clause might be connected to the other (for example if Tom has just broken Aunt Sally's vase), you can also fix it by putting a **conjunction** (such as "and" or "but") between the two thoughts:

Aunt Sally ran into the room, but Tom was already gone.

If there is some connection between the two clauses, but it is not really a matter of cause and effect, you can break up the two thoughts with a semicolon instead of a period.

Aunt Sally arrived home several hours later; Tom was already gone.

A **run-on** sentence is pretty much the same thing as a comma splice, without the comma:

Aunt Sally swept up the shards of glass she was furious.

Again, the easiest way to solve the problem is to break the sentence up into two new sentences.

Aunt Sally swept up the shards of glass. She was furious.

A run-on sentence is often much longer than our example, running on and on, so that, if you were to read it out loud, you might actually run out of breath, and wonder whether perhaps it would have been better to have split it up into more than one sentence. That last sentence, of course, was a run-on as well.

Here's How They Look on the ACT

There is not much difference between the decision to enter politics and the decision to jump into a pit full of <u>rattlesnakes, in fact,</u> you might find a friendlier environment in the snake pit.

3. **A.** NO CHANGE
   B. rattlesnakes. In fact,
   C. rattlesnakes in fact
   D. rattlesnakes, in fact

Here's how to crack it:

Check the punctuation. As soon as you see that one or more of the answer choices gives you the option of breaking the sentence up into two pieces, you should immediately consider whether there might be a comma-splice or run-on problem. Are the two clauses surrounding the punctuation both independent? Yes! This is probably a comma splice error. Now, the question is how to fix it. Only one of the answer choices breaks the long sentence into two little ones. Answer choice B is probably correct. Remember, however, that there are other ways to fix a comma splice; to be certain, try out the other answer choices in the sentence. Perhaps one of them will use a conjunction to bridge the two clauses. Is that the case here? No. Therefore the correct answer is choice **B**.

The college's plans for expansion included a new science building and a new <u>dormitory if</u> the funding drive were successful there would be enough money for both.

4. **F.** NO CHANGE
   G. dormitory, if
   H. dormitory; if,
   J. dormitory. If

Here's how to crack it:

If you could start from scratch, there are lots of different ways you could have expressed the thoughts in this passage. However, as always, you must find the way that the ACT test writers decided to express them.

Again, the answer choices provide an immediate clue: in some, the sentence is broken up into two smaller sentences. Check to see if there are independent clauses on either side of the punctuation. Bingo: this is a run-on sentence. Which choices can we eliminate? F and G bite the dust. Both H and J successfully break up the two clauses. (Remember, a semicolon will often do the trick if the subject of the two clauses is related.)

Is there anything else wrong with either of them? Come to think of it, the comma at the end of choice H is unnecessary. The correct answer is **J**.

MISPLACED MODIFIERS

A modifying phrase needs to be near what it is modifying. If it gets too far away, it can get misplaced:

> *Sweeping up the shards of glass, the missing key to the jewelry box was found by Aunt Sally.*

As written, this sentence gives the impression that the *missing key* was sweeping up the shards of glass. When a sentence begins with a modifying phrase (a group of words without a subject), the noun being modified must follow the phrase. *Who* was sweeping up the shards of glass? Aunt Sally, of course. The correct version of this sentence would be:

> *Sweeping up the shards of glass, Aunt Sally found the missing key to her jewelry box.*

A more subtle version of the same type of error:

> *Ecstatic and happy, Aunt Sally's key opened the jewelry box for the first time in weeks.*

At first glance, it looks like the modifying phrase "ecstatic and happy" is modifying Aunt Sally. However, what is the real subject of this sentence, as written? The key. "Aunt Sally's" is actually modifying the key. The correct version of this sentence would be:

> *Ecstatic and happy, Aunt Sally was able to use her key to open the jewelry box for the first time in weeks.*

Here's how a misplaced modifier might look on the ACT:

Because there was no sun tan oil left in the bottle, <u>which</u> had to drape towels over our shoulders.

5. **A.** NO CHANGE
   B. one
   C. we
   D. that

Here's how to crack it:

"Which" is a relative pronoun that turns the last half of the sentence into a phrase modifying bottle. A bottle can't drape towels over shoulders, so this is a misplaced modifier. There's also another problem: the first half of the sentence is a dependent clause (it began with "because"). This means that neither half of the sentence can stand on its own. We need to make one of the groups of words in this sentence into an independent clause, and we don't have a lot of options, since only one word in the entire sentence is underlined. Which choices create an independent clause in the second half of the sentence? If you said B or C, you are absolutely correct. So cross off A and D. Now, we want to be consistent. Let's look at answer choice B. Does "one" go with the pronoun "our" used later in the sentence? No. If the sentence had read "one had to drape towels over one's shoulders," this would have been correct. Since it doesn't, we can forget B. Does "we" agree with "our"? Yes. So the answer is choice **C**.

How Do You Spot Misplaced Modifiers?

That's easy! If the underlined portion of the sentence is part of a modifying phrase, check to make sure it modifies the correct noun. If the underlined portion of the sentence includes the noun that is supposed to be modified, check to make sure it is the correct noun.

CONSTRUCTION SHIFTS

A related type of error is what the ACT writers call construction shifts. These resemble misplaced modifiers in that the modifier is in the wrong place, but construction shifts require no words to be changed. Instead, the modifying word or phrase simply has to be moved over slightly:

Stepping to avoid the large puddle, I
<u>carefully</u> tripped and fell.
6

6. **F.** NO CHANGE
   G. (Place after *stepping*)
   H. (Place after *and*)
   J. (Place after *fell*)

Here's how to crack it:

These questions just require a little common sense. "Carefully" is an adverb. It must modify a verb. The only question for us is, which verb? Only a stunt man trips or falls "carefully." This effectively disposes of answer choices F, H, and J. If we put "carefully" after "stepping" does the sentence make sense? Yes, so the answer is **G**.

How Do You Spot Construction Shifts?

That's easy. The answer choices in construction shifts are either presented as shown above, or like this:

7. **A.** NO CHANGE
   B. stepping carefully over the puddle I tripped and fell.
   C. stepping over the puddle I tripped and carefully fell.
   D. stepping over the puddle I tripped andfell carefully.

In either case, it is easy to see that the only difference in each of the answer choices is the position of the word "carefully." This should alert you to consider the position of the modifier.

PARALLEL CONSTRUCTION

There are two major types of parallel construction errors tested on the ACT. They both involve some kind of list. You might see a list of **verbs**:

> When Tom finally came home, Aunt Sally kissed him, hugged him, and gives him his favorite dessert after dinner.

The sentence above is wrong because all of the items on the list must be in the same tense. The first two verbs in the example above ("kissed" and "hugged") are in the past tense, but the third verb ("gives") is in the present tense. It is not "parallel" with the other two. The correct sentence should read:

> When Tom finally came home, Aunt Sally _kissed_ him, _hugged_ him, and _gave_ him his favorite dessert after dinner.

You also might see a list of **nouns**:

> Three explanations for Sid's locking himself in his room were _a desire_ to do his homework, _a sense_ that he needed to hone his college essays, and _hating_ his brother Tom, who always gets away with murder.

The sentence above is wrong because while "a desire" and "a sense" are both nouns, "hating" seems to be functioning like a verb. Is there a more noun-like way to say the same thing? If you said "a hatred," you were absolutely right. Now the sentence is parallel. Here's the corrected version:

> Three explanations for Sid's locking himself in his room were _a desire_ to do his homework, _a sense_ that he needed to hone his college essays, and _a hatred_ for his brother Tom, who always gets away with murder.

The lists do not have to have _three_ nouns or _three_ verbs. Sometimes there are only two:

> _To see_ the beauty of a sunset in Venice is _experiencing_ perfection.

This is wrong because if the first half of the sentence begins with the infinitive "to see," the second half of the sentence must do the same thing:

> *To see the beauty of a sunset in Venice is to experience perfection.*

How Do I Spot Parallel Construction Problems?

That's easy. First, as you read the passage be on the lookout for a series of actions or nouns. Now that you know what to look for, you may spot an error even without having to go to the answer choices. Second, look for changes in verb tense, or the way in which nouns are set up, among the answer choices.

SENTENCE CONSTRUCTION DRILL

In the drill below, you will find only questions that focus on sentence construction. Before you start, take a few moments to go back over the review material and techniques. If you don't spot an error as you read, remember that the answer choices may help to suggest the error you should look for.

When you see the gingerbread houses of Roskilde with their neatly thatched roofs, the gardens filled with <u>flowers, blooms,</u> and the happy smiles on the fresh-faced inhabitants, it is difficult to believe that this town was once the home of a more warlike people—the Vikings.

Roskilde's main museum is devoted to those early <u>inhabitants, the Vikings</u> once wandered throughout Europe, and by some reports, may have <u>travel</u> all the way to North America as well.

The museum sits on a site at the edge of Roskilde <u>fiord. Where</u> the Viking ships were once launched on voyages of conquest and plunder. Until twenty years ago used only by the fishermen who still ply their trade in the fiord, <u>tourists now arrive in buses at the craggy shoreline</u> to watch local artisans

1. **A.** NO CHANGE
   B. flowers and blooms,
   C. flowers; blooms
   D. flowers, blooms

2. **F.** NO CHANGE
   G. inhabitants the Vikings
   H. inhabitants. The Vikings
   J. inhabitants, the Vikings,

3. **A.** NO CHANGE
   B. travels
   C. traveled
   D. had traveled

4. **F.** NO CHANGE
   G. fiord. Where,
   H. fiord, where
   J. fiord; where

5. **A.** NO CHANGE
   B. the craggy shoreline must now be shared with tourists who arrive in buses
   C. tourists now arrive at the craggy shore line in buses
   D. the craggy shoreline must now share itself with tourists who arrive in buses

build Viking ships <u>in the traditional</u>
<u>manner.</u>[6]

High above the fiord is Roskilde
Cathedral, built by the famous Viking
King Harold Blue-toothe <u>in the 1200's</u>
<u>the king</u>[7] is said to have converted to
Christianity when a visiting priest was
able to cure his toothache.

In one corner of the cathedral is a
column on which the heights of some
other famous historical figures who
visited the cathedral are recorded. The
tallest (over seven feet tall, if the
markings are to be believed) was Peter
the Great; the shortest was a King of
<u>Siam; who</u>[8] one hopes was only a boy at
the time.

6. **F.** NO CHANGE
   G. (place after *artisans*)
   H. (place after *Build*)
   J. (place after *watch*)

7. **A.** NO CHANGE
   B. in the 1200's. The king
   C. in the 1200's, the king
   D. in the 1200's, the king,

8. **F.** NO CHANGE
   G. Siam. Who
   H. Siam, whom
   J. Siam, who

Here's how to crack them:

Question 1: Did you notice as you were reading that the passage begins with a *list* of nice things about the town of Roskilde? Lists often mean **parallel construction**. Because this is a list of *things,* or nouns, we need to check if everything on the list is presented in the same way. The list is composed of:

- the gingerbread houses of Roskilde with their neatly thatched roofs

- the gardens filled with flowers

- blooms

- the happy smiles on the fresh-faced inhabitants

Which one of these seems a little out of place? Each of them begins with "the" except for the third item on the list. And come to think of it, the third item is a lot shorter. Is "blooms" by itself a nice thing about Roskilde or does it really belong with the gardens back in the previous item on the list?

Let's look at the answer choices. We see several ways to connect the two nouns. Different nouns in the answer choices indicate that this could be a parallel construction problem (or possibly a misplaced modifier). Answer choice A implies that there are four items on the list, but these items are not set up the same way. Let's get rid of it. Choice D is essentially just the same, but even worse, there is no comma after "blooms." Choice C splits the sentence in two. Can the second half of the sentence stand on its own? No way. Answer choice B puts the blooms back in the garden, and clears up all problems of parallel construction. The correct answer is **B**.

Question 2: The answer choices here provide an immediate clue: one of the choices breaks the sentence up into two pieces, while the others leave it intact. Changes in punctuation may mean a **comma splice**. They don't always, of course, but we should always check. Can the clauses on both sides of the punctuation stand alone? Yes they can. Aha! This is definitely a comma splice. We are now probably giving serious thought to answer choice H, which splits the sentence in two.

However, since there is more than one way to fix a comma splice, we should check the other answer choices just to see if any of them are better than H. Choice G takes the comma splice and removes the comma, turning it into a run-on sentence. This is no better. Choice J merely inserts another pause after "the Vikings" which does not help matters. The correct answer is **H**.

Question 3: Here the sentence, which is partially underlined, contains a *list* of actions:

The Vikings a) once wandered and b) may have travel

Are the two verbs in the same tense? No. What did we really need here? If you said "traveled" you are absolutely correct.

If you missed this as you were reading it the first time, the answer choices provided great clues. Each was just another form of a verb. Any time you see verb changes in the answer choices, you should immediately think **parallel construction**. Each choice is in a different tense. Just read through them until you get a match with "wandered." The correct answer is **C**.

Question 4: Punctuation again! Three of the choices break up the sentence, one doesn't. Let's see which is better this time. Again, we ask ourselves, can the clauses on both sides of the punctuation stand by themselves? This time, the answer is no. The clause that begins "Where the Viking ships…" is dependent. This is a **sentence fragment**. We need to combine the two thoughts. Our only option is answer choice **H**.

Question 5: The answer choices here give us a choice of nouns. This could be a parallel construction problem or it could be a misplaced modifier. Since there is no list in this case, let's check for a misplaced modifier. How does the sentence begin?

> *"Until twenty years ago used only by the fishermen who*
> *still ply their trade in the fiord,..."*

This is a long modifying phrase. The noun that comes next in the sentence must be what is being modified. Are "tourists" what the fishermen used until twenty years ago? No! This is a **misplaced modifier**. We can eliminate answer choices A and C. In choice D, the shore must share itself. Can a shore do something like that? In choice B, the construction indicates that the fishermen and the tourists must do the sharing. The correct answer is **B**.

Question 6: We can spot the *type* of error ACT is looking for this time by going straight to the answer choices. This is one of those **phrase shift** questions. Let's move "in the traditional manner" around in the sentence and find the best fit. You say it was just fine where it was? You're right. The answer is **F**. NO CHANGE.

Question 7: More punctuation! Again, our choices either put the sentence together or break it apart. Can the two phrases on either side of the punctuation stand on their own? The answer this time is "yes." We have another run-on sentence. There is only one choice that breaks the two clauses up: the correct answer is **B**.

Question 8: More of the same. Can "who one hopes was only a boy at the time," stand on its own? No. We are down to choices H and J. The correct answer is **J**. How do you decide between "who" and "whom"?

To find out, let's review the elements of basic grammar.

CHAPTER 5

Grammar and Usage

The grammar questions on the ACT test your ability to recognize the proper (or improper) uses of the different parts of speech. We will not review *all* the rules of grammar (several long, dense books exist on the subject if you're really interested). Instead, we will go over the grammatical rules that are tested most frequently on the ACT: noun-pronoun agreement, pronoun case agreement, subject-verb agreement, verb tense, proper placement of adjectives and adverbs, and the correct use of idiom.

PRONOUNS

Pronouns—words like *he, she, it, they*—are used to replace nouns. The ACT writers like to see if you understand the rules of pronouns—there will probably be two or three pronoun questions on the test you take.

The First Pronoun Rule: Agreement

A pronoun must always agree with the noun it refers to. Sound straightforward? Try to spot the error in the sentence below.

> *Any young boy who watched the first moon landing probably spent the next few years wishing that they could become an astronaut.*

In spoken English, people make pronoun agreement errors all the time. In written English you have to be more precise. As you look at the sentence above, try to decide which noun is being referred to by the word "they." If you decided that "they" was referring to "boy," you were absolutely correct. However, since "boy" is singular, the pronoun referring to "boy" has to be singular as well. "He" would more correctly refer back to "boy."

> *Any young boy who watched the first moon landing probably spent the next few years wishing that he could become an astronaut.*

Following is a chart of some commonly used singular and plural pronouns:

Singular Pronouns				Plural Pronouns		
Subject	Object	Possessive		Subject	Object	Possessive
I	me	my		we	us	our
you	you	mine		you	you	ours
he	him	your		they	them	your
she	her	yours				yours
it	it	his				their
		hers				theirs
		its				

Here's another example:

> *Neither of the two young girls with whom I watched the*
> *first moon landing expressed their feelings out loud, but I*
> *knew that all three of us wanted to be astronauts too.*

"Neither" is also a pronoun, but like the other indefinite pronouns (*either, each, anyone, and everyone*) "neither" is always singular. Think of "neither" as meaning neither one. Therefore, in this sentence, it is incorrect to use the possessive pronoun "their." We should use "her" instead:

> *Neither of the two young girls with whom I watched the*
> *first moon landing expressed her feelings out loud, but I*
> *knew that all three of us wanted to be astronauts too.*

The following indefinite pronouns are all singular:

either	no one
neither	everyone
	everybody
each	somebody
anyone	anybody

Let's look at an example in ACT format:

Although the American bald eagle has been on the endangered species list for years, <u>they have been</u> sited in wildlife preserves¹ much more frequently during the past two years.

1. A. NO CHANGE
   B. they are
   C. it can be
   D. it has been

Here's how to crack it:

As you read the sentence, look to see if there is a pronoun in the underlined portion. If you find one, check to make sure the pronoun agrees with the noun to which it is referring. What does the "they" refer to here? Obviously, it must refer to "the American Bald eagle." Although the sentence is clearly talking about the American bald eagle in its *general* sense, we need to use a singular pronoun to agree with the singular noun. Thus, we can eliminate choices A and B. Choices C and D both contain the correct pronoun, "it." How do we decide which one to pick? Note the difference between C and D. Choice C uses the present tense, while choice D uses a type of past tense. According to the sentence, when were these birds sited? "In the past two years." Which answer do you want to pick? If you said Choice **D**, you were absolutely correct.

Even if you missed the pronoun as you read the sentence, you almost certainly would have noticed that the *answer choices* offered you two different pronouns. The answer choices are always great clues to what might be going on in the ACT test writers' minds.

THE SECOND PRONOUN RULE: CASE

If a pronoun is the subject of a sentence, it must be expressed as a subject. Subject pronouns include *I, we, you, he, she, it, they,* and who. If a pronoun is the object of a sentence, or the object of a preposition, it must be expressed as an object. Object pronouns include *me, us, you, him, her, it, them,* and whom.

Which choice best fits the sentence below?

> *(She/her) bought a souvenir NASA sweatshirt.*

Since the person who buys the shirt is the subject of the sentence, the correct pronoun would be "she."

> *Jane bought a souvenir NASA sweatshirt for (he/him).*

Since the person who receives the shirt is the object of the preposition "for," the correct pronoun would be "him."

ACT's favorite pronoun case errors involve the use of *who* and *whom,* both of which are called relative pronouns. Let's look at a correct example first:

> *The TV announcer, who was quite an expert, told us many*
> *interesting facts about the lunar mission.*

The group of words "who was quite an expert" is functioning here as an adjective describing the TV announcer. Is this group of words a phrase or a clause? You may remember that a phrase cannot contain a subject but a clause must contain both a subject and a verb. In this group of words, the relative pronoun "who" functions as a subject, which means that this group of words is a clause. You should always use "who" when the relative pronoun is functioning as the subject of a clause, or as the subject of the entire sentence. "...whom was quite an expert" would be completely wrong here.

Now try an incorrect example:

> *Before the moon landing, the TV announcer gave some*
> *additional background on the astronauts, about who we*
> *were all quite interested.*

If you spot *who* following a preposition (in this case, "who" follows the word "about") on the ACT, it will almost certainly turn out to be incorrect. In most cases, a pronoun following a preposition is supposed to be the object of that preposition. The sentence should read

> *Before the moon landing, the TV announcer gave some additional background on the astronauts, about whom we were all quite interested.*

Let's try an example in ACT format:

The students, <u>who had been studying the space program</u>, were thrilled to witness the lunar landing.

2. **A.** NO CHANGE
   B. about whom had been studying the space program,
   C. whom had been studying the space program,
   D. who had been studying the space program

Here's how to crack it:

The group of words "who had been studying the space program" is functioning as an adjective clause describing the students. Is "who" the subject of this adjective clause? Yes it is, so we are down to answer choices A (NO CHANGE) and D, both of which contain the correct form of the pronoun—"who." How do the two remaining choices differ? Answer choice A contains a comma after "program" while choice D does not. Is the comma necessary? We look back at the passage and see that a comma precedes the clause, which is a nonrestrictive clause. (You'll recall from the punctuation section that a nonrestrictive clause is one that is not necessary in order for the sentence to make sense.) Here "The students were thrilled to witness the lunar landing" would be perfectly acceptable. Nonrestrictive clauses require commas on either side of them, so answer choice **A**, NO CHANGE, is correct.

How Do You Spot Pronoun Errors?

Look for pronouns! Whenever you see a pronoun in the underlined portion of the sentence— or in the *answer choices*— you must first determine which noun the pronoun is replacing. If the pronoun is replacing a singular noun, it must be singular; if it is replacing a plural noun, it must be plural.

If the pronoun is being used as a subject, it must be in its subject form. If the pronoun is being used as an object, it must be in its object form.

If *who* or *whom* appears in the underlined portion of the passage—or in the answer choices— you must determine whether the pronoun is the subject or the object of the clause in which it appears. If it is the subject, *who* is correct. If it is the object, *whom* is correct. Generally, if the relative pronoun follows a preposition, the correct form will be "whom."

SUBJECT-VERB AGREEMENT

The verb of a sentence must always agree with its subject. If a sentence contains a singular subject, the verb that goes with it must also be singular. If a sentence contains a plural subject, then the verb that goes with it must also be plural. Let's look at an example:

> *The best moment during a broadcast filled with many great moments were when the astronaut stepped out of the lunar lander and bounced on the moon.*

The subject of this sentence is "moment," which is singular. See if you can find the main verb of the sentence. If you said "were" you were absolutely correct. Since the subject is singular, the verb should also be singular. The correct form of the verb should be "was."

> *The best moment during a broadcast filled with many great moments was when the astronaut stepped out of the lunar lander and bounced on the moon.*

Now if the original sentence had been written like this…

> *The best moment were when the astronaut stepped out of the lunar lander and sort of bounced on the moon.*

…the error sure would have been a lot easier to spot.

ACT test writers like to stick lots of modifying phrases and clauses between the subject and the verb, in the hope that you will have forgotten what the subject was by the time you get to the verb. The best way to check subject-verb agreement is to put mental parentheses around all the words between the subject and the verb so you can see if they really agree.

PRONOUN-VERB AGREEMENT

Sometimes, the subject of a sentence turns out to be a pronoun; don't let that throw you. The verb must still agree with the subject, even if it is just a pronoun. Let's look at an example:

> *Each of these moments have played in my mind again and again as I try to recapture the excitement of that momentous day in June.*

The subject of this sentence is "each," which you'll recall is singular (along with *either, neither, each, everybody, everyone, etc.*). The verb is "have played," which is plural. The subject (in this case a pronoun) and the verb don't agree. How do you fix the sentence?

Each of these moments has played in my mind again and again as I try to recapture the excitement of that momentous day in June.

How Do You Spot Subject-Verb Agreement Errors?

That's easy. Isolate the subject and the verb of the sentence. To see the relationship between the subject and the verb, try putting parentheses around any words, phrases or clauses in between. As always, it is a good idea to remember that the answer choices themselves can provide valuable clues. If the underlined portion of a sentence contains a verb, you should check to see whether the answer choices contain different forms of that verb. If they do, you have a potential subject-verb error.

VERB TENSE

Verb tense tells us when the action of the sentence is taking place— in the past, in the present, or in the future.

In general, the ACT test writers like continuity. If a passage begins in one tense, it tends to stay in the same tense. If you notice that an underlined sentence suddenly departs from the tense in which the rest of the passage is written, you may have found a tense error. Let's review the different verb tenses.

The **present tense** indicates an action that is happening right now:

He runs the 440 in 50 seconds.

The simple **past tense** indicates an action that took place entirely in the past:

He ran the 440 in 50 seconds last week.

The **present perfect tense** indicates an action that started in the past, but which may continue into the present:

He has run the 440 in under 50 seconds in the last four races.

The **past perfect tense** indicates an action that happened in the past and that preceded another action also in the past:

He had run 100 yards of the race when he twisted his ankle.

The **future tense** indicates an action that will take place at some point down the road:

> *He will run the race next Saturday.*

The **future perfect tense** indicates that an action will be completed by a definite time in the future:

> *He will have finished the race by next Sunday.*

HOW DOES THE ACT TEST VERB TENSE?

The ACT test writers don't care whether you know the names of the verb tenses, or even, sometimes, whether you know in which tense a particular passage should be written.

What the ACT writers want to see is whether you can spot *inconsistencies* in verb tense (they are testing a form of agreement here). If a verb in a non-underlined portion of the sentence is in one tense, the verb in the underlined portion will tend to be in the same tense. What's wrong with the following sentence?

> *Sam is walking down the street when he found a large suitcase.*

The verbs "is walking" and "found" are in two different tenses. "Is walking" is in the present tense, and "found" is in the past tense. One or the other has to change.

The new sentence can either read:

> *Sam is walking down the street when he finds a large suitcase.* ⋅

> or

> *Sam was walking down the street when he found a large suitcase.*

On the ACT, you generally will not be asked to make a decision as to which tense (in this case past or present) would be most appropriate for the sentence. Only one of the verbs will be underlined, and it will be up to you to look at the other verb in the sentence, or the verbs in surrounding sentences to decide how to change the underlined verb.

HOW DO YOU SPOT VERB AGREEMENT ERRORS?

That's easy. If you see a verb in the underlined portion of the sentence— or in any of the answer choices— you should immediately anticipate that the error could be one of two types: subject-verb agreement (which we've already spoken about) or tense.

You should begin by asking yourself whether the verb agrees with its subject.

If that is not the problem, then ask yourself whether the verb's tense is consistent with the tense of other verbs in the sentence or in surrounding sentences. If there is an inconsistency, then you've probably spotted the error.

ADJECTIVES AND ADVERBS

Adjectives modify nouns. Adverbs modify verbs. The ACT sometimes tests to see whether you know the difference between adjectives and adverbs. You may remember from grade school a method that often helps to decide if a word is an adjective—simply put the word you aren't sure about into the following sentence: "He (or she or it) is very _____." If the word fits the blank, then the word is an adjective. Let's try it out.

He is very <u>intelligent</u>.

He is very <u>intelligently</u>.

"Intelligent" fits the blank in the first sentence, so intelligent must be an adjective. "Intelligently" does not fit the blank in the second sentence. In fact, "intelligently" is an adverb. You can often recognize an adverb by the "-ly" at the end of the word.

She thinks intelligently.

A comparative adjective is often used when a sentence is comparing two things.

Juanita is taller than Jane.

("Taller" is a comparative adjective.)

In general, if an adjective has only one syllable, you can make it comparative by adding an "-er" to the end of the word. If an adjective has more than one syllable, you can usually make it comparative by adding a "more" or a "less" in front of the adjective.

Sid is more careful than Tom.

Tom is less careful than Sid.

A comparative adverb is often used when a sentence is comparing two actions.

Juanita dances more gracefully than Jane.

("More gracefully" is a comparative adverb.)

To make most adverbs comparative, you also need to add a "more" or "less" in front of the adverb.

Sid behaves more correctly than Tom does.

Tom behaves less correctly than Sid does.

When more than two things are being compared, a sentence often needs a superlative adjective:

Of the many men in the room, John is the strongest.
("Strongest" is a superlative adjective.)

To make a comparison among three or more people or things, add "-est" to the adjective.

When more than two actions are being compared, a sentence often needs a superlative adverb:

Compared to the other boys in the school, Sid behaves the most correctly. ("Most correctly" is a superlative adverb.)

IDIOMATIC EXPRESSIONS

Why do we say, "I am in love *with* you," instead of, "I am in love *for* you?" The answer is,

"Well, just because!"

Each idiomatic expression is a law unto itself. There are no general rules to go by. Of course, it would be difficult to memorize every single idiom in the English language, at least on short notice. Fortunately, it turns out that you already know most of the idioms that come up on the ACT.

Here's an example:

My sculpture is based after Rodin's Thinker.

Do you base something "after?" No, the correct expression would be

My sculpture is based on Rodin's Thinker.

How Do You Spot Idiomatic Errors?

You already know most of the idiomatic expressions likely to appear on the ACT. The only problem will be spotting the error in the first place. As always, the answer choices provide excellent clues. Let's look at how that last example would have looked on the ACT.

My sculpture <u>is based after</u> Rodin's [3]
Thinker.

3. A. NO CHANGE
    B. is based over
    C. is based on
    D. based on

Here's how to crack it:

Even if you didn't spot the error as you read the sentence, when you went to the answer choices you would have noticed that the question seemed to be mostly concerned with the preposition that followed the word "based."

The best way to check out a potential idiom error is to try making up your own sentence using the idiomatic expression.

> *My term paper is based after the discoveries of Edison.*

Does that sound correct? No! We need to say "is based on..." Answer choice D, while it uses the correct idiomatic expression, is a sentence fragment. Thus the best answer is choice **C**.

In the drill below, you will find questions focusing only on grammar. Before you start, take a few moments to go back over the review material and techniques. If you don't spot an error as you read, remember that the answer choices may help to suggest the error you should look for.

Have you ever had a day when you realized in retrospect that it would have been better if one had stayed in bed? Yesterday was one of those days. I woke up at 10:30 to find that my alarm clock has failed to go off. I was already an hour and a half late for work. I jumped into my clothes and ran to my car, only to discoverthat I had left the lights on the previously evening and

the car wouldn't start. Each of the first three taxis I saw were too far away to

hail. The taxi driver who finally picked me up didn't have change of a ten dollar bill. When I finally arrived at the office, my boss was not only furious that I was late, and she was also mad that I had forgotten to bring the report I had been preparing at home. Of all the bad days I have experienced in my life, this was the worse.

1. A. NO CHANGE
   B. if you had
   C. if one has
   D. had one

2. F. NO CHANGE
   G. have failed
   H. had failed
   J. having failed

3. A. NO CHANGE
   B. on the evening previously
   C. on the evening previous
   D. on the previous evening

4. F. NO CHANGE
   G. was
   H. are
   J. is

5. A. NO CHANGE
   B. whom finally picked me up
   C. whom picked me up finally
   D. who finally picks me up

6. F. NO CHANGE
   G. and her
   H. but he
   J. but she

7. A. NO CHANGE
   B. was the more worse
   C. was the worst
   D. was the worser

Here's how to crack them:

Question 1: Looking at the answer choices, you might notice that there are two potential errors to check: pronoun agreement and tense. Why? Because the answers contained two different pronouns and two different verb tenses. Let's check pronouns first. In the original underlined portion of the sentence, "one" is a pronoun. Does it agree with the other pronouns in the same sentence? Not really. The author begins the passage by addressing "you." It is confusing and incorrect to change to "one" in the same sentence. Which answer choice avoids the use of "one"? The correct answer is **B**.

Question 2: Checking the answer choices, we see that the question seems to revolve around verb tense. The sentence is describing something that happened yesterday, so we can expect that the sentence should be in some form of the past tense. Two events take place in this sentence. The author woke up, and the alarm clock failed to go off. Which of these two events happened first, thus causing the other? If you said that the failure of the alarm clock took place before the author woke up, you were absolutely correct. When two events occur in the past, but one occurs before the other, the sentence requires the past perfect. The correct answer is choice **H**.

Question 3: The answer choices here seem to offer us the choice of the adverb "previously" or the adjective "previous." To decide which is correct, we need to know which word the "previously" (or "previous") is referring to. The word being modified here is "evening" which we all know is a noun. The correct modifier of a noun is an adjective. This eliminates choices A and B. Now, does an adjective normally precede or follow the noun it modifies? The correct answer is **D**.

Question 4: The answer choices here indicate that we have to consider either of two errors: tense or subject-verb agreement. Let's check subject-verb agreement first. Find the subject of the sentence. If you said the subject was "each" you were absolutely correct. "Of the first three taxis I saw" is modifying "each." Now, check the verb. "Each... were." In our review, we said that the word "each" is always singular—but the verb in this case is plainly plural. Aha! we have found the error. Check the answer choices to see which ones are singular. Our only remaining choices are G) was and J) is. In what general tense is this passage written? Check the tense of the verbs in surrounding sentences. The correct answer is choice **G**.

Question 5: Clearly this question is testing our understanding of the "who/whom" issue. Remember that the difference between the pronouns "who" and "whom" lies in whether they are being used as subjects or objects in the clause or phrase that contains them. "Who finally picked me up" is a clause modifying the taxi driver. What is the subject of the clause? If you said "who" you are absolutely correct. Thus, "who" is fine just the way it is. We can eliminate choices B and C both of which contain "whom." Now let's see what the difference is between choices A and D. Again, it comes down to tense. Is this passage being told in the present tense? No. The correct answer is **A**. NO CHANGE.

Question 6: The answer choices are offering you a variety of options having to do with "and" or "but." This is an idiom question. Try making up your own sentence using the idiomatic expression in question.

>   *My sister Jane is not only stupid...*

How would you finish this sentence? Or put it this way: what would be *the next word* in the sentence after "stupid?"

>   *My sister Jane is not only stupid,* but *she is also a pain.*

Choices F and G bite the dust. The answer is either H or J. In the sentence you just made up, did you use "she" or "her" after the "but"? Chances are you used "she." "She is also a pain" is a clause. Since "she" is the subject of the clause, we have to use the subject form, "she," instead of the object form, "her." The same is true for the sentence in the passage. The correct answer is choice **J**.

Question 7: This question is about the proper use of the superlative. The answer choices (including "worser" and "worst" give you a pretty good indication that this is the case. If you are discussing two bad options, you would have to decide which of them was *worse*. It you are discussing three or more bad options, you would have to decide which of them was *the worst*. The correct answer is choice **C**.

Punctuation

Punctuation marks signal pauses and transitions in speech. While you've probably learned dozens of punctuation rules over the last eight years or so, you'll only need to know a select few for the ACT. In this chapter we'll show you only the rules you'll need to know.

COMMAS

More than half of the punctuation questions on the ACT concern the proper use of commas (,). Too few commas in a sentence can create confusion as to where one thought ends and another begins. Too many commas break up the flow of the sentence.

THE FIRST COMMA RULE: THE SERIAL COMMA

Commas are used to separate items in a series. Let's look at an example:

> *When Mary walked into the classroom she saw a school teacher, a doctor, a woman eating a bagel and a bird.*

A comma should be placed after each item in a series. Thus, we need a comma after the phrase "a woman eating a bagel." As this sentence stands, you might get the impression that the woman was eating the bird as well!

In informal writing, it is often considered acceptable to leave out the comma between the "and" and the final item in a list. However, the ACT test writers prefer a more formal version of English (no surprise there), so use a comma to separate every item in a series, including the last one.

> *When Mary walked into the classroom she saw a school teacher, a doctor, a woman eating a bagel, and a bird.*

How Do You Spot Serial Comma Errors?

To spot serial comma errors, look at the entire sentence, not just the portion that is underlined. What you are searching for is a series or list of items or actions. If you spot one of these series, make sure there is a comma between each item in the series.

THE SECOND COMMA RULE:
SEPARATING CLAUSES AND PHRASES

The ACT also tests your ability to use commas correctly when two clauses, or a clause and a phrase, appear in the same sentence.

Two Independent Clauses

As you'll recall from the sentence structure chapter, independent clauses are those that could form a complete sentence on their own. Identify the two independent clauses in the sentence below:

> *Mary wondered why there was a bird in the classroom and she decided to ask the teacher what the bird was doing indoors.*

When two independent clauses appear in the same sentence, they are usually joined by a conjunction (a word like *and, or, but, for, nor,* or *yet*). Thus, the two independent clauses above are "Mary wondered why there was a bird in the classroom" and "She decided to ask the teacher what the bird was doing indoors." A comma belongs before the conjunction that joins the two independent clauses:

> *Mary wondered why there was a bird in the classroom, and she decided to ask the teacher what the bird was doing indoors.*

An Independent Clause and a Dependent Clause

Commas are also used to separate independent clauses from dependent clauses. You'll remember that a dependent clause is one that cannot stand on its own as a sentence. Identify the dependent clause in the sentence below:

> *Before Mary could reach the teacher she saw the woman offer the bird part of the bagel.*

The first clause, "Before Mary could reach the teacher," cannot stand by itself, and therefore is a dependent clause. "She saw the woman offer the bird part of the bagel" can stand by itself, and is an independent clause. The two must be separated by a comma.

> *Before Mary could reach the teacher, she saw the woman offer the bird part of the bagel.*

An Independent Clause and a Long Modifying Phrase

Commas are also used to separate independent clauses from modifying phrases of more than just a couple of words. A modifying phrase modifies, or describes, something else, usually a noun. Identify the modifying phrase in the sentence below:

Hungry and excited the bird snapped up the bagel.

"Hungry and excited" is a a modifying phrase (it modifies the noun "bird"). "The bird snapped up the bagel" is an independent clause. The two must be separated by a comma.

Hungry and excited, the bird snapped up the bagel.

How to Spot Comma Errors in Clause/Phrase Separation

As you saw in the last example, sometimes the error can be the *lack* of a comma, which you might think would be very difficult to spot. Fortunately, as always, the answer choices provide you with excellent clues. If some of the answer choices insert a comma into the sentence, while others don't, that is reason enough to check to see if we need to separate two clauses or a clause and a long phrase.

THE THIRD COMMA RULE: SEPARATING "RESTRICTIVE" AND "NON-RESTRICTIVE" ELEMENTS

A "restrictive" clause or phrase is essential to the meaning of a sentence, and does not need to be separated from the rest of the sentence by commas:

People who snore are advised to sleep on their side.

"Who snore" is essential to the meaning of this sentence. The sentence is not saying that *all* people should sleep on their side; just the ones who snore.

An "unrestrictive" clause or phrase is not essential to the meaning of a sentence. It merely adds a parenthetical thought, and thus needs to be separated from the rest of the sentence by commas:

My Grandfather, who snores loudly, always sleeps in his longjohns.

Identify the nonrestrictive clause in the sentence below:

> *Mary who by now was very confused stopped in front of the*
> *woman.*

The nonrestrictive clause is "who by now was very confused." This clause modifies the noun that precedes it—in this case "Mary" —but is not essential to the meaning of the sentence. "Mary stopped in front of the woman" can stand on its own. To set off the clause from the rest of the sentence, you need to surround it with a *pair* of commas.

> *Mary, who by now was very confused, stopped in front of*
> *the woman.*

Identify the restrictive clause in the sentence below:

> *"Only a person who is a little peculiar would feed a bagel*
> *to a bird!" thought Mary.*

"Who is a little peculiar" is a restrictive clause, because it adds essential information to the sentence. Thus, it does *not* require separation by commas.

How Do You Spot a Restrictive/Nonrestrictive Comma Error?

As always, the answer choices provide you with a very small "menu" of options to choose from. If you see differences in punctuation among the choices, check to see whether the underlined portion of the sentence is part of a restrictive or nonrestrictive phrase or clause.

SEMICOLONS

Semicolons (;) are punctuation marks used to put two or more clauses together to form one big sentence. A semicolon falls somewhere between a heavy comma and a light period.

When Do You Use a Semicolon?

Use a semicolon instead of a period to connect two related independent clauses. Identify the two independent clauses in the sentence below:

> *Just then the woman screamed the bird jumped up and*
> *perched on her head.*

The first independent clause is "Just then the woman screamed." The second independent clause is "the bird jumped up and perched on her head." In the absence of a conjunction (these two could be connected by the word *and*), a semicolon is used to join the two independent clauses. Of course it would have been equally correct to put a period after the first independent clause; however, the use of a semicolon suggests to the reader that the two clauses are closely related.

> *Just then the woman screamed; the bird jumped up and*
> *perched on her head.*

So, How Do You Spot a Semicolon Error?

If the underlined portion *or any of the answer choices* contains a semicolon, you should ask yourself whether the sentence contains two related independent clauses not joined by a conjunction. If it does, the semicolon is probably correct. You might be wondering how you would decide if the ACT gave you a choice between a semicolon and a period. Don't worry. Because the test writers know that semicolons and periods are often interchangeable, the ACT will almost certainly never give you that choice.

COLONS

Colons (:) are usually used after a complete statement to introduce a list of related details. In the following sentence, try to decide where the statement ends and the details begin.

> *Maria just purchased all the*
> *camping supplies for our trip,*
> *a back pack, a sleeping bag,*
> *and a pair of hiking boots.*

"Maria just purchased all the camping supplies for our trip" is the complete statement in the sentence above. (It is also an independent clause.) "A back pack, a sleeping bag, and a pair of hiking boots" are the related details. A colon belongs between the two.

> *Maria just purchased all the*
> *camping supplies for our trip:*
> *a back pack, a sleeping bag,*
> *and a pair of hiking boots.*

How Do You Spot a Colon Error?

If the underlined phrase *or the answer choices* contain a colon, you should ask yourself:

Is a list of some kind introduced by an independent clause?

If so, a colon preceding the list or statement is correct. If not, a colon is probably incorrect.

DASHES

Dashes (—) separate a word or group of words from the rest of the sentence. Dashes are used either to indicate an abrupt break in thought, or to introduce an explanation or afterthought.

In the example below, which group of words should be separated from the rest of the sentence?

> *I tried to express my gratitude not that any words could be adequate but she just nodded and walked away.*

The clause "not that any words could be adequate" must be isolated from the rest of the sentence.

> *I tried to express my gratitude—not that any words could be adequate—but she just nodded and walked away.*

When the group of words that needs isolating is in the middle of a sentence, dashes function like a pair of less formal parentheses. However, when the phrase that needs isolating is at the end of the sentence instead, only one dash is required.

> *Just outside the door to the cabin we heard the howling of wolves— a sound which made our hair stand on end.*

How Do You Spot Dash Errors?

If the underlined portion or any of the *answer choices* contains a dash, compare the dash to the punctuation marks available in the other answer choices. Ask yourself whether the sentence contains a sudden break in thought, an explanation, or an afterthought. Remember that if the group of words that need isolating is in the middle of the sentence, there should be a *pair* of dashes. If the group of words is at the end of the sentence, there should be only one.

APOSTROPHES

An apostrophe (') is used either to indicate possession or to mark missing letters in a word.

When it is used to indicate possession, it appears either right before or right after the "s" at the end of the possessive noun:

> *Peter's car is extremely expensive.*
> *Women's issues will be important in the next election.*
> *The girls' room will be renovated this summer.*

The apostrophe tells us that the car belongs to Peter. If the noun in possession is singular—as in the case of Peter—the apostrophe falls before the "s." If it is plural and it doesn't end in "s"—as in the case of women—the apostrophe falls before the "s." If it is plural and it ends in "s"—as in the case of "girls"—the apostrophe falls after the "s." Note: Don't worry too much about the plural nouns—ACT seems more interested in your ability to form singular possessives correctly.

The ACT folks also seem very interested in whether you know when an apostrophe is *unnecessary*—some of the questions testing this type of apostrophe require you to *drop* the apostrophe. Remember, in order for the apostrophe to be correct when forming a possessive, the noun containing it must be followed by another noun, or an adjective and a noun.

> *Peter's car*
> *Women's issues*
> *Girls' room*

If the noun containing the apostrophe is followed by a verb, no apostrophe is needed:

> *Students must have identification cards.*

The apostrophe is also used to indicate missing letters in a word:

> *I'm sorry. I couldn't make it to your party.*

In the sentences above, the apostrophe takes the place of "a" (*I'm* instead of *I am*) and the place of "o" (*couldn't* instead of *could not*). Words that use apostrophes in this way are called contractions. Other common contractions: words like *don't, isn't, won't*, etc.

Its/It's

The most common apostrophe error you'll see on the ACT is the misuse of the words *it's* and *its,* which have their own special rules.

The word *it's*—with an apostrophe—is used when you want to say "it is."

> *It's important.* (It is important.)

The word *its*—without an apostrophe—is (in this case only) the possessive form of the word "it."

> *The baby bear could not find its mother.*

We realize this is a little confusing, because with every other noun or pronoun you use an apostrophe to form the possessive form. The ACT writers realize that it's confusing too—that's why it's on the test!

How Do You Spot Apostrophe Errors?

If a word in the underlined portion or any of the *answer choices* contains an apostrophe, you should ask yourself whether the apostrophe is being used to form a contraction, or to make a noun *followed by another noun* possessive. In either case, the apostrophe is probably correct. Any other use of an apostrophe is probably wrong.

Unless...

You see the words *it's* or *its* in the underlined portion *or any of the answer choices*. In this case, remember the special rules we've just discussed.

What About !(")*?

It seems that the ACT test writers just aren't that interested in whether you know how to use exclamation points, parentheses, asterisks, and question marks correctly. They mention in their guide that the ACT tests some of these points, but not one of the three real ACTs in the very same book contains any such questions.

Quotation marks sometimes surround words in the underlined portion and the answer choices, but when they do appear they show up in every answer choice (you aren't given the option of removing them), and seem designed to distract you from some other form of punctuation being tested.

As a result, we think you're safe spending your time worrying about other kinds of punctuation. The most common punctuation errors on the ACT deal with commas, semicolons, colons, dashes, and apostrophes: learn how to use *these* correctly, and you should be covered punctuation-wise.

HOW DO YOU SPOT PUNCTUATION ERRORS?

That's easy. Look for changes in punctuation among the answer choices. These changes tell you what the ACT test writers are up to. Look at the following example:

A) NO CHANGE
B) cities environmental problems
C) city's environmental problems
D) citys' environmental problems

Clearly, this question is about the proper use of the apostrophe. Read the entire sentence, and use the rules you've learned in this chapter to pick the best answer.

ONE LAST NOTE

There are some forms of punctuation that can be used interchangeably. As we stated above, a semicolon can sometimes take the place of a period. Dashes can sometimes be used instead of parentheses. Sometimes a colon could be replaced by a dash. We haven't discussed these possibilities at length because on the ACT you will never be asked to make a decision between two correct alternatives. If two kinds of punctuation could both be considered correct, only one will appear among the answer choices.

PUNCTUATION DRILL

In the drill below, you will find questions that focus only on punctuation. Before you start, take a few moments to go back over the review material and techniques. If you don't spot an error as you read, remember to use the answer choices to help you determine the problem.

Passage I

My most memorable vacation as a childwas a trip I took to the Grand Canyon with my grandfather. I was only eleven at <u>the time; and</u> I'd never been outside the city of Boston. My

1. **A.** NO CHANGE
   B. at the time and
   C. at the time, and
   D. at the time. And

<u>grandfather, a true adventurer,</u> decided that it was time for me to discover the great West. My romantic picture of the <u>west complete with cowboys and Indians</u> was a little out of date, but the incredible scenery took my breath

2. **F.** NO CHANGE
   G. grandfather, a true, adventurer,
   H. grandfather: a true adventurer
   J. grandfather, a true adventurer

3. **A.** NO CHANGE
   B. west—complete with cowboys and Indians—
   C. west—complete with cowboys and Indians
   D. west; complete with cowboys and Indians,

away.<u>On our first day we</u> decided that the best way to explore the vast beauty of the canyon would be to take a mule-packed trip down one of the trails. As I rode along <u>on my mules back</u>, I noticed that each rock stratum displayed a

4. **F.** NO CHANGE
   G. On our first day we,
   H. On our first day, we
   J. On, our first day, we

5. **A.** NO CHANGE
   B. on my mules' back
   C. on our mule's back
   D. on my mule's back

distinctive <u>hue; gray</u> and violet in some places, dark brown and green in others. The rock layers of the Grand

6. **F.** NO CHANGE
   G. hue. Gray
   H. hue, gray
   J. hue: gray

Canyon are mostly made of <u>limestone, freshwater shale and sandstone.</u> The Grand Canyon was truly magnificent. As I looked up from the floor of the

7. **A.** NO CHANGE
   B. limestone, freshwater, shale, and sandstone.
   C. limestone, freshwater shale, and sandstone.
   D. limestone freshwater shale and sandstone.

canyon, <u>it's imposing</u> peaks made me realize how small I really was.

8. **F.** NO CHANGE
   G. its imposing
   H. its' imposing
   J. its, imposing

Here's how to crack them:

Question 1: In the underlined portion, the semicolon breaks up two independent clauses. Of course, that is acceptable behavior for a semicolon, but only if there is no conjunction between them. Thus, we can get rid of answer choice A. Looking at the answer choices, none of the alternatives gets rid of the conjunction. Therefore, we cannot break the two clauses into two separate sentences. This allows us to eliminate choice D. When you have two independent clauses linked by a conjunction, what kind of punctuation is required? If you said a comma, you were absolutely right. The correct answer is **C**.

Question 2: Notice that the underlined portion contains two commas. When do we need two commas in a sentence? When we want to set off a clause or phrase that describes a noun in more detail, but that is not vital to the meaning of the sentence (a nonrestrictive element). Let's remove the phrase "a true adventurer" from the sentence. Do we lose any vital information? No. Therefore, the correct answer choice is F. If you weren't sure how to correct the underlined portion, you could have looked at your answer choices. Answer choice G has three commas. Do they make the sentence any clearer? No. The comma after the word "true" is unnecessary. Answer choice H is incorrect because a colon should come after a complete thought and precede a list of related details. Answer choice **J** only supplies *one* comma. Remember, nonrestrictive elements need a *pair* of commas.

Question 3: Since the wording is exactly the same in each of the answer choices, it is easy to see that this question can only concern punctuation. Choice D creates an incomplete sentence: "My vision of the west;" Since this cannot stand alone, we can forget choice D. The phrase "Complete with cowboys and Indians" is supposed to be a parenthetical description of the author's vision of what the west would be like. As the underlined sentence stands, it is unclear where the main clause ends and the parenthetic thought begins, so cross off choice A. If there had been a pair of parentheses in one of the answer choices, that could well have been the correct answer, but there were no parentheses in any of the choices. What is another way to surround a parenthetical thought? If you suggested dashes, you were absolutely correct. Now, look at the difference between choices B and C. In B, there are *two* dashes surrounding the parenthetic thought. In choice C, there is only one at the beginning of the phrase. The correct answer is choice **B**.

Question 4: Again, we can be pretty sure that this is a question about punctuation. Let's look at the entire sentence. It begins with a long introductory phrase, followed by an independent clause. Do we need any punctuation between a long phrase and a clause? Sure. We need a comma. The only answer choice that correctly positions the comma between the phrase and the clause is choice **H**.

Question 5: If you look at the answer choices, you'll realize that this question is concerned with the proper use of the apostrophe. Whose back is it? It is the mule's back. We need the possessive form here. Thus, choice A is immediately gone. Choice C uses the pronoun "our." Does this agree with the first part of the sentence? No, the rest of the sentence is about the first-person author. Forget choice C. In choice B, "mules'" gives the impression that she is riding more than one mule at the same time. The correct answer is choice **D**.

Question 6: This sentence contains an independent clause followed by a list of related details, so the best punctuation mark to connect the two is the colon. A period or semicolon would be inappropriate since the sentence does not contain two independent clauses. So, answer choices F and G are eliminated. A comma would not be sufficient: the related details should be set off in order to avoid creation of a run-on sentence. So, answer choice H is eliminated. The best answer to this question is choice **J**.

Question 7: Here we have a series of items that need commas. Eliminate answer choice D because it doesn't have any commas. The original sentence, answer choice A, is missing a comma after the word "shale." In answer choice B, the adjective "freshwater" is split from the noun "shale." A comma should be placed after the words "limestone," and "freshwater shale." Therefore, the correct answer choice is **C**.

Question 8: Does the sentence require the word "its" or" it's"? If you use the word "it's," the sentence would be the same as: *It is* imposing peaks. This is clearly wrong. The word "its" refers back to the Grand Canyon. Thus, answer choice F is wrong. A comma is unnecessary after the word "its" in J since it breaks up the thought of the sentence. Two down and two to go. Is an apostrophe needed after the word "its"? Definitely not! There is no such word as "its'." Therefore the correct answer choice is **G**.

CHAPTER 7

Rhetorical Skills

Thirty-five of the seventy-five ACT English questions test rhetorical skills. These questions are not necessarily harder than the types we've been discussing up to now; they're just different. Rather than ask you about specific points of grammar, rhetoric questions get into the realm of style and editing. A few will concern the passage as a whole—save these for last. For the most part, the test writers have placed them after the specific questions anyway.

The *Official Guide to the ACT* suggests two strategies for rhetoric questions that, frankly, we disagree with.

First, the *Official Guide* suggests that you read or skim the entire passage quickly for content, and then start answering the questions. We think this is a waste of time. You don't get any points for *reading* these passages. The proctor is not going to walk around the room saying, "Ah, excellent reading form there. Five points." You get points for *answering questions* correctly. Since most of the questions (including many of the rhetoric questions) can be answered just by looking at the particular sentence that contains the underlined portion related to that question, you might as well wade in there and start racking up points.

Second, *The Official Guide* suggests that it might be a good idea to answer the general rhetoric questions first. *The Guide* points out that if a general question asks you to rearrange the order of paragraphs, your new order will make it easier for you to answer other questions. Unfortunately, we think it's equally distracting to try to read a passage for content when every other sentence has something grammatically wrong with it.

General questions are more complicated and there are fewer of them. We recommend that you leave them for last. By the time you've finished the specific line questions, you'll have had longer to absorb what's going on in the passage as a whole.

The ACT test writers break rhetorical skills down into three subcategories: strategy, organization, and style.

STRATEGY

There are twelve strategy questions on the ACT; many of these concern **transitions.** Transition questions pop up throughout the passage, not just at the end. They are probably the easiest of the rhetorical skills questions.

A transition is sometimes needed at the *beginning* of a clause, sentence or paragraph, as the writer attempts to move smoothly from one thought to another. Writers use what are called sentence connectors to get from one thought to the next. There are really only three main sentence connectors in the world: **but**, **also**, and **thus**.

Try filling in each of the blanks below with one of these three words.

> Fred and Sue were looking forward to going to dinner at a Chinese restaurant with their friends: _____ their friends wanted to go to an Italian restaurant.

> When European children hear the word "Chicago," the first thing they think of is gangsters; _____ it must be a disappointment to them when they get off the plane and see that no one is wearing spats or carrying a tommy gun.

> The campers were very tired. _____ they were very hungry.

Here's how to crack it:

There's a food fight brewing in the first sentence. To indicate that the friends are in disagreement with Fred and Sue, we need a word implying *contradiction*. That word is "but."

In the second sentence, we want to imply a *cause and effect* relationship. The first part of the sentence is meant to cause the second half. The word that suggests this is "thus."

The third example connects two sentences. Surely the two are related, but much less directly than in either of the first two examples. Our transition word needs to stress that the second idea is an *addition* to the first. The word is "also."

Of course there are lots of different ways of saying but, thus, and also. Here's a partial list:

> **but (contradiction)**—however, quite the contrary, despite, rather, notwithstanding, contrarily, on the other hand, on the contrary, although, yet, nevertheless
>
> **thus (cause and effect)**—hence, and so, therefore, consequently, for example, because of, finally, in conclusion
>
> **also (in addition)**—in addition, for example, furthermore, another, and, first, second, moreover, by the same token, besides, so too, also, in addition, similarly

Each of these words has a slightly different shade of meaning—we don't mean to imply that all the "but" words, for example, are interchangeable. On the other hand, the answer choices in a transition question generally won't give you a choice between three different kinds of buts. Your choice will be between a but and three also's, or a thus and three buts.

HOW DO YOU SPOT TRANSITION QUESTIONS?

The underlined portion in a transition question is almost always at the *beginning* of a new clause, sentence, or paragraph.

The answer choices themselves will help you to spot transition questions. They are, invariably, made up of different sentence connectors from the list we just gave you. You have to decide which sentence connector is appropriate.

Now go back to the passage. Think **but**, **thus**, or **also**. Which type of sentence connector would be most appropriate to express the transition from one thought to the other? Now look at the answer choices to see which version of the sentence connector you want is available to you this time.

Here's an example:

Funds provided by the Stafford program are not considered scholar-ships; <u>so too,</u> they are part of the extended student loan system.

1. **A.** NO CHANGE
   B. in addition,
   C. rather,
   D. moreover

Here's how to crack it:

There are two clues that might immediately point you in the right direction on this question: the underlined portion is at the *beginning* of a new clause; it also contains one of the sentence connectors we just listed. If you still aren't sure what type of question this is, look at the other answer choices. What do we see? More sentence connectors. This is a transition question.

As the passage stands, what type of transition is being used? "So too" is an **also**. Is this what we need? No. The next clause is not an *additional* thought, but rather a contrary thought. If we eliminate any answer choices that contain **also**'s, A, B, and D all bite the dust. The answer must be **C**.

Note that in this case it might have been harder to decide among the answer choices if one of them had been a **thus**. Fortunately, that was not an option.

THE OTHER STRATEGY QUESTIONS

Other strategy questions read as if they have been lifted from the reading comprehension section of the ACT:

- Which of the following answers best summarizes the main point of the passage?

- Is the use of formal English appropriate in the context of this passage?

- If the passage were revised to present conflicting viewpoints, which of the following changes would best represent the other side of the author's argument?

These are content questions, and difficult to talk about without the passage they came from. Unless you have some immediate gut feeling about the answer, these questions are better left for the second pass, when your understanding of the passage may be more complete. If you are still stuck, eliminate as many answers as you can, and guess. You may find that some of the reading comprehension techniques will help you answer these remaining strategy questions.

ORGANIZATION

There are two kinds of organization questions. The first asks you to reorder sentences within a paragraph. The second asks you to reorder paragraphs within the passage as a whole. Let's talk about sentences within a paragraph first. Here's an example:

[1] Van Gogh, particularly in his later paintings, creates thick swirls of paint which perhaps mirror the emotional storm raging within. [2] DuFevre piles the paint onto the canvas in thick swatches which rise off the canvas by a good half inch at times. [3] Perhaps the most telling similarity between Van Gogh and DuFevre, the little-known modern surrealist, lies in their use of brushstrokes. [4] It is almost as if he is challenging Van Gogh to a contest to determine who was more emotionally disturbed.

2. Which of the following ordering of sentences will make the paragraph most logical?

F. NO CHANGE
G. 1, 3, 2, 4
H. 1, 4, 3, 2
J. 3, 1, 2, 4

Here's how to crack it:

Although you might not think so at first, these questions are actually easier when they ask you to reorder *all* of the sentences in the paragraph as they do here. Rather than trying to figure out the order of all four sentences, why not figure out which of the sentences ought to come *first*. This should eliminate several of the answer choices and make your job much easier. Read through the sentences again looking for the thought which is capable of launching the entire paragraph. We need the topic sentence—the main idea which the other sentences support.

If you think the main idea is in Sentence [3], you are absolutely correct. The third sentence suggests a similarity between two painters which is explained and amplified in the other sentences. Which of the answer choices has Sentence [3] in the lead-off position? Only one. The answer must be choice **J**.

If you can't decide which of the choices comes first, another tack is to pair sentences that you can connect in some way. For example, in the paragraph above, you might have looked at Sentence [4] and noticed that the pronoun "he" could only refer to DuFevre. This implies that Sentence [4] comes right after Sentence [2]. This would eliminate answer choices F and H.

ORDERING WHOLE PARAGRAPHS

When the ACT test writers ask you to reorganize the paragraphs in a passage, they always position the question at the end of the passage after all the other specific questions. That's exactly where this question belongs. Don't spend large amounts of time rereading the entire passage. If, as you were reading the first time, you were struck by something strange in the ordering of paragraphs, go back and look at that place; otherwise, do some quick elimination and guess.

Again, you don't need to be sure of the position of *all* the paragraphs in order to do some clever elimination. Look for either the first paragraph, or a pair of paragraphs that you are pretty sure go together, and use POE.

Here's a small-scale example. Let's assume that you've read a passage and summarized each of the paragraphs in your head. Here are the summaries:

Summary of Paragraph 1:

Most people believe eating healthy nutritious food is good for you.

Summary of Paragraph 2:

Carrying the heavy boxes home, I pulled a muscle.

Summary of Paragraph 3:

I recently went to the health food store and bought big boxes of wheat germ, carrot juice, and tofu.

Summary of Paragraph 4:

But you can take this health kick too far, as I discovered.

3. Which of the following ordering of paragraphs best organizes this passage?

A. NO CHANGE
B. 1, 4, 3, 2
C. 4, 2, 1, 3
D. 2, 3, 4, 1

Here's how to crack it:
There are several ways to approach this question. You could look for the first paragraph of the passage. You could try to establish some relationship between any two of the paragraphs. You could try to spot the *last* paragraph of the passage. Let's begin by trying to establish some relationship between any two paragraphs. In this passage, is there any observable cause and effect going on? Yes. Lifting the boxes caused a pulled muscle in the narrator. He couldn't pull the muscle until after he bought the boxes, which means Paragraph 2 must come after Paragraph 3. This option exists in only one of the answer choices. It begins to look as if answer choice **B** must be correct. To check, we can look to see what answer B offers us as the beginning and end paragraphs. However, bear in mind that you don't want to spend too much time on any one question. Reading an entire passage again with a new beginning is a laborious task. Practice good triage technique, and leave this one for later.

STYLE

The largest number of style errors stems from **redundancy.** Put simply, redundancy means saying the same thing twice.

HOW TO SPOT REDUNDANCY

Some redundancy errors are easier to see than others. Here are a couple of easy examples:

> *Cheap and inexpensive gifts can be found in the shopping district.*

> *Weak and without strength, the old car could not make it up the hill.*

In both of the examples above, two adjectives are saying exactly the same thing. Since there is really no need for both, the best way to correct the sentences would be to remove one of the superfluous adjectives:

> *Inexpensive gifts can be found in the shopping district.*

> *The weak old car could not make it up the hill.*

Slightly more difficult:

> *After birth, the newborn babies are weighed by a nurse.*

> *In the year 1992...*

These examples would be perfectly acceptable in normal speech. However, newborn babies have obviously just been born, and 1992 is already a year. To fix these sentences, simply remove one of the superfluous items:

> *After birth, the babies are weighed by a nurse.*

> *In 1992...*

A comprehensive list of all the possible redundancies would be too long to do you any good. All you have to do in questions like these is spot the redundancy, and that's easy enough. Look for repetition in the underlined portion of the sentence or among the answer choices. When you see it, expunge it ruthlessly.

The Vietnam veterans were recently <u>memorialized by a memorial</u> sculpture in Washington[4].

4. **F.** NO CHANGE
   G. memorialized by a
   H. memorialized with a new memoria
   J. memorialized in a recent

Here's how to crack it:
This is an obvious case of redundancy. We need to find an answer choice which does not repeat itself. Choice J seems possible until we realize that "recently memorialized in a recent sculpture" merely makes the same error with another word (recently). The only possible answer is choice **G**.

THE OTHER STYLE QUESTIONS
A small number of style questions relate to the tone of the passage overall, and to the suitability of individual words. There are relatively few of these questions, and again, we counsel that unless you have a strong feeling that you have a handle on these questions, you circle them and come back to them later.

SUMMARY

1. Do the questions in order, leaving only tougher rhetoric questions for the end. If you're having trouble with a particular question, leave it and come back. Often a later question will remind you of the error in an earlier one.

2. Search the answer choices for clues. Note how the choices differ from each other, and use that information to determine the error(s) being tested.

3. Look for one error at a time. It is a good idea to first narrow the choices down on the basis of errors in sentence structure and grammar, then use punctuation to make your selection between the remaining choices. For instance, if the choices offer you a list of items or actions, first check for parallel construction, then look for correct use of serial commas.

4. Don't forget that NO CHANGE is the answer a little less than a quarter of the time—if you can't find anything wrong with the underlined portion, it may be correct as written.

5. If "OMIT the underlined portion" is offered as an answer choice, examine it very closely. It has a high probability of being correct.

6. Read carefully—it is easy to overlook a comma or apostrophe when you're working quickly.

RHETORIC DRILL

[1]

The golden age of television means many things to many people; <u>and to</u> the small band of actors, writers, and directors who would rise <u>to prominence</u> in the late 50's and early 60's, without a doubt it meant the "live" television shows like *Playhouse 90* where many of them <u>initially worked for the first time.</u>

[2]

[1] Each week, a new "teleplay" was created from scratch—written, cast, rehearsed and performed. [2] *Playhouse 90* was truly a remarkable training ground for the young talents. [3] Such future luminaries as Paddy Chayefsky,

1. **A.** NO CHANGE
   B. thus to
   C. but to
   D. In addition to

2. **F.** NO CHANGE
   G. prominent famousness
   H. famous prominence
   J. famousness

3. **A.** NO CHANGE
   B. initially for the first time worked
   C. for the first time worked initially
   D. worked for the first time.

Marlon Brando, and Patricia Neal worked long hours honing to a knife edge their craft. [4] In some cases, when there were problems with the censors, it would have to be created twice. 5

[3]

Despite the frantic pace, accidents happened frequently. David Niven once revealed that during an early show, he inadvertently locked his costume in his dressing room two minutes before air time. As the announcer announced the opening credits, the sound of axes splintering the door to Niven's dressing room could be heard in the background.

4. **F.** NO CHANGE
   G. to an edge
   H. edges
   J. OMIT the underlined portion

5. Which of the following sequences would best organize the sentences in Paragraph 2?

   A. NO CHANGE
   B. 1, 2, 4, 3
   C. 2, 1, 4, 3
   D. 3, 4, 1, 2

6. **F.** NO CHANGE
   G. Due to
   H. In spite of
   J. Thus

Items 7, 8, and 9 ask questions about the passage as a whole.

7. If the writer wished to make the tone of Paragraph 3 more lighthearted, she could change the word "accidents" to

   A. NO CHANGE
   B. casualties
   C. mishaps
   D. grave errors

8. Which of the following would best summarize the passage as a whole?

   F. The golden age of television meant many things to many different people.
   G. Early television shows like *Playhouse 90* provided the training ground where talented new actors could learn their craft.
   H. The golden age of television had many amusing moments.
   J. The rise of Paddy Chayefsky, Marlon Brando, and Patricia Neal helped to make *Playhouse 90* a success.

9. Which of the following sequences of paragraphs would make the structure of the passage as a whole the most logical?

   A. NO CHANGE
   B. 3, 2, 1
   C. 3, 1, 2
   D. 2, 3, 1

Here's how to crack them:

Question 1: The underlined portion and the answer choices all contain sentence connectors. This is a **transition** question. Do we need an *also*, a *but*, or a *thus*? It seems pretty clear we need a *but*. The answer is **C**.

Question 2: Several of the answer choices here seem to use similar words. We should consider **redundancy** immediately. G and H are clearly redundant. Answer choice J ("famousness") seems incorrect. Thus the best answer is **F**, NO CHANGE.

Question 3: The underlined portion and the answer choices all seem to contain similar words, so again we should consider **redundancy**. There is no need to say both "initially" and "for the first time" in the same sentence. Answer choice D is the only choice that does not do this.

Question 4: At first this might strike you as an idiom question. In fact, **style** questions often resemble idiom questions. The metaphor of an actor sharpening his or her skills is effective, but how far do we want to take it? Is it necessary to say "to a knife edge" to get across the point? The answer is **J**. OMIT the underlined portion.

Question 5: As with all **organization** questions, we should try to spot either the beginning sentence, or any pair of sentences we can link together. There is a certain cause and effect visible between Sentence [1] and Sentence [4]. Which of the answer choices puts them next to each other in that order? Only one. The answer would seem to have to be C. Does that make sense? Let's read the paragraph in the new order just to be sure.
It begins by saying *Playhouse 90* was a training ground. Each week a new teleplay was created from scratch. Sometimes, it was created twice. Future stars worked there in order to get experience. The paragraph seems to hold together. The answer is **C**.

Question 6: We see more sentence connectors, so we are again prepared for **transition**. "(Blank) the frantic pace, accidents happened frequently." Let's try out the words in the answer choices. Could "despite" fill in the blank? No. We want more of a causal word (a "thus" word). Answer choice **G**. "Due to" is the correct answer.

Question 7: How do we change the **tone** of Paragraph [3] with one word? Well, "accidents" sounds a little drastic. Which choice minimizes the sound of that word? If you said **C**, "mishaps," you were absolutely correct.

Question 8: This is one to leave for last. **Summary** questions always take a while. Answer choice F merely repeats the first half of the first sentence of the passage, entirely missing *Playhouse 90*. Answer choice G seems real good. Answer choice H concentrates on the third paragraph only. Answer J concentrates solely on the three actors and writers mentioned. Are they the primary focus of the passage? Not really. The answer is **G**.

Question 9: Another question to leave until the end. **Organization of paragraphs** requires an overview of the entire passage. As always, try to find one paragraph you feel you can label as first or last, and proceed from there. The correct answer is **A**. NO CHANGE.

PART III

How to Beat the ACT Math Test

WHAT TO EXPECT IN THE MATH SECTION

You will have 60 minutes to answer 60 multiple-choice questions based on "... topics covered in typical high school classes." For those of you who aren't sure if you went to a typical high school, these questions break down into rather precise areas of knowledge.

There are always exactly:

- 24 problems from pre-algebra and elementary algebra. *Included are questions based on definitions of terms (integers, prime numbers, etc.), fractions, decimals, ratios, percents, averages, word problems, quadratic equations.*

- 18 problems from intermediate algebra and coordinate geometry.

  Included are questions based on exponents, square roots, factoring, writing equations, inequalities, simultaneous equations, and graphing.

- 14 problems from geometry.

  Included are questions based on angles, lengths, triangles, parallel lines, area, perimeter, circles, and volume.

- 4 problems from basic trigonometry.

  Questions based on SOHCAHTOA, and some other relatively easy trigonometry formulas.

WHAT NOT TO EXPECT IN THE MATH SECTION

You won't find any logarithms, imaginary numbers, or calculus of any kind. For those of you who may have taken the SAT, you also won't find any of the devious tricks which plague that test. The ACT, by contrast, is pretty fair.

THE PRINCETON REVIEW APPROACH

Because the test is so predictable, the best way to prepare for ACT math is with:

1. A thorough review of the very specific information and question types that come up again and again.

2. An understanding of The Princeton Review test-taking strategies and techniques.

In each chapter of the math section you'll find a mixture of review and technique, with a sprinkling of ACT-like problems. At the end of each chapter will be a summary of the chapter and a drill designed to pinpoint your math test-taking strengths and weaknesses. In addition to working through the problems you'll find in this book, we strongly suggest you practice our techniques on some real ACT practice tests.

Let's begin with some general strategy.

EASY, MEDIUM, DIFFICULT

Sixty minutes for sixty questions. This seems fairly straightforward, but don't let the symmetry of these two numbers fool you; some problems will take much less than a minute—and others could take forever if you let them.

The first few questions are designed to be easier than the rest of the test, then the questions get a bit tougher and stay that way for the remainder of the section. At least, this is ACT's intention. However, what the people at ACT think is easy may not strike you the same way. Similarly, you might find some of the problems in the middle or end of the test to be a piece of cake.

So you are going to have to figure out for yourself which are the easy, medium, and difficult questions in this section.

MATH TRIAGE

In Chapter Two we introduced the concept of triage. Let's apply this concept to ACT math. Here's a problem:

1. Cynthia, Peter, Nancy, and Kevin are all carpenters. Last week, each built the following number of chairs:

   Cynthia–36   Peter–45   Nancy–74   Kevin–13

   What was the average number of chairs the carpenters built last week?

   A. 39
   B. 42
   C. 55
   D. 59
   E. 63

NOW, LATER, MUCH LATER, NEVER

Do you want to do this problem *now*? That is the question you should constantly be asking yourself during the exam. If you finish reading a problem and immediately know how to solve it, then of course you should do it right away.

If you finish reading a problem and immediately know that you will never, ever, understand that question, then write R.I.P. next to it, pick an answer at random, and never look at it again.

If you aren't sure, you *might* want to *start* doing the problem to see if something will jog your memory. However, if you look at your watch and see that thirty seconds have gone by and you still don't have a handle on the problem, it's time to throw it to the back of the line. Put a big circle around it and move on. You haven't wasted the thirty seconds, you've invested them. When you come back to the question later, after you've done all the problems that you found easy, you will already have read it once, thought about it, perhaps made some beginning calculations. You won't be starting from scratch at all.

I'M ALMOST DONE . . .

The temptation to get stubborn and stay with a particular problem can be very strong. But if it takes you four minutes to solve question 5, that might mean you will never get a chance to look at several other problems later in the test that you might have found easy.

As we mentioned in Chapter Two, you might have the "oh yeah!" revelation on this problem before you finish the section!

THAT WAS AN EASY ONE

Of course to solve the problem about the four carpenters, you were probably not going to have to depend on revelation. Did you want to do it right away? Sure. It was a moderately easy average problem.

Here's how to crack it:

To find the average of a set of numbers, add the numbers together and divide by the number of terms.

$$\frac{\text{sum of numbers to be averaged}}{\text{number of terms}} = \text{average}$$

In this case, the thing we don't know is the average, but we do know everything else, so let's put the numbers into our formula:

$$\frac{36 + 45 + 74 + 13}{4} = \text{average}$$

(By the way, we will cover average problems more fully in Chapter Nine. The answer to this question is **B**.)

How do you distinguish an easy problem from a tough one? In part by deciding whether it can be done in one or two steps, or whether it will require three or more steps.

HERE'S A MEDIUM ACT PROBLEM

22. Four carpenters built an average of 42 chairs each last week. If Cynthia built 36 chairs, Nancy built 74 chairs, and Kevin built 13 chairs, how many chairs did Peter build?

    F. 24
    G. 37
    H. 45
    J. 53
    K. 67

This is still an average problem, but it has become less straightforward now, and will require an extra step to get the final answer.

Here's how to crack it:

Let's put the information we have into the same formula we used above:

$$\frac{36 + 74 + 13 + \text{Peter}}{4} = 42$$

You might want to substitute the variable x for Peter. Note that medium and difficult average problems often give you the number of terms and the average. What they *don't* give you—and the important thing to figure out—is the *sum* of the numbers to be averaged.

If we multiply both sides by 4, we get the sum of all four numbers.

$$36 + 74 + 13 + \text{Peter} = 168$$

To find out Peter's hours, we just have to add the other hours and subtract from 168. 168 - 123 = 45. The answer is **H**.

HERE'S A HARD ACT PROBLEM

41. Four carpenters each built an average of 42 chairs last week. If no chairs were left uncompleted and if Peter, who built 50 chairs, built the greatest number of chairs, what is the *least* number of chairs one of the carpenters could have built?

    A. 18
    B. 19
    C. 20
    D. 39.33
    E. 51

The concept *behind* this question is really no more difficult than either of the first two problems. It is still about averages. But now there are several more steps involved, including a small leap of faith. You can tell it's more difficult than the first two questions partly because of the language it uses: "If no chairs were left uncompleted" is closing a potential loophole. Easy problems are usually too simple to have loopholes. "What is the *least*" implies the need for reflection.

Here's how to crack it:

Let's put what we know into the same formula we have used twice already:

$$\frac{50 + x + y + z}{4} = 42$$

The only individual we know something specific about is Peter. We've represented the other three carpenters as *x*, *y*, and *z*. Since the sum of all four carpenters adds up to 168, we now have:

$$50 + x + y + z = 168$$

By itself, an equation with three variables can't be solved, so unless we can glean a bit more information from the problem, we're stuck, and it's time to put a circle around the problem and move on.

Let's assume you skipped the problem temporarily, and have now come back to it after completing all the problems you thought were easy.

The problem asks for the *least* number of chairs one carpenter could build. To figure this out, let's have the other two carpenters build the *most* number of chairs they could build. According to the problem, Peter constructed 50, and no one else built as many as he did. So let's say two of the other carpenters constructed 49 each—the largest possible amount they could build and still have built less than Peter. By making carpenters *x* and *y* construct as many chairs as possible, we can find out the *minimum* number of chairs carpenter *z* would have to make.

Now the problem looks like this:

$$50 + 49 + 49 + z = 168$$

If we add $50 + 49 + 49$ and subtract it from 168, then $z = 20$, and the correct answer choice is **C**.

PROCESS OF ELIMINATION

Even if you weren't sure how to do that last problem, you might have been able to eliminate one answer choice right away using the major technique we introduced in Chapter Three: POE. Remember, ACT doesn't take away any points for wrong answers, so it is in your interest to guess on every question you can't solve using other methods. But your guesses will be a lot more valuable if you can eliminate some of the answer choices first. The problem said Peter built the greatest number of chairs—50 of them. Therefore, could any of the other carpenters have built *more* than that? No, so answer choice E didn't make sense.

COMMON SENSE

You can frequently get rid of several answer choices in an ACT math problem without doing much actual math. Let's look at an example:

> 3. There are 600 school children in the Lakeville
> district. If 54 of them are high school seniors,
> what is the percentage of high school seniors in
> the Lakeville district?
>
> A. .9%
> B. 2.32%
> C. 9%
> D. 11%
> E. 90%

Here's how to crack it:

This is not an advanced problem. ACT wants us to write a simple equation, and we will review just how to do that in the arithmetic chapter. But before we do any heavy math, let's see if we can get rid of some answer choices using common sense.

The question asks us to find a percentage of 600. Just to get a rough fix on where we are, what is 10% of 600? If you said 60, you are right. To find 10% of anything, you simply move the decimal point over one place to the left. If 60 is 10%, then 54 must be slightly less than 10%. Which answer choices don't make sense? D and E don't work because we need something less than 10%. On the other hand, we need something only *slightly* less than 10%. Could the answer be A or B? No. On this problem, it was just as easy to eliminate wrong answers as it was to solve for the right answer. The answer is **C**.

On most ACT problems, you will only be able to eliminate one or two answer choices by using common sense, but it's still vital that you always think about what a reasonable answer might be for a particular problem—*before* you solve it mathematically. This is because the ACT has some trap answers waiting for you.

PARTIAL ANSWERS

Sometimes students think they have completed a problem before the problem is actually done. The test writers at ACT like to include trap answer choices for these students. Here's an example:

4. A bus line charges $5 each way to ferry a passenger between the hotel and an archeological dig. On a given day, the bus line has a capacity to carry 255 passengers from the hotel to the dig and back. If the bus line runs at 90% of capacity, how much money did the bus line take in that day?

F. $1147.50
G. $1250
H. $2295
J. $2550
K. $2625

Here's how to crack it:

The first step in this problem is to determine how much money the line would make if it ran at total capacity. If there were 255 passengers, each of whom paid $10 (remember, the bus company charges $5 each way), that would be $2550.

If you were in a hurry, you might decide at this point that you were already done and go straight to the answer choices. And there is answer choice J, beckoning seductively. Unfortunately, of course, J is not the right answer. The bus line is only running at 90% of capacity. To get the real answer, we have to find 90% of $2550.

You also might have missed, or put aside temporarily, the information that each passenger has to pay coming *and* going, in which case you might have multiplied 255 by 5 to get $1275, and then found 90% of that, $1147.50—which just happens to be answer choice **F**.

Both answer choices F and J were partial answers. Students who picked one of these answers did not make a mistake in their math, nor did they misunderstand the overall concept of the problem; they simply stopped before they were completely finished. All you had to do to $1147.50 to get the right answer was double it, so that you included both trips. All you had to do to $2550 to get the right answer was to take 90% of it.

HOW TO AVOID PARTIAL ANSWERS

You can prevent yourself from picking partial answers by doing two things:

1. SLOW DOWN. It isn't going to help to do a problem so quickly that you miss important information.

2. When you finish a problem, always reread the last line to make sure you've answered the question the ACT test writer asked.

ARE PARTIAL ANSWERS FAIR?

You might decide that it is not very sporting of ACT to try to trip students up with partial answer choices. On the other hand, if this had been a short-answer test, students might well have made exactly the same mistake on their own. Besides, if partial answers represent the downside of multiple- choice testing, there is a tremendous upside as well: let's see how POE could have helped us on this last problem.

YOU BET!

POE allows us to eliminate crazy answer choices. Remember, we said the first step in the problem was to find out how much total money was taken in on that day. If you read carefully, you realized that each of the 255 passengers had to pay $10. This is a total of $2550. To get the final answer, of course, we had to get 90% of $2550.

Was it necessary to work the problem out exactly?

Let's look at the answer choices.

J. $2550 represents the total capacity. It is a trap, so eliminate it. The correct answer must be a bit less than $2550. Could the answer be **K.** $2625? Impossible.

We know the answer should be a bit less than $2550. Could it be as small as F. $1147.50 or G. $1250? No way.

RED HERRINGS

Of the sixty problems in this section, perhaps as many as two will contain extra information that is not, strictly speaking, necessary to solve the problems. The test writers want to see if you can distinguish important information from filler. Since there are so few of these questions, it isn't necessary to examine each new piece of information with a magnifying glass to see if it might be a red herring. In almost every problem on the ACT you will need *all* the information given in order to solve it. However, if you're staring at a particular number which doesn't seem to have anything to do with the solution of the question you're doing— well, every once in a while it might not. Here's an example:

5. Susan's take-home pay is $300 per week, of which she spends $80 on food and $150 on rent. What fraction of her take-home pay does she spend on food?

A. $\dfrac{2}{75}$

B. $\dfrac{4}{15}$

C. $\dfrac{1}{2}$

D. $\dfrac{23}{30}$

E. $\dfrac{29}{30}$

Here's how to crack it:

The last line tells us what we need to do. A fraction is a part over a whole. In this case, the whole is $300. The part is the amount of money spent on food:

$$\frac{\$80}{\$300} \quad \text{which reduces to} \quad \frac{4}{15}$$

Where does the $150 fit in? It doesn't. The question isn't asking about rent. The test writers just threw that in to confuse you. Note that if you got confused and found the fraction of the take-home salary that was paid in rent, $150/$300, you would pick answer choice C. The correct answer is **B**.

SUMMARY

1. The math section of the ACT contains 60 questions to do in 60 minutes. It breaks down into:

   pre-algebra and elementary algebra—24 questions
   intermediate algebra and coordinate geometry—18 questions
   geometry—14 questions
   trigonometry—4 questions

2. To answer the greatest number of questions correctly, it helps to use triage to decide whether to do a problem now, or whether to wait until later. Triage enables you to decide if a problem is easy, medium, or hard. Easy problems generally have only one or two steps. Medium problems generally have two or three steps. Difficult problems have more steps, and may call for further analysis.

3. You can use the Process of Elimination, or POE, to cancel out wrong answer choices. Sometimes it is easier to get rid of wrong answers than to find the correct answer.

   - Incorrect answers are sometimes partial answers—answers you arrive at on the way to the final solution if you quit before you were really done.

   - Incorrect answers sometimes don't really make sense if you look at them in the cold light of day. Frequently, you can eliminate several answer choices because they are nowhere near what common sense says the answer would have to be.

   - Incorrect answers are also sometimes based on red herrings—pieces of information which are not really necessary to solve the problem.

CHAPTER 8

Basics

Look at the following problem:

1. How many even prime numbers are there between 0 and 100?

   A. 0
   B. 1
   C. 2
   D. 3
   E. 4

This is a very easy problem—provided you know what the terms "even" and "prime" mean. Without a knowledge of these terms, the problem is impossible. Let's begin our math review by going over all the basic math terms and operations covered on the ACT. (By the way, the answer to that last question is answer choice **B**.)

BASIC TERMS

Real Numbers

Real numbers are all the numbers you think of when you think of numbers: $5, \frac{1}{4}$, 7.9, 100, -43, etc., etc. They include everything *except* imaginary numbers, which are no longer tested on the ACT anyway. In other words, *all* the numbers on this test will be real—and real numbers include all the other types of numbers we will cover below.

Rational Numbers

Any number that can be written as a fraction is called a rational number. But this does not just mean what we normally think of as fractions. $\frac{1}{2}$ is a rational number, but so is 2 because we can write it as $\frac{2}{1}$. So is $\frac{26}{23}$. In fact, it is easier to think of rational numbers as being everything except. . . .

Irrational Numbers

An irrational number cannot be written as a fraction; there aren't that many of them. π is irrational. Like other irrational numbers, it goes on forever. While you may think of π as 3.14, it can be written out to as many decimal places as you feel like writing down: 3.141592 etc. etc.—and as many places as you take it, you will never find a repeating pattern.

Other irrational numbers? Any square root of a number that does not have a square root. For example, $\sqrt{3}$, or $\sqrt{2}$. By contrast, $\sqrt{4}$, which reduces to 2, is a rational number.

Integers

Integers include everything *except* what we normally think of as fractions or decimals: 2, 134, -56, 0, and 7 are all integers. $\frac{1}{2}$, 6.7, and $\frac{-31}{4}$ are not.

Positive and Negative

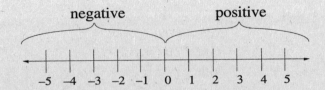

Positive numbers are to the right of the zero on the number line above. Negative numbers are to the left of zero on the number line above. Zero itself is neither negative nor positive.

Note that positive numbers get bigger as they move away from 0. Negative numbers get smaller. For example, -3 is smaller than -1.

There are three rules regarding the multiplication of positive and negative numbers:

$$positive \times positive = positive$$
$$positive \times negative = negative$$
$$negative \times negative = positive$$

When you add a positive number and a negative number, you're subtracting the number with the negative sign in front of it from the positive number.

$$5 + (-3) = 2$$

When you add two negative numbers, you're adding the two numbers as if they were positive and then putting a negative sign in front of the sum.

$$-3 + -4 = -7$$

Even and Odd Numbers

Even numbers are integers that can be divided evenly by 2:

$$-4, -2, 0, 2, 4, 6 \text{ etc.}$$

Odd numbers are integers that cannot be divided evenly by 2:

$$-5, -3, -1, 1, 3, 5 \text{ etc.}$$

Note that 0 is even. There are several rules regarding multiplication and addition of even and odd numbers:

even × even = even
odd × odd = odd
even × odd = even
even + even = even
odd + odd = even
even + odd = odd

Digits

There are ten digits: 0,1,2,3,4,5,6,7,8,9

The number 364 has three digits—3, 6, and 4. In this number, the 4 is called the *ones* digit, or *units* digit. The 6 is called the *tens* digit. The three is called the *hundreds* digit.

The number 4.56 has three digits—4, 5, and 6. The 4 is called the *ones* digit or *units* digit. The 5 is called the *tenths* digit, and the 6 is called the *hundredths* digit.

Prime Numbers

A prime number can be divided evenly only by itself and by 1. Thus 2, 3, 5, 7, 11, and 13 are all prime numbers. The number 2 is the only even prime number. Neither 0 nor 1 is a prime number.

Absolute Value

The absolute value of a number is the distance between that number and 0 on the number line. The absolute value of 6 is expressed as | 6 |.

| 6 | = 6

| -6 | = 6

Variables and Coefficients

In the expression $3x + 4y$, x and y are called **variables** because we don't know what they are. 3 and 4 are called **coefficients**.

BASIC OPERATIONS

Divisibility Rules

If a number can be divided evenly by another number, it is said to be divisible by that number. A good way to save time actually dividing is to know the rules of divisibility for some common numbers:

2: A number is divisible by 2 if its units digit can be divided evenly by 2 (in other words, if it is even). 46 is divisible by 2. So is 3,574.

3: A number is divisible by 3 if the sum of its digits can be divided evenly by 3. We can instantly tell that 216 is divisible by 3 because the sum of the digits (2 + 1 + 6) is divisible by 3.

4: A number is divisible by 4 if the number formed by its last two digits (tens digit and units digit) is also divisible by 4. Thus, 316 is divisible by 4 because 16 is divisible by 4. 728 is also divisible by 4 because 28 is divisible by 4.

5: A number is divisible by 5 if its last digit (units place) is either 0 or 5. For example, 60, 85, and 15 are all divisible by 5.

6: A number is divisible by 6 if it is also divisible by the factors of 6—2 and 3. For example, 228 is divisible by 6 because it is even (divisible by 2) and the sum of its digits is divisible by 3.

Operations

Sum means addition.
   The sum of 3 and 4 is 7.

Product means multiplication.
   The product of 5 and 2 is 10.

Difference means subtraction.
   The difference between 7 and 3 is 4.

Quotient means division.
   If you divide 14 by 7, the quotient is 2.

Factors and Multiples

A number is a *factor* of another number if it can be divided evenly *into* that number. Is 3 a factor of 15? Yes, because 3 can be divided evenly into 15. The complete list of factors of 15 is 1, 3, 5, and 15.

A number is a *multiple* of another number if it can be divided evenly *by* that number. For example, multiples of 15 include 15, 30, 45, and 60.

What is the only factor of 15 that is also a multiple of 15? 15.

STANDARD SYMBOLS

Symbol	Meaning
$=$	*is equal to*
$\neq$	*is not equal to*
$<$	*is less than*
$>$	*is greater than*
$\leq$	*is less than or equal to*
$\geq$	*is greater than or equal to*

Exponents

An exponent is a short way of writing the value of a number multiplied several times by itself. 4 x 4 x 4 x 4 x 4 can also be written as 4^5. This is expressed as "4 to the fifth power." The large number (4) is called the base, and the little number (5) is called the exponent.

There are several rules to remember about exponents:

Multiplying numbers with the same base

When you multiply numbers that have the same base, you simply add the exponents.

$$6^2 \times 6^3 = 6^{(2+3)} = 6^5 \qquad \left(y^2\right)\left(y^3\right) = y^{(2+3)} = y^5$$

Dividing numbers with the same base

When you divide numbers that have the same base, you simply subtract the bottom exponent from the top exponent.

$$\frac{4^7}{4^2} = 4^5 \qquad \frac{x^7}{x^2} = x^5 \qquad \frac{y^3}{y^5} = \frac{1}{y^2}$$

Negative powers

In that last example, we also could have written the result as y^{-2}. A negative power is simply the reciprocal of a positive power. (The reciprocal of 3 is $\frac{1}{3}$.)

$$3^{-1} = \frac{1}{3} \qquad 3^{-2} = \frac{1}{9} \qquad 3^{-3} = \frac{1}{27}$$

Fractional powers

When a number is raised to a fractional power, the numerator (the number above the line in a fraction) functions like a real exponent, while the denominator (the number below the line in a fraction) tells you what power radical to make the number. (Radicals will be defined on page 110.)

$$9^{\frac{1}{2}} = \sqrt{9} = 3 \qquad 8^{\frac{2}{3}} = \sqrt[3]{8^2}$$

Raising a power to a power

When you raise a power to a power, you simply multiply the exponents.

$$(4^2)^6 = 4^{(2 \cdot 6)} = 4^{12} \qquad (y^3)^2 = y^{(3 \cdot 2)} = y^6$$

The zero power

Anything to the zero power is 1.

$$4^0 = 1 \qquad x^0 = 1$$

Distributing exponents

When several numbers are inside parentheses, the exponent outside the parentheses must be distributed to all of the numbers within.

$$(4y)^2 = 4^2 y^2 = 16y^2$$

But Watch Out For . . .

There are several operations that *seem* like they ought to work with exponents but don't.

Does $x^2 + x^3 = x^5$? NO!!

Does $x^4 - x^2 = x^2$? NO!!!

Does $\dfrac{x^2 + y^3 + z^4}{x^2 + y^3} = z^4$? NO!!!!

In fact, none of these three expressions can be reduced.

You would expect that raising a number to a power would increase that number, and usually it does, but there are exceptions:

- If you raise a positive fraction of less than 1 to a power, the fraction gets smaller.

$$\left(\frac{1}{2}\right)^2 = \frac{1^2}{2^2} = \frac{1}{4}$$

- If you raise a negative number to an odd power, the number gets smaller.

$$(-3)^3 = (-3)(-3)(-3) = -27$$

(remember –27 is smaller than –3)

- If you raise a negative number to an even power, the number becomes positive.

$$(-3)^2 = (-3)(-3) = 9$$

RADICALS

The **square root** of a positive number x is the number that, when squared, equals x. For example, the square root of 16 equals 4 (or–4) because $4 \times 4 = 16$ (or $-4 \times -4 = 16$). On the ACT, you will not have to worry about negative square roots—for our purposes, the square root of 16 is just 4.

The symbol for a positive square root is $\sqrt{}$. A number inside the $\sqrt{}$ is also called a radical.

$$\sqrt{16} = 4$$
$$\sqrt{9} = 3$$

The **cube root** of a positive number x is the number that, when cubed, equals x. For example, the cube root of 8 equals 2 because $2 \times 2 \times 2$ equals 8.

$$\sqrt[3]{8} = 2$$
$$\sqrt[3]{27} = 3$$

There are several rules to remember about radicals:

- $\sqrt{x} \cdot \sqrt{y} = \sqrt{xy}$

  For example, $\left(\sqrt{12}\right)\left(\sqrt{3}\right) = \sqrt{36}$ or 6.

  $$3\sqrt{5} \cdot 6\sqrt{2} = 18\sqrt{10}$$

- $\sqrt{\dfrac{x}{y}} = \dfrac{\sqrt{x}}{\sqrt{y}}$

  For example, $\sqrt{\dfrac{3}{16}} = \dfrac{\sqrt{3}}{\sqrt{16}} = \dfrac{\sqrt{3}}{4}$

- To simplify a radical, try factoring.

  $$\sqrt{32} = \sqrt{16}\sqrt{2} = 4\sqrt{2}$$

  $$2\sqrt{5} + 4\sqrt{125} = 2\sqrt{5} + 4\left(\sqrt{25} \cdot \sqrt{5}\right) =$$
  $$2\sqrt{5} + (4)(5)\left(\sqrt{5}\right) = 22\sqrt{5}$$

- The square root of a positive fraction less than 1 is actually larger than the original fraction.

  For example,

  $$\sqrt{\dfrac{1}{4}} = \dfrac{1}{2}$$

- Always try to have a ballpark idea of how big the number you are dealing with actually is. $\sqrt{63}$ is a bit less than $\sqrt{64}$ or 8. $\sqrt[3]{9}$ is a bit more than $\sqrt[3]{8}$ or 2.

  Some good approximations to remember:

  $\sqrt{1} = 1$

  $\sqrt{2} = 1.4$

  $\sqrt{3} = 1.7$

  $\sqrt{4} = 2$

BASICS DRILL

1. Which of the following expresses the prime factorization of 54?

   A. 9×6
   B. $3 \times 3 \times 6$
   C. $3 \times 3 \times 2$
   D. $3 \times 3 \times 3 \times 2$
   E. 5.4×10

2. $\dfrac{(-5)(4)|-6|}{-3} =$

   F. -120
   G. -40
   H. 40
   J. 60
   K. 120

3. The number 1134 is divisible by all of the following except

   A. 3
   B. 6
   C. 9
   D. 12
   E. 14

4. $(-2)^3 + (3)^{-2} + \dfrac{8}{9} =$

   F. -7

   G. $-1\dfrac{7}{9}$

   H. $\dfrac{8}{9}$

   J. $1\dfrac{7}{9}$

   K. 12

5. $27^{\frac{2}{3}} =$

   A. -9
   B. -4
   C. 9
   D. 18
   E. 81^3

6. $\dfrac{(xy)^3 z^0}{x^3 y^4} =$

   F. $\dfrac{1}{y}$

   G. $\dfrac{z}{y}$

   H. z

   J. xy

   K. xyz

7. When is $\dfrac{11 - a}{2}$ an integer?

   A. Only when a is negative
   B. Only when a is positive
   C. Only when a is odd
   D. Only when a equals 0
   E. Only when a is even

8. How many even integers are there between −4 and 4?

   F. 1
   G. 3
   H. 4
   J. 5
   K. 7

9. If the four-digit number 47w6 is divisible by 6 (w represents the tens digit), which of the following could be the value of w?

   A. 2
   B. 3
   C. 4
   D. 6
   E. 8

10. If $9^x = \dfrac{1}{3}$, then $x =$

   F. −3
   G. −2
   H. −1

   J. $\dfrac{-1}{2}$

   K. $\dfrac{-1}{3}$

Here's how to crack them:

Question 1: Answer choice C does not equal 54, so we can eliminate it right away. Answers A, B, and E all equal 54, but each of these choices includes a factor that is not prime. The correct answer is **D**.

Question 2: The absolute value of –6 is 6, so after we multiply, the numerator equals –120. If you picked answer choice F, it was because you thought you were already done, but we haven't finished the problem yet. We still have to divide by the denominator, –3. A negative number divided by a negative number must be positive, so we can cancel out choices F and G. The correct answer is **H**.

Question 3: We could just divide each of these numbers into 1134, but there's a shortcut: Think rules of divisibility. Is 1134 divisible by 3? Yes. By 6? Yes. By 9? Yes. 12 breaks down in two factors: 3 and 4. We already know the number is divisible by 3. Is it divisible by 4? NO! If you don't remember these rules, go back and review divisibility. The correct answer is **D**.

Question 4: $(-2)^3$ equals –8. $(3)^{-2}$ equals $\frac{1}{9}$. $\frac{1}{9} + \frac{8}{9}$ equals 1. $-8 + 1 = -7$. The correct answer is **F**.

Question 5: The cube root of 27 equals 3. 3 squared equals 9. The correct answer is **C**.

Question 6: $(xy)^3$ equals x^3y^3. Anything to the zero power equals 1, so z disappears from the numerator. The correct answer is **F**.

Question 7: To make this expression even, we need an even numerator. Why? Because it is going to be divided by 2. How can we insure that the numerator of this fraction is even? The value a must be odd. The correct answer is **C**.

Question 8: Just count on your fingers. Is 0 even? Yes. The correct answer is **G**.

Question 9: For the four-digit number to be divisible by 6, it must also be divisible by the prime factors of 6: 2 and 3. We already know it is divisible by 2, because the last digit is even. If the sum of the four digits is divisible by 3, so is the entire number. Which of the answer choices makes the four-digit number divisible by 3? The correct answer is **C**.

Question 10: If you get confused by the fractional roots or negative roots, you might start by trying the simpler answer choices first. A negative power is just the reciprocal of a positive power. Putting answer choice F into the equation gives us $\left(\dfrac{1}{9}\right)^3$. Does that equal $\dfrac{1}{3}$? No way. We can use the same method to eliminate answers G and H. If you aren't sure how to put answer choices J and K into the equation, just guess. At this point, the odds are fifty-fifty. Then go back and review fractional powers. The correct answer is just the reciprocal of the fractional power. The correct answer is **J**.

CHAPTER 9

Arithmetic

Did you know that the ACT tests ancient history? You don't believe us? O.K., when was the last time you took a test in school that asked you to add fractions or subtract decimals? We're talking fourth grade here. Because it's been so long, we think it's a good idea for you to read through this chapter carefully (even the part about adding fractions). Sometimes specific rules from a subject you learned a long time ago can vanish from your mind when you need them most. Also, the test writers at ACT sometimes like to take simple concepts and construct hard problems around them.

Here are the specific arithmetic topics tested on the ACT:

1. Order of operations
2. Fractions
3. Decimals
4. Percentages
5. Ratios
6. Averages

In this chapter, we will first discuss the fundamentals of each topic and then show you how ACT constructs questions based on those fundamentals.

ORDER OF OPERATIONS

In a problem that involves several different operations, the operations must be performed in a particular order. Here's an easy way to remember the order of operations:

Please Excuse My Dear Aunt Sally

First, you do operations enclosed in **P**arentheses; then you take care of **E**xponents; then you **M**ultiply, **D**ivide, **A**dd, and **S**ubtract.

Try this one:

$$((-5)+4)^2 \left(\frac{8}{2}\right) + 4 - 8 =$$

How about this one?

$$(-8) + \left(\frac{8}{2}\right)(4-5)^2 + 4 =$$

If you did these in the correct order, you should have gotten the same answer both times: 0.

The Associative Law: In adding a string of numbers, you can add them in any order you like. The same thing is true when you are multiplying a string of numbers.

$$5 + 6 + 7 \text{ is the same as } 7 + 6 + 5.$$
$$2 \times 3 \times 4 \text{ is the same as } 3 \times 4 \times 2.$$

The Distributive Law: Some combinations of addition and multiplication can be written in two different formats—which often prove extremely useful in finding ACT answers.

The distributive law states that:

$$a(b + c) = ab + ac$$
$$\text{and that}$$
$$a(b - c) = ab - ac.$$

If a problem gives you information in "factored" format —$a(b + c)$—you should distribute it immediately. If the information is given in distributed form—$ab + ab$—you should factor it.

An ACT problem might look like this:

1. For all $x \neq -2$, $\dfrac{2x + 4}{x + 2} = ?$

    A. $x + 2$
    B. x
    C. 2
    D. $x + 4$
    E. 4

Here's how to crack it:
Let's use the distributive property on the numerator of this fraction, and rewrite it in factored form:

$$\frac{2(x+2)}{(x+2)}$$

$\dfrac{(x+2)}{(x+2)}$ just equals one. Therefore, we can cancel out both terms and the answer must be choice **C**.

FRACTIONS

Fractions can be thought of in two ways.

A fraction is just another way of expressing division. The expression $\frac{1}{2}$ means 1 divided by 2. $\frac{x}{y}$ is nothing more than x divided by y. A fraction is made up of a numerator and a denominator. The numerator is on top, the denominator is on the bottom.

$$\frac{1}{2} \quad \frac{\text{numerator}}{\text{denominator}}$$

The other way to think of a fraction is as a part over a whole.

$$\frac{1}{2} \quad \frac{\text{part}}{\text{whole}}$$

In the fraction $\frac{1}{2}$ we have one part out of a total of two parts.

In the fraction $\frac{3}{7}$ we have 3 parts out of a total of 7 parts.

REDUCING FRACTIONS

To make a large fraction smaller, see if the numerator and the denominator share a common factor. It may save time to find the largest factor they share, but this isn't crucial. Whatever factor they share can now be canceled. Let's take the fraction $\frac{6}{8}$. Is there a common factor? Yes, 2.

$$\frac{6}{8} = \frac{\cancel{2} \times 3}{\cancel{2} \times 4} = \frac{3}{4}$$

Get used to reducing all fractions (if they can be reduced) before you do any work with them. It saves a lot of time and prevents errors that crop up when you try to work with big numbers.

COMPARING FRACTIONS

Sometimes a problem will involve deciding which of two fractions is bigger.

Which is bigger, $\frac{2}{5}$ or $\frac{4}{5}$? Think of these as parts of a whole. Which is bigger, 2 parts out of 5, or 4 parts out of five? $\frac{4}{5}$ is clearly bigger. In this case it was easy to tell because they both had the same whole, or the same denominator.

What about this one? Which is bigger, $\frac{2}{3}$ or $\frac{3}{7}$? To decide, we need to find a common whole, or denominator. You change the denominator of a fraction by multiplying it by another number. In order to keep the entire fraction the same, however, you must multiply the numerator by the same number.

Let's change the denominator of $\frac{2}{3}$ into 21.

$$\frac{2 \times 7}{3 \times 7} = \frac{14}{21}$$

$\frac{14}{21}$ still has the same value as $\frac{2}{3}$ (it would reduce to $\frac{2}{3}$), because we multiplied the fraction by, $\frac{7}{7}$ or one.

Let's change the denominator of $\frac{3}{7}$ into 21 as well.

$$\frac{3 \times 7}{7 \times 3} = \frac{9}{21}$$

$\frac{9}{21}$ still has the same value as $\frac{3}{7}$ (it would reduce to $\frac{3}{7}$), because we multiplied the fraction by $\frac{3}{3}$, or one.

Now we can compare the two fractions. Which is bigger, $\frac{14}{21}$ or $\frac{9}{21}$? Clearly $\frac{14}{21}$ (or $\frac{2}{3}$) is bigger than $\frac{9}{21}$ (or $\frac{3}{7}$). Why did we decide on 21 as our common denominator? The easiest way to get a common denominator is to multiply the denominators of the two fractions you wish to compare: $7 \times 3 = 21$.

Let's do it again. Which is bigger,

$$\frac{2}{3} \text{ or } \frac{4}{7} \text{ or } \frac{3}{5} ?$$

To compare these fractions directly you need a common denominator, but finding a common denominator that works for all three fractions would be complicated and time consuming. It makes more sense to compare these fractions two at a time. Let's start with $\frac{2}{3}$ and $\frac{4}{7}$. An easy common denominator is 21.

$$\frac{2}{3} \qquad\qquad \frac{4}{7}$$

$$\frac{2}{3} \times \frac{7}{7} = \frac{14}{21} \qquad\qquad \frac{4}{7} \times \frac{3}{3} = \frac{12}{21}$$

Since $\frac{2}{3}$ is bigger, let's compare it with $\frac{3}{5}$. This time, the easiest common denominator is 15.

$$\frac{2}{3} \qquad\qquad \frac{3}{5}$$

$$\frac{2}{3} \times \frac{5}{5} = \frac{10}{15} \qquad\qquad \frac{3}{5} \times \frac{3}{3} = \frac{9}{15}$$

So $\frac{2}{3}$ is bigger than $\frac{3}{5}$, which means it's also the biggest of the three.

THE BOW TIE

A more streamlined way to do this is to use the "bow tie." Let's compare the last two fractions again. We get the common denominator by multiplying the two denominators together:

$$\frac{2}{3} \longrightarrow \frac{3}{5} = \frac{}{15}$$

We get the new numerators by multiplying as shown below:

$$\overset{\text{\textcircled{\scriptsize 10}}}{\frac{2}{3}} \bowtie \overset{\text{\textcircled{\scriptsize 9}}}{\frac{3}{5}} = \frac{}{15}$$

So $\frac{2}{3}$ is bigger.

ADDING AND SUBTRACTING FRACTIONS

Now that we've reviewed finding a common denominator, adding and subtracting fractions is simple. Let's use the bow tie to add $\frac{2}{5}$ and $\frac{1}{4}$.

$$\overset{\textcircled{8}}{\frac{2}{5}}\bowtie\overset{\textcircled{5}}{\frac{1}{4}}=\frac{8+5}{20}=\frac{13}{20}$$

Let's use the bow tie to subtract $\frac{2}{3}$ from $\frac{5}{6}$.

$$\overset{\textcircled{15}}{\frac{5}{6}}\times\overset{\textcircled{12}}{\frac{2}{3}}=\frac{15-12}{18}=\frac{3}{18}\text{ or }\frac{1}{6}$$

MULTIPLYING FRACTIONS

To multiply fractions, line them up and multiply straight across.

$$\frac{5}{6}\times\frac{4}{5}=\frac{20}{30}=\frac{2}{3}$$

Was there anything we could have canceled or reduced *before* we multiplied? Yes. We could cancel the 5 on top and the 5 on the bottom. What's left is $\frac{4}{6}$, which reduces to $\frac{2}{3}$.

Sometimes rusty students think they can cancel or reduce in the same fashion *across an equal sign*. For example:

$$\frac{\cancel{5}x}{6}=\frac{4}{\cancel{5}}\qquad\text{No!}$$

You *cannot* cancel the 5's in this case, or reduce the $\frac{4}{6}$. When there is an equal sign, you have to cross multiply, which yields $25x=24$, so x in this case would equal $\frac{24}{25}$.

DIVIDING FRACTIONS

To divide one fraction by another, just invert the second fraction and multiply:

$$\frac{2}{3} \div \frac{3}{4} \text{ is the same thing as } \frac{2}{3} \times \frac{4}{3} = \frac{8}{9}$$

You may see this same operation written like this:

$$\frac{\dfrac{2}{3}}{\dfrac{3}{4}}$$

Again, just invert and multiply. Try the next example:

$$\frac{6}{\dfrac{2}{3}}$$

Think of 6 as $\frac{6}{1}$, and so we do the same thing:

$$\frac{6}{1} \times \frac{3}{2} = \frac{18}{2} = 9$$

CONVERTING TO FRACTIONS

An integer can always be expressed as a fraction by making the integer the numerator and 1 the denominator. $8 = \frac{8}{1}$

Sometimes the ACT gives you numbers that are mixtures of integers and fractions, for example $3\frac{1}{2}$. It is often easier to work with these numbers by converting them completely into fractions. Here's how you do it: since the fraction is being expressed in halves, let's convert the integer into halves as well. $3 = \frac{6}{2}$. Now just add the $\frac{1}{2}$ to the $\frac{6}{2}$. $3\frac{1}{2} = \frac{7}{2}$.

NOW, HOW DOES THE ACT TEST FRACTIONS?

An ACT fraction problem combines several of the elements we've just discussed. Here's an example of a typical problem:

1. After $\dfrac{4\frac{1}{3}}{2\frac{3}{5}}$ has been simplified to a single fraction in lowest terms, what is the denominator?

   A. 2
   B. 3
   C. 5
   D. 9
   E. 13

Here's how to crack it:

First, let's convert the mixture of integers and fractions into fractions. $4\frac{1}{3} = \frac{13}{3}$, $2\frac{3}{5} = \frac{13}{5}$. Remember, to divide fractions, simply flip and multiply $\frac{13}{3} \times \frac{5}{13}$. The 13's cancel, leaving $\frac{5}{3}$. The answer is choice **B**.

More complicated fraction problems might test your ability to recognize that every fraction implies another fraction—what's left over. If a glass is $\frac{3}{5}$ full, what part of the glass is empty? $\frac{2}{5}$.

1. On Friday, Jane does one-third of her homework. On Saturday, she does one-sixth of the remainder. What fraction of her homework is still left to be done?

   F. $\dfrac{4}{9}$

   G. $\dfrac{1}{2}$

   H. $\dfrac{5}{9}$

   J. $\dfrac{5}{6}$

   K. $\dfrac{7}{12}$

Here's how to crack it:

Jane did $\frac{1}{3}$ on Friday. How much is still left to be done? That's right: $\frac{2}{3}$. On Saturday she did $\frac{1}{6}$ *of the remainder*. In math, the word "of" always means multiply, so let's set this up:

Friday	Saturday
$\frac{1}{3}$	$\frac{1}{6} \times \frac{2}{3} = \frac{2}{18}$
$\frac{1}{3}$	$\frac{2}{18}$ or $\frac{1}{9}$

If we find a common denominator,

$$\frac{3}{9} + \frac{1}{9} = \frac{4}{9}$$

So altogether, she has done $\frac{4}{9}$ of the assignment. If you thought you were done at this point, you might have picked answer choice F, but the question doesn't ask how much was done, but rather how much remained *undone*. How much is left? $\frac{5}{9}$. The answer is choice **H**.

POE NOTES

In that last problem, answer choice F was a *partial* answer designed to catch people who thought they were done before they really were. Choice G, on the other hand, was designed to catch people who slightly misunderstood the question. If you missed the words "of the remainder" as you read the question, you probably added $\frac{1}{6}$ to $\frac{1}{3}$, and got $\frac{1}{2}$.

DECIMALS

A fraction can be written as a decimal and vice versa. Take the fraction $\frac{3}{5}$. Remember what we said before, a fraction is just another form of division:

$$\frac{3}{5} = 3 \div 5 = .6 \qquad 5\overline{)3.0}^{.6}$$

You can also express any decimal as a fraction:

$$.4 = \frac{4}{10} \qquad .03 = \frac{3}{100}$$

ADDING AND SUBTRACTING DECIMALS

To add or subtract decimals, just line up the decimal points, and proceed as if it were regular addition or subtraction. To add 9.25, 3.2, and 8.567:

$$
\begin{array}{r}
9.250 \\
3.200 \\
+\ 8.567 \\
\hline
21.017
\end{array}
$$

It helped to add zeros to fill out the decimal places of the numbers with fewer digits. 3.2 is the same as 3.200.

MULTIPLYING DECIMALS

To multiply decimals, simply ignore the decimal points, and multiply your numbers. When you've finished, count all the digits to the right of the decimal points in the original numbers you multiplied. Now place the decimal point in your answer so that there are the same number of digits to the right of it. Here's an example:

$$
\begin{array}{r}
2.32 \\
\times.03 \\
\hline
.0696
\end{array}
$$

$3 \times 232 = 696$. There were a total of four digits to the right of the decimal point in the original numbers, so now we place the decimal so that there are four digits to the right in the answer.

DIVIDING DECIMALS

The best way to divide one decimal by another is to convert the number you are dividing *by* (in mathematical terminology, the divisor) into a whole number. You do this simply by moving the decimal point as many places as necessary.

This works as long as you also remember to move the decimal point in the number that you are *dividing* (in mathematical terminology, the dividend) the same number of spaces.

Here's an example: To divide 12 by .6, set it up the way you would an ordinary division problem:

$$.6\overline{)12}$$

To convert .6 into a whole number, move the decimal point over one place to the right. Now, you must move the decimal place in 12 one place as well. Now the operation looks like this:

$$6\overline{)120} \qquad 6\overline{)\overset{20}{120}}$$

SCIENTIFIC NOTATION

The purpose of scientific notation is to express very large numbers or very small numbers without endless strings of zeros:

$$3.24 \times 10^2$$

All you have to do to simplify this expression is move the decimal point over to the right by the same number as the power of ten. In this case, two places. If the power of ten is negative, you move the decimal point to the left instead.

$$3.24 \times 10^3 = 3240$$
$$3.24 \times 10^2 = 324$$
$$3.24 \times 10^{-1} = .324$$
$$3.24 \times 10^{-2} = .0324$$

An ACT scientific notation problem might look like this:

1. $\left(9 \times 10^{-3}\right) - \left(2 \times 10^{-2}\right) = ?$

    A. −0.007
    B. −0.07
    C. −0.011
    D. −0.11
    E.   0.11

Here's how to crack it:

$$9 \times 10^{-3} = .009$$
$$2 \times 10^{-2} = .02$$

$$
\begin{array}{r}
.009 \\
-\ .02 \\
\hline
-.011
\end{array}
$$

The answer is **C**.

RATIOS

There are relatively few ratio problems on the ACT. The important thing to remember is the difference between a ratio and a fraction. While a fraction is a $\dfrac{\text{part}}{\text{whole}}$, a ratio is a $\dfrac{\text{part}}{\text{part}}$.

Take the ratio of $\dfrac{3 \text{ dogs}}{4 \text{ cats}}$.

What is the whole in this problem? If you said the total number of animals, or 7, you were absolutely correct. So what fractional part of the animals is dogs? Let's change the ratio $\left(\dfrac{\text{part}}{\text{part}}\right)$ into a fraction $\left(\dfrac{\text{part}}{\text{whole}}\right)$. The part made up of dogs is 3. The whole is 7. Thus the fraction part of the animals composed of dogs is $\dfrac{3}{7}$.

Other ratio problems don't need to be converted to fractions:

1. If the ratio of $2x$ to $5y$ is $\frac{1}{20}$, what is the ratio of x to y?

   A. $\frac{1}{40}$

   B. $\frac{1}{20}$

   C. $\frac{1}{10}$

   D. $\frac{1}{8}$

   E. $\frac{1}{4}$

Here's how to crack it:

$$\frac{2x}{5y} = \frac{1}{20}$$

To isolate $\frac{x}{y}$ on the left side of this equation, what do we have to do to it? Let's multiply both sides by $\frac{5}{2}$.

$$\frac{5}{2} \times \frac{2x}{5} = \frac{1}{20} \times \frac{5}{2}$$

$$\frac{x}{y} = \frac{5}{40}$$

Which reduces to $\frac{1}{8}$. The answer is choice **D**.

PERCENTAGES

A percentage is just a fraction in which the denominator is always equal to 100. Fifty percent means 50 parts out of a whole of 100. Since fractions can be expressed in different ways, $\left(\dfrac{1}{2} = \dfrac{2}{4} = \dfrac{25}{50} = \dfrac{50}{100}\right)$, any fraction can be turned into a percentage. To do this, you set one $\dfrac{\text{part}}{\text{whole}}$ equal to another $\dfrac{\text{part}}{\text{whole}}$. If four out of five dentists recommend a particular brand of toothpaste, what percentage of the dentists recommend the toothpaste?

$$\frac{\text{part}}{\text{whole}} = \frac{4}{5} = \frac{x}{10}$$

We cross multiply, and find that $x = 80$.

PERCENTAGE SHORTCUTS

In the last problem, we could have saved a little time if we had realized that $\dfrac{1}{5} = 20\%$. Therefore, $\dfrac{4}{5}$ would be 4×20 or 80.

Here are some fractions and decimals whose percent equivalents you should know:

$$\frac{1}{5} = .2 = 20\%$$

$$\frac{1}{4} = .25 = 25\%$$

$$\frac{1}{3} = .333... = 33\frac{1}{3}\%$$

$$\frac{1}{2} = .5 = 50\%$$

Another fast way to do percents is to move the decimal place. To find 10% of any number, move the decimal point of that number over one place to the left.

10% of 500 = 50
10% of 50 = 5
10% of 5 = .5

To find 1% of a number, move the decimal point of that number over two places to the left.

1% of 500 = 5
1% of 50 = .5
1% of 5 = .05

You can use a combination of these last two techniques to find even very complicated percentages, by breaking them down into easy-to-find chunks:

20% of 500: 10% of 500 = 50, so 20% is twice 50, or 100

30% of 70: 10% of 70 = 7, so 30% is three times 7, or 21

32% of 400: 10% of 400 = 40, so 30% is three times 40, or 120

1% of 400 = 4, so 2% is two times 4, or 8

32% of 400 = 128

Here's what an ACT percentage problem might look like:

1. At a restaurant, diners enjoy an "early bird" discount of 10% off their bill. If a diner orders a meal regularly priced at $18, and leaves a tip of 15% of the discounted meal, how much does he pay in total for the meal?
   A. $13.50
   B. $16.20
   C. $18.63
   D. $18.90
   E. $20.70

Here's how to crack it:
10% of 18 = $1.80. If we subtract this from the cost of the meal, we have the discounted price of $16.20. This is answer choice B, but we aren't done yet. The diner leaves a tip of 15% of the $16.20.

10% of 16.20 is $1.62
5% is half again of that, or   0.81
                                                         $2.43

The diner's total cost is $16.20 plus $2.43, which equals $18.63, or answer choice **C**.

POE NOTES

Even before you began this problem you could have eliminated one answer choice through POE. Did you spot it? Answer choice A was way too small. The diner is getting a discount of only 10% off the $18.00 and he must still pay the tip, which will add a bit more money. Could the answer be as low as $13.50? Cross off answer choice A.

Even if you didn't notice that answer choice A was too small, once you figured out that 10% of $18.00 was $16.20, you could have eliminated answer choices A and B, because there was still the tip to pay, so the total had to be bigger than $16.20.

AVERAGES

To find the average of a set of n numbers you simply add the numbers and divide by n. For example, the average of 9, 12, and 6 is

$$\frac{9+12+6}{3} = \frac{27}{3} \quad \text{or} \quad 9$$

Whenever you see the word average, you should think:

$$\frac{\text{sum of everything}}{\text{number of things}} = \text{average}$$

An ACT average problem might look like this:

1. Over 9 games, a baseball team had an average of 8 runs per game. If the average number of runs for the first 7 games is 6 runs per game, and the same number of runs were scored for each of the last 2 games, how many runs were scored during the last game?

   A. 5
   B. 15
   C. 26
   D. 30
   E. 46

Here's how to crack it:

Let's put the information from the first line of this problem into our trusty average equation:

$$\frac{\text{sum of everything}}{9} = 8$$

What is the sum of everything for these 9 games? 9×8, or 72.

Now let's put the information from the second line into the average equation:

$$\frac{\text{sum of everything}}{7} = 6$$

What is the sum of everything for these 7 games? 7×6, or 42.

If all 9 games added up to 72, and 7 of these games added up to 42, then the remaining 2 games added up to 72 minus 42, or 30. In case you are feeling smug about having gotten this far, the ACT test writers made 30 answer choice D.

But of course, if you read the last line, you know that they only want the runs scored in the *last* game. Since the same number of runs were scored in each of the last two games, the answer is $\frac{30}{2}$ or 15, answer choice **B**.

THE WEIGHTED AVERAGE

ACT test writers have a particular weakness for "weighted average" problems. First, let's look at a regular unweighted average question:

If Sally received a grade of 90 on a test last week, and a grade of 100 on a test this week, what is her average for the two tests?

Piece of cake, right? The answer is 95. You added the scores and divided by 2. Now, let's turn the same question into a weighted average question:

If Sally's average for the entire year last year was 90, and her average for the entire year this year was 100, is her average for the two years combined equal to 95?

The answer is, "not necessarily." If Sally took the same number of courses in both years then yes, her average is 95. But what if last year she took 6 courses while this year she took only 2 courses? Can you compare the two years equally? ACT likes to test your answer to this question. Here's an example:

1. The starting team of a baseball club has 9 members who have an average of 12 home runs apiece for the season. The second-string team for the baseball club has 7 members who have an average of 8 home runs apiece for the season. What is the average number of home runs for the starting team and the second-string team combined?

   A. 7.5
   B. 8
   C. 10
   D. 10.25
   E. 14.2

Here's how to crack it:

The ACT test writers want to see whether you spot that this is a *weighted* average problem. If you thought the first string team was exactly equivalent to the second string, then you merely had to take the average of the two averages, 12 and 8, to get 10. In weighted average problems, the ACT test writers always include the average of the two averages among the answer choices—and it is always wrong. 10 is answer choice C. Cross off C.

The two teams are not equivalent because there are *different* numbers of players on each team. To get the true average, we'll have to find the total number of home runs and divide by the total number of players. How do we do this? By going to the trusty average formula as usual. The first line of the problem says that the 9 members on the first team have an average of 12 runs apiece:

$$\frac{\text{sum of everything}}{9} = 12$$

So the sum of everything is 9×12 or 108.

The second sentence says that the 7 members of the second team have an average of 8 runs each.

$$\frac{\text{sum of everything}}{7} = 8$$

So the sum of everything is 7×8 or 56.

Now, we can find the true average. Add all the runs scored by the first team to all the runs scored by the second team: $108 + 56 = 164$. This is the true sum of everything. We divide it by the total number of players ($9 + 7 = 16$).

The answer is 10.25, or answer choice **D**.

POE NOTES

While we could eliminate answer choice C in that last problem because it represented the "unweighted" average, there were several other answers we might have eliminated through POE. If the average of the first team was 12 and the average of the second team was 8, it stood to reason that the correct answer would be somewhere between those two numbers. Could the answer really have been higher than 12? Answer choice E bites the dust. Could the answer really have been equal to or lower than 8? Answer choices A and B fall by the wayside.

ARITHMETIC SUMMARY

1. The six main topics of arithmetic are

    • Order of operations

    • Fractions

    • Decimals

    • Percentages

    • Ratios

    • Averages

2. Arithmetic operations must be performed in a particular order. Here's an easy way to remember the order of operations: **P**lease **E**xcuse **M**y **D**ear **A**unt **S**ally. First, you do operations enclosed in parentheses; then you take care of exponents; then you multiply, divide, add, and subtract.

3. When you add or multiply a group of numbers, you can put them in any order that suits you. This is called the associative law.

4. The distributive law states that a(b + c) = ab + ac and that a(b - c) = ab - ac. On the ACT, if you see a problem in one form, you will make the problem much easier by immediately putting it in the other form.

5. A fraction can be thought of as a $\dfrac{\text{part}}{\text{whole}}$.

6. You must know how to reduce, multiply, divide, compare, add, and subtract fractions. The bow tie is a great method for doing all of the last three items mentioned.

7. Every fraction implies another fraction—what is left over. If a glass is $\dfrac{3}{5}$ empty, it is $\dfrac{2}{5}$ full.

8. A decimal is just another way to express a fraction.

9. You must know how to add, subtract, multiply, and divide decimals, as well as be familiar with scientific notation.

10. A ratio is different in one respect from a fraction: a ratio is a $\dfrac{\text{part}}{\text{part}}$. If the ratio of cats to dogs is $\dfrac{3}{4}$, the whole is 7.

11. A percentage is just a fraction in which the denominator is always equal to 100. Most percentage problems can be set up to look like this:

$$\frac{\text{part}}{\text{whole}} = \frac{x}{100}$$

12. In average questions, you should immediately think:

$$\frac{\text{sum of everything}}{\text{number of things}} = \text{average}$$

13. The ACT has a particular weakness for weighted averages. Be on the lookout for them.

ARITHMETIC DRILL

1. The ratio of boys to girls at the Milwood school is 4 to 5. If there are a total of 27 children at the school, how many boys attend the Milwood school?

   A.   4
   B.   9
   C.   12
   D.   14
   E.   17

2. Linda computed the average of her biology test scores by adding the totals of the 5 scores together and dividing by the number of tests. She discovered her average score was an 88. Unfortunately, she completely forgot one entire test on which she scored an 82. What is the true average of Linda's biology tests?

   F.   82
   G.   85
   H.   86
   J.   87
   K.   88

3. In the process of milling grain, 3% is lost due to spillage, and another 5% is lost because of mildew. If the mill starts out with 490 tons of grain, how much (in tons) remains to be sold after milling?

   A.   425
   B.   426
   C.   420.5
   D.   440
   E.   450.8

4. $5\frac{1}{3} - 6\frac{1}{4} = ?$

F. $\dfrac{-11}{12}$

G. $\dfrac{-1}{2}$

H. $\dfrac{-2}{7}$

J. $\dfrac{1}{2}$

K. $\dfrac{9}{12}$

5. $1,245 \div .05 = ?$

A. 200
B. 2490
C. 2,500
D. 24,900
E. 25,000

Here's how to crack them:

Question 1: A ratio is a $\dfrac{\text{part}}{\text{part}}$. Since the only actual number of students that we have is a whole, we will need to convert the ratio into a fraction. If the ratio is 4/5, then the whole is 9. The equation we need is $\dfrac{4}{9} = \dfrac{x}{27}$. $x = 12$ and the answer is **C**.

Question 2: First let's do some quick elimination. The average of the first 5 tests is 88. Since the sixth test is less than 88, the final average must also be less than 88. Scratch answer choice K. Now, let's get to work. As usual, the key number in an average question is the sum of all the tests. If the first tests have an average question of 88, the sum of all five tests is 5 times 88, or 440. She scored 82 on the sixth text. To get the true average, we add 82 to 440 which equals 522. Dividing 522 by 6—the total number of tests—we get 87. The correct answer is **J**.

Question 3: The mill lost a total of 8%. To find the correct answer, we just have to take away 8% of 490. That isn't much. In fact, it's just a bit less than 10%. Can we eliminate any answer choices? 10% of 490 is 49. 490 minus 49 is 441. The correct answer must be a little more than 441. There is only one answer greater than 441. The correct answer is **E**.

Question 4: First, let's convert these numbers into improper fractions. $5\frac{1}{3}$ equals $\frac{16}{3}$. $6\frac{1}{4}$ equals $\frac{25}{4}$. Clearly, when we subtract the second number from the first, the result will be negative. Cross off answer choices J and K since they are both positive. To find the exact answer, we need a common denominator. How about 12? The first number becomes $\frac{64}{12}$. The second number becomes $\frac{75}{12}$. The correct answer is **F**.

Question 5: If you picked answer choice B, you forgot to take away two decimals from *both* numbers before you divided. The correct answer is **D**.

CHAPTER 10

Algebra

Algebra is all about solving for an unknown quantity. The unknown is usually represented by a variable such as x or y. There are two general kinds of algebra questions on the ACT. The first kind asks you to solve for a particular x. The second kind asks you to solve for a more cosmic x. Let's begin with the particular.

WHEN X HAS A PARTICULAR VALUE: THE BASIC EQUATION

Here is a classic example of the most basic particular equation:

$$3x + 7 = 28$$

There is only one number in the world that will satisfy this equation. To find it, we need to isolate x on one side of the equation and get all of the numbers on the other side. To get rid of the 7 which is being added on the left side, we must do the opposite of addition and *subtract* 7 from the left side. However, in order to avoid changing the entire equation, we also have to subtract 7 from the right side. Whatever is done to one side must also be done to the other.

$$
\begin{array}{rcr}
3x + 7 & = & 28 \\
-7 & & -7 \\
\hline
3x & = & 21
\end{array}
$$

In order to get rid of the 3 which is being multiplied on the left side, we must do the opposite of multiplication and *divide* the left side by 3. If we are dividing the left side by 3, we must also divide the right side by 3.

$$\frac{3x}{3} = \frac{21}{3} = 7$$

$$x = 7$$

But in this last problem, we left out one very important thing: ACT questions always have multiple choice answers. Let's look at this question the way it would have appeared on the actual test:

1. If $3x + 7 = 28$, what is x?
   A. 4
   B. 5
   C. 6
   D. 7
   E. 8

You might say, "Well, what's the difference? It's the same problem." But in fact, it's not the same problem at all.

MOST PARTICULAR *X* PROBLEMS CAN ALSO BE SOLVED *BACKWARD*

Algebra is a wonderful discipline, and we *do* want you to be able to solve problems like the one above algebraically, particularly when they are easy. However, there is another way to do most particular *x* problems, a way that can, in some cases, save you huge amounts of time and trouble. It's called "Working Backward."

If we asked you to *guess* the value of *x* in this question, it might take you a long, long time. After all, there's only going to be one number in the whole world that satisfies this equation, and there are billions and billions of numbers to choose from. Or are there?

In fact, on the ACT, there are always just five: the five possible answer choices—and one of them has to be the correct answer. Let's try doing the problem backward. To do this, you take the answer choices one at a time, and put them into the equation to see which one makes the equation work. Which choice should we begin with?

The one in the middle. Numeric answers are always presented in order on this test, from least to greatest. There are three steps to working backward:

1. **Start with the middle answer – in this case, choice C.**
2. If C is too big, go down to answer choice B.
3. If C is too small, go up to answer choice D.

Here's the problem again:

1. If $3x + 7 = 28$, what is *x*?

   A. 4
   B. 5
   C. 6
   D. 7
   E. 8

Here's how to crack it:

Let's start with answer choice C: $3(6) + 7$ equals only 25. Could this be the right answer? No, it's *supposed* to equal 28. Do we need a smaller or a larger *x*? Since we need a larger number, we can immediately knock out answer choices A and B. Let's try answer choice **D**. 3 times $(7) + 7 = 28$. Bingo! We have our answer.

Note that if answer choice D had still been too small, the only possible answer would have been choice E. One of the great things about working backward is that you will have to do only two actual calculations. You start with C. If C is correct, you're done. If C is too big, then you're down to A and B. Now you try B. If B is correct, you're done. If it isn't, you're still done. The answer must be the only remaining choice: A.

LET'S DO IT AGAIN

Here's another problem:

2. If $600 was deposited in a bank account for one year and earned an interest of $42, what was the percentage interest rate earned?

    F. 6.26%
    G. 7.00%
    H. 8.00%
    J. 9.00%
    K. 9.50%

Here's how to crack it:

Of course, we *could* write an equation. On the other hand, one of these answer choices is correct, and all we have to do is find out which one it is. Why not work backward?

We'll start, as always, in the middle, this time with H. If the interest rate is 8%, then 8% of $600 should equal $42. Remember the quick way to do percents we taught you in arithmetic? What's *one* percent of 600? That's right, 6. So what is eight percent? 8 times 6, which equals $48. Is this the correct answer? It's a little too big. We wanted $42. Great, we can cross out H, and while we're at it, we might as well cross off answers J and K—they're even bigger. Let's try G. What is 7% of 600? One percent is 6, so seven percent would be 7 times 6, or $42. Yes! We're done. The answer is **G**.

HOW DO YOU KNOW WHEN TO WORK BACKWARD?

You can *always* work backward when you see numbers in the answer choices, and when the question asked in the last line of the problem is relatively straightforward. For example, if there are numbers in the answer choices, and the question asks, "What is *x*?", you can work backward.

However, if the question asks instead, "What is the difference between *x* and *y*?" then you probably don't want to work backward. In this case, the answers won't give us a value for either *x* or *y*; we only know the *difference* between them.

THE REVERSE QUESTION

Sometimes, the ACT test writers will make your job even easier by giving you the value for the variable within the question itself:

1. What is the value of $3x^2 + 5x - 7$ when $x = -1$?

   A. -15
   B. -9
   C. -1
   D. 5
   E. 15

Here's how to crack it:

There is still only one number in the world which will satisfy this question, because—in this case—you know what the particular value of x is supposed to be. This time the ACT test writer is asking you to find the value of the entire polynomial. (A polynomial is just a fancy word for a bunch of numbers and variables.) These problems are about as easy as this test gets.

Note that it would be pointless to work backward on this problem, since the answer choices don't give you possible values for x, but rather for the entire polynomial. Simply plug -1 into the polynomial and solve:

$$3(-1)^2 + 5(-1) - 7 =$$
$$3 \qquad -5 \ -7 = -9$$

NOW, THERE'S A CHOICE

When x has a particular value, you have a choice: you can solve for x or you can work backward. There are times when one technique is more suitable than the other, but as we cover different algebra topics in this chapter—factoring, quadratics, inequalities—we will keep returning to the concept of working backward. You will find it extremely useful, particularly on the more difficult questions that you might not want to take the time to solve the old-fashioned way.

WHEN X HAS NO PARTICULAR VALUE: THE COSMIC EQUATION

Now let's look at the following problem:

1. What is 5 more than the product of 4 and a certain number x?

   A. $4x - 5$
   B. $4x$
   C. $-x$
   D. $5x - 4$
   E. $4x + 5$

In this problem, there is *no* one value for *x*. *x* could be 5 or 105 or −317. In fact, the ACT test writers are asking you to write an equation that will answer this question no matter what the "certain number" is.

In other words, this is kind of a cosmic problem. The correct answer choice will be correct *for any value of x*.

There are two methods to deal with a cosmic problem.

ONE METHOD IS TRANSLATION

The people at ACT would like you to write a mathematical equation based on the words they've written down in English. This is not that hard, as it turns out. Unlike an English-French Dictionary or a Chinese-English Dictionary, an ACT English-Math dictionary would be very short. In fact, here it is, in its entirety:

ACT English $\longrightarrow$	**ACT Math**
is (any form of the verb to be) is the same as	=
of product times	× (multiplication)
what	*x, y, z* (your favorite variable)
a certain number	*x, y, z* (your company name here)
percent	over 100
30 percent	$\dfrac{30}{100}$
more than	+ (addition)
less than	− (subtraction)

Let's translate the problem word for word:

"what is 5 more than the product of 4 and a certain number *x*"
$$5 \qquad + \qquad 4x \; = \; ?$$

Does this equal any of the answer choices? Yes, the answer is choice **E**.

While translation is a fine way to solve this particular problem, we want you to try thinking about cosmic problems in a slightly different way. If this problem is truly cosmic—if the correct answer is correct for *every* value of "a certain number"—then it should be equally correct for *one* value.

THE OTHER METHOD IS PLUGGING IN

Why don't we pick a value?

Let's make $x = 7$.

The advantage of using a specific number is that our minds do not think naturally in terms of variables. We don't go into a store and ask for an x-pack of Coca-Cola. We have a specific number in mind.

There are three steps involved in plugging in:

1. **Pick numbers for the variables in the problem.**

2. Using your numbers, find an answer to the problem.

3. Plug your numbers into the answer choices to see which choice equals the answer you found in step 2.

Here's the problem again:

1. What is 5 more than the product of 4 and a certain number x?

   A. $4x - 5$
   B. $4x$
   C. $-x$
   D. $5x - 4$
   E. $4x + 5$

Here's how to crack it:

Let's make $x = 7$. In the space over the x in the problem above, write down "7." Now, let's figure it out. The product of 4 and 7 is 28. 5 more than 28 is 33. So, if $x = 7$, then the answer to the question is 33. We're done. All we have to do now is check to see which of the answer choices equals 33.

Let's start with A. Since $x = 7$, $4(7) - 5 = 23$. Not the answer.

Let's look at E. Since $x = 7$, $4(7) + 5 = 33$. The answer is **E**.

You might be thinking, "Wait a minute. It was easier to solve this problem algebraically. Why should I plug in?" There are a couple of reasons:

1. This was an easy problem. Plugging in makes even difficult problems easy.

2. The test writers at ACT try to anticipate how you might screw this problem up using algebra. If you make one of these common mistakes, your answer will be among the answer choices, and you will pick it and get it wrong.

HOW DO YOU SPOT A COSMIC PROBLEM?

Any problem with variables in its answer choices is a cosmic problem. You may not choose to plug in on every one of these, but you *could* plug in on *all* of them.

There are other cosmic problems that do not have variables in the answer choices. For example:

1. At a baseball game, h hot dogs are divided equally among 9 people, but there are 2 hot dogs left over. If there were $(h + 5)$ hot dogs for the 9 people, how many hot dogs would be left over?
   A. 3
   B. 4
   C. 5
   D. 7
   E. 9

Here's how to crack it:

At first glance, you might think this was a "working backward" question. However, the question is not asking how many hot dogs there were, but how many were *left over*. This would be difficult to solve by working backward.

The real clue to solving this problem is that it never tells you how many hot dogs there were in the first place. The number is represented by a variable. In other words, this is a cosmic problem too. Let's plug in. Why don't we make $h = 12$?

You say we can't? Oh, good point. The problem tells us that after we share the number h among 9 people there were 2 hot dogs left over. 12 would give us a remainder of 3, one too many. What would be a good number for h? 11 would be fine. What other number could we use? 20 would work, because 20 divided by 9 also leaves a remainder of 2.

Let's stick with 11. Write the 11 in near the h in the problem above, so you don't forget which number you chose. Now, the problem wants to know how many hot dogs would have been left over if the original number had been $(h + 5)$. If $h = 11$, then $(h + 5)$ equals 16. If there are 9 people who share these 16 hot dogs, how many are left over? 7. The answer is choice **D**.

Would the problem have worked if we had chosen another number? Sure, as long as we chose a number which when divided by 9 gives a remainder of 2. Let's try it with $h = 20$. They want to know how many hot dogs would be left over if there had been $(h + 5)$ hot dogs or 25. 9 goes evenly into 25 twice, with a remainder of...you guessed it—7.

SOME NUMBERS ARE BETTER THAN OTHERS

In that last problem, only certain numbers could be plugged in for h— numbers which agreed with the conditions set forth in the problem.

In most cosmic problems, you can pick any number you like. However, there are some numbers that work better than others. In general, you might want to stick to small numbers just because they're easier to work with. If a problem is about days and weeks, 7 might be a particularly good number. If the problem is about percents, 100 might be a good number.

Some numbers to avoid are 0, 1, and numbers that are already being used in the problem. Why? If you plug in one of these numbers, you may find that more than one answer choice appears to be correct.

SO NOW THERE'S ANOTHER CHOICE

When x has *no* particular value, you also have a choice: you can translate or you can plug in. There are times when one technique is more suitable than the other, but as we cover the different algebra topics in this chapter we will keep returning to the concept of plugging in.

FACTORING

Many ACT problems involve factoring of one kind or another. Here is the most basic kind of factoring problem:

$$x^2 + 7x + 12 = ?$$

To factor this expression, put it into the following format, and start by looking for the factors of the first and last terms.

$$
\begin{aligned}
&x^2 + 7x + 12 = \\
&(\quad)(\quad) = \\
&(x\quad)(x\quad) = \\
&(x\quad 3)(x\quad 4) = \\
&(x + 3)(x + 4)
\end{aligned}
$$

The ACT test writers might use that last expression to make a problem like this:

1. If $\dfrac{x^2 + 7x + 12}{(x+4)} = 5$, then $x = ?$

    A. 1
    B. 2
    C. 3
    D. 5
    E. 6

This is a specific x question. If we factor the top expression as we did a moment ago, we get:

$$\dfrac{(x + 3)(x + 4)}{(x + 4)} = 5$$

Now we can cancel the $(x + 4)$'s, with the result that $x + 3 = 5$. To get rid of the 3, we subtract it from both sides. Now $x = 2$, and the answer is **B**.

POE NOTES

1. If you were having trouble factoring $x^2 + 7x + 12$, it might have helped to wonder why—of all the numbers in the world—ACT picked $(x + 4)$ as the denominator of its problem. It was almost bound to be one of the factors of the polynomial in the numerator.

2. Note that like all specific x problems, this could also have been solved by **working backward**:

1. $\dfrac{x^2 + 7x + 12}{(x + 4)} = 5$, then $x = ?$

    A. 1
    B. 2
    C. 3
    D. 5
    E. 6

The question asks, "what is x?" Let's start with answer choice C—3.

$$\frac{(3)^2 + 7(3) + 12}{(3 + 4)}$$

$$= \frac{9 + 21 + 12}{7}$$

$$= \frac{42}{7} = 6$$

Since the answer was supposed to be 5, we know that we need a smaller x. Eliminate answer choices C, D, and E. Let's try 2:

$$\frac{(2)^2 + 7(2) + 12}{(2 + 4)}$$

$$= \frac{4 + 14 + 12}{6}$$

$$= 5$$

Again, the answer is choice **B**.

The same kind of equation could have been used in a **cosmic problem**:

1. For all $x \neq 3$, which of the following is equivalent to the expression $\dfrac{x^2 - x - 12}{x + 3}$?

   F. $x - 4$
   G. $x - 2$
   H. $x + 2$
   J. $x + 4$
   K. $x + 6$

Again, we could solve this by factoring:

$$x^2 - x - 12 =$$

$$(\quad)(\quad)$$
$$(x\quad)(x\quad)$$
$$(x\quad)(x\quad)$$
$$(x - 4)(x + 3)$$

Therefore we can write the problem as $\dfrac{(x - 4)(x + 3)}{x + 3}$.

The $(x + 3)$'s cancel and we get $(x - 4)$, or answer choice **F**.

1. As in the preceding problem, if you were having trouble factoring $x^2 - x - 12$, it might have helped to wonder why—of all the numbers in the world—ACT picked $(x + 3)$ as the denominator of its problem. It was almost bound to be one of the factors of the polynomial in the numerator.

2. Because this was a cosmic problem (variables in the answer choices), we also could have done this problem by **plugging in**.

Here's how. Let's choose a value for x. How about 3?

$$\frac{(3)^2 - (3) - 12}{(3+3)}$$

$$= \frac{9 - 3 - 12}{6}$$

$$= \frac{-6}{6}$$

$$= -1$$

Now all we had to do was plug 3 (our value for x) into the answer choices to see which one gets us the answer −1. Let's try choice **F**. $x - 4$. Bingo!

$$3 - 4 = -1.$$

FACTORING: ADVANCED PRINCIPLES

More advanced factoring problems set a factorable expression equal to zero. This is called a **quadratic equation**.

$$x^2 + 7x + 6 = 0$$
$$(\quad)(\quad) = 0$$
$$(x\quad)(x\quad) = 0$$
$$(x\quad 6)(x\quad 1) = 0$$
$$(x +6)(x + 1) = 0$$

Quadratic equations often have *two* values that solve the equation. In this example, x could be either -6 or -1. These two solutions are sometimes called the **roots** of the equation. Let's try an ACT type quadratic equation:

1. What is the positive value of x in the equation $2x^2 - 4x - 6 = 0$?

   A. -1
   B. 2
   C. 3
   D. 4
   E. 6

Here's how to crack it:

Before we can factor the expression the way we did in the previous problems, we need to reduce it. Look to see if all of the terms have any factor in common. Yes, each of the terms can be divided by 2.

$$\frac{2x^2}{2} - \frac{4x}{2} - \frac{6}{2} = \frac{0}{2}$$

Let's rewrite the equation:

$$2(x^2 - 2x - 3) = 0$$

Now we can factor. The expression becomes:

$$2(x + 1)(x - 3) = 0$$

x could equal -1, or 3. Unfortunately, both our values are among the answer choices. Which one is correct? If we reread the question, we realize that we were asked to find the *positive* value of x. Therefore, the answer is 3, answer choice **C**.

1. Because the problem asked us for a *positive* value, we should have crossed out answer choice A even before we factored the expression. If we had done this, we would not have been tempted by it when we finished factoring and discovered it was one of the solutions to the problem.

2. This was a particular *x* problem. That's right, you could have **worked backward**. Start with answer choice C, and put it back into the equation. Does $2(3)^2 - 4(3) - 6 = 0$? It sure does. The answer must be C.

A note of warning: When you work backward with a quadratic problem, remember that there may be two solutions. The problem will usually find a way to ask you for only one of them, but sometimes the test writers will ask you for the *sum* or the *product* of the two solutions. Remember what we said before: if a question asks, "what is *x*?" you can work backward; if a question asks, "what is *x* + *y*?" then you probably can't.

THE ACT'S TWO FAVORITE QUADRATICS

The test writers are really fond of two quadratic equations in particular. The first is called the difference of perfect squares (although the name isn't important):

$$x^2 - y^2 = (x + y)(x - y)$$

For some reason, they use this one all the time, and you should just memorize it. The idea is that whenever you see this expression in the form on the left, you should immediately put it into the form on the right. If you see it in the form on the right, you should immediately put it into the form on the left. That's all there is to it. Here's an example:

1. If $\dfrac{x^2 - 9}{x + 3} = 1$, then $x = ?$

      A. 10
      B. 15
      C. 17
      D. 19
      E. 20

Here's how to crack it:

Do you recognize the form of the top left expression? Great, so let's factor it:

$$\frac{(x+3)(x-3)}{(x+3)} = 12$$

Now we can cancel the $(x + 3)$ terms, and are left with $x - 3 = 12$. The answer is 15, or answer choice **B**.

POE NOTES

Could you have worked backward to solve this problem? Yes, although it wouldn't have been much fun squaring those large numbers. In this case it was definitely faster to solve by factoring—if you recognized the difference of perfect squares.

The other quadratic formula ACT test writers are fond of is this one:

$$x^2 + 2xy + y^2 = (x + y)(x + y)$$

Like the difference of perfect squares, the important thing is to recognize the two forms that this equation takes. Whichever form is used in the problem, the solution lies in immediately putting it into its *other* form. Memorize both forms and look for them on the test.

SIMULTANEOUS EQUATIONS

If you see one equation with two variables, can you solve for either variable? For example, if $x + y = 4$, do we know exactly what x and y equal? No. If x is 2 then y is 2, but if x is 3 then y is 1. You can *never* solve one equation with two variables. However, if there are *two* equations, each of which contains the same two variables, then you can solve using a process known as simultaneous equations. An easy problem might look like this:

If $4x + 2y = 5$ and $6x - 2y = 15$, then what is x?

To solve, set one equation above the other and add or subtract one equation to or from the other so that one of the variables disappears.

$$
\begin{array}{r}
4x + 2y = 5 \\
+\ 6x - 2y = 15 \\
\hline
10x \qquad = 20, \text{ so } x = 2.
\end{array}
$$

In more difficult simultaneous equations, you'll find that neither of the variables will disappear when you try to add or subtract the two equations. In such cases you must multiply both sides of one of the equations by some number in order to get the coefficient in front of the variable you want to disappear to be the same in both equations.

This sounds more complicated than it really is. A difficult problem might look like this:

1. What is the value of y in the system of equations below?

$$3x + 4y = 5$$
$$6x + 2y = 2$$

    A. $\dfrac{4}{3}$

    B. $\dfrac{8}{3}$

    C. 6

    D. 7

    E. 9

Here's how to crack it:

Line up the two equations:

$$3x + 4y = 5$$
$$6x + 2y = 2$$

Since we want to end up with a value for y, we need to make x disappear. To do this, let's multiply the entire top equation by 2. Now we have:

$$6x + 8y = 10$$
$$6x + 2y = 2$$

When we subtract one equation from the other, all the x's will disappear.

$$
\begin{array}{r}
6x + 8y = 10 \\
-6x - 2y = -2 \\
\hline
6y = 8
\end{array}
$$

$y = \dfrac{8}{6}$ or $\dfrac{4}{3}$, and the answer is choice **A**.

INEQUALITIES

There is one difference between an inequality and an equality. You solve for both in exactly the same way, except that when you multiply or divide both sides of an equality by a *negative* number, the direction of the inequality sign flips. Here's an example:

$$3x + 7 > 28 \qquad\qquad -3x + 7 > 28$$
$$\underline{-7 \qquad -7} \qquad\qquad \underline{-7 \qquad -7}$$
$$3x \qquad 21 \qquad\qquad -3x \qquad 21$$
$$\frac{3x}{3} \qquad \frac{21}{3} \qquad\qquad \frac{-3x}{-3} \qquad \frac{-21}{-3}$$
$$x \quad > \quad 7 \qquad\qquad\quad x \quad < \quad -7$$

Because most inequalities on the ACT involve graphing, we will be discussing them in more detail in the Graphing and Coordinate Geometry chapter.

ALGEBRA SUMMARY

1. There are two main types of algebra questions on the ACT: particular value questions which ask you to solve for a particular x, and no particular value questions, otherwise known as cosmic problems.

2. On particular value questions you can use algebra OR you can **work backward** from the answer choices. Working backward is frequently easier. When you work backward always begin with the middle answer choice, to see if you need a larger number or a smaller number. You can always work backward if you see specific numbers in the answer choices and the question in the last line is relatively straightforward.

3. On cosmic problems, you can use algebra OR you can **plug in**. Plugging in is frequently easier. You can always plug in if you see variables in the answer choices, or if the problem itself does not depend on specific numbers.

4. You must know how to factor quadratic equations. Two of ACT's favorites are $x^2 + 2xy + y^2 = (x + y)^2$ and $x^2 - y^2 = (x + y)(x - y)$. Remember that many quadratic problems can be solved by working backward or plugging in.

5. In solving simultaneous equation problems, add or subtract one equation to or from another so that one of the two variables disappears.

6. When you solve for an inequality, remember that if you multiply or divide by a negative number, the sign flips.

ALGEBRA DRILL

1. If $x = -3$, then $\dfrac{(x+3)\,(x-3)}{9} = ?$

   A. 0
   B. 1
   C. 3
   D. 5
   E. 6

2. What is the larger value of x in the equation $x^2 - 4x + 3 = 0$?

   F. 1
   G. 2
   H. 3
   J. 4
   K. 5

3. If $x + 2y = 8$ and $\dfrac{x}{2} - y = 10$, then $x = ?$

   A. –7
   B. 0
   C. 10
   D. 14
   E. 28

4. For all $x \neq -9$, $\dfrac{x^2 + 6x - 27}{(x+9)} = ?$

   F. $x + 9$
   G. $x - 3$
   H. $x + 3$
   J. $2x - 4$
   K. $2x + 3$

5. If 2 less than 3 times a certain number is the same as 4 more than the product of 5 and 3, what is the number?

   A. 7
   B. 10
   C. 11
   D. 14
   E. 15

6. A certain number of books are to be given away at a promotion. If $\frac{2}{5}$ of the books are distributed in the morning, and $\frac{1}{3}$ of the remaining books are distributed in the afternoon, what fraction of the books remain to be distributed the next day?

F. $\frac{1}{5}$

G. $\frac{2}{5}$

H. $\frac{1}{3}$

J. $\frac{5}{7}$

K. $\frac{8}{9}$

Here's how to crack them:

Question 1: If $x = -3$, then the first term of the denominator $(x + 3)$ equals 0. 0 times any number equals 0, so the correct answer is **A**.

Question 2: If we factor the equation we get $(x - 3)(x - 1) = 0$. x could be either 3 or 1. Since we are being asked for the larger value, the correct answer is **H**. Note that you could have **worked backward** on this question.

Question 3: Since this question contains two equations with two different variables, this is a simultaneous equations question. Let's get rid of the denominator of the second equation. Multiply the entire equation by 2. We get:

$$x + 2y = 8$$
$$x - 2y = 20$$

If we add the two equations together, we get $2x = 28$, or $x = 14$. The correct answer is **D**.

Question 4: If we factor, we get

$$\frac{(x + 9)(x - 3)}{(x + 9)}$$

The $(x + 9)$'s cancel out, so the correct answer is **G**. Note that you could have **plugged in** on this question.

Question 5: The correct translation of the equation is $3x - 2 = 5(3) + 4$. Thus, the correct answer is **A**.

Question 6: "A certain number" sounds pretty cosmic to us. This is a **plug in** question. Let's pick a number of books. Since we will be dividing by 5 and by 3, a good number might be 15. $\frac{2}{5}$ of 15 = 6. If 6 are gone, then 9 remain to be given out the next day. The next day, $\frac{1}{3}$ of 9 are given out: This equals 3. If 3 are given out the next day, that leaves 6. The question asks for the *fraction* of books which remain. Every fraction is a part over a whole. The part is 6; the whole is 15. $\frac{6}{15}$ reduces to $\frac{2}{5}$. The correct answer is **G**.

CHAPTER 11

Geometry

Geometry questions account for a greater percentage of the ACT math test than do any other type of question. However, the amount of actual information being tested is extremely small. You can forget most of the geometry you learned in high school: there will be no proofs, no theorems, virtually no problems in three dimensions. Instead, you will find a few concepts being tested over and over again. All of these concepts will be covered in this chapter, along with illustrations of how the ACT test writers use the concepts to construct their questions.

Even if geometry was your least favorite subject in school, you should count on getting most of the ACT geometry questions correct after you've finished reading this chapter. They just aren't that tough.

Before we begin our review, however, there is an important question to ask:

TO SCALE OR NOT TO SCALE?

That is the question. In the instructions to the math portion of the ACT, the test writers say that the diagrams are "NOT necessarily drawn to scale." On the other hand, in the ACT's own *Official Guide,* one of the suggested strategies is to use the diagrams to estimate the correct answer. The book says that "some of the figures are reasonably accurate."

We didn't think measuring the diagrams would be a very successful strategy if some of them were accurate and some of them weren't. So, we carefully measured the diagrams on every geometry problem of every ACT test we could get our hands on. The results? EVERY diagram was drawn EXACTLY to scale. When we asked an ACT spokesperson about this, he said that ACT diagrams were never intended to be misleading, but that there might be rare instances in which it was impossible to draw a problem to scale. Since we couldn't find a single one of these problems, you should consider it a very rare possibility indeed.

POE AND CRAZY ANSWERS

In the previous chapters you've seen how POE can be used to prevent picking careless or partial answers when you know how to do a problem. You've also seen how POE can narrow down the range of reasonable answers when you *don't* know how to do a problem and just need to guess.

In geometry, because the problems are *always* drawn to scale, it will be possible to get very close approximations of the correct answers *before you even do the problems.*

HOW BIG IS ANGLE *NLM*?

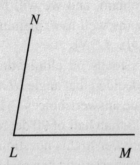

Obviously, you don't know exactly how big this angle is, but it would be easy to compare it with an angle whose measure you *did* know exactly. Let's compare it with a 90 degree angle:

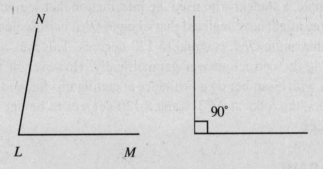

Angle *NLM* is clearly a bit less than 90 degrees. Now look at the following problem, which asks about the same angle *NLM*.

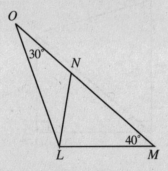

1. In the figure above, *O*, *N*, and *M* are collinear.
    If the lengths of $\overline{ON}$ and $\overline{NL}$ are the same, and the measure of angle *LON* is 30 degrees and angle *LMN* is 40 degrees, what is the measure of angle *NLM*?

    A. 40
    B. 80
    C. 90
    D. 120
    E. 150

Here's how to crack it:

This is a relatively easy problem, and we will be showing you its geometric solution later in the chapter (as well as explaining terms like "collinear," and which angle is meant by angle *LON).*

For now, however, let's focus on eliminating answer choices that don't make sense. We've already decided that angle *NLM* is a bit less than 90 degrees, which means we can eliminate answer choices C, D, and E. How much less than 90 degrees? 40 degrees is less than half of 90 degrees. Could angle *NLM* be that small? Of course not. The answer to this question must be **B**.

In this case, it wasn't necessary to do any real geometry at all in order to get the question right. Why did the ACT test writers make the other answers so crazy? They wanted to include some partial answers for people who tried to do the problem geometrically, but who stopped before they were really done.

For example, a student who used the information that segments $\overline{ON}$ and $\overline{NL}$ were the same, might have realized that triangle *ONL* is isosceles (has two equal sides), and that angle *ONL* is equal to 120 degrees. This was a necessary first step to getting the correct answer geometrically. However, if the student felt carried away with his or her own brilliance at getting this far, and looked straight to the answers, the folks at ACT wanted 120 degrees to be one of the possible answer choices.

LET'S DO IT AGAIN

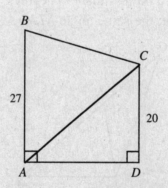

2. In the figure above, if $\overline{AB}$ = 27, $\overline{CD}$ = 20, and the area of triangle *ADC* = 240, what is the area of polygon *ABCD*?

F.   420
G.   480
H.   540
J.   564
K. 1128

Here's how to crack it:

Again, we will be solving this problem using geometry a little later in the chapter. For now, let's concentrate on eliminating crazy answers. This polygon is not a conventional figure, but if we had to choose one figure that the polygon resembled, we might pick a rectangle. Try drawing a line at a right angle from the line segment *AB* so that it touches point *C*, thus creating a rectangle. It should look like this:

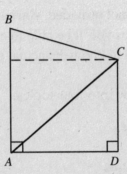

The area of polygon *ABCD* is equal to the area of the rectangle you've just formed, plus a little bit at the top. The problem tells you that the area of triangle *ADC* is 240. What is the area of the rectangle you just created? If you said 480, you are exactly right, whether you knew the geometric rules which applied or whether you just measured it with your eyes.

So the area of the rectangle is 480. Roughly speaking then, what should the area of the polygon be? A bit more. Let's look at the answer choices. F and G are either less than or equal to 480. Get rid of them. H and J both seem possible. They are both a bit more than 480. Let's hold on to them. Answer choice K seems pretty crazy. We want more than 480, but 1128 is ridiculous.

Thus on this problem, which was of medium difficulty, we were able to eliminate three of the five answer choices without doing any real geometry. Now what should you do? If you know how to do the problem, you do it. If you don't or if you are running out of time, you guess and move on.

IMPORTANT APPROXIMATIONS

In some cases, you may want to estimate problems that contain answer choices with radicals or π. Here are some useful approximations:

$$\sqrt{1} = 1$$
$$\sqrt{2} = 1.4$$
$$\sqrt{3} = 1.7$$
$$\sqrt{4} = 2$$
$$\pi = 3$$

WHAT SHOULD I DO IF THERE IS NO DIAGRAM?

Draw one. It's always easier to understand a problem when you can see it in front of you. If possible, draw your figure to scale so that you can estimate the answer as well.

GEOMETRY REVIEW

By using the diagrams ACT has so thoughtfully provided, and by making your own diagrams when they are not provided, you can often eliminate several of the answer choices. In some cases you'll be able to eliminate every choice but one. Of course, you will also need to know the actual geometry concepts that ACT is testing.

We've divided our review into four topics:

1. Angles and lines
2. Triangles
3. Four-sided figures
4. Circles

ANGLES AND LINES

Here is a line:

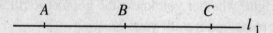

A line extends forever in either direction. This line, called l_1, has three points on it, *A*, *B*, and *C*. These three points are said to be **collinear** because they are all on the same line. The piece of the line in between points *A* and *B* is called a line **segment**. ACT will refer to it as segment *AB* or simply $\overline{AB}$. *A* and *B* are the **endpoints** of segment *AB*.

A line forms an angle of 180 degrees. If that line is cut by another line, it divides that 180 degrees into two pieces that together add up to 180 degrees:

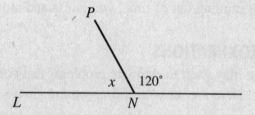

In the previous diagram, what is the value of *x*? If you said 60 degrees, you are correct. To find angle *x*, just subtract 120 degrees from 180 degrees.

An angle can also be described by points on the lines which intersect to form the angle, and the point of intersection itself, with the middle letter corresponding to the point of intersection. For example, in the previous diagram, angle *x* could also be described as angle *LNP*. If there are 180 degrees above a line, there are also 180 degrees below the line, for a total of 360 degrees.

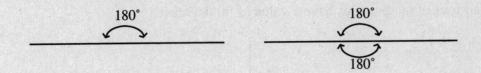

When two lines intersect, they form four angles, represented below by letters *A*, *B*, *C*, and *D*. Angles *A* and *B* together form a straight line, so they add up to 180 degrees.

Angles like these are called **supplementary**. Angles *A* and *C* are opposite from each other, and always equal each other, as are angles *B* and *D*. Angles like these are called **vertical** angles.

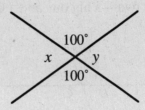

In the figure above, what is the value of angle *x*? If you said 80 degrees, you're right. Together with the 100 degree angle, *x* formed a straight line. What is the value of angle *y*? If you said 80 degrees, you're right again. These two angles are vertical and must equal each other.

The four angles together add up to 360 degrees.

When two lines meet in such a way that 90 degree angles are formed, the lines are called **perpendicular**. The little box at the point of the intersection of the two lines below indicates that they are perpendicular. It stands to reason that all four of these angles have a value of 90 degrees.

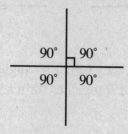

When two lines are drawn so that they could extend into infinity without ever meeting, they are called **parallel**. In the figure below l_1 is parallel to l_2. The symbol for parallel is ‖.

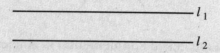

When two parallel lines are cut by a third line, eight angles are formed, but in fact, there are really only two—a big one and a little one. Look at the diagram below:

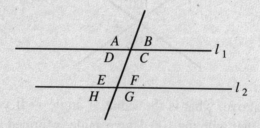

If angle $A = 110$ degrees, then angle B must equal 70 degrees (together they form a straight line). Angle D is vertical to angle B, which means that it must also equal 70 degrees. Angle C is vertical to Angle A, so it must equal 110.

The four angles E, F, G, and H are in exactly the same proportion as the angles above. The little angles are all worth 70 degrees. The big angles are all worth 110 degrees.

Try the following problem:

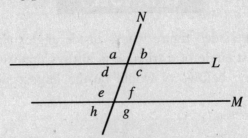

1. In the figure above, line L is parallel to line M. Line N intersects both L and M, with angles a, b, c, d, e, f, g, and h as shown. Which of the following lists includes all the angles which are supplementary to angle a?

   A. Angles b, d, f, and h
   B. Angles c, e, and g
   C. Angles b, d, and c
   D. Angles e, f, g, and h
   E. Angles d, c, h, and g

Here's how to crack it:

An angle is supplementary to another angle if the two angles together add up to 180 degrees. Since angle a is one of the eight angles formed by the intersection of a line with two parallel lines, we know that there are really only two angles: a big one and a little one. Angle a is a big one. Thus only the large angles would be supplementary to it. Which angles are those? The correct answer is choice **A**.

TRIANGLES

A triangle is a three-sided figure whose inside angles always add up to 180 degrees. The largest angle of a triangle is always opposite to its largest side. Thus in triangle *xyz* below, *xy* would be the largest side, followed by *yz*, followed by *xz*.

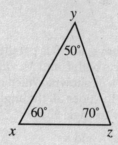

The ACT likes to ask about certain kinds of triangles in particular:

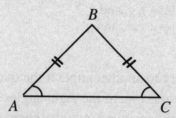

An **isosceles** triangle has two equal sides. The angles opposite those sides are also equal. In the isosceles triangle below, if angle *A* = 50 degrees, then so does angle *C*. If side *AB* = 6, then so does side *BC*.

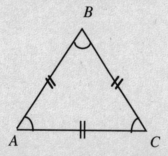

An **equilateral** triangle has three equal sides, and three equal angles. Since the three equal angles must add up to 180 degrees, all three angles of an equilateral triangle are always equal to 60 degrees.

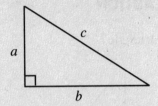

A **right triangle** has one inside angle which is equal to 90 degrees. The longest side of a right triangle (the one opposite the 90 degree angle) is called the **hypotenuse**.

Pythagoras, the Greek mathematician, discovered that the sides of a right triangle are always in a particular proportion, which can be expressed by the formula $A^2 + B^2 = C^2$, where A and B are the shorter sides of the triangle, and C is the hypotenuse. This discovery is called the Pythagorean theorem.

There are certain right triangles that the test writers at ACT find endlessly fascinating. Let's test out the Pythagorean theorem on the first of these:

$$3^2 + 4^2 = C^2$$

$$9 + 16 = 25$$

$$C^2 = 25 \text{ so } C = 5$$

The ACT test writers adore the 3-4-5 triangle, and use it frequently, along with its multiples, such as the 6-8-10 triangle and the 9-12-15 triangle. Of course, you can always use the Pythagorean theorem to figure out the third side of a right triangle—as long as you have the other two sides—but since ACT problems almost invariably use "triples" like the ones we've just mentioned, it makes sense just to memorize them.

The ACT's most commonly used right-triangle triples:

- 3-4-5 (and its multiples)

- 5-12-13

- 8-15-17

- 7-24-25

TWO SMALL NOTES OF CAUTION

1. Is this a 3-4-5 triangle?

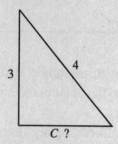

No, because the hypotenuse of a right triangle must be its *biggest* side—the one opposite the 90 degree angle. In this case, we must use the Pythagorean theorem to discover side C: $3^2 + C^2 = 16$. $C = \sqrt{7}$.

2. Is this a 5-12-13 triangle?

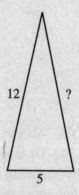

No, because the Pythagorean theorem—and triples—apply only to *right* triangles. We don't know anything about the third side of this triangle.

THE ISOSCELES RIGHT TRIANGLE

As fond as the test writers are of triples, they are even fonder of two other right triangles. The first is called the **isosceles right** triangle. The sides and angles of the isosceles right triangle are always in a particular proportion:

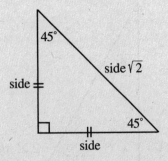

You could use the Pythagorean theorem to prove this (or you could just take our word for it). Whatever the value of the two equal sides of the isosceles right triangle, the hypotenuse is always equal to one of those sides times $\sqrt{2}$. Here are two examples:

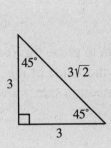 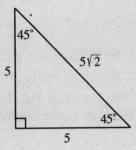

THE 30-60-90 TRIANGLE

The other right triangle tested frequently on the ACT is the **30-60-90** triangle, which also always has the same proportions:

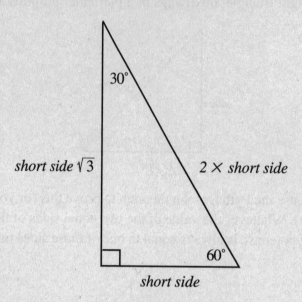

You can use the Pythagorean theorem to prove this (or you can just take our word for it). Whatever the value of the short side of the 30-60-90 triangle, the hypotenuse is always twice as big. The medium side is always equal to the short side times $\sqrt{3}$. Here are two examples:

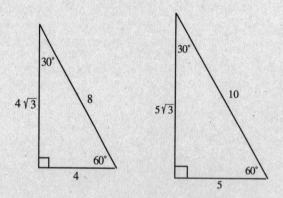

Because these triangles are tested so frequently, it makes sense to memorize the proportions, rather than waste time deriving them each time they appear.

TWO MORE NOTES OF CAUTION

1. In the isosceles right triangle below, are the sides equal to $3\sqrt{2}$?

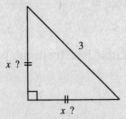

No. Remember, in an isosceles right triangle,

hypotenuse = the side $\times \sqrt{2}$.

In this case,

3 = the side $\times \sqrt{2}$.

If we solve for the side, we get

$\dfrac{3}{\sqrt{2}}$ = the side.

For arcane mathematical reasons, we are not supposed to leave a radical in the denominator, but we can multiply top and bottom by $\sqrt{2}$ to get $\dfrac{3\sqrt{2}}{2}$.

2. In the right triangle below, is x equal to $4\sqrt{3}$?

No. Even though it is one of ACT's favorites, you have to be careful not to see a 30-60-90 where none exists. In the triangle above, the short side is half of the *medium* side, not half of the hypotenuse. This is some sort of right triangle all right, but it is not a 30-60-90.

AREA

The **area** of a triangle can be found using the formula

$$\text{area} = \frac{\text{base} \times \text{height}}{2}$$

where height is the perpendicular line from the base of the triangle to its highest point.

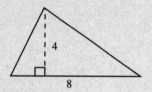 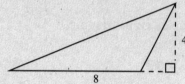 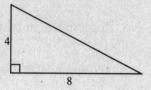

In all three of the above triangles, the area is:

$$\frac{8 \times 4}{2} = 16$$

TWO FURTHER NOTES OF CAUTION

1. Sometimes the height of a triangle can be *outside* the triangle itself, as we just saw in the second example.

2. In a right triangle, the height of the triangle can also be one of the sides of the triangle, as we just saw in the third example. However, be careful when finding the area of a *non-right* triangle. Simply because you know two sides of the triangle does not mean that you have the height of the triangle.

SIMILAR TRIANGLES

Two triangles are called similar if their angles have the same degree measures and if their sides are in the same proportion. For example, the two triangles below are similar.

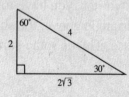 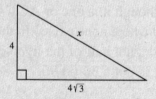

Because the sides of the two triangles are in the same proportion, you can find the missing side, x, by setting up a proportion equation.

$$\frac{2}{4} = \frac{4}{x}$$

(small triangle) (big triangle); $x = 8$

ACT TRIANGLE PROBLEMS

Most of the triangle problems on the ACT combine *several* of the triangle concepts we've just gone over. Be flexible, and look for clues as to which concepts are being tested. Here are some triangle problems as they might appear on the ACT:

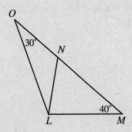

1. In the figure above, O, N, and M are collinear. If the length of $\overline{ON}$ and $\overline{NL}$ are the same, and the measure of angle LON is 30 degrees and angle LMN is 40 degrees, what is the measure of angle NLM?

A. 40
B. 80
C. 90
D. 120
E. 150

Here's how to crack it:

We saw this problem at the beginning of the chapter, and managed to solve it without using any geometry. Now let's solve it geometrically. Since $\overline{ON}$ is equal to $\overline{NL}$, we know that triangle ONL is isosceles. If angle $O = 30$ degrees then so does angle L, and therefore angle ONL is equal to 120 degrees. Because this angle and angle LNM add up to a straight line, LNM must be equal to 60 degrees. Angle LNM plus angle LMN add up to 100 degrees, meaning that the angle we are looking for (NLM) is equal to 80 degrees and the answer is **B**.

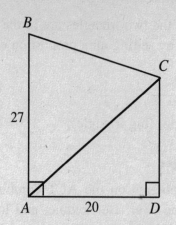

2. In the figure above, if $\overline{AB} = 27$, $\overline{CD} = 20$, and the area of triangle $ADC = 240$, what is the area of polygon $ABCD$?

F. 420
G. 480
H. 540
J. 564
K. 1128

Here's how to crack it:

Again, we saw this problem at the beginning of the chapter, and managed to eliminate three of the five answer choices through POE. Now let's solve it geometrically. The polygon in question is made up of two triangles. We are told that the area of triangle ADC is 240.

The formula for the area of a triangle $= \dfrac{\text{base} \times \text{height}}{2}$.

We don't know the base of this triangle, but we do know the height and the total area. Can we figure out the base? Of course.

$$\frac{(B)(20)}{2} = 240$$

$$B = 24.$$

Now let's look at the other triangle. We need to find its area, because the sum of the areas of the two triangles equals the area of the polygon we are looking for. If we turn the polygon on its side so that BA is on the bottom, we have the base of the triangle ABC. Do we know the height? Yes! The base of triangle ADC also happens to be equal to the height of triangle ABC: 24.

All that's left is to plug the base and height into the area formula to get the area of triangle ABC. $\dfrac{(27)(24)}{2} = 324$.

The area of the polygon is $324 + 240 = 564$, or answer choice **J**.

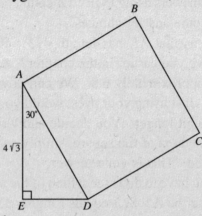

1. In the figure above, square $ABCD$ is attached to triangle ADE as shown. If angle EAD is equal to 30 degrees, and $\overline{AE}$ is equal to $4\sqrt{3}$, then what is the area of square $ABCD$?

   A. $8\sqrt{3}$
   B. 16
   C. 64
   D. 72
   E. $64\sqrt{2}$

Here's how to crack it:

The triangle in this diagram is a 30-60-90. Since angle A is the short angle, the side opposite that angle is equal to 4 and the hypotenuse is equal to 8. Because that hypotenuse is also the side of the square, the area of the square must be 8 times 8 or 64. This is answer choice **C**.

If you didn't remember the ratio of the sides of a 30-60-90 triangle, could you have eliminated some answers using POE? Of course. Let's see if we can use the diagram to eliminate some answer choices.

The diagram tells us that AE has length $4\sqrt{3}$. Remember the important approximations we gave you earlier in the chapter? A good approximation for $\sqrt{3}$ is 1.7. So $4\sqrt{3}$ = approximately 6.8. We can now use this to estimate the sides of square $ABCD$. Just using your eyes, would you say that AD is longer or shorter than AE? It's a bit longer. You decide and write down what you think it might be. To find the area of the square, simply square whatever value you decided the side equaled. This is your answer.

Now, all you have to do is see which of the answer choices still make sense. Could the answer be A? $8\sqrt{3}$ equals roughly 13.6. Is this close to your answer? No way. Could the answer be answer choice B, which is 16? Still much too small. Could the answer be answer choice C, which is 64? Quite possibly. Could the answer be 72? It might be. Could the correct answer be $64\sqrt{2}$? An approximation of radical 2 = 1.4, so $64\sqrt{2}$ equals 89.6. This seems rather large. Thus, on this problem, by using POE we could eliminate answer choices A, B, and E.

FOUR-SIDED FIGURES

The interior angles of any four-sided object (also known as a quadrilateral) add up to 360 degrees. The most common four-sided figures on the ACT are the rectangle and the square, with the parallelogram and the trapezoid coming in a far distant third and fourth.

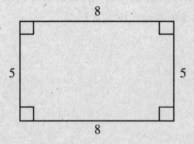

A **rectangle** is a four-sided object whose four interior angles are each equal to 90 degrees. The area of a rectangle is base times height. Therefore, the area of the rectangle above is 8 (*base*) × 5 (*height*) = 40. The perimeter of a rectangle is the sum of all four of its sides. The perimeter of the rectangle above is 8 + 8 + 5 + 5 = 26.

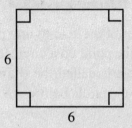

A **square** is a rectangle whose four sides are all equal in length. You can think of the area of a square therefore as side^2. The area of the above square is 6 (*base*) × 6 (*height*) = 36. The perimeter is 24.

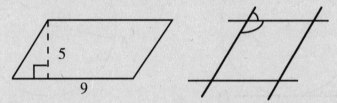

A **parallelogram** is a four-sided figure made up of two sets of parallel lines. We said earlier that when parallel lines are crossed by a third line, eight angles are formed, but that in reality there are only two—the big one and the little one. In a parallelogram, sixteen angles are formed, but there are still, in reality, only two.

The area of a parallelogram is also *base × height,* but because of the shape of the figure, the height of a parallelogram is not necessarily equal to one of its sides. Height is measured by a perpendicular line drawn from the base to the top of the figure. The area of the parallelogram above is 9 × 5 = 45.

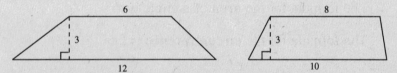

A **trapezoid** is a four-sided figure, of which two sides are parallel. Both of the figures above are trapezoids. The area of a trapezoid is the *average of the two parallel sides × the height*, or $\frac{1}{2}$(*Base* 1 +*Base* 2)(*Height*), but on ACT problems involving trapezoids there is almost always some easy way to find the area without knowing the formula (for example, by dividing the trapezoid into two triangles). In both trapezoids above, the area is 27.

CIRCLES

The distance from the center of a circle to any point on the circle is called the **radius**. The distance from one point on a circle, through the center of the circle, to another point on the circle is called the **diameter**. The diameter is always equal to twice the radius. In the circle below, *AB* is called a **chord**. *CD* is called a **tangent** to the circle.

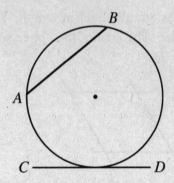
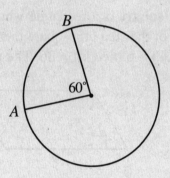

The curved portion of the circle between points *A* and *B* is called an **arc**. The angle formed by drawing lines from the center of the circle to points *A* and *B* is said to be **subtended** by the arc. There are 360 degrees in a circle, so that if the angle we just mentioned equaled 60 degrees, it would take up $\frac{60}{360}$ or $\frac{1}{6}$ of the degrees in the entire circle. It would also take up $\frac{1}{6}$ of the area of the circle and $\frac{1}{6}$ of the outer perimeter of the circle, called the circumference.

The formula for the **area** of a circle is πr^2.

The formula for the **circumference** is $2\pi r$.

In the circle below, if the radius is 4, then the area is 16π, and the circumference is 8π.

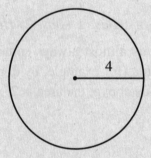

The key to circle problems on the ACT is to look for the word or phrase that tells you what to do. If you see the word circumference, immediately write down the formula for circumference, and plug in any numbers the problem has given you. By solving for whatever quantity is still unknown, you have probably already answered the problem.

1. If the area of a circle is 16 meters, what is its radius in meters?

   A. $\dfrac{8}{\pi}$

   B. 12π

   C. $\dfrac{4\sqrt{\pi}}{\pi}$

   D. $\dfrac{16}{\pi}$

   E. $144\pi^2$

Here's how to crack it:

As soon as you see the word "area," start thinking $\pi r^2 = 16$. The problem is asking for the radius, so you have to solve for r. If you divide both sides by π you get:

$$r^2 = \frac{16}{\pi}$$

$$r = \sqrt{\frac{16}{\pi}}$$

$$= \frac{4}{\sqrt{\pi}}$$

$$= \frac{4\sqrt{\pi}}{\pi}$$

which is answer choice **C**.

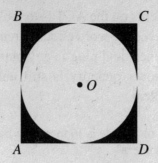

2. In the figure above, the circle with center O is inscribed inside square $ABCD$ as shown. If a side of the square measures 8 units, what is the area of the shaded region?

    F. $8 - 16\pi$
    G. 8π
    H. 16π
    J. $64 - 16\pi$
    K. 64π

Here's how to crack it:

Since the side of the square measures 8 units, what is the area of the square? 64 square units.

POE NOTES

Before we do any more real math, let's take a moment to look at the diagram. What portion of the entire square would you say is shaded? Could it be as much as $\frac{1}{2}$? No, so we're looking for an answer that is less than half of 64—in other words, less than 32. Most of the answer choices are in terms of π, but a rough approximation of π is 3. Let's go through the choices and see if there are any we can eliminate.

    F. $8 - 16(3) = -40$. This is clearly crazy. You can't have a negative area.

    G. $8(3) = 24$. Let's hold on to this one.

    H. $16(3) = 48$. No. We need an answer less than 32.

    J. $64 - 16(3) = 16$. Let's hold on to this one too.

    K. $64(3) = 192$. This is larger than the entire square. No way.

Using POE you can eliminate three of the choices. If you're running out of time, or don't remember how to do the problem geometrically, guess and move on.

To solve the problem the way ACT expects you to, you must find the area of the circle and subtract it from the square. What is left over is the shaded region. The formula for the area of a circle is πr^2. Do we know the radius of this circle? Sure. Because the circle is inscribed in the square, the side of the square has the same measure as the diameter of the circle. In other words, the radius of the circle is 4, and the area of the circle is 16π. Subtracting the area of the circle from the area of the square, we get $64 - 16\pi$, which is answer choice J.

GEOMETRY SUMMARY

ACT test writers have a particular weakness for "weighted average" problems. First, let's look at a regular unweighted average question:

1. There are only a limited number of geometry concepts tested on the ACT. Don't bother to study information that will not appear.

2. To the best of our knowledge, all geometry diagrams on this test are drawn to scale. This means you can use **estimation** to eliminate crazy answers.

3. If there is no diagram included in a problem, you should draw your own.

4. There are several things to know about angles and lines:

    A. A line is a 180-degree angle.

    B. When two lines intersect, four angles are formed, but in reality there are only   two.

    C. When two parallel lines are cut by a third line, eight angles are formed, but in reality there are still only two.

5. There are several things to know about triangles:

    A. A triangle has three sides and three angles, the sum of which equals 180-degrees.

B. An isosceles triangle has two equal sides, and two equal angles opposite those sides.

C. An equilateral triangle has three equal sides, and three equal angles, all of which equal 60 degrees.

D. A right triangle has one 90-degree angle. In a right triangle problem you can use the Pythagorean theorem to find the lengths of sides.

E. Some common right triangles are 3-4-5, 5-12-13, 8-15-17, 7-24-25.

F. ACT test writers also like the isosceles right triangle, whose sides are always in the ratio 1: 1: $\sqrt{2}$, and the 30-60-90 triangle who sides are always in the rato 2:1:$\sqrt{3}$.

G. Similar triangles have the same angle measurements, and the same proportion.

H. The area of a triangle is equal to $\dfrac{\text{base} \times \text{height}}{2}$.

6. Four-sided objects are called quadrilaterals and have four angles which add up to 360 degrees. There are several important things to remember:

A. The area of a rectangle, a square, or a parallelogram can be found using the formula: *base ¥ height = area.*

B. The perimeter of any object is the sum of the lengths of its sides.

C. The area of a trapezoid is equal to the average of the two bases times the height.

7. In a circle problem, the two important things to remember are:

A. Area = πr^2

B. Circumference = $2\pi r$.

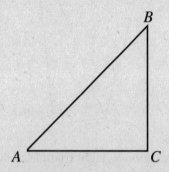

1. In triangle *ABC* above, angle *A* = angle *B*, and angle *C* is twice the measure of angle *B*. What is the measure, in degrees, of angle *A*?

   A. 30
   B. 45
   C. 50
   D. 75
   E. 90

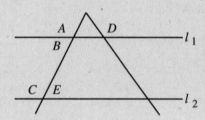

2. In the figure above, $l_1 \parallel l_2$. Which of the labeled angles must be equal to each other?

   F. *A* and *C*
   G. *D* and *E*
   H. *A* and *B*
   J. *D* and *B*
   K. *C* and *B*

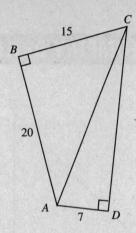

3. In the figure above, right triangles ABC and ACD are drawn as shown. If $\overline{AB} = 20$, $\overline{BC} = 15$, and $\overline{AD} = 7$, then $\overline{CD} = ?$

   A. 21
   B. 22
   C. 23
   D. 24
   E. 25

4. If the area of circle A is 16π, then what is the circumference of a circle B if its radius is $\frac{1}{2}$ that of circle A?

   F. 2π
   G. 4π
   H. 6π
   J. 8π
   K. 16π

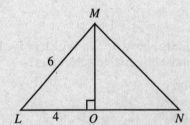

5. In the figure above, $\overline{MO}$ is perpendicular to $\overline{LN}$, $\overline{LO}$ is equal to 4, $\overline{MO}$ is equal to $\overline{ON}$, and $\overline{LM}$ is equal to 6. What is $\overline{MN}$?

   A. $2\sqrt{10}$
   B. $3\sqrt{5}$
   C. $4\sqrt{5}$
   D. $3\sqrt{10}$
   E. $6\sqrt{4}$

Here's how to crack them:

Question 1: Let's say angle *A* equals *x* degrees. Angle *B* also equals *x* degrees. Angle *C* is therefore 2*x* degrees. We have a total of 4*x* degrees. Since there are 180 degrees in a triangle, 4*x* = 180. *x* equals 45, and therefore the correct answer is **B**. Note that you could have **worked backward on** this problem.

Question 2: When two parallel lines are cut by a third line, there are really only two angles formed—a big one and a little one. We need to find an answer choice with two big angles or two little angles. Remember, any answer choice with angle *D* in it must be wrong because this angle is not formed by two parallel lines being cut by a third. The correct answer is **F**.

Question 3: You could use the Pythagorean theorem to solve this question, but you will be done much faster if you know the triples ACT likes to use. The triangle on the left is a version of a 3-4-5 triangle: 15-20-25. The triangle on the right is a 7-24-25 triangle. The correct answer is **D**.

Question 4: The radius of circle *A* is 4. If circle *B* has a radius that is half of circle A, its radius is 2. Therefore the circumference is 4π. The correct answer is **G**.

Question 5: This time we have to use the Pythagorean theorem, because all we know about triangle LMO is that it is a right triangle. Using the Pythagorean theorem, we find that MO is equal to $\sqrt{20}$ or $2\sqrt{5}$. Triangle *MON* is isoceles, so the hypotenuse is equal to the side times $\sqrt{2}$. The correct answer is **A**.

Graphing and Coordinate Geometry

Coordinate geometry, the fancy name for graphing, is a way of thinking about an equation, or the solutions to an equation, as a kind of picture. The simplest equations involve only one variable, and can be represented on a number line. Often, these equations involve inequalities.

GRAPHING INEQUALITIES

Here's a simple inequality:

$$3x + 5 > 11$$

As you know from reading the algebra chapter of this book, you solve an inequality in the same way that you solve an equality. By subtracting 5 from both sides and then dividing both sides by 3, you get the expression:

$$x > 2$$

This can be represented on a number line as shown below:

The open circle at 2 indicates that x can include every number greater than 2, but not 2 itself, or anything less than 2.

If we had wanted to graph $x \geq 2$, the circle would have to be filled in, indicating that our graph includes 2 as well:

An ACT graphing problem might look like this:

1. Which of the following represents the solution of the inequality $-5x - 7 < x + 5$?

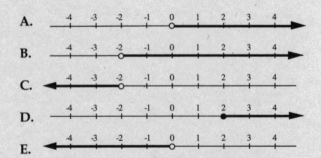

Here's how to crack it:

The test writers want you first to simplify the equation, and then figure out which of the answer choices represents a graph of the solution set of the equation. To simplify, get all the x's on one side of the equation.

$$
\begin{array}{rcl}
-5x - 7 & < & x + 5 \ ? \\
\underline{-x} & & \underline{-x} \\
-6x - 7 & < & 5 \\
& \underline{+7} & \underline{+7} \\
-6x & < & 12
\end{array}
$$

Now, divide both sides by -6. Remember that when you multiply or divide an inequality, the sign flips over.

$$\frac{6x}{-6} < \frac{12}{-6}$$
$$x > -2$$

Which of the choices answers the question? If you chose answer choice **B**, you're right!

POE NOTES

You could have done this (and most other inequality graphing problems) just as easily by **working backward**. Look at the possible answer choices. The test writers at ACT tend to surround the correct answer with at least one *almost* correct answer. Why don't we begin by checking to see if any numbers appear more than once as origin points in the answer choice graphs? The only number which repeats here is –2 which appears in answer choices B and C. Let's plug –2 into our inequality and pretend for a moment that it is an equality.

$$\text{Does } -5(-2) - 7 = (-2) + 5 \ ?$$
$$10 - 7 = 3 \ ?$$

Yes! Now, to decide whether the answer is B or C, just pick a number which is in one answer but not the other. For example, in answer choice C, 4 is part of the solution set. By plugging –4 into the inequality, we will see if answer choice

C is correct. If it isn't, then the answer is B.

$$-5(-4) - 7 < (-4) + 5$$
$$20 - 7 < 1$$
$$13 < 1$$

Is this true? No, so the answer must be **B**.

GRAPHING IN TWO DIMENSIONS

More complicated graphing questions concern equations with two variables, usually designated x and y. These equations can be graphed on a Cartesian grid which looks like this:

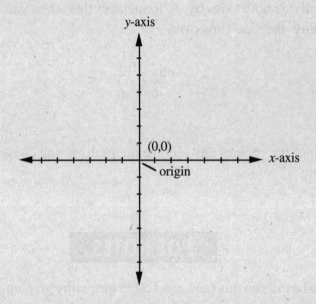

Every point (x,y) has a place on this grid. For example, the point A (3,4) can be found by counting over on the x–axis 3 places to the right of (0,0)—known as the origin—and then counting on the y-axis 4 places up from the origin, as shown below. Point B (5, –2) can be found by counting 5 places to the right on the x–axis and then down 2 places on the y-axis. Point C (–4, –1) can be found by counting 4 places to the left of the origin on the x-axis and then 1 place down on the y–axis.

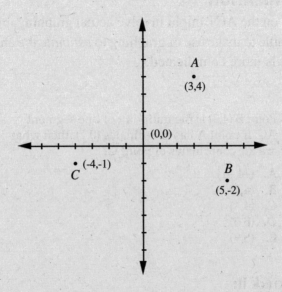

The grid is divided into four quadrants, which for no good reason go counterclockwise:

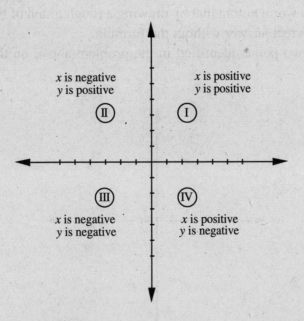

- In the first quadrant, *x* and *y* must both be positive.

- In the second quadrant, *x* must be negative but *y* must be positive.

- In the third quadrant, *x* and *y* are both negative.

- In the fourth quadrant, *x* is positive, but *y* is negative.

GRAPHIC GUESSTIMATION

A few questions on the ACT might involve actual graphing, but it is more likely that you will be able to make use of graphing to *estimate* the answer to a question that ACT thinks is more complicated.

> **1.** Point B (4,3) is the midpoint of line segment AC. If point A has coordinates (0,1), then what are the coordinates of point C?
>
> **A.** (–4,–1)
> **B.** (4,1)
> **C.** (4,4)
> **D.** (8,5)
> **E.** (8,9)

Here's how to crack it:

You may or may not remember the midpoint formula: the ACT test writers are expecting you to use it to solve this problem. We'll go over it in a moment, along with the other formulas you'll need to solve coordinate geometry questions. However, it is worth noting that by drawing a rough graph of this problem, you can get the correct answer without the formula.

Find the two points identified in the problem above on the grid provided below:

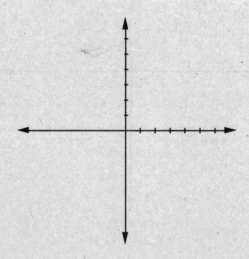

B is supposed to be the midpoint of a line segment AC. Draw a line through the two points you've just plotted and extend it upward until B is the midpoint of the line segment. It should look like this:

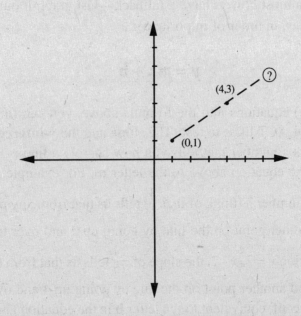

The place where you stopped drawing is the approximate location of point C. Now let's look at the answer choices to see if any of them are in the ballpark.

A. (-4,-1): These coordinates are in the wrong quadrant!

B. (4,1): This point is way below where it should be.

C. (4,4): This point does not extend enough to the right.

D. (8,5): Definitely in the ballpark. Hold on to this answer choice.

E. (8,9): Possible, though the *y*-coordinate seems a bit high.

Which answer choice do you want to pick? If you said answer choice **D**, you are right.

By the way, the folks at ACT will not allow you to bring graphing paper (or any other kind of scrap paper) with you to the real test, so get used to making your graphs and other calculations in the margins of the test booklet.

THE IMPORTANT COORDINATE GEOMETRY FORMULAS

By memorizing a few formulas, you will be able to answer virtually all of the coordinate geometry questions on this test. Remember, too, that in coordinate geometry you almost *always* have a fallback—just graph it out.

The formulas, in order of importance:

$$y = mx + b$$

By putting (x,y) equations into the formula above, you can find two pieces of information that ACT likes to test: The **slope** and the **y-intercept**.

The **slope** is a number that tells you how sharply a line is inclining, and is equivalent in the equation above to the letter **m**. For example, in the equation $y = 3x + 4$, the number 3 (think of it as $\frac{3}{1}$) tells us that from any point on the line, we can find another point on the line by going up 3 and over to the right 1.

In the equation $y = -\frac{4}{5}x - 7$, the slope of $-\frac{4}{5}$ tells us that from any point on the line, we can find another point on the line by going up 4 and over 5 to the left.

The **y-intercept**, equivalent to the letter **b** in the equation above, is the point at which the line intercepts the y-axis. For example, in the equation $y = 3x + 4$, the line will strike the y-axis at a point 4 above the origin. In the equation $y = 2x - 7$, the line will strike the y-axis at a point 7 below the origin.

A typical ACT $y = mx + b$ question might give you an equation in another form and ask you to find either the slope or the y-intercept. Simply put the equation into the form we've just shown.

1. What is the slope of the line based on the equation $5x - y = 7x + 6$?

    A. –2
    B. 0
    C. 2
    D. 6
    E. –6

Here's how to crack it:

Isolate y on the left side of the equation. To do this, subtract $5x$ from both sides.

$$5x - y = 7x + 6$$
$$\underline{-5x \qquad -5x}$$
$$-y = 2x + 6$$

We aren't quite done. The format we want is $y = mx + b$, *not* $-y = mx + b$. Let's multiply both sides by -1.

$$y = -2x + 6$$

The slope of this line is -2, and the answer is **A**.

THE SLOPE FORMULA

You can find the slope of a line, even if all you have are two points on that line, by using the slope formula.

$$\text{slope} = \frac{\text{change in } y}{\text{change in } x}$$

1. What is the slope of the straight line passing through the points (-2,5) and (6,4) ?

   A. $-\dfrac{1}{16}$

   B. $-\dfrac{1}{8}$

   C. $\dfrac{1}{5}$

   D. $\dfrac{2}{9}$

   E. $\dfrac{4}{9}$

Here's how to crack it:
Find the change in y and put it over the change in x. The change in y is the first y coordinate minus the second y-coordinate. The change in x is the first x minus the second x:

$$\frac{y[1] - y[2]}{x[1] - x[2]} \qquad \begin{array}{l} 5 - 4 = 1 \\ -2 - 6 = -8 \end{array}$$

The correct answer choice is **G**.

MIDPOINT FORMULA

If you have the two endpoints of a line segment, you can find the midpoint of the segment by using the midpoint formula.

$$(x[m], y[m]) = \frac{x[1] + x[2]}{2}, \frac{y[1] + y[2]}{2}$$

It looks a lot more intimidating than it really is.

To find the midpoint of a line, just take the *average* of the two x coordinates, and the *average* of the two y coordinates. For example, the midpoint of the line segment formed by the coordinates (3,4) and (9,2) is just

$$\frac{(3+9)}{2} = 6 \text{ and } \frac{(4+2)}{2} = 3$$
$$\text{or } (6,3)$$

Remember the first midpoint problem we did? Here it is again:

1. Point B (4,3) is the midpoint of line segment
   AC. If point A has coordinates (0,1) then what
   are the coordinates of point C?

   A. (–4,–1)
   B. (4,1)
   C. (4,4)
   D. (8,5)
   E. (8,9)

Here's how to crack it:

You'll remember that it was perfectly possible to solve this problem just by drawing a quick graph of what it ought to look like. However, to find the correct answer using the midpoint formula, we first have to realize that, in this case, we already *have* the midpoint. We are being asked to find one of the endpoints.

The midpoint is (4,3). This represents the average of the two endpoints. The endpoint we know about is (0,1). Let's do the x-coordinate first. The average of the x-coordinates of the two endpoints equals the x-coordinate of the midpoint.

So $\frac{(0 + ?)}{2} = 4$. What is the missing x-coordinate? 8. Now, let's do the y-coordi-

nate. $\frac{(1 + ?)}{2} = 3$. What is the missing y-coordinate? 5. The answer is **D**.

If you had trouble following that last explanation, just remember that you already understood this problem (and got the answer) using graphing. Never be intimidated by formulas on the ACT. There is usually another way to do the problem.

THE DISTANCE FORMULA

We hate the distance formula. We keep forgetting it, and even when we remember it, we feel like fools for using it because there are much easier ways to find the distance between two points. We aren't even going to tell you what the distance formula is.

If you need to know the distance between two points, you can always think of that distance as being the hypotenuse of a right triangle. Here's an example:

1. What is the distance between the points A (2,2) and B (5,6) ?

   A. 3
   B. 4
   C. 5
   D. 6
   E. 7

Here's how to crack it:
Let's make a quick graph of what this ought to look like.

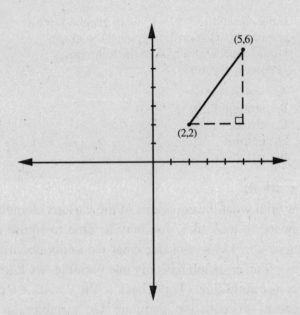

If we extend lines from the two points to form a right triangle under the line segment AB, we can use the Pythagorean theorem to get the distance between the two points. What is the length of the base of the triangle? 3. What is the length of the height of the triangle? 4. So what is the length of the hypotenuse? 5. Of course, as usual, it was one of the triples of which ACT is so fond. The answer is **C**.

CIRCLES, ELLIPSES, AND PARABOLAS, OH MY

You should probably have a *vague* idea of what the equations for these figures look like; just remember that there are very few questions concerning these figures, and when they do come up you can almost always figure them out by graphing.

The equation for a circle looks like this:

$$x^2 + y^2 = 1$$

The equation for an ellipse (just a squat looking circle) looks like this:

$$\frac{x^2}{25} + \frac{y^2}{16} = 1$$

The equation for a parabola (just a U-shaped line) looks like this:

$$y = x^2$$

1. If the equation $x^2 = 1 - y^2$ were graphed in the standard (x,y) coordinate plane, the graph would represent which of the following geometric figures?

   A. square
   B. straight line
   C. circle
   D. ellipse
   E. parabola

Here's how to crack it:

If you're familiar with what the equations of the various elements in the answer choices are supposed to look like, you may be able to figure the problem out without graphing at all. Let's consider what we know about the equations of geometric figures. If an equation has only one variable, we know that the graph of the equation is a straight line. (Think back to the $y = mx + b$ problems we did earlier.) However, in this equation, there are two variables, so we can rule out answer choice B. There is no equation for a square, so we can rule out answer choice A. If only one of the variables were squared, this might be a parabola, but in this problem *both* are squared, which means we can eliminate answer choice E. If both variables were squared, but both were also divided by numbers, then this might be an ellipse, but in this case neither were divided by numbers, so we can get rid of answer choice D.

We are left with answer choice **C**. We can rearrange the equation to make it look more like the classic circle equation if we add y[squared] to both sides:

$$x^2 + y^2 = 1.$$

ESTIMATING NOTE

Of course, we could also just plug some numbers into the equation and plot them out on a homemade (x,y) axis in the margin of the test booklet. Let's try this on the grid below.

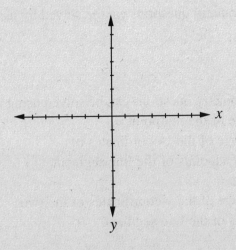

The easiest way to start is to let one of the variables equal 0. If $x = 0$, then y must equal 1. So one point of this equation is $(0,1)$. If we let $y = 0$, then x must equal 1. So another point of this equation is $(1,0)$. Plot out some other points of the equation. How about $(-1,0)$ and $(0, -1)$? What kind of geometric figure does it appear that we have? If you said a circle, you were absolutely correct.

GRAPHING AND COORDINATE GEOMETRY SUMMARY

1. In graphing an inequality, solve for the variable, and look for the number-line graph that expresses the equation. Remember, you can often **work backward** on inequality graphing questions.

2. Graphing on an *x/y* axis is most useful as a way to **estimate** the correct answers to coordinate geometry questions.

3. Some coordinate geometry equations can be solved by putting them into the format $y = mx + b$, where m is the slope of the line and b is the y intercept.

4. Some coordinate geometry questions can be solved by using the slope formula:
$$\text{slope} = \frac{\text{change in } y}{\text{change in } x}$$

5. Other coordinate geometry questions can be solved using the midpoint formula:
    The x-coordinate of the midpoint =
    　　　the average of the x-coordinates of
    　　　the two endpoints of the line segment.
    The y-coordinate =
    　　　the average of the y-coordinates of the two
    　　　endpoints of the line segment.

6. You can always find the distance between two points by drawing a line between them and making this the hypotenuse of a right triangle.

7. Every once in a while ACT asks a question based on the equations of circles, ellipses, and parabolas. If you need a very high score, it might help to memorize these equations, but remember, these questions can frequently be done by using graphing to estimate the correct answer.

1. Which of the following represents the solution of the inequality $-3x - 6 > 9$?

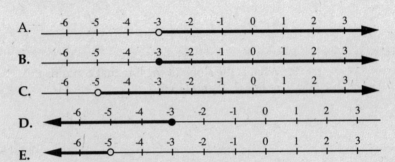

2. What is the midpoint of the line segment whose endpoints are represented on the coordinate axis by the points (3,5) and (–4,3)?

   F. (–2,–5)

   G. $(-\frac{1}{2}, 4)$

   H. (1,8)

   J. $(4, -\frac{1}{2})$

   K. (3,3)

3. What is the slope of the line represented by the equation $10x + 2x = y + 6$?

   A. 10
   B. 12
   C. 14
   D. 15
   E. 16

4. What is the length of the line segment whose endpoints are represented on the coordinate axis by the points (–2,–1) and (1,3) ?

F. 3
G. 4
H. 5
J. 6
K. 7

5. What is the slope of the line that contains the points (6,4) and (13,5) ?

A. $-\dfrac{1}{8}$

B. $-\dfrac{1}{9}$

C. $\dfrac{1}{7}$

D. 1
E. 7

Here's how to crack them:

Question 1: We can immediately cancel choices B and D because the equation does not contain a greater than *or equal to* sign. If you chose answer choice C, you forgot that in inequalities the sign flips when you multiply or divide by a negative number. The correct answer is **E**.

Question 2: If you don't remember the formula for finding a midpoint, just make a rough graph. Which quadrant should the answer be in? If you said the second, you were absolutely correct. The *x*-coordinate should be negative, the *y*-coordinate should be positive. Which answer choices are possible? There's only one. The correct answer is **G**.

Question 3: We need to put this into the standard $y = mx + b$ form. In this case, the equation becomes $y = 12x - 6$. The slope is 12, and the answer is **B**.

Question 4: Forget the distance formula. Instead, try sketching out a graph. Make the line between the two points the hypotenuse of a right triangle. It turns out to be a 3-4-5 triangle. The correct answer is **H**.

Question 5: Just use the slope formula—the difference in *y* over the difference in *x*. The correct answer is **C**.

CHAPTER 13

Trigonometry

There are only four trigonometry questions on the ACT. As we said before, since these questions are among the easiest on the test, you should plan to do them even if you never took trigonometry. To do that you will need to know a couple of specific facts. Don't worry about what they mean or why they are true. After the ACT, if you're still interested, there will be lots of time to read books on trigonometry. You could even take a course in college.

All the trigonometry questions on this test involve the relationships between the sides of a right triangle. In the right triangle below, the angle x can be expressed in terms of the ratios of different sides of the triangle.

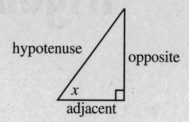

The **sine** of angle $x = \dfrac{\text{length of side opposite angle } x}{\text{length of hypotenuse}}$

The **cosine** of angle $x = \dfrac{\text{length of side adjacent angle } x}{\text{length of hypotenuse}}$

The **tangent** of angle $x = \dfrac{\text{length of side opposite } x}{\text{length of side adjacent } x}$

There is a very handy acronym to remember all this:

SOHCAHTOA

Sine is **o**pposite over **h**ypotenuse. Cosine is **a**djacent over **h**ypotenuse. Tangent is **o**pposite over **a**djacent. So in the triangle below, the sine of angle θ would be $\dfrac{4}{5}$. The cosine of angle θ would be $\dfrac{3}{5}$. The tangent of angle θ would be $\dfrac{4}{3}$.

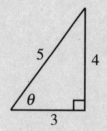

YOU'RE ALMOST DONE

There are three more relationships to memorize. They involve the reciprocals of the previous three.

$$\text{The } \textbf{cosecant} = \frac{1}{\text{sine}}$$

$$\text{The } \textbf{secant} = \frac{1}{\text{cosine}}$$

$$\text{The } \textbf{cotangent} = \frac{1}{\text{tangent}}$$

And one last thing, while we're at it:

$$\textbf{sine}^2\boldsymbol{\theta} + \textbf{cosine}^2\boldsymbol{\theta} = 1$$

YOU'RE DONE

That wasn't too grueling was it? Please feel free to cut out the wallet-sized diploma (suitable for framing) below, and carry it everywhere with pride and distinction.

> ### •*Princeton Review Diploma*•
> This is to certify that
>
> _____
>
> has completed the
> entire ACT trigonometry canon.

Let's try a couple of problems:

1. What is sine θ, if tangent $\theta = \frac{4}{3}$?

    A. $\frac{3}{4}$

    B. $\frac{4}{5}$

    C. $\frac{5}{4}$

    D. $\frac{5}{3}$

    E. $\frac{7}{3}$

Here's how to crack it:

It helps to sketch out the right triangle, and fill in the information we know:

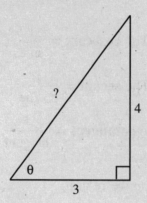

What kind of right triangle is this? That's right—a 3-4-5. Now, we need to know the sine of the angle θ: opposite over hypotenuse, or $\dfrac{4}{5}$, which is answer choice **B**.

1. For all θ, $\dfrac{\cos\text{ine }\theta}{\sin^2\theta\ +\ \cos\text{ine}^2\theta} = ?$

   A. sine θ
   B. cosecant θ
   C. cotangent θ
   D. cosine θ
   E. tangent θ

Here's how to crack it:

sine²θ + cosine²θ always equals 1. $\dfrac{\cos\text{ine}}{1}$ = cosine. The answer is **D**.

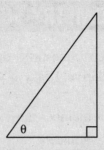

2. In a right triangle shown above, the secant of
angle θ is $\frac{25}{7}$. What is the sine of angle θ?

F. $\frac{3}{25}$

G. $\frac{5}{25}$

H. $\frac{7}{25}$

J. $\frac{24}{25}$

K. $\frac{25}{7}$

Here's how to crack it:

The secant of any angle is the reciprocal of the cosine, which is just another way
to say that the cosine of angle θ is $\frac{7}{25}$:

Secant $= \frac{1}{\cos}$ so $\frac{1}{\cos} = \frac{25}{7}$, which means that $\cos = \frac{7}{25}$.

Cosine means adjacent over hypotenuse. Let's sketch this out:

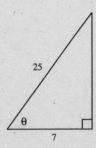

As you can see, we now have two sides of a right triangle. Can we find the
third side? If you said this was one of the triples we told you about before, you
were absolutely correct, although you also could have derived this by using the
Pythagorean theorem. The third side must be 24. The question asks for the sine
of θ. Sine = opposite over hypotenuse, or $\frac{24}{25}$, which is answer choice **J**.

TRIGONOMETRY SUMMARY

1. There are only four trigonometry questions on the ACT. They only deal with right triangles, and they are relatively easy if you know a few formulas.

2. SOHCAHTOA will help you remember most of the formulas:

   Sine = $\dfrac{\text{opposite}}{\text{hypotenuse}}$; cosine = $\dfrac{\text{adjacent}}{\text{hypotenuse}}$; tangent = $\dfrac{\text{opposite}}{\text{adjacent}}$.

3. The cosecant = $\dfrac{1}{\text{sine}}$, the secant = $\dfrac{1}{\text{cosine}}$, and the cotangent = $\dfrac{1}{\text{tangent}}$.

4. $\text{sine}^2\theta + \text{cosine}^2\theta = 1$.

TRIGONOMETRY DRILL

1. In triangle ABC below, the tangent of angle θ equals

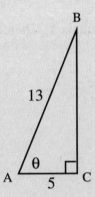

   A. $\dfrac{5}{12}$

   B. $\dfrac{12}{13}$

   C. $\dfrac{17}{12}$

   D. $\dfrac{12}{5}$

   E. 3

2. If the cotangent of an angle θ is 1, then the tangent of angle θ is

   F. -1
   G. 0
   H. 1
   J. 2
   K. 3

3. If $x + \sin^2\theta + \cos^2\theta = 4$, then $x = ?$

   A. 1
   B. 2
   C. 3
   D. 4
   E. 5

Here's how to crack them:

1. This is a 5-12-13 triangle. The tangent of an angle is opposite over adjacent. The correct answer is **D**.

2. The cotangent of an angle is the reciprocal of the tangent. If the tangent is 1, then so is the cotangent. The correct answer is **H**.

3. $sine^2\theta + cosine^2\theta$ always equals 1. Therefore x must equal 3. The correct answer is **C**.

PART IV

How to Beat the ACT Reading Test

The ACT reading test presents four passages and forty questions: that's ten questions per passage. You get thirty-five minutes for the whole section, which means you have about nine minutes to cover each passage and the questions that follow it.

The passages are edited bits of books and magazines and according to ACT they're "typical of what a college freshman might be required to read…." And the questions? ACT says they test your ability to "understand" the passages.

BUT THAT'S NOT REALLY TRUE

No one ever achieved a great insight by spending eight or nine pressured minutes reading an isolated fragment of a book or article. Serious writers don't intend their work to be read in fragments, or in so hurried a fashion as reading tests require. (Imagine that you were asked to read a *fragment* of the history of the relations between the United States, Germany, and Japan during the twentieth century. Suppose, in particular, that you're only asked to read about their cooperative relations in the years 1985–1990. You'd be missing the history of their relationship during the years 1940–1945—World War II—which means you'd be missing a rather important piece of the story.)

Furthermore, serious *readers* take time to *think* about the things they read. How far would Albert Einstein have gotten if someone interrupted his reading every eight or nine minutes to announce that he should "close his book because time is up"? As a college student, you'll be asked not only to read, but also to think about what you read—and then to reread—and then to think some more. Any professor will tell you that understanding takes thought, and thought usually takes time.

When you take the ACT reading test you're not asked to understand. You're not asked to do anything you'll ever do in college. You're just asked to take a "reading test."

THE ACT READING TEST: CRACKING THE SYSTEM

You'll raise your reading score if you're "wise" to the test and if you think strategically. We're first going to show you how ACT reading questions are built. Then we'll show you how to use that knowledge to select correct answers.

You'll learn to:

(1) attack the passages in the order that best suits *you*

(2) see through the camouflage that hides *correct* answer choices

(3) identify *incorrect* answer choices and eliminate them quickly

(4) answer questions without really reading passages

(5) put all of these techniques together in order to approach every passage and question with a step-by-step strategy that leads systematically to a correct answer.

Reading Test Triage: Ordering the Passages

The reading test has four passages, one each from the fields of:

(1) natural science,

(2) social studies,

(3) the humanities, and

(4) literature.

Students differ in their abilities to tackle these different passage types and it's important that you decide which passages are easiest and hardest for you. That way you can decide which passages to do first (the easier ones) and which to do last (the harder ones).

Natural science passages are filled with lots of details and dry technical descriptions:

> It is further noteworthy that the terrestrial vertebrate's most significant muscles of movement are no longer located lateral to the vertebral column as they are in the fish, but rather in ventral and dorsal relation to it. This trend in terrestrial evolution is highly significant and means that the terrestrial vertebrate's principle movements are fore and back, not side to side. The trend is well documented in the whale, an aquatic animal whose ancestors are terrestrial quadrupeds. The whale, in other words, has "returned" to the sea secondarily, after an ancestral stage on the land. Unlike the fish, and in accordance with its ancestry, it propels itself by moving the tail up and down, not side to side. In a sense, the whale moves himself by bending up and down at the waist. Indeed, that very analogy is recalled by the mythical mermaid figure who seems to represent a humanlike line returned to the water secondarily like the whale.

The questions usually track the text pretty closely and don't require you to make inferences:

1. Which of the following best represents a general trend associated with mammalian evolution?

   A. Enhancement of bodily movement from right to left and left to right
   B. Minimization of muscle groups oriented lateral to the vertebral column
   C. The development of propulsive fins from paired limbs
   D. Secondary return to the sea

Some people have a flair for the ACT's natural science passages and some people find them extremely tedious and difficult. (And by the way, it isn't necessarily good science students who do well with these passages nor poor science students who have trouble with them.) If among all of the passage types you find science the easiest, you should make it a rule to address the science passage *first*. If, on the other hand, you find science passages the most difficult, save them for *last*.

The *literature passage* is kind of opposite to the natural science passage. It tells a fictitious story and it's supposed to be packed with hints and suggestions about characters and their motivations:

> Allen's grandmother was readying herself to leave. She was, in fact, putting the final touches on her make-up which, as always, looked to Allen as though someone had thrown it on her face with a shovel. Mrs. Mandale then placed her newly purchased bracelet over her wrist when a look of troubled ambivalence came over her. "Perhaps this bracelet isn't right for me," she said. "I won't wear it."
>
> Waiting, now, for thirty minutes, Allen tried to be tolerant. "It is right for you," he said. "It matches your personality. Wear it." The bracelet was a remarkable illustration of poor taste. Its colors were vulgar and the conformation lacked any sign of thoughtful design. The truth is it did match his grandmother's personality. All that she did and enjoyed was tasteless, and induced in Allen a quiet hopelessness.

Literature questions often require that you "read between the lines" and draw inferences about the way characters feel or behave:

1. Allen most likely encouraged his grandmother to wear her bracelet because he:

   A. found it colorful and approved of its appearance.
   B. found its appearance pathetic and wished his grandmother to look petty.
   C. was impatient with his grandmother for spending time worrying about the bracelet.
   D. felt the bracelet matched his grandmother's personality.

Some people have a flair for *these* kinds of passages and questions. Others find them unclear and confusing. If you find literature passages easiest, do them *first*. If you find them most difficult, do them *last*.

Social studies and humanities passages are sort of a cross between natural science and literature. Often, the author has *views* about the subject he's discussing, and you might be asked to draw inferences about them. You might also be asked questions about details:

> Religion is so fundamental a part of human existence that one might easily forget to ask how it started. Yet it had to start somewhere and there had to be a time when human beings or their apelike ancestors did not entertain notions of the supernatural. Hence the historian should want to probe the origins of religious belief.
>
> It is doubtful that morality played a part in the beginnings of religious belief. Rather, religion is traceable to far more fundamental a human and animal characteristic. Storms, floods, famine, and other adversities inspired *fear* in the hearts of primitive peoples as well they should have. Curiously, humankind early took the position that they might somehow subject such catastrophes to their control. Specifically, they believed they might control it by obedience and submission and by conforming their behavior to its mandates. Worship, ritual, sacrifice of life, and property became means through which early peoples sought to cajole the powers and avoid the blights and miseries they dreaded. As Petronius, in Lucretius's tradition remarked, "it was fear that first made the gods."

1. According to the passage, natural disasters contributed to the development of religion by:

    A. motivating human beings to acquire some command over their environment.
    B. making human beings distinguish themselves from animals.
    C. causing human beings to sacrifice their lives and goods.
    D. providing a need for ritual and tradition.

2. The author believes that the origins of religion:

    F. are extremely easy to ascertain and understand.
    G. should not be questioned by historians because religion is fundamental to civilized life.
    H. are directly tied to apelike subhuman species.
    J. should be the subject of serious historical inquiry.

Mark Twain had magnificent style, and with *The Adventures of Huckleberry Finn* he built the gateway to American fiction. *Huckleberry Finn* treats extraordinarily serious themes and it reflects the author's coming of age. Although they don't represent truly mature works, other Twain Mississippi River stories, published before Huck Finn, afford Americans a clear, collective picture of pre-civil war life in the Mississippi Valley.

With the coming and going of the civil war, however, Twain adopted a revised agenda and this was reflected in the style and subject matter of his writing. The post-war era demanded that he address himself to the nation's social squalor. His work was more intellectualized, artificial, and at times angry. The author himself had faced several personal tragedies in series and these too might have contributed to the metamorphosis.

1. According to the passage, which of the following statements is true of *The Adventures of Huckleberry Finn*?

    A. It appeared after the publication of other Mark Twain stories describing life on the Mississippi River.
    B. It was the first full-length book that Mark Twain published.
    C. It would have been quite different if Mark Twain had not suffered personal tragedy.
    D. It had no serious themes and addressed no serious issues.

2. In the author's opinion, *The Adventures of Huckleberry Finn*:

    F. should not be read by children.
    G. contributed less to American literature than did Twain's post-war writings.
    H. is less adult in its subject matter than were Twain's post-war writings.
    J. reveals that Mark Twain had grown since writing his early Mississippi River stories.

You should order your work according to its degree of difficulty *for you*.

If you find literature passages especially easy and science passages especially tough you should probably address the passages in this order:

1	Literature
2/3	Social Studies & Humanities (either order)
4	Natural Science

If you find *both* literature and natural science particularly difficult, do the social studies and humanities passages first (in either order) and then do the literature and science passages in this order:

1/2	**Social Studies / Humanities (either order)**
3/4	**Literature / Science (either order)**

If you find both literature and science passages especially easy, order your work like this:

1/2	**Literature / Science (either order)**
3/4	**Social Studies / Humanities (either order)**

HOW TO TELL WHICH PASSAGES YOU FIND EASY AND HARD

Use the *Official Guide to the ACT*. Go through the sample ACTs and determine which you find easy to do and which you find difficult to do. Whatever holds true on the sample ACTs will probably hold true when you take the ACT for real.

Now that we've talked about the ordering of the passages and questions, let's talk about the whole point of taking the ACT—finding right answers.

THE RIGHT ANSWER MIGHT BE CAMOUFLAGED

Look at these two phrases:

"rationally conceived idea"
"concept born of reason"

The two phrases don't have a single word in common, but if you think about it you'll probably agree that they kind of mean the same thing. Lots of ACT reading questions test your ability to see that one sentence or phrase means more or less the same as another even though the wording is quite different. They test whether you can see that a sentence has been *paraphrased*, which means—reworded.

READ THIS PASSAGE; IT'S VERY SHORT

Regardless of personal religious belief, no true student of history can emerge from study without a scholarly appreciation for the significant role of religion in the development of human civilization.

Now that you've read the passage, answer this question:

1. Which of the following represents the author's belief regarding religion and the study of history?

    A. Many historians develop a deep suspicion of totalitarian societies and the way in which they abuse human rights.
    B. Most historians have a profound distaste for ancient documents and torn papers.
    C. True historians develop an appreciation for the role of religion in the course of human development.
    D. Few historians develop insight into the manner in which political leaders gain power.

It's pretty easy to see that **C** is right, and that A, B, and D are wrong. Choice C features the author's words and accurately reflects his meaning. Options A, B, and D are totally wild. They have nothing whatsoever to do with anything in the passage. This question is pretty straightforward. The wrong answers are clearly wrong and the right answer is clearly right.

ACT QUESTIONS AREN'T LIKE THAT

ACT questions won't usually provide you with a correct answer that reprints the author's own words. Instead, the author's statements will be camouflaged by *rewording*. That means you must be on the look-out for answer options that don't *seem* right because the author's sentences have been reworded. Let's take the question we just answered and turn it into an ACT question by rewriting the answer choices.

1. Which of the following represents the author's belief regarding the role of religion in the study of history?

    A. Few historians have gained a complete appreciation for the development of religion.
    B. Historians should not allow their personal religious beliefs to affect the historical conclusions with which they emerge.
    C. Serious historians regard religious belief as a significant force in man's social evolution.
    D. A true student of religious history should not ignore a general study of human development.

Answer choice C is still the correct answer, but that's not so easy to figure out anymore. Unless you're on the lookout for camouflage, you might not appreciate the similarity between these two statements:

1. ...no true student of history can emerge from study without a scholarly appreciation for the significant role of religion in the development of human civilization.

and

2. Serious historians regard religious belief as an important force in man's social evolution.

These two statements don't have a single word in common. Yet, when you think about it:

"serious historians"	*is camouflage for*	"true student of history"
"important force"	*is camouflage for*	"significant role"
"man's social evolution."	*is camouflage for*	"development of human civilization."

Answer choice C presented the author's statements—camouflaged.

SEE THROUGH THE CAMOUFLAGE

You'll raise your ACT score if you learn first to recognize camouflage, and then to see through it. So, let's practice. Each of the very short readings below comes from an ACT-type passage. We want you to:

- read each one,

- think carefully about what it means,

- *with that meaning in mind* consider the meaning of each answer choice, and

- determine which one constitutes the author's statements—camouflaged.

The human condition is unequal, distributing its gifts and penalties according to a wildly haphazard scheme of unfairness. One is not what he deserves to be but, simply—what he is.

1. According to the passage, it is true that the human condition:

   A. is a precious gift and should not be treated haphazardly.
   B. does not allocate its burdens and benefits according to merit.
   C. will become more predictable as human beings learn to appreciate it.
   D. is sometimes unjust, due to fundamental aspects of human nature.

Here's how to crack it:

What does the author say?

The author says that life's pleasures and hardships are not given out fairly—according to what people deserve. Instead, they're given out randomly. The author is saying that you don't get what you deserve. You just get what you get.

With that in mind, let's look at the answer options and see which one makes the same statement in a different way.

What do the choices mean?

Answer choice A means that life is a very valuable thing and that people should not be careless with it.

That's not what we're looking for.

Answer choice B says just what the author has said—in different words. Think about it:

"allocate"	*is camouflage for*	"distributing"
"burdens and benefits"	*is camouflage for*	"gifts and penalties"
"merit."	*is camouflage for*	"deserves."

Answer choice C means that people who appreciate life will find that it offers fewer surprises.

The author did not say that.

Answer choice D means that human nature is the cause of life's unfairness.

Interesting, but that's not what the author wrote.

Only answer choice **B** comes close to expressing the author's meaning.

That's why it's right.

Poverty, deformity, illness, loss, weakness, and mistreatment impose themselves relentlessly on individual lives. That circumstance begs the historian to ask why humans have for the most part accepted the situation so peaceably.

1. The passage indicates that persistent poverty and illness:

   A. are caused partially by humanity's overriding concern with acceptance and peace.
   B. are due in some part to faulty understanding of history.
   C. should make historians question the role of the individual in human affairs.
   D. should provoke historical inquiry into humanity's willingness to tolerate adversity.

Here's how to crack it:

What does the author say?

The author says, first of all, that people have always had a lot of trouble in their lives. He then says that historians should try to figure out why they're so willing to put up with it.

What do the choices mean?

Answer choice A means that people have trouble because they're too concerned with peace.

Ridiculous, but more important, it's not what the author wrote.

Answer choice B means that people have trouble because they don't understand history.

Not so ridiculous, but the author made no such statement.

Answer choice C means that all of this trouble should make historians try to figure out the place of individuals in society.

Whatever that means, it's not what we're looking for.

Now look at answer choice D. It's just what the doctor ordered. It's the author's statement—camouflaged. Think about it:

"should provoke historical inquiry"	*is camouflage for*	"begs the historian to ask"
"willingness to tolerate adversity."	*is camouflage for*	"why humans…accepted the situation so peaceably."

So answer choice **D** is right.

Religious belief allows the unlucky on some very important level to treat their misery as insignificant in the grand scheme of things, for they look to something higher: the approval of their God and the faith that they will not in the end be forsaken.

1. The passage states that religious belief helps people by:

   A. allowing them to accept the idea that they have been forsaken.
   B. providing them with faith that they will overcome their difficulties.
   C. diminishing the importance they might place on their day–to–day pain.
   D. emphasizing that spiritual strength is more significant than luck.

Here's how to crack it:

What does the author say?

The author says that religious belief helps people whose lives are difficult. It causes them to focus on the wish to please their God, which means that they place relatively little importance on the troubles they face in their lives.

What do the choices mean?

Answer choice A means that religious believers don't mind being forsaken.

Sorry, not what we're looking for.

Answer choice B means that religion helps people believe they'll get over their problems.

Sounds good, but it's not the meaning we're after.

Answer choice C means that religious believers don't think their troubles are so important.

That's what the author said! Choice C represents the author's statements camouflaged. Think about it:

| "diminishing the importance" | *is camouflage for* | "treat…as insignificant |
| "pain." | *is camouflage for* | "misery." |

Answer choice D means that religious believers think spiritual strength is more important than luck.

The author does not say anything like that.

Only answer choice C reflects the author's meaning.

That's why it's right.

Distracters

GETTING WISE TO DISTRACTERS

PROCESS OF ELIMINATION

You'll raise your ACT reading score if you're good at spotting not only right answers, but *wrong* answers too. In the standardized test business, wrong answers are called "distracters," and that's a perfect name for them. Distracters are designed to *misdirect your thinking*—to break your concentration and throw you off course. Even if you do have a pretty good grasp of the passage and the question you're trying to answer, distracters can make you lose sight of both. *But if you're wise to distracters* you can quickly eliminate them and make your way rapidly to the right answer.

FOUR KINDS OF DISTRACTERS

You should know about the four kinds of distracters that show up on the ACT reading test. We're going to show you how each one operates so you'll know how to use them to your advantage.

DISTRACTER TYPE 1: DISTORTIONS

Many distracters steal words directly from the passage and use them to create a statement that does *not* reflect the content of the passage. These distracters use the author's words but *distort* his meaning, so we call them distortions.

Read this statement:

> *"Tom loves going to the movies with Mary."*

It's easy to write a bunch of sentences that do not reflect the statement's meaning, even though they use the words "Tom," "love," "movies," and "Mary." For example, consider this:

> *"Tom fell in love with Mary at the movies."*

or this:

> *"Tom and Mary love movies."*

or this:

> *"Tom and Mary generally enjoy seeing movies about love."*

or this:

> *"Tom and Mary go to the movies to make love."*

(OK, the ACT would not include this, but you get the idea.)

If you think about *meaning,* not one of these statements resembles the one we started with. Each *distorts* the original by taking its words and rearranging them. Yet they all sort of "sound like" the original because they use the same words.

Each one of the distortions we just read would make a good ACT distracter. Suppose you've just read an ACT passage that contains the statement we just worked with: "Tom loves to go to the movies with Mary." Now imagine that you get a question like this:

1. According to the passage, which of the following statements is true regarding Tom and Mary?

   A. Tom fell in love with Mary at the movies.
   B. Tom enjoys viewing motion pictures with Mary as companion.
   C. Tom and Mary generally enjoy seeing movies about love.
   D. Both Tom and Mary love going to the movies.

Notice that answer choices A, C, and D use words that come straight from the passage. *They're all wrong.* Which one is right? Answer choice **B**: it presents the author's meaning—in camouflage.

Don't Let Distortions Trap You

Don't be suckered by answer choices that take words and phrases directly from the passage. Be suspicious of them: they're often distortions.

Look at these four excerpts from ACT-like passages. Each one is followed by five statements. Three of the five are distortion distracters. The other two accurately reflect the author's meaning; they *don't* distort. For each passage, decide which three statements distort, and which two do not.

Read this natural science excerpt:

> As an explanation for the age and origin of the solar system, the nebular hypothesis lost ground at the turn of the twentieth century over questions about the distribution of angular momentum.

What does the author say?

- The nebular hypothesis was intended to explain the age and origin of the solar system.

- It lost influence at the beginning of the twentieth century.

- That happened because people raised questions about the distribution of angular momentum, and the nebular hypothesis did not provide adequate answers.

Now evaluate these statements:	*Distorts*	*Does Not Distort*
1. According to the nebular hypothesis, the solar system was created by distributions of angular momentum.	☐	☐
2. The nebular hypothesis came under question at the beginning of the twentieth century.	☐	☐
3. The nebular hypothesis was challenged because of issues related to angular momentum.	☐	☐
4. Knowledge about the solar system's angular momentum was first distributed in the twentieth century.	☐	☐
5. The nebular hypothesis was poorly understood until the twentieth century when theories of angular momentum gained ground.	☐	☐

Statements 1, 4, and 5 distort the author's meaning. The words come straight from the passage, but the meaning definitely does not. The author does *not* say that:

- the distribution of angular momentum created the solar system.

- someone first distributed knowledge about angular momentum in the twentieth century.

- people didn't understand the nebular hypothesis until the twentieth century.

Statements 2 and 3 do not distort. The author *does* say that:

- the nebular hypothesis was questioned (lost ground) at the beginning of the twentieth century.

- the nebular hypothesis was questioned because of concerns relating to angular momentum.

Read this social studies excerpt:

> With revolutionary improvements in health care technologies, modern medicine's expansive arsenal has undoubtedly created an improved state of national health. Although the incidence of degenerative disease is on the rise, that is primarily because degenerative diseases are characteristic of old age and the population is living, on average, longer than did its parents and grandparents.

What does the author say?

- There's been great progress in medicine.

- It's true that there's more degenerative d-0=isease around than there used to be.

- That's because degenerative diseases usually affect the elderly, and people are living long enough to *get* these diseases.

	Distorts	*Does Not Distort*
Now evaluate these statements:	☐	☐
1. Modern medicine has increased the individual's average life span.	☐	☐
2. Revolutionary health care techniques have produced degeneration in the state of national health.	☐	☐
3. Few people doubt the degenerative disease tends to decrease longevity.	☐	☐
4. Today's health care technologies have bettered the national health.	☐	☐
5. With today's tools and techniques the physician can cure degenerative diseases that once caused early death.		

Statements 2, 3, and 5 distort the author's meaning. The words are familiar, but they've been rearranged to say something that has nothing to do with the passage. The author does *not* say:

- modern medicine has had a negative effect on health care.

- most people think degenerative disease makes for longer life.

- modern medicine allows physicians to cure degenerative diseases.

Statements 1 and 4 do not distort. The author *does* say:

- modern medicine has increased the average life span.

- modern medicine has improved the national health.

Read this literature excerpt:

> Mrs. Mandale's physician repeatedly reminded his patient of her diabetes and had ordered her on several occasions to lose weight. Hence, Allen found himself escorting her once each week to her weight watching group.
>
> Mrs. Mandale was not among the heavier women in her group. She never announced her weight, however, because, "a true lady did not discuss such personal matters." The group was one of Mrs. Mandale's few pleasures, but she feared walking unaccompanied in the city at night and asked that Allen take her each week to "group." She pointed out that she had done much for him, that her very health was involved, and that he should be willing to extend himself for her.

What does the author say?

- Allen's grandmother has diabetes.

- For that reason her doctor ordered her to lose weight.

- To lose the weight she participates in a weight watching group.

- She's not one of the heavier women in the group.

- Even so, she won't reveal her weight, because she thinks true ladies shouldn't discuss such personal issues.

- The weight watching group is one of Mrs. Mandale's few pleasures.

- The weight watching group is conducted at night and Mrs. Mandale does not like to walk in the city by herself at night.

- Mrs. Mandale thinks she's done a lot for Allen so she asks him to take her to her weight watching group each week.

Now evaluate these statements:	*Distorts*	*Does Not Distort*
1. Mrs. Mandale is willing to reveal her weight only because she weighs less than others in her weight watching group.	☐	☐
2. The doctor recommends that Allen's grandmother not walk alone at night.	☐	☐
3. Mrs. Mandale finds her weight reduction group more enjoyable than most of her other activities.	☐	☐
4. Mrs. Mandale thinks that other women in her weight watching group are not as lady-like as she is.	☐	☐
5. Mrs. Mandale believes she has been a positive force in her grandson's life.	☐	☐

Statements 1, 2, and 4 distort the author's meaning. The key words come straight from the passage, but the statements are distortions. The author does *not* say that:

- Mrs. Mandale is willing to reveal her weight. (He says just the opposite.)

- the doctor advised Mrs. Mandale against walking alone at night.

- Mrs. Mandale believes herself to be more of a lady than the other women in the group.

Statements 3 and 5 do not distort. The author *does* say that:

- the weight watching group is one of the few pleasures Mrs. Mandale has.

- Mrs. Mandale thinks she has done a lot for her son.

Read this humanities excerpt:

> Before the Civil War, Frances Ellen Watkins Harper was the best known of black abolitionist writers. Her greatest true novel, *Iola Leroy,* or *Shadows Uplifted,* appeared in 1892. The work was transitional: it treats both the pre-civil war and post-civil war periods. Although it describes the evils of slavery its principle purpose was considerably different from some of the earlier novels for which Mrs. Harper became famous. In *Iola Leroy,* Mrs. Harper wished to promote justice and interracial tolerance. For that reason, the novel treats some issues with more idealism than realism.
>
> Referring to her own novel, Mrs. Harper wrote: "I have woven a story whose mission will not be in vain if it awakens in the hearts of our countrymen a stronger sense of justice and a more Christlike humanity."

What does the author say?

- Mrs. Harper was a black abolitionist writer—the most famous of her time.

- Her earlier novels dealt primarily with the evils of slavery.

- Her best novel was *Iola Leroy,* which was also called *Shadows Uplifted.*

- That novel dealt with the periods before and after the civil war—*Iola Leroy* dealt with the evils of slavery, but Mrs. Harper primarily intended the novel to promote justice and tolerance among races.

- Because that was her purpose, she sometimes treated issues not in a realistic manner, but in an idealistic manner instead.

Statements 2, 3, and 4 distort the author's meaning. The words come right out of the passage, but the meanings have nothing to do with it. The author definitely does *not* say that:

- *Iola Leroy* was Mrs. Harper's *first* true novel, or that Mrs. Harper was not well known until that novel appeared.

- Mrs. Harper's pre-war novels concerned justice and not slavery.

- Mrs. Harper lost fame after the civil war.

Statements 1 and 5 do not distort. The author *does* indicate that:

- *Iola Leroy* concerned both the pre-civil war and post-civil war periods.

- Mrs. Harper was an abolitionist before the war and that her post-war novel *Iola Leroy* was intended to improve relations among the races.

DISTRACTER TYPE 2: THE SWITCH

Some ACT distracters take the truth and switch it around. We cleverly call this "the switch." Don't let it fool you. For instance read this:

1. Professor Thorne generally explains a technological discovery first in terms of its history and then in terms of the science on which it was founded.

We've learned that Professor Thorne discusses history *first,* and science *second.*

Now, look at this statement:

2. Professor Thorne generally explains a technological discovery first in terms of the science on which it was founded, and then in terms of its history.

Statement 2 looks like Statement 1, but it's backwards. Professor Thorne is doing things in the wrong order: science first and history second. Statement 2 takes the truth and turns it around. That's the essence of "the switch."

But the ACT Writers Get Sneaky

When the ACT writers throw a switch into the answer choices they don't always write something like Statement 2, which takes the author's statement and literally reverses the order of its words. Sometimes they *change* the wording and at the same time, turn the meaning upside down. Read Statement 1 again, and then look below at Statement 3.

3. After Professor Thorne describes the scientific aspects of a technological breakthrough he explains the historical context in which the breakthrough was made.

It's not so easy to see at first, but Statement 3 is a switch. It doesn't use the words "first," or "then," and it begins with the word "after." But think about what it says. Professor Thorne discusses history *after* discussing science. That would mean that he discusses science first and history second. That's opposite to what you're told in the passage.

Now read this:

4. Irrespective of population, every state elects two members to the United States Senate. The most populous state and the least populous state thus have equal representation in that important legislative body. In contradistinction, the House of Representatives is population based and the number of representatives elected by any state depends on the number of citizens residing in it.

Here's a switch:

5. Representation in the United States Senate is dependent on state population.

From Statement 4 we learned that:

- Representation in the Senate is *not* based on population.

- Representaion in the House *is* based on population. Statement 5 is exactly opposite to the original. It's a switch.

Now evaluate these statements:	*Distorts*	*Does Not Distort*
1. *Iola Leroy* depicts situations occurring before and after the civil war.	☐	☐
2. Frances Ellen Watkins Harper was not well known as an abolitionist until the appearance of her first true novel, *Iola Leroy*.	☐	☐
3. Although best known as abolitionist literature, Mrs. Harper's pre-war novels usually concerned justice, not slavery.	☐	☐
4. Mrs. Harper was well-known before the civil war but in the post-war period her fame diminished considerably.	☐	☐
5. Frances Ellen Watkins Harper opposed slavery before the war and attempted to improve relations among blacks and whites after the war.	☐	☐

Eliminate the Switch

You're looking at a question. You spot two distortions and you eliminate them. That leaves you with two choices and you aren't sure which is right. One thing you should do is determine whether one of them is a switch. If it is, then the *other* one is right. Here are two passage excerpts, each one followed by two to three questions. For each question, determine which answer choice is the switch. Read this social studies excerpt:

Twenty and thirty thousand years ago *Homo Sapiens* was an uncommon animal, wandering alone or in small groups in a constant search for food. Primitive humans lived by the hunt and modern nutritionists like to ob-
5 serve that with meat as dietary staple, they were seldom iron-deficient as are many farm-based populations to- day. But the absence of iron deficiency was perhaps the only advantage to the hunting lifestyle of the time. The hunter, it should be remembered, may find himself the
10 hunted, and by anything approaching our own standards today, primitive human life was unstable and inces- santly hazardous.

In this regard, however, the advent of agriculture improved the human condition. Between ten and twenty
15 thousand years ago human beings discovered the use of herding and of growing, which apparently served as inspiration to man's mechanical facilities. Relatively crude weapons of hunt were replaced by more refined farming implements. To be sure, farming is subject to
20 the uncertainties of weather and climate but it ulti- mately allows humans a greater degree of control over their food supply and relieves them from the dangers of the hunt.

1. In terms of the tools and implements made by primitive man, the passage suggests that:

   A. farming tools were less sophisticated than hunting weapons.
   B. [Already eliminated]
   C. Agriculture is associated with more advanced tool- making skills.
   D. [Already eliminated]

Look at answer choice A. It says farming tools are less sophisticated than hunting weapons. Now look at the passage, lines 18–19. It says that hunting implements were crude and that farming implements were more refined. Choice A has it backwards—it's a switch. *Eliminate it!*

1. According to the passage, a life based on agriculture:

    A. [Already eliminated]
    B. provides humans with more iron than is provided by hunting.
    C. [Already eliminated]
    D. offers a greater degree of certainty than does a hunting lifestyle.

Look at answer choice B. It says that agriculture provides more iron than does hunting. The author does discuss iron deficiency, but she says that hunters were *not* iron deficient, and that farmers *are*. Choice B is a switch. *Eliminate it!*

Read this natural science excerpt:

In certain critical respects the magnificence of science lies not in its discovery of what is true but in its identification of that which is not. Pivotal points in scientific learning are those at which some long-held
5   assumption is openly examined, and exposed as a falsehood. Copernicus, Kepler, Galileo, and ultimately Newton established that the sun, not the earth, is the fixed center of the solar system and that the earth orbited the sun, thus invalidating the views of Aristotle
10 and Ptolemy, which were largely unquestioned before that time.

Toward the turn of this century Michelson, Morley, Lorentz, and Einstein successfully challenged a host of assumptions about the absolute quality of space and
15 time. Then, in the nineteen twenties, theories put forward by Heisenberg, Schrodinger, and Dirac together created the science of quantum mechanics and thus destroyed time-honored views about position and velocity. Even Einstein had difficulty accepting
20 Heisenberg's theory which dealt a lethal blow to the cherished notion, advocated especially by LaPlace, that science could aspire to complete knowledge of the state of the universe and thus predict its future.

In 1929 Hubble, versed in the writings of Olbers a
25 hundred years before him, showed that the universe was finite but expanding and more or less did away with the prevailing belief that the universe had either to be finite and static or infinite.

1. According to the passage, Ptolemy differed from Copernicus in that:

    A. Ptolemy envisioned a stationary earth and Copernicus did not.
    B. [Already eliminated]
    C. [Already eliminated]
    D. Ptolemy postulated that the earth followed an orbit about the sun and Copernicus did not.

Look at answer choice D. It says that Ptolemy imagined the earth orbiting the sun, and that Copernicus did not imagine the earth orbiting the sun. Now look at lines 6–9 of the passage. They tell us that Copernicus (and others) did *not* believe in a fixed earth. They thought the earth orbited the sun. That view *invalidated* Ptolemy's view. In other words, Ptolemy thought otherwise. He thought the earth was fixed and that the sun orbited the earth. Choice D is a switch. *Eliminate it!*

1. According to the passage, Heisenberg's theory:

   A. [Already eliminated]
   B. challenged traditional beliefs about position and velocity.
   C. described a universe that could be understood and predicted.
   D. [Already eliminated]

Look at answer choice C. It says that Heisenberg's principle makes the universe seem predictable. Now read the passage, lines 19–23. They say that Heisenberg's theory *dealt a blow* to the idea that science could attain complete knowledge of the universe and predict its future. Heisenberg's principle *destroyed* the belief that science might completely understand the state of the universe. That means choice C is a switch. *Eliminate it!*

Sometimes the Switch Involves a Sneaky Word Substitution

Sometimes the switch involves the substitution of a wrong word (or name) for a right one. The answer choice *looks* correct but isn't because one word doesn't belong. Recall the natural science passage and look at this question:

1. The Aristotelian conception of the solar system was:

   A. inconsistent with Newtonian and Galilean insights.
   B. at odds with Copernican and Ptolemic views.
   C. [Already eliminated]
   D. [Already eliminated]

Look at answer choice B. It indicates that Aristotle's views were different from those of Ptolemy *and* Copernicus. Now look at lines 6–11 of the passage. They tell us that Copernicus, Kepler, Galileo, and Newton challenged the views of Aristotle and Ptolemy. In other words, Aristotle and Ptolemy believed one thing and the other four, including Copernicus, believed another. "Ptolemic" belongs in the answer choice, but "Copernican" does not. Answer choice B is a switch. *Eliminate it!*

Sometimes the Switch Gives You a
Simple Shortcut to the Right Answer

If the answer choices happen to feature two statements which are basically opposites, then one of them is usually right (and the other, of course, is the switch). That means you can eliminate the remaining two answer options automatically.

For instance, consider the natural science excerpt we just read, and look at these answer choices:

1. Blah, blah, blah...

   A. important in that it shows certain propositions to be true.
   B. important in that it shows certain propositions to be false.
   C. less precise than most scientists believe.
   D. extremely misleading to those who fail to question its premises.

Notice that answer choices A and B are opposites. Without even looking at the question you can conclude that one of them is the right answer. Why? Because the ACT writers are predictable that way. They don't present opposing statements unless one of them is right. Answer choices C and D are wrong, and you can eliminate them.

Now, let's look at the question.

1. In the first paragraph the author makes the point that natural science can be:

   A. important in that it shows certain propositions to be true.
   B. important in that it shows certain propositions to be false.
   C. less precise than most scientists believe.
   D. extremely misleading to those who fail to question its premises.

Here's how to crack it:

You know that either answer choice A or B is right. Eliminate C and D. At this point, even if you guessed wildly between A and B you'd stand a 50/50 chance of being right. But you don't have to guess wildly. In the first sentence of the paragraph the author states that "In certain critical respects the magnificence of science lies not in its discovery of what is true but in its identification of that which is not." Answer choice B makes the same statement—in camouflage. Answer choice A is the switch. Answer choice **B** is right.

DISTRACTER TYPE 3: EXTREMES

If an answer choice indicates that something is *always* so, *invariably* so, or *never* so—it's usually wrong. We call such choices *extremes* and you should be very suspicious of them.

Words like "completely," "perfectly," and "absolutely" also signal an extreme.

Extremes tend to be wrong because they're usually *debatable*, and the ACT writers know that. Think about these statements:

> *Patients who are chronically depressed never enjoy their lives.*

Never? *Ever?* It's pretty hard to prove the truth of such a statement.

It's one thing to say that depressed patients *have difficulty* enjoying their lives or that they *tend not* to enjoy their lives. But to say they never enjoy their lives just can't be correct.

> *A political leader should seek to make peace at all costs.*

All costs? No matter what? That's pretty tough to defend. Such a statement is too debatable to constitute a right answer on the ACT.

> *In order to lead a productive life a citizen must devote all of his energy to his work.*

All of his energy? Come on. That statement is too easy to dispute and the ACT writers know it. They can't call it correct.

Extreme statements are easy to write and they're very useful to standardized test writers. When a standardized test writer has trouble thinking of a wrong answer choice for one of her questions, she constructs an extreme.

Without reading any passage, consider this question and determine which answer choice is an extreme.

1. The author's claim that "cause is relative only to perspective" introduces his argument that:

    A. mental well-being depends on physical strength.
    B. how something is perceived depends on its nature.
    C. psychological health requires a perfect upbringing.
    D. psychiatric condition depends on numerous factors, environmental and internal.

Here's how to crack it:

Answer choice C is an extreme. The idea that anything has to be "ideal" or "perfect" or "absolutely precise" or "completely objective" or "totally honest" is usually contrary to ACT philosophy. *Eliminate it!*

Look at this question and determine which answer choice or choices are extremes.

2. The author believes that practicing psychiatrists:

    F. cannot possibly help patients unless they are completely objective.

    G. are hopelessly confused over the genesis of mental illness.

    H. are scientists notwithstanding the uncertainties that surround psychiatry.

    J. should for the time being treat mental disease in terms of environment.

Answer choices F and G are extremes. The phrases "cannot possibly," "completely objective," and "hopelessly confused" should tip you off.

Read this next question and determine which answer choice or choices are extremes.

3. According to information presented in the third paragraph, an individual organism will not survive to reproductive age unless:

    A. all of its compensatory mechanisms are in ideal balance.

    B. it has adequate homeostatic and feedback responses.

    C. it is capable of complete adaptation to every form of stress.

    D. other individuals of the same species fail to reproduce.

Answer choices A and C are extremes. "Ideal balance," "complete adaptation," "every...stress"—are the tip-offs.

DISTRACTER TYPE 4: CHOICES THAT SOUND TOO "NICE"

Some distracters will appeal to you simply because they sound "nice," even though they have little to do with the question or the passage. Such distracters might draw on something you already know, or on the surface they might just seem reasonable and correct. Think for instance, about statements like these:

Ultimately, the voting public knows its own best interest.

Structure is important, but it should not be imposed in such a way as to stifle creativity.

The ideal society is one that allows for individual difference, but at the same time creates a people united in interest.

All people have a right to live and die with dignity.

These thoughts are so "nice" and "sensible" as to seem practically beyond challenge. Some students read them and think "this must be right." Sometimes these kinds of statements do represent the correct answer. But at other times they don't. When you find yourself drawn toward such an answer choice you should check back with the question and ask yourself whether the answer choice is just a sweet and easy sentiment or whether it really *answers* the question you are asked.

For example, look at this literature excerpt and consider the question that follows.

> "And then the men!" said Jonathan, "the men coming aboard drunk, and having to be pounded sober!..." "Well, what can you do?" he went on. "If you don't strike, the men think you're afraid of them...." Jonathan Tinker was plainly part of the horrible tyranny which we all know exists on shipboard; and his listener respected him the more that, though he had heart enough to be ashamed of it, he was too honest not to own it.

1. Jonathan's listener respected him because he believed:

   A. [Already eliminated]
   B. Jonathan did not attempt to conceal his participation in maritime abuse.
   C. Jonathan had a good heart and basically cared for his men.
   D. [Already eliminated]

Look at answer choice C. What could be more correct than a good heart and an honest concern for other people? Answer choice C is tempting, but it isn't right. Nice or not, the author does not state that the listener's respect for Jonathan had anything to do with a good heart or a concern for his men. Read the last two lines of the passage. The listener respected Jonathan because he had the honesty to "own" his acts. He acknowledged his participation in the tyranny.
Read this social studies excerpt :

> The thought that older citizens might be denied health care on the basis of cost effectiveness is very troublesome and probably not acceptable to modern American society. Yet there is precedent for such poli-
> 5 cies in other westernized nations. In Sweden, for example, where the overwhelming majority of health care is funded by the government, patients over the age of 55 are not eligible for long-term life-saving renal dialy-

sis. The nation has made a decision to invest a certain
10 amount of its resources in renal dialysis and it does not
consider it sensible to provide the service to kidney
patients over a certain age. Because Sweden is founded
largely on egalitarian principles, a citizen over 55 is not
permitted access to renal dialysis even if he is willing
15 to pay for it on his own. The society does not believe
that wealth should play a role in longevity. Presently the
United States has inaugurated a number of systems
aimed at controlling health care costs and avoiding
waste. These include requirements that patients obtain
20 a second opinion before undergoing surgery and utilize
review systems aimed at shortening hospital stays. To
date, however, no agency or insurer in the United States
premises its willingness to pay for health care on the age
or the youth of the patient.

1. In Sweden, which of the following measures is designed to promote egalitarianism?

A. [Already eliminated]
B. The Swedish government denies certain life-
saving medical resources to older citizens.
C. [Already eliminated]
D. The Swedish government attempts to provide the
same health care to all citizens regardless of
wealth or age.

Here's how to crack it:

Look at answer choice D. Very, very attractive. What could be nicer than equal
health care for all? But look at lines 5–15. In Sweden, we are told, citizens over
55 are denied access to renal dialysis. D is wrong and **B** is right.

CHAPTER 15

The Four-Step System

Now that you've learned how to recognize right and wrong answer choices, we're going to teach you a four-step process that leads you systematically to correct answers. We take time to explain each step *slowly,* so we can be sure you learn it. Because of that you might at first think our system lengthy or cumbersome. It isn't. It's streamlined and efficient. When we're all through, you'll see how speedily it works. (Think about how long it takes to tie a shoe. Now think about how long it takes to *tell*—not show—someone how to tie a shoe.)

We'll begin by answering this simple question:

Why Are ACT Passages Hard to Follow?

You know how to read. So why is it so tough to read an ACT passage? It's tough, first of all, because the passage is pulled out of the middle of some larger work: you're reading it *out of context.* It's also tough to read an ACT passage because you don't know *why* you're reading it. You don't know what you're looking for or what you're supposed to "understand."

Stop thinking about the ACT for a second and suppose someone offers you a $20/hour job. She points from her office window to a building sitting on a nearby lot. Then she hands you a key and says,

"Check the place out and come back with a report."

That sounds easy enough, except for one thing.

You Don't Know What You're Looking For

What are you supposed to "check out?" The landscaping? The driveway? Are you looking for chipped paint? Leaky pipes? Broken windows?

You have no idea. So you roam around the place. An hour goes by and you roam back to your boss's office. She asks:

"Are there any mice in the basement?"

You tell her you don't know.

"In a whole hour you couldn't look in the basement and see if there were any mice?"

Of course you could have, but you didn't know she wanted you to. You had a simple job and you blew it. Why? Because you never really knew what the job *was.* You didn't know what you were supposed to do.

The same sort of thing holds true for ACT reading passages. The passages are usually tough to read because you don't know what you're supposed to look for. They become much easier if you solve that problem. Having said that, we're ready to tell you about the first two steps of our system.

FIND THE CRITICAL WORDS AND PHRASES

Step 1 should take you about thirty seconds and here's what it's all about. *Before you read the passage*, look at the questions (but not the answer choices) and underline their *critical words* or phrases. Look, for instance, at this question. (We'll help you ignore the answer choices by turning them all into "blah, blah, blah.")

1. Jeremy Bentham probably would have said that lawyers:

    A. blah, blah, blah...
    B. blah, blah, blah...
    C. blah, blah, blah...
    D. blah, blah, blah...

The question has some pretty ordinary words like "probably," "would," "have," and "that." We might find those words in a lot of different questions. The *critical words* special to *this* question are: "Jeremy Bentham" and "lawyers." So, when we say "critical words," we mean the words, phrases, or names that kind of stand out and tell you what the question's about. Look at this question and underline the critical words or phrases.

2. The author states that the common law differs from the civil law in that:

    F. blah, blah, blah...
    G. blah, blah, blah...
    H. blah, blah, blah...
    J. blah, blah, blah...

There are of course some ordinary words like "author," "states," "from," "differs." This question's *critical* phrases are "common law" and "civil law."

Try three more.

1. According to the passage, Peters differs from Jefferson in that:

    A. blah, blah, blah...
    B. blah, blah, blah...
    C. blah, blah, blah...
    D. blah, blah, blah...

2. As discussed in the passage, the integrative movement produced:

    F. blah, blah, blah...
    G. blah, blah, blah...
    H. blah, blah, blah...
    J. blah, blah, blah...

3. According to the passage, edema and hypoproteinemia:

   A. blah, blah, blah...
   B. blah, blah, blah...
   C. blah, blah, blah...
   D. blah, blah, blah...

- In Question 1, the critical words are *Peters* and *Jefferson*.

- In Question 2, the critical phrase is *integrative movement*.

- In Question 3, the critical words are *edema* and *hypoproteinemia*.

By the way, when you find critical words, don't worry about their meaning. You don't have to know who Peters is or what edema means. Your job at Step 1 is to see that some name, word, or phrase is the *focus* of a question. Its meaning doesn't matter.

SOME QUESTIONS DON'T HAVE CRITICAL WORDS

When you follow Step 1, you're going to notice that some questions don't really have any critical words. Look at these three:

1. Among the following assertions, which represents the writer's opinion, and not a fact?

   A. blah, blah, blah...
   B. blah, blah, blah...
   C. blah, blah, blah...
   D. blah, blah, blah...

2. Which of the following conclusions is drawn by the passage?

   F. blah, blah, blah...
   G. blah, blah, blah...
   H. blah, blah, blah...
   J. blah, blah, blah...

3. The author's discussion would best support which of the following statements?

   A. blah, blah, blah...
   B. blah, blah, blah...
   C. blah, blah, blah...
   D. blah, blah, blah...

As you can see, none of these three questions offers any critical words. "Writer," "opinion," "support," and "conclusion" are pretty ordinary. We might find them in lots of different questions. What do you do with these questions when you're pursuing Step 1? You ignore them. Among the ten questions that follow a passage, usually eight or nine will offer you critical words. *Those* are the questions you're looking for when you follow Step 1.

Take a look at these ten questions. (We've deleted the answer choices completely.) Figure out which five have critical words and which five don't.

1. Among the following assertions, which represents the writer's opinion, and not a fact?

2. As discussed in the passage, Quentin Bell believes that historians and critics:

3. According to the passage, academicism and mannerism:

4. Which of the following conclusions is drawn by the passage?

5. The third paragraph of the passage makes the point that:

6. According to the passage, Renoir differs from Daleur in that:

7. The author's discussion would best support which of the following statements?

8. In lines 33–42, the author implies that:

9. In the author's view the phrase "modern art" means:

10. According to the author, subjectivism affected Rodin in which of the following ways?

Questions 2, 3, 6, 9, and 10 have critical words: "Quentin Bell," "academicism," "mannerism," "Renoir," "Daleur," "modern art," "subjectivism." On the other hand, questions 1, 4, 5, 7, and 8 are more general. They don't have critical words. If you were to encounter these 10 questions while pursuing Step 1, you'd focus on 2, 3, 6, 9, and 10. You'd ignore 1, 4, 5, 7, and 8.

STEP 2

SCAN THE *PASSAGE* FOR CRITICAL WORDS

Step two of our system should take you about thirty seconds. In Step 2, you *scan* the passage very quickly looking for *the same critical words* you noticed at Step 1. You don't *read* the passage, you scan it. That means you pass your eyes over all of it, trying only to spot the critical words. Every time you see a critical word, underline it.

Here's part of a humanities passage followed by five questions. We want you:

- first to follow Step 1: look at the questions and notice the critical words.

- then to follow Step 2: scan the passage and underline those same critical words wherever you see them.

At Step 2, you should also underline any words or phrases that seem to be very much *like* the critical words you find in the questions. For instance, if a question uses the phrase "modern art forms," and the phrase "modern styles of art" appears in the passage, you should underline it.

Rodin was surely a great artist but he was not an innovator as was Cezanne; prevailing tides of subjectivism came over him. Rodin's mission was to reinvest sculpture with the integrity it lost when Michelangelo had died. Rodin succeeded in this mission. His first true work, The *Age of Bronze* (1877), marked the beginning of the end of academicism, mannerism and decadence that had prevailed since Michelangelo's last sculpture, the *Rondanini Pieta*.

Yet it is largely Cezanne, not Rodin, who was artistic ancestor to Picasso, Gonzalez, Brancusi, Archipenko, Lipchitz, and Laurens, and they are unquestionably the first lights in the "new art" of sculpture. This "new art," of course, is the sculpture we call "modern." It is modern because it breaks with tradition and draws little on that which preceded it.

When I speak of "modern" sculpture I do not refer to every sculptor nor even to every highly talented sculptor of our age. I do not exclude, necessarily, the sculptors of an earlier time. Modern sculpture, so far as I am concerned, is any that consciously casts tradition aside and seeks forms more suitable to the senses and values of its time. Renoir and Daumier are, in this light, modern sculptors notwithstanding the earlier time at which they worked. Daleur and Carpeaux are not modern although they belong chronologically to the recent era. Professor Quentin Bell argues that historians and critics name as "modern" those sculptors in whom they happen to be interested and that the term when abused in that way has no historical or artistic significance. That, I think, is not right. The problem is that Professor Bell thinks "modern" means "now," when in fact it means "new."

1. As discussed in the passage, Quentin Bell believes that historians and critics:

   A. blah, blah, blah...
   B. blah, blah, blah...
   C. blah, blah, blah...
   D. blah, blah, blah...

2.	According to the passage, academicism and manner-
ism:

F.	blah, blah, blah...
G.	blah, blah, blah...
H.	blah, blah, blah...
J.	blah, blah, blah...

3.	According to the passage Renoir differs from Daleur in
that:

A.	blah, blah, blah...
B.	blah, blah, blah...
C.	blah, blah, blah...
D.	blah, blah, blah...

4.	In the author's view, the phrase "modern art" means:

F.	blah, blah, blah...
G.	blah, blah, blah...
H.	blah, blah, blah...
J.	blah, blah, blah...

5.	According to the author, subjectivism affected Rodin in
which of the following ways?

A.	blah, blah, blah...
B.	blah, blah, blah...
C.	blah, blah, blah...
D.	blah, blah, blah...

In the first question, you see the name Quentin Bell (whoever he is). In the second, you notice the words "academicism" and "mannerism" (whatever they mean). In question 3 the critical words are "Renoir" and "Daleur," and in question 4 the critical phrase is "modern art." For question 5 you should notice the words "subjectivism" and "Rodin."

SO YOUR UNDERLINED PASSAGE SHOULD LOOK SOMETHING LIKE THIS

<u>Rodin</u> was surely a great artist, but he was not an innovator as was Cezanne; prevailing tides of <u>subjectivism</u> came over him. Rodin's mission was to reinvest sculpture with the integrity it lost when Michelangelo had died. Rodin succeeded in this mission. His first true work, *The Age of Bronze* (1877), marked the beginning of the end of <u>academicism</u>, <u>mannerism</u>, and decadence that had prevailed since Michelangelo's last sculpture, the *Rondanini Pieta*.

Yet it is largely Cezanne, not <u>Rodin</u>, who was artistic ancestor to Picasso, Gonzalez, Brancusi, Archipenko, Lipchitz, and Laurens, and they are unquestionably the first lights in the "new art" of sculpture. This "<u>new art</u>," of course, is the sculpture we call "<u>modern</u>." It is modern because it breaks with tradition and draws little on that which preceded it.

When I speak of "modern" sculpture I do not refer to every sculptor nor even to every highly talented sculptor of our age. I do not exclude, necessarily, the sculptors of an earlier time. Modern sculpture, so far as I am concerned, is any that consciously casts tradition aside and seeks forms more suitable to the senses and values of its time. Renoir and Daumier are, in this light, modern sculptors notwithstanding the earlier time at which they worked. Daleur and Carpeaux are not modern although they belong chronologically to our era. Professor Quentin Bell argues that historians and critics name as "modern" those sculptors in whom they happen to be interested and that the term when abused in that way has no historical or artistic significance. That, I think, is not right. The problem is that Professor Bell thinks "modern" means "now," when in fact it means "new."

Let's Do It Again

Here's another short passage followed by four questions. Follow Steps 1 and 2 just as you did before.

Such relatively reliable insights as we have into the nature of Halley's comet's nucleus derive largely from the work done by the Giotto imaging team. Named for the spacecraft from which six key photographs of the
5   comet were taken at distances ranging from 14,430 to 2,730 kilometers, the team forged a single composite photograph under the directorship of H. Use Keler. As the photograph is normally held, north is up and the sun is at the left.

10   Discernibility of detail varies at different points in the photograph. The greatest resolution, 100 meters, is found in the upper left portion of the image and the poorest resolution, 400 meters, is found at the lower right. This circumstance and other of the photograph's
15   features largely reflect the "instructions" that were given to the Giotto camera, which had been systematically programmed to track the brightest feature in its visual field. This, for example, explains why the greatest detail in the composite photograph is of the
20   nucleus's uppermost aspect; it was photographed when Giotto was closest to the comet.

The Giotto photographs have allowed investigators to conclude that the surface of the nucleus is rough. This conclusion emanates from the observation that the bor-
25   der area between light and dark portions of the comet is irregular. In addition, the light side reveals a large crater and a hill. The most noticeable of the comet's features relate to the movement of dust away from selected portions of the comet's nucleus toward the sun.
30   The resulting dust jets are brightly colored and likely arise from points and places that lack surface crust which then would expose the deeper lying ices to the sun.

5. According to the passage, the nuclear surface of
    Halley's comet is believed to be:

    A. blah, blah, blah...
    B. blah, blah, blah...
    C. blah, blah, blah...
    D. blah, blah, blah...

6. As described in the passage, Giotto's camera was
    specifically programmed to:

    F. blah, blah, blah...
    G. blah, blah, blah...
    H. blah, blah, blah...
    J. blah, blah, blah...

7. As used in the passage, the word *resolution* (line 11)
    means:

    A. blah, blah, blah...
    B. blah, blah, blah...
    C. blah, blah, blah...
    D. blah, blah, blah...

8. The passage indicates that H. Use Keler:

    F. blah, blah, blah...
    G. blah, blah, blah...
    H. blah, blah, blah...
    J. blah, blah, blah...

For question 5, the critical phrase is "nuclear surface." For question 6 it's "Giotto's camera," and for question 7 it's "resolution." For question 8 it's H. Use Keler.

Your Underlined Passage Should Look Something Like This

Such relatively reliable insights as we have into the nature of <u>Halley's comet's</u> nucleus derive largely from the work done by the <u>Giotto</u> imaging team. Named for the spacecraft from which six key photographs of the
5   comet were taken at distances ranging from 14,430 to 2,730 kilometers, the team forged a single composite photograph under the directorship of <u>H. Use Keler</u>. As the photograph is normally held, north is up and the sun is at the left.

10   Discernibility of detail varies at different points in
      the photograph. The greatest <u>resolution</u>, 100 meters, is
      found in the upper left portion of the image and the
      poorest <u>resolution</u>, 400 meters, is found at the lower
      right. This circumstance and other of the photograph's
15   features largely reflect the "instructions" that were
      given to the <u>Giotto camera</u>, which had been systemati-
      cally programmed to track the brightest feature in its
      visual field. This, for example, explains why the great-
      est detail in the composite photograph is of the
20   nucleus's uppermost aspect; it was photographed when
      Giotto was closest to the comet.

      The <u>Giotto photographs</u> have allowed investigators
      to conclude that the <u>surface of the nucleus</u> is rough. This
      conclusion emanates from the observation that the bor-
25   der area between light and dark portions of the comet
      is irregular. In addition, the light side reveals a large
      crater and a hill. The most noticeable of the comet's
      features relate to the movement of dust away from
      selected portions of the comet's nucleus toward the sun.
30   The resulting dust jets are brightly colored and likely
      arise from points and places that lack surface crust
      which then would expose the deeper lying ices to the
      sun.

How Steps 1 and 2 Help You

If you were actually to read a passage from beginning to end you'd never know, as you read, which words or lines you're supposed to understand. Furthermore, when you then went to look at questions about Renoir, H. Use Keler, or the Giotto camera, you'd have to start hunting through the passage to find those words and to figure out what they're all about. By following Steps 1 and 2 you help yourself in two important ways:

(1) you avoid wasting time trying to read and comprehend the whole passage; and

(2) you identify those places in the passage likely to provide answers to the questions you're going to be asked. It's *those* portions of the passage that you'll read carefully when the time comes to answer questions.

Here's What We Mean

Below is a small piece of the sculpture passage with our underlining in it. There's also a question you've seen before, except this time it has answer choices. Read the question carefully, and look at the answer choices. Then take a look back at the sentence and read *it* very carefully. Think about what it means and figure out which answer choice expresses the same thing—in camouflage. That's the right answer.

Professor <u>Quentin Bell</u> argues that historians and critics name as "<u>modern</u>" those sculptors in whom they happen to be interested and that the term when abused in that way has no historical or artistic significance.

1. As discussed in the passage, Quentin Bell believes that historians and critics:

    A. should be open-minded to new and innovative art forms.
    B. misuse art and fail to understand its history.
    C. are generally uninterested in modern art.
    D. attach the phrase "modern art" to those sculptors that intrigue them.

The correct answer to this question is D, and reading the whole passage definitely would *not* help you answer it any more quickly or accurately. The answer is wholly contained in a single sentence. The author says that Professor Quentin Bell (whoever he is) thinks historians and critics give the name "modern" to the sculptors in whom they happen to be interested. Choice D expresses that same thought—in camouflage.

YOU WON'T *ALWAYS* FIND THE ANSWER IN A SINGLE SENTENCE

When you're looking for an answer, you might have to go to the underlined words and "read around" a little. You might have to read the sentences that appear immediately before and after the one that has your mark. Sometimes, you'll have to read a whole paragraph.

Here again is the short passage about comets. It's followed by two questions you've already seen, except this time they have answer choices. Follow Steps 1 and 2, and then answer the questions.

Such relatively reliable insights as we have into the nature of <u>Comet Halley's</u> <u>nucleus</u> derive largely from the work done by the <u>Giotto</u> imaging team. Named for the spacecraft from which six key photographs of the

5   comet were taken at distances ranging from 14,430 to 2,730 kilometers, the team forged a single composite photograph under the directorship of <u>H. Use Keler</u>. As the photograph is normally held, north is up and the sun is at the left.

10   Discernibility of detail varies at different points in the photograph. The greatest <u>resolution</u>, 100 meters, is found in the upper left portion of the image and the poorest <u>resolution</u>, 400 meters, is found at the lower right. This circumstance and other of the photograph's

15   features largely reflect the "instructions" that were

given to the Giotto camera, which had been systematically programmed to track the brightest feature in its
visual field. This, for example, explains why the greatest detail in the composite photograph is of the
20 nucleus's uppermost aspect; it was photographed when
Giotto was closest to the comet.

The Giotto photographs have allowed investigators
to conclude that the surface of the nucleus is rough. This
conclusion emanates from the observation that the bor-
25 der area between light and dark portions of the comet
is irregular. In addition, the light side reveals a large
crater and a hill. The most noticeable of the comet's
features relate to the movement of dust away from
selected portions of the comet's nucleus toward the sun.
30 The resulting dust jets are brightly colored and likely
arise from points and places that lack surface crust
which then would expose the deeper lying ices to the
sun.

1. According to the passage, the nuclear surface of
    Halley's comet is believed to be:

    A. smooth since the interface of light and dark shows
        high resolution.
    B. rough, since a visible border area is irregularly
        shaped.
    C. smooth at some points and rough at others,
        depending on the relative degrees of light and
        dark.
    D. undetectable since even the most sophisticated
        instruments have limitations.

2. As described in the passage, the Giotto camera was
    specifically programmed to:

    F. send "instructions" to Halley's comet regarding
        detail and resolution.
    G. identify the portions of the comet that had rela-
        tively low light intensity.
    H. detect areas of Halley's comet that bordered on
        light and dark.
    J. photograph those areas of Halley's comet that gave
        off the most light.

Here's how to crack them:

The first question concerns the "nuclear surface" of Halley's comet. That
precise phrase does not appear in the passage, but the phrase "surface of the
nucleus" shows up on line 23. That sentence and the one immediately following
it give you the answer to the first question.

The Giotto photographs have allowed investigators
to conclude that the surface of the nucleus is rough. This
conclusion emanates from the observation that the border area between light and dark portions of the comet
is irregular.

These two sentences are telling you that Halley's comet has light and dark areas, and that the border between these areas is irregular. When scientists noticed this they concluded that the surface of the nucleus was rough. You don't have to understand *why* that observation led to that conclusion. You just have to realize that these two sentences are telling you it did. Once you realize that you know that the correct answer is **B**.

The second question refers to "the Giotto camera." So, when we first scanned the passage we underlined the word Giotto everywhere it appeared. Look at the sentence that specifically mentions the "Giotto's camera." What does it say?

> This circumstance and other of the photograph's features largely reflect the "instructions" that were given to the Giotto camera, which had been systematically programmed to track the brightest feature in its visual field.

The Giotto camera was systematically programmed to track the brightest feature in its visual field. Among the answer options, **J** is best. "Brightest feature" is camouflage for "areas …that gave off the most light."

STEP 3

SKIM AND SCRIBBLE

Step 3 should take you about sixty seconds. In Step 3, you skim the passage, and in the margin of each paragraph you scribble a few words that describe its main idea. When we say "skim" we mean you should read fast, so fast that you're uncomfortable, and not at all sure you comprehend the passage in detail. (Remember, you're not trying to *understand* the passage. You're trying to earn a high score on the ACT.) As you speed through each paragraph you should:

- direct a little more attention to the first two sentences than to the remainder, and

- ask yourself: what, basically, is this paragraph about?

Then, in two or three words scribble an answer in the margin.

Here are three paragraphs from a *humanities* passage. Let's skim and scribble.

1) If we were to start fresh in the study of sculpture or any art we might observe that the record is largely filled by works of relatively few great contributors. Next to the influences of these great geniuses time periods themselves are of little significance. The study of art and art history are properly directed to the achievements of outstanding individual artists, not the particular decade or century in which any may have worked.

2) Nonetheless, when we study art in historical perspective we select a convenient frame of reference through which diverse styles and talents are to be compared. Hence we write of "movements" and attempt to understand each artist in terms of the one to which he "belongs." Movements have limited use, but we should not talk of realism, impressionism, cubism, or surrealism as though they genuinely had lives of their own to which the artist was answerable. We regard the movement as the governing force and the artist as its servant. Yet it is well to remember that the movements do not necessarily present themselves in orderly chronological series and the individual artist frequently weaves her way into one and out of another over the course of a single career.

3) Great artists are not normally confined by the "movements" that others may name for them. Rather they transcend the conventional structure working now in one style, then in another, and later in a third. Picasso's work, for example, echoes many of the artistic movements, and other artists too work their way from one style through another. Indeed, artists are people and any may decide to alter her style for no more complex a reason than that which makes most people want to "try something new" once in a while.

Paragraph 1

The paragraph seems to be about the fact that individual artists are more important than the time periods in which they work. So, you scribble:

artist > periods

That's enough.

Paragraph 2

The second paragraph has something to do with artistic "movements." What should you scribble?

movements

Paragraph 3

The third paragraph tells us that great artists don't really conform to movements. They vary their styles over time. So, for paragraph 3 you scribble:

artists switch styles

Enough said, and enough scribbled.

After practice, skim and scribble should take you about one minute per passage.

USE TRIGGER WORDS

When you're skimming a passage, pay attention to words that *signal a change in direction.* In line 1 of the second paragraph, for instance, we see the word "nonetheless," which means the author is about to criticize, negate, or "take something away" from thoughts previously expressed. "Nonetheless" is what we call a *trigger word.* Trigger words tell you the author is about to "go somewhere," and you should watch where he's going. Sometimes a trigger word means the author is reaching some sort of conclusion ("therefore," "hence").

Here are fifteen trigger words:

Despite • However, • In spite of (a trigger *phrase)* • Nonethe-less • On the other hand (a trigger *phrase)* • On the contrary (a trigger *phrase)* • Yet • Notwithstanding • But • Ironically • Rather • Unfortunately • Therefore • Hence • Consequently

An alarm should go off every time you see one of these words. Trigger words will help you figure out what a paragraph is all about. The "nonetheless" at the beginning of paragraph two indicates that the author's going to say something that kind of opposes what he said in the first paragraph. He says there's some purpose in thinking of art in terms of "movements," even though he has already said the individual artist is more important than time periods.

Try Another Skim And Scribble

Here are four paragraphs from the comet passage. Skim and scribble. See if you can do it in a minute.

On the other hand, the Giotto photographs reveal virtually nothing of the interior of the comet's nucleus or its rotational period. For instance, it is not known, even, whether the interior of the nucleus had a density greater than or less than 1 gram per cubic centimeter, which is the density of water. Hans Rickman has attempted to estimate the comet's density, hoping, with good reason, that this information would ultimately lead to better understanding of the nuclear interior. Rickman recognized that if he could gain estimates of the comet's mass and volume he would be able to derive an estimate of density from the simple physical formulas relating mass, volume, and density: he would divide the volume into the mass and arrive at an estimate.

The comet's overall dimensions were already known to an approximation and on this basis Rickman took the volume as 500-550 cubic kilometers. He then employed a rather ingenious method of estimating the nuclear mass. Rickman considered the fact that the comet was losing gas at all times and that the expulsion produced a thrust. He then reasoned, according to simple law, that mass times the thrust due to expelled gas had to equal the product [rate at which mass was lost by expulsion of gas and dust] and the velocity of the expelled substance. Rickman then derived estimates of these values from the comet's motion and from the rate at which the comet visibly produced water. Rickman arrived at a value of 0.1 to 0.3 grams per cubic centimeter for the density of Halley's nucleus.

Using an analogous technique, R.Z. Sagdeev and colleagues arrived at a value of 0.2 to 1.5 grams per cubic centimeter. Stanton J. Peale, however, wrote that he had little confidence in the estimates of mass and volume that had been used in connection with the density calculations. He believed that little could be said about the nuclear density except that it was approximately equal to 1 gram per cubic centimeter.

Zdenek Sekanina and Stephen M. Larson studied the rotational period by first processing images of 1920 photographs in an attempt to improve the image of spiral dust features. They assumed that the spiral dust characteristics were caused by emission from distinct parts of the nuclear surface and that these areas were visible when rotation brought them into sunlight and were invisible in the dark of the cometary night. On these premises, the pair estimated that Halley has a rotation period of 2.2 days, and some spacecraft data have seemed to confirm the figure. However, Robert L.

Millis and David G. Schleicher estimated a rotational period of 7.4 days by resort to filters that allowed them to explore fluorescence of CN, C and C_2 emissions and the continuum emission from dust particles. Other investigators have reported additional approximations of Halley's rotational period and the issue remains, for the time being, clouded.

The first paragraph has something to do with the inside of the comet. Maybe it's about density too. So we scribble:

interior, density

The second paragraph seems to provide details about what someone named Rickman did to calculate the density of the comet's interior.

Rickman, details, density

The third paragraph concerns what other scientists said and did in response to Rickman's work.

other peop.

The last paragraph has something to do with calculating the comet's rotational period.

rotat. per.

So, that's what we're talking about. It doesn't take long. Steps 1 through 3 together should take, maybe, one and a half to two minutes.

SUMMARY: STEPS 1, 2, AND 3

- **Step 1—Note Critical Words**: Look quickly at questions. Notice critical words. Ignore questions that don't have critical words.
  Approximate Time: 30 seconds

- **Step 2—Scan and Underline:** Scan passage and underline critical words.
  Approximate Time: 30 Seconds

- **Step 3—Skim and Scribble**: Read the passage at racing speed giving special attention to the first two to three sentences of each paragraph. For each paragraph, scribble in the margin a few words that describe the main subject.

  Approximate Time: 60 seconds

AFTER STEPS 1, 2, AND 3

After you've spent about two minutes completing Steps 1, 2, and 3, the passage will be underlined and scribbled. The next thing you do is go back to the questions.

Here's the full humanities passage about modern sculpture. It's underlined and scribbled, and it's complete with ten questions. Even though we've already completed Steps 1–3 for you, you should run through them again yourself so you're familiar with the underlining and scribbling. After you do that we'll discuss Step 4, which is called "the loop."

      If we were to start fresh in the study of sculpture or any art we might observe that the record is largely filled by works of relatively few great contributors. Next to the influences of these great geniuses time periods themselves
5 are of little significance. The study of art and art history are properly directed to the achievements of outstanding individual artists, not the particular decade or century in which any may have worked.

      Nonetheless, when we study art in historical perspec-
10 tive we select a convenient frame of reference through which diverse styles and talents are to be compared. Hence we write of "<u>movements</u>" and attempt to understand each artist in terms of the one to which he "belongs." <u>Move-ments</u> have limited use, but we should not talk of <u>realism</u>,
15 <u>impressionism</u>, <u>cubism</u>, or <u>surrealism</u> as though they genu-inely had lives of their own to which the artist was answer-able. We regard the movement as the governing force and the artist as its servant. Yet it is well to remember that the movements do not necessarily present themselves in or-
20 derly chronological series and the individual artist fre-quently weaves her way into one and out of another over the course of a single career.

      Great artists are not normally confined by the "move-ments" that others may name for them. Rather they tran-
25 scend the conventional structure working now in one style, then in another, and later in a third. <u>Picasso</u>'s work, for example, echoes many of the artistic movements, and other artists who work their way from one style through another. Indeed, artists are people and any may decide to alter her
30 style for no more complex a reason than that which makes most people want to "try something new" once in a while.

      In studying <u>modern sculpture</u> one is tempted to begin a history with <u>Auguste Rodin</u> (1840–1917) who was a contemporary of <u>Cezanne</u>. Yet the two artists did not, in
35 artistic terms, belong to the same period. Their strategies and objectives differed. Although <u>Rodin</u> was surely a great artist he did not do for sculpture what <u>Cezanne</u> did for painting. In fact, although <u>Cezanne</u> was a painter, he had a more lasting effect on sculpture than did <u>Rodin</u>.

artists > periods

movements

artists switch style

*Cezanne > Rodin
as modern artist*

40   Cezanne's work constitutes a reaction against impressionism and the confusion he thought it created. He
searched persistently for the "motif." Cezanne strived for
clarity of form and was able to convert his personal per-
ceptions into concrete, recognizable substance. He is justly
45 considered to have offered the first glimmer of a new art—
a new classicism.

Cezanne was
innovative

    Rodin was surely a great artist but he was not an
innovator as was Cezanne; prevailing tides of subjectivism
came over him. Rodin's mission was to reinvest sculpture
50 with the integrity it lost when Michelangelo had died.
Rodin succeeded in this mission. His first true work, *The
Age of Bronze* (1877), marked the beginning of the end of
academicism, mannerism, and decadence that had prevailed since Michelangelo's last sculpture, *the Rondanini
55 Pieta.*

Rodin not an
innovator

    Yet it is largely Cezanne, not Rodin, who was artistic
ancestor to Picasso, Gonzalez, Brancusi, Archipenko,
Lipchitz and Laurens, and they are unquestionably the first
lights in the "new art" of sculpture. This "new art," of
60 course, is the sculpture we call "modern." It is modern
because it breaks with tradition and draws little on that
which preceded it.

Cezanne = first
modern sculptor

    When I speak of "modern" sculpture I do not refer to
every sculptor nor even to every highly talented sculptor
65 of our age. I do not exclude, necessarily, the sculptors of
an earlier time. Modern sculpture, so far as I am concerned,
is any that consciously casts tradition aside and seeks forms
more suitable to the senses and values of its time. Renoir
and Daumier are, in this light, modern sculptors notwith-
70 standing the earlier time at which they worked. Daleur and
Carpeaux are not modern although they belong chronologically to the recent era.

modern = innovative

    Professor Quentin Bell argues that historians and critics
name as "modern" those sculptors in whom they happen to
75 be interested and that the term when abused in that way has
no historical or artistic significance. That, I think is not
right. The problem is that Professor Bell thinks "modern"
means "now," when in fact it means "new."

Bell is wrong
modern = new not
now

1. Which of the following conclusions is drawn by the
    passage?
    A. Cezanne had greater influence on modern sculpture
        than did Rodin.
    B. Rodin made no significant contribution to modern
        sculpture.
    C. Daumier should not be considered a modern
        sculptor.
    D. Carpeaux should be considered a modern sculptor.

2. As discussed in the passage, Quentin Bell believes that historians and critics:

    F. have no appreciation for the value of modern art.
    G. abuse art and its history.
    H. should evaluate works of art on the basis of their merit without regard to the artist's fame.
    J. attach the phrase "modern art" to those sculptors that intrigue them.

3. The author expresses the idea that:

    A. art should never be studied in terms of movements.
    B. true artists are seldom understandable in terms of a single movement.
    C. lesser artists do not usually vary their styles.
    D. great artists are always nonconformists.

4. According to the passage, academicism and mannerism:

    F. were readily visible in Rodin's earliest work.
    G. are partially manifest in the *Rondanini Pieta*.
    H. characterized the work of artists who followed Michelangelo.
    J. were primarily part of the Bronze Age.

5. Among the following assertions, which represents the writer's opinion, and not a fact?

    A. Realism, impressionism, cubism, and surrealism are recognized artistic movements.
    B. Cezanne is said to have had a primary role in creating a new art.
    C. A true modern artist is one who transcends tradition.
    D. Rodin and Cezanne were contemporaries.

6. According to the passage, Renoir differs from Daleur in that:

    F. Daleur had no inspiration and Renoir was tremendously inspired.
    G. Renoir's work was highly innovative and Daleur's was not.
    H. Daleur was a sculptor and Renoir was not.
    J. Renoir revered tradition and Daleur did not.

7. According to the fifth paragraph, Cezanne's work is characterized by:

    A. a return to subjectivism.
    B. a pointless search for form.
    C. excessively personal expressions.
    D. rejection of the impressionistic philosophy.

8. In lines 52–54, the author implies that:

    F. mannerism reflects a lack of integrity.
    G. Rodin disliked the work of Michelangelo.
    H. Rodin embraced the notion of decadence.
    J. Rodin should have resisted the appeal of subjectivism.

9. In the author's view, the phrase "modern sculpture" means sculpture that:

    A. postdates the *Rondanini Pieta.*
    B. is not significantly tied to work that comes before it.
    C. shows no artistic merit.
    D. genuinely interests contemporary critics.

10. According to the author, subjectivism affected Rodin in which of the following ways?

    F. It ended his affiliation with mannerism.
    G. It caused him to lose his artistic integrity.
    H. It limited his ability to innovate.
    J. It caused him to become decadent.

QUESTIONS THAT POINT

With the passage underlined and scribbled, go back to the questions, but don't go necessarily to question 1. *Go first to the questions that point you to an answer.* Look at questions 1–10 on the last passage. Questions 2, 4, 6, 7, 8, 9, and 10 *point to the answer.* Questions 2, 4, 6, 7, 9, and 10 have critical words. For those questions we've already *underlined* the relevant sections of the passage, and we know where to look.

- Question 7 sends us directly to the relevant paragraph (and also features the critical word "Cezanne").

- Question 8 *directs* us to the relevant portion of the passage by citing line numbers.

- Questions 1, 3, and 5 don't point anywhere. We'll save them for last.

Now we're ready to answer questions, which means we're ready for:

STEP 4

THE LOOP

Step four should take you about forty seconds.

- Go to the first question that points. Read it.

- Go to the appropriate portion of the passage. (Either you've underlined it or the question sends you there.)

- Read it *carefully.* Understand it as best you can.

- Go back to the question and look at the answer choices.

Now, suppose something strikes you as correct. *Be suspicious*. Ask yourself if you're falling for a distortion or a switch, or something too "nice." If you consider those possibilities and still think the answer is right, choose it and go to the next question.

Now, suppose that when you come back to the question *nothing* strikes you as right. Fine. Try to eliminate answers that are *wrong*. Look for a distortion, a switch, a statement in the extreme, and *eliminate*! (In the process the right answer might strike you, in which case you'll choose it and move on.)

If you don't settle on an answer, take a *second pass through the loop*.

- Go back to the appropriate portion of the passage.

- Read it again. Understand it as best you can.

- Come back to the question.

- Look at the choices that still remain (some were eliminated a few seconds earlier, during your first pass through the loop).

If one of the choices now strikes you as correct, choose it. If nothing strikes you as correct, see if you can eliminate—*and then guess among whatever answer choices remain.*

PRACTICE THE LOOP

We'll start with question 2 because question 1 doesn't point.

2. As discussed in the passage, Quentin Bell believes that historians and critics:

   F. have no appreciation for the value of modern art.
   G. abuse art and its history.
   H. should evaluate works of art on the basis of their merit without regard to the artist's fame.
   J. attach the phrase "modern art" to those sculptors that intrigue them.

Here's how to crack it:

We go to the relevant part of the passage, which we've already underlined.

Professor <u>Quentin Bell</u> argues that historians and critics name as "<u>modern</u>" those sculptors in whom they happen to be interested and that the term when abused in that way has no historical or artistic significance.

- We read it carefully and try to understand it.

- We go back to the question.

Suppose nothing strikes us as right. Fine. We look for answers that are *wrong*. Answer choice F is a statement in the extreme ("<u>no</u>" appreciation). We eliminate it!

Choice H is very "nice," and very irrelevant. We eliminate it!

We're left with G and J, and we're not sure which is right.

So we take a second pass through the loop.

- We go back to the relevant part of the passage and read it again.

- We return to the question and try to choose again between G and J.

We're still not sure, so we try to eliminate one of the choices. Answer choice G, we now see, is a distortion. (The author uses the word "abuse," but he doesn't say that anyone abuses art or its history.) We eliminate G. That leaves **J**, so we choose it.

Altogether we've spent thirty to fifty seconds answering question 2.

WE'RE READY FOR QUESTION 4

Use the loop to answer question 4:

4. According to the passage, academicism and mannerism:

    F. were readily visible in Rodin's first true work.
    G. are partially manifest in the *Rondanini Pieta*.
    H. characterized the work of artists who followed Michelangelo.
    J. were primarily part of the Bronze Age.

Here's how to crack it:

We go to the pertinent part of the passage:

> <u>Rodin</u> was surely a great artist but he was not an innovator as was Cezanne; prevailing tides of <u>subjectivism</u> came over him. <u>Rodin</u>'s mission was to reinvest sculpture with the integrity it lost when Michelangelo had died. <u>Rodin</u> succeeded in this mission. His first true work, *The Age of Bronze* (1877), marked the beginning of the end of <u>academicism</u>, <u>mannerism</u>, and decadence that had prevailed since Michelangelo's last sculpture, the *Rondanini Pieta*.

- We read it *carefully* and try to understand it.

- We go back to the question.

We're not sure of the answer, but we realize that choices F and J are distortions, so *we eliminate them*! We're left with G and H.

Now, we take a second pass through the loop.

- We go back to the relevant part of the passage and read it again.

- We return to the question.

The last sentence tells us that academicism, mannerism, and decadence were around *since Michelangelo produced his last sculpture*. Answer choice H says the same thing—in camouflage. We choose **H** and move on.

USE THE LOOP TO ANSWER QUESTION 6

6. According to the passage, Renoir differs from Daleur in that:

   F. Daleur had no inspiration and Renoir was tremendously inspired.
   G. Renoir's work was highly innovative and Daleur's was not.
   H. Daleur was a sculptor and Renoir was not.
   J. Renoir revered tradition and Daleur did not.

Here's how to crack it:

- We read the important part of the passage carefully.

> When I speak of "modern" sculpture I do not refer to every sculptor nor even to every highly talented sculptor of our age. I do not exclude, necessarily, the sculptors of an earlier time. Modern sculpture, so far as
> 5 I am concerned, is any that consciously casts tradition aside and seeks forms more suitable to the senses and values of its time. Renoir and Daumier are, in this light, modern sculptors notwithstanding the earlier time at which they worked. Daleur and Carpeaux are not mod-
> 10 ern although they belong chronologically to the recent era.

- We come back to the question.

- F is a statement in the extreme. *We eliminate it!*

- H is a switch. (The passage tells you that "Renoir and Daumier are modern sculptors." That means Renoir *was* a sculptor.) *We eliminate it!*

- We take a second pass.
  The author writes that modern sculpture is any that "casts tradition aside..." Then he writes that Renoir is a modern sculptor, and Daleur is not. That means Renoir casts tradition aside and Daleur does not. Choice G says the same thing in camouflage, so **G** is right. (J is a distortion.)

Now, use the loop to answer questions 7–10.

LET'S SEE HOW YOU DID

7. According to the fifth paragraph, Cezanne's work is characterized by:

    A. a return to subjectivism.
    B. a pointless search for form.
    C. excessively personal expressions.
    D. rejection of the impressionistic philosophy.

Here's how to crack it:

We go to paragraph 5:

> Cezanne's work constitutes a reaction against impressionism and the confusion he thought it created. He searched persistently for the "motif." Cezanne strived for clarity of form and was able to convert his personal perceptions into concrete, recognizable substance. He is justly considered to have offered the first glimmer of anew art—a new classicism.

- Go back to the question. Answer choice B is extreme (and ridiculous). *Eliminate it!* With our eye on A, C, and D, we take a second pass. The first sentence tells us that Cezanne reacted against impressionism. Choice D says the same thing—in camouflage.

Question 8: **F** is right.

- G, H, and J, are distortions.

Question 9: **B** is right.

- A and D are distortions. C is a statement in the extreme.

Question 10: **H** is right.

- F, G, and J are distortions.

What If You *Can't* Settle on an Answer?

Simple. You guess. If you've taken two (or maybe three) passes through the loop, and you still can't decide on an answer, look at the choices still remaining, take a guess, and move on. Remember: having eliminated one or two choices, you've raised the odds that your guess will be right.

THE QUESTIONS WE DIDN'T ANSWER: 1, 3, AND 5

We held questions 1, 3, and 5 for last because they don't point. Now it's time to answer them. For questions that don't point, you:

- use the *answer choices* to tell you what the question is about and

- use your scribbles to get you to the right part of the passage.

Here are the answer choices for question 1:

> **A.** Cezanne had greater influence on modern sculpture than did Rodin.
> **B.** Rodin made no significant contribution to modern sculpture.
> **C.** Daumier should not be considered a modern sculptor.
> **D.** Carpeaux should be considered a modern sculptor.

Apparently this question has a lot to do with the phrase modern sculpture. For paragraph 8 we scribbled:

> *what's modern art*

So, you go to paragraph 8. From there on, you follow the loop.
The correct answer is **A**.

- Answer choice B is extreme

- Answer choices C and D are both switches.

Let's look at question 3. Here are the answer choices:

> **A.** art should never be studied in terms of movements.
> **B.** true artists are seldom understandable in terms of a single movement.

C. lesser artists do not usually vary their individual styles.

D. great artists are always nonconformists.

Apparently, the question has something to do with movements and style. It calls our attention to paragraphs 2 and 3 where we scribbled:

(2) Movements
(3) Artists Switch Styles

It turns out that the answer is in paragraph 3. It's B.

- Answer choices A and D are extreme.

- Answer choice C is a distortion.

Now, what about question 5? Question 5 is a *Fact vs. Opinion* question and we're going to discuss it separately in our next section.

SUMMARY: STEPS 1–4

Step 1—Find the Critical Words

Time: 30 seconds

Step 2—Scan the Passage for Critical Words

Time: 30 seconds

Step 3—Skim and Scribble

Time: 60 seconds

Step 4—The Loop

Time: 40 seconds

SPECIAL QUESTION TYPE: FACT VS. OPINION

When you take the ACT reading test, you'll probably have one or two questions that ask you to distinguish between a fact and the author's opinion:

5. Which of the following statements is the author's opinion and not a fact?

A. blah, blah, blah...
B. blah, blah, blah...
C. blah, blah, blah...
D. blah, blah, blah...

You'll probably be able to answer fact vs. opinion questions without looking at the passage. Just look at the answer choices and remember that in ACT's mind:

- A statement is a "fact" if you can say this about it: It's either true or it isn't.

- A statement is an "opinion" if you can say this about it: People might disagree.

Fact: Trees are alive. (Either it's true or it isn't.)
Opinion: Trees are beautiful. (People might disagree.)
Fact: In order to serve as President of the United States, one must be thirty-five years old or older. (Either it's true or it isn't.)
Opinion: Those with greater political experience make better Presidents. (People might disagree.)
Fact: Professor George Rosen spent his professional life studying the history of medicine. (Either it's true or it isn't.)
Opinion: The history of medicine is at least as important as medicine itself. (People might disagree.)

Look at these five statements. Decide which ones sound like fact, and which sound like opinions.

1. World War II proceeded for several years before the United States sent its troops to engage in combat.

2. The United States would have been better advised to enter World War II in 1939.

3. World War II was the most tragic military conflict in history.

4. With respect to World War II, Germany surrendered to the allies before Japan did.

5. During World War II many of the allied nations experienced domestic shortages in steel and rubber.

The ACT writers would say that statements 1, 4, and 5 represent facts.

- Statement 1: The United States did not involve itself in World War II combat until several years after the war had begun.

Either it's true or it isn't.

- Statement 4: Germany surrendered before Japan did.

Either it's true or it isn't.

- Statement 5: The allied nations experienced shortages.

Either it's true or it isn't.

On the other hand, statements 2 and 3 represent what the ACT writers would call opinions.

- Statement 2: Who's to say that the United States should have entered the war earlier. One person might think so. Another might disagree.

People might disagree.

- Statement 3: Who's to say which war was most "tragic"? Different people have different ideas about tragedy. One person might think the most tragic war of all was World War II. Another might think it was the American Civil War, and a third might believe that all wars are equally tragic.

People might disagree.

Here are five more statements. Decide which ones sound like fact and which sound like opinions.

6. Painting and drawing are not usually called performing arts.

7. Most professional musicians do not really have genuine musical talent.

8. To compare a painter to a pianist is like comparing a dining table to a desk.

9. Most people who aspire to be actors are employed part time in fields outside of acting.

10. There have been very few great actors in the last century.

The ACT writers would say that statements 6 and 9 represent facts.

- Statement 6: People use the term "graphic art" to describe painting and drawing.

  Either it's true or it isn't.

- Statement 9: Most aspiring actors have jobs outside of the acting field.

  Either it's true or it isn't.

The ACT writers would say that statements 7, 8, and 10 represent opinions.

- Statement 7: Who's to say that someone does or doesn't have talent?

  People might disagree.

- Statement 8: Who's to say that these two comparisons are alike?

  People might disagree.

- Statement 10: Who's to say whether an actor is or isn't "great"?

  People might disagree.

Now, let's look at question 5 from the previous section, and decide which of the answer choices represents "opinion."

5. Among the following assertions, which represents the writer's opinion, and not a fact?

   A. Realism, impressionism, cubism, and surrealism are recognized artistic movements.
   B. Cezanne is said to have had a primary role in creating a new art.
   C. A true modern artist is one who transcends tradition.
   D. Rodin and Cezanne were contemporaries.

Choice C is the ACT answer. Who's to say that someone is or is not a "true" modern artist?

Fact vs. Opinion: Don't Use the Loop

When you're answering a fact vs. opinion question, don't use the loop. Just look for the choice that makes you want to say "People might disagree."

SPECIAL QUESTION TYPE: STATE OF MIND QUESTIONS

When you take the ACT, you'll probably get a few questions that ask you to describe an attitude or state of mind. Often, the answer choices have just one word:

1. The author's attitude toward...blah, blah, blah...is best described as:

    A. skeptical
    B. approving
    C. concerned
    D. hopeful

In a literature passage these questions pertain not to the author, but to some character. Read this final paragraph of a literature passage and look at the question that follows it.

> So they parted with a shake of the hand, Jonathan Tinker saying that he believed he should go down to the vessel and sleep aboard, if he could sleep, and murmur-
> 5 ing at the last moment the hope of returning the compliment, while the contributor walked homeward, weary to the flesh, but, in spite of his sympathy for Jonathan Tinker, very elated in spirit. The truth is, and however disgraceful to human nature, let the truth be told, he had recurred to his primal satisfaction in the
> 10 man as calamity capable of being used for such and such literary ends, and, while he pitied him, rejoiced in him as an episode of real life quite as striking and complete as anything in fiction.

1. As final response to his conversation with Jonathan Tinker, the contributor experienced a feeling of:

    A. worry
    B. amusement
    C. gratification
    D. disappointment

If this kind of item throws you, it's probably because you start thinking about the distracters and lose sight of the question.

Here's how to crack it:

- Think about the person and the situation about which you're being asked.

- Turn the item into four true/false questions by saying to yourself:

TRUE   FALSE   "This guy was _____."

and fill in the blank with each of the answer choices. When you hit a statement that's true, you've got the ACT answer.

Let's try it.

- We think about the contributor as he is described in the last paragraph, and we say to ourselves (very quickly):

TRUE   FALSE   "This guy was <u>worried</u>."

TRUE   FALSE   "This guy was <u>amused</u>."

TRUE   FALSE   "This guy was <u>gratified</u>."

TRUE   FALSE   "This guy was <u>disappointed</u>."

Answer choices A, B, and D yield statements that sound *false*. There's nothing in the paragraph to suggest that this guy was worried or disappointed, and he's not particularly amused either. (He didn't, for example, "chuckle," or "grin.") The paragraph tells us that the contributor experiences "satisfaction," and that he "rejoices." Answer choice **C** yields a statement that sounds *true*.

Try another one:

Many decisions of the United States Supreme Court are inconsistent with the precedents by which they are theoretically balanced. It is true that the court has some
5   freedom to overrule its own precedents, but in such cases it is expected to announce, forthrightly, that it has determined a particular precedent to be erroneous, and that such precedent is renounced.

Contrary to what should be so, however, there are
10   a great many occasions on which the Supreme Court does in fact disavow its own precedents without acknowledging that it has done so. Instead, the Court contrives some implausible distinction between the precedent and the case before it, and purports dishon-
15   estly to abide by a precedent it has in fact determined to repudiate.

1. In this passage, the author's attitude toward the United States Supreme Court is best described as one of:

     A. criticism
     B. disbelief
     C. appreciation
     D. surprise

Here's how to crack it:

- We consider what the author has said about the Supreme Court's attitude toward precedent. She objects to the dishonesty through which the Court sometimes avoids precedent while pretending to honor it.

- We make four true/false questions:

TRUE   FALSE   "This woman is <u>critical</u>."

TRUE   FALSE   "This woman is in a state of <u>disbelief</u>."

TRUE   FALSE   "This woman is <u>appreciative</u>."

TRUE   FALSE   "This woman is <u>surprised</u>."

The correct answer choice is A. The author thinks that if the Supreme Court decides not to abide by a precedent, it should do so honestly. Contrary to what should be so, the author explains, the courts rejects precedents while pretending to honor them. She's making a criticism.

PART V

How to Beat the ACT Science Reasoning Test

THE SCIENCE REASONING TEST

Remember that tough biology test for which you had to memorize dozens of facts about photosynthesis? When you sat down to take the test, you either knew the answers or you didn't. Well that's not the case on the science portion of the ACT. Even though the word "science" appears in the title, this section doesn't resemble the science tests you've had in high school. The ACT science reasoning test presents you with science-based reading passages and requires that you answer questions about them. Rather than test your knowledge of science, it's supposed to test your ability to "think about science."

Of course, a little science knowledge doesn't hurt. If a passage is about photosynthesis, you'll undoubtedly do better if you know something about photosynthesis. But remember, the information you need to answer each question is supposed to be contained within the passage itself. So if science has never been your strength, don't worry. In this chapter, we're going to show you techniques that will help you master scientific reasoning, even if you don't know anything about photosynthesis, bacteria, the periodic table, or quantum mechanics.

What Does the Science Reasoning Section Look Like?

The science reasoning section has seven passages, each of which is followed by five to seven questions. The passages cover material drawn from biology, chemistry, physics, and the physical sciences (including geology, astronomy, and meteorology). They vary in organization and difficulty, as well as in the scientific reasoning skills they test.

Sound intimidating? It really isn't—all you need is the ability to answer questions strategically.

You've already developed some of these skills during science lab in school. Others you can borrow from what we've taught you in the ACT reading chapter. (If you had any trouble mastering those skills, this is a good time to review them and make them stick.) The only additional skill you'll need is a basic understanding of math to help you read and interpret charts, figures, and graphs.

You'll have thirty-five minutes to answer forty questions. That's about five minutes a passage! It's like a car race, you have to move fast but you don't want to crash. In this section, we'll teach you how to do exactly that.

WHAT ARE THE PASSAGES LIKE?

All of the passages fall within three basic categories.

Data Representation

These passages provide you with one or more charts, tables, graphs, or illustrations, and are intended to test your ability to understand and interpret the information that's presented. There are usually three data representative passages per test.

Experimental Reasoning

These passages describe several experiments and their results to see whether you can follow the procedures in each experiment (or experiments) and interpret them. There are usually three experimental reasoning passages per test.

Alternative Viewpoints

These passages present two conflicting views on a research hypothesis. You will be asked about the conflict, and the evidence supporting each view. The ACT writers may also ask you to figure out what kind of evidence might actually *resolve* the conflict. There will be only one alternative viewpoints passage per test.

WHAT ARE THE QUESTIONS LIKE?

The questions test your ability to interpret scientific data and fall into three categories.

Understanding

These questions test your ability to *paraphrase* specific parts of the passage. They're like the questions that you see on the reading test, and they usually require that you focus on *one* sentence or paragraph. You might be asked to think about *what* happened in the passage, *why* it happened, and what the underlying *assumptions* are behind it.

Analysis

These questions call for a deeper understanding of the information in the passage, "deeper" meaning that you have to consider more than one part of the passage. You'll be required to recognize relationships between different pieces of information in the passage. For instance, you might be asked to put two thoughts together and figure out *why* something happened, or what's *going* to happen.

Generalization

These questions require that you see things in perspective ("the bigger picture"). You're asked to understand how events described in the passage may relate to situations *not* described in the passage. For instance, a passage may describe an experiment and the results. One question might ask you to predict the result if the experiment was performed under different conditions. Or suppose a passage describes an experimental finding. A question might ask you to assess the impact of the finding on the "real world."

HERE'S OUR STEP-BY-STEP GAME PLAN FOR TACKLING SCIENCE REASONING PASSAGES

We have a step-by-step game plan for reading ACT science passages and answering questions about them. We'll outline the plan first, then discuss each step in detail.

Step 1. Scan the passage

Before you read the passage, take a quick look at the format. Your first task is to identify the *passage type*. Is it a data representation, experimental reasoning, or alternative viewpoints passage? In a minute we'll show you how to do that. If there are tables, illustrations, or graphs, familiarize yourself with their content. This should only take you about twenty seconds. (Remember, time is limited.) After you have scanned the passage, *then* you should go back and read the text. As you're reading the passage, *underline* key words so you can refer to them later on.

Step 2. Look at each question and identify its type

Once you've read the passage, you should move on to the questions. To which category does each question belong? Identify each as either an understanding, analysis, or generalization question. Why? Because knowing the question type will help you eliminate distracters and zero in on the right answer.

Step 3. Guesstimate

Some of the questions will require you to do some pretty simple calculations. Sometimes you can come up with the right answer choice by "guesstimating," which means making a rough estimate. (Remember this from our geometry chapter?) This technique works particularly well on problems that require you to interpret graphs.

Step 4. Use Process of Elimination (POE)

As on all sections of the ACT, you should use POE to eliminate incorrect answer choices. Once you have eliminated a couple of answer choices, you'll be able to spend a little time on the remaining choices and make a pretty good guess.

DON'T FORGET TO PACE YOURSELF

In order to finish the science reasoning section you'll have to move along at a good clip. That means you'll have to answer the questions strategically. Remember the "triage" rule? Well, it applies to the science reasoning section as well. As always, you should answer the easiest questions first. If you find yourself spending lots of time on a particular question—move on. You can always come back to it later.

Which questions are the easiest? Fortunately, the questions that accompany each science passage tend to be arranged in order of difficulty. The easier ones are in the beginning and the harder questions are toward the end.

ONE MORE NOTE

Some questions are fairly long themselves. They're like "mini passages" and usually accompany experimental reasoning and alternative viewpoints passages. These take a lot of time to do, so leave them for the end.

Now that we've outlined our general step-by-step strategy, we'll show you how to apply the strategy to the three passage types that you'll see on the ACT science reasoning test.

Data Representation

These passages use charts, tables, graphs, diagrams, or illustrations to convey information. Often the figures will have an explanatory key or footnote to help you better understand the information presented in the passage.

STEP 1. SCAN THE PASSAGE

You'll notice that the text is pretty skimpy on a data representation passage. (Some passages contain only three sentences.) Since charts, tables, or graphs make up the major part of the passage, you'll need to examine them carefully. What does "carefully" mean? It means using some of the skills you've developed in everyday life.

What do you do when you have to take a bus to a place you've never been? You look at a bus map. In order to understand the map, you have to figure out how it's designed, and what the signs and symbols mean. Well, the same rule applies to the graphs, tables, and charts you'll see on the ACT.

SCANNING A GRAPH: LOOK AT THE VARIABLES AND UNITS

When you see a graph, table, or chart, you should ask yourself two questions:

(1) What are the variables? (sunlight? temperature? number of plants?)?

(2) How are they measured? (in grams? quarts? meters?) Keep in mind that values can also be represented as percentages.

Let's look at an example.

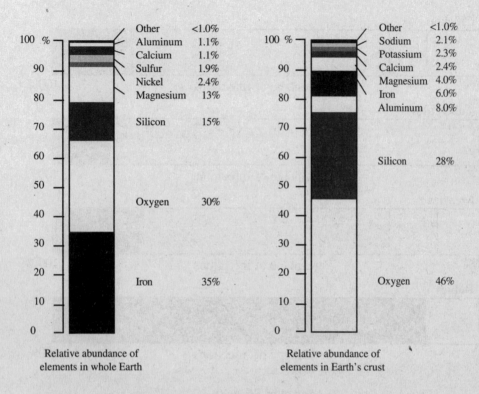

Figure 1.
Relative abundance by weight of elements in the whole Earth and in the Earth's crust.

We see two bar graphs that describe the composition of the whole Earth compared to the Earth's crust.

(1) What are the variables?

The variables are iron, oxygen, silicon, aluminum, magnesium, and other miscellaneous elements.

(2) How are they measured?

Do you see the numbers on either side of the bar graphs? They tell you the values are given in percentages (%). The graph on the left describes the percent (by mass) of an element in the whole Earth. The one on the right describes the percent (by mass) of an element in the Earth's crust.

Now, let's see if you can work with a slightly more complicated graph.

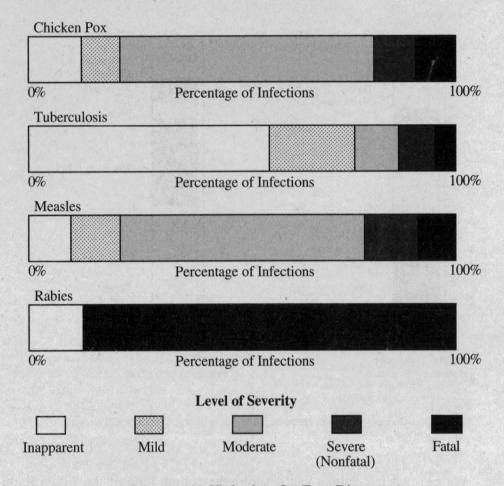

Percentage of Infections for Four Diseases

FIRST: SCAN THE BAR GRAPHS

(1) What are the variables?

There are four diseases: chicken pox, tuberculosis, measles, and rabies.
Did you notice the small boxes under the bar graphs? They make up a key which gives you more information about the variables. The graph is about diseases, and the key describes levels of *severity*.
Now, how many levels are there?
There are five levels: inapparent, mild, moderate, severe, and fatal.

(2) How are they measured?

The values are in percentages, just as before.

NOT EVERY GRAPH IS A BAR GRAPH

The ACT is chock full of graphs. There are all types, so you must learn how to read not only bar graphs, but graphs in general. We started with bar graphs because they're usually easy to understand. But all graphs illustrate how one variable affects another. Now let's look at the ACT's favorite type of graph: the coordinate graph.

Coordinate Graphs

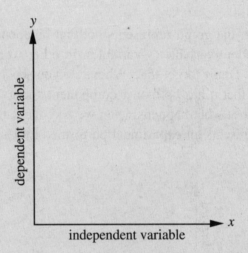

Look at the coordinate graph above. It has a horizontal axis (*x-axis*) and a vertical axis (*y-axis*). The *x*-axis usually contains the independent variable, the thing that's being manipulated (or changed purposely). The *y*-axis contains the dependent variable, the thing that is affected when the independent variable is changed.

Now, let's look at what happens when we put some points on the graph.

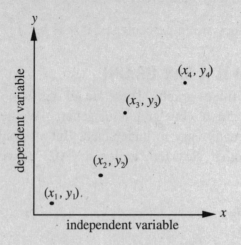

Every point on the graph represents both an independent variable (*x*-variable) and a dependent variable (*y*-variable). In other words, each point represents an (*x,y*) pair. Don't forget that. Whenever you see a point on a graph you should remember that it has both an *x*-component and a *y*-component.

Now let's look at what happens when we take the same graph and indicate that the graph represents an experiment performed by Dr. Frankenstein.

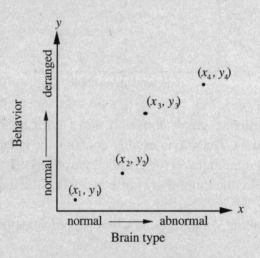

Dr. Frankenstein's Experiment

Take a look at the axes. The variables are brain type and behavior. The brain type is an independent variable and is represented along the *x*-axis. The brain type affects the monster's behavior which is represented along the *y*-axis.

When building his monster, Dr. Frankenstein can use the brain of either a normal person or a psychopath. In this experiment (x_1, y_1) represents a normal brain (the independent variable) with a normal behavior (dependent variable). Another point (x_4, y_4) represents a psychopath's brain, and the associated tendency to burn down villages.

Let's look, for example, at point (x_2, y_2) on the graph. When the monster is given this brain type (x_2), what type of behavior does he exhibit? Does he behave normally, or does he burn down villages?

Point (x_2, y_2) represents a fairly normal brain, and, consequently, a reasonably well-behaved individual.

Unfortunately, most graphs on the ACT won't be as interesting as the one about Dr. Frankenstein's experiment. However, we'll show you how interpreting even the most boring graphs can be just as easy.

KNOW THREE KINDS OF COORDINATE GRAPHS

On the ACT, you will see three kinds of coordinate graphs.

Linear Graphs

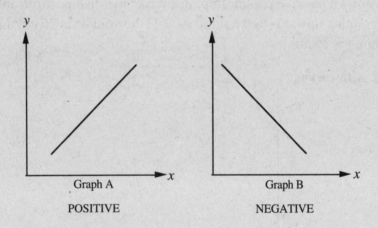

The graphs above show a linear relationship. Linear is a fancy word meaning that the points follow a straight line. A positive linear relationship occurs when an **increase** in x (as you move to the right along the *x-axis*) leads to an **increase** in y (Graph A). A negative, or inverse, relationship occurs when an **increase** in x leads to a **decrease** in y (Graph B).

Let's see if you can recognize the relationship below.

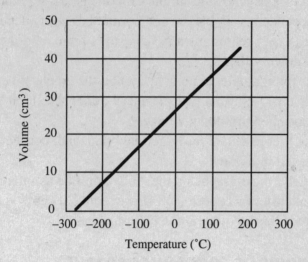

Does the graph show a positive or a negative linear relationship between temperature and volume?

If you answered positive, you're right. If, for some reason, you forget which graph shows a positive relationship, just remember that positive means that the line is pointing upwards to the right. At 0°C the volume is 26 cm³ and at 100°C the volume is 35cm³.

Graphs with curves

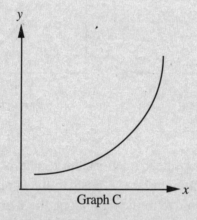

Graph C

Another common graph displays a curve, as shown in Graph C. The curve above means that for every increase in x, the y values are becoming larger and larger. The changes in y are **exponential** (just like in math, the number doubles or triples) and become greater and greater the more x increases. Let's look at an example.

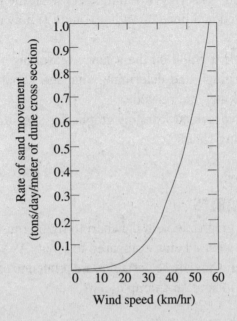

When the wind speed is 40 km/hr, what is the rate of sand movement?

The answer is 0.3. Now, let's see what happens when the wind speed is 50 km/hr. The rate of sand movement increases to 0.6. Did you notice that the rate of sand movement doubled? Now what happens when the wind speed is 60 km/hr? The rate of sand movement increased a whole lot! As you pick larger values for wind speed, the rate of sand movement will shoot up in value.

Scatter Diagrams

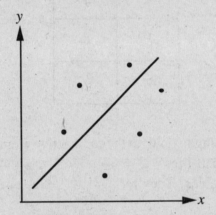

The ACT test writers expect you to understand one more graph. This graph is called a scatter diagram. See the line that runs through the center of the graph? It's called a "best-fit" line. It tells you that if you took the average of all the points on the graph and lined them up, they would form the straight line above.

Therefore, the graph tells you two things: (1) what the points would look like if they were averaged and lined up (a line), and (2) how they *really* look on the graph (scattered).

So when you see a graph on the science reasoning section of the test, you should look at the graph and determine what the variables are, how they are measured, and how they are related.

Now that we have tackled scanning graphs, let's see if we can apply the same technique to scanning charts.

SCANNING A CHART:
LOOK AT THE VARIABLES

Just as we did with graphs, look at the chart to figure out what the variables are. You want to know what's being compared to what. As you read the chart take the time to understand how these variables are related to each other (don't skimp on this part). Let's look at an example:

Number of half-lives expired for radioactive thorium	Remaining fraction of original thorium sample
0	1
1	$\frac{1}{2}$
2	$\frac{1}{4}$
3	$\frac{1}{8}$
4	$\frac{1}{16}$

This chart has something to do with the radioactive element thorium, which has something called a "half-life."

What are the variables? They're:

(A) the number of half-lives expired, and

(B) the remaining fraction of the original thorium sample.

As you can see, the more half-lives that expire the less we have of the original thorium sample.

SCANNING AN ILLUSTRATION:
LOOK AT THE VARIABLES

Instead of a chart or graph, sometimes the ACT writers will give you an illustration. Sometimes these illustrations will have text within the picture, but usually they will *not* have a specific explanation accompanying them. The ACT writers want to see if you can follow a flow chart or interpret a diagram. Here's an example.

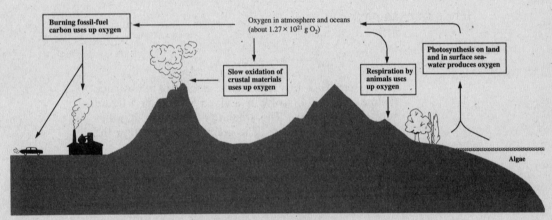

The Cycle of Oxygen Through the Atmosphere

Figure 2

This figure illustrates the oxygen cycle. Based on this figure, which of the processes releases oxygen into the atmosphere? Look at the arrows associated with each box. The information inside every box is the variable. Which of the boxes has an arrow that shows that oxygen is released into the atmosphere? The box labeled "photosynthesis on land and in surface sea-water produces oxygen."

Now what if the ACT writers ask you what kinds of living organisms produce oxygen? According to this diagram, the answer is algae. The direction of the arrow indicates that oxygen is moving from algae and the ground to the atmosphere. All the other arrows are pointing *away* from the atmosphere.

Now that you know how to scan the passage let's go right to the questions. Remember that there are only three basic question types, each addressing a different skill.

UNDERSTANDING

The majority of these questions test your ability to *understand* the passages. They want you to explain, describe, and identify some of the basic scientific concepts or assumptions that underlie the information provided in the passage. Other times the ACT writers are looking for a summary of the passage. Usually, you'll only need to look at *one* portion of a passage to answer the question. This means that the correct answers tend to be specific and refer back to a *specific* part of the passage. So, for understanding questions, *identify the piece of information needed*.

Here's an example:

Passage A

The term *solubility* refers to the amount of a substance (solute) that will dissolve in a given amount of a liquid substance (solvent). The solubility of solids in water varies with temperature. The graph below displays the water solubility curves for six crystalline solids.

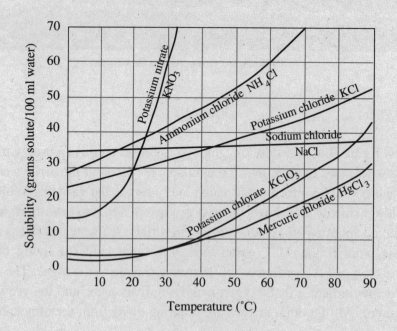

1. Which of the following factors affect(s) the degree to which KCl is soluble in water?

   A. Only the quantity of KCl added to 100 grams of water
   B. The quantity of KCl added to 100 grams of water and the temperature of the solution
   C. Only the amount of solvent present in the solution
   D. The weight of KCl

Here's how to crack it:

This question requires that you understand the variables—what's being compared to what. The variables are:

(A) the solution's temperature and

(B) solubility, or the mass of solute that will dissolve in 100 ml of water.

The passage stated that when we talk about solubility we're talking about the amount of solute that will dissolve in a given amount of a solvent. The *question* asks you *what*, according to this graph, affects the solubility of solids in water? Let's look at the variables. The graph shows you, that for KCl the solubility varies with the amount of the solid in 100 grams of water and, with the solution's temperature. That's why the answer is **B**.

TRANSLATING CHARTS TO GRAPHS

One more note: sometimes you will be given a question that asks "Which of the following graphs would best represent the results in the passage?" If you're given a chart, you'll probably have to translate the information into a graph. This means you'll have to convert information in a table into a graph.

Luckily, we've just learned a few things about graphs and tables. Now we have to learn how to read a table and *translate* this information into a graph. To make a graph, draw both axes and label the axes as x and y. Remember, the x-axis is the independent variable and the y-axis is the dependent variable. After you have drawn your axes, you can begin to plot some points on the graph.

Let's see if we can translate the information in the chart about radioactive thorium into a graph.

Number of half-lives expired for radioactive thorium	Remaining fraction of original thorium sample
0	1
1	$\frac{1}{2}$
2	$\frac{1}{4}$
3	$\frac{1}{8}$
4	$\frac{1}{16}$

The first thing to do is draw your axes.

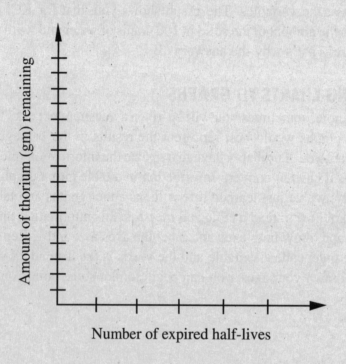

What is the independent variable? It's the number of expired half-lives. Label your x-axis with the numbers 0 through 4. Now, what is the dependent variable? It's the amount of thorium left after each expired half-life. Label the y-axis with the numbers $\frac{1}{16}$ to 1. Now you can plot the values on the graph and connect the dots!

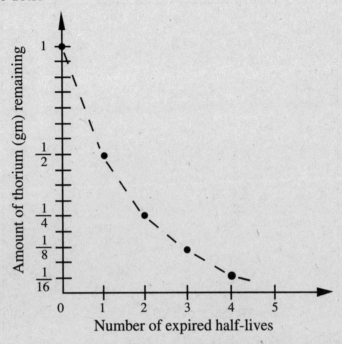

Now, let's see if *you* can translate a table into a graph.

An investigator conducted a study to determine the relationship between temperature and pH of the enzyme chymotrypsin. Her findings are listed in the table below.

Temp. (°C)	pH Level
47	2
42	5
37	7
32	4
27	3

Chymotrypsin acidity:
temperature dependence

Use the space below to draw a graph that represents the relationship between temperature and pH in this experiment.

THIS IS WHAT YOUR GRAPH SHOULD LOOK LIKE

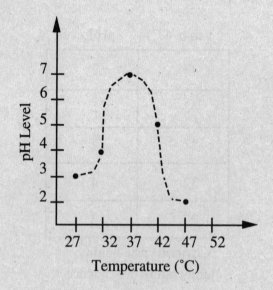

Did you label your axes? Temperature is the independent variable and pH is the dependent variable. Now here's where it can get a little tricky. You *should* have labeled your *x*-axis with the units *increasing* as you move to the right. If you plotted your numbers differently, you probably got the wrong answer. Now, are you ever going to have to draw a graph on the ACT? No, but you will have to *recognize* which of the graphs in the answer choices best represents the information in the chart or passage. These questions are fairly easy if you practice how to read the axes, and look at the points (or lines) on the graphs.

Analysis

For this type of question you're supposed to have a little deeper understanding of the passage. The question will usually require you to look at *several* pieces of information to get the right answer. Basically, you're being asked to figure out how different pieces of information are related to each other. So for analysis questions:

DRAW ON MORE THAN ONE PIECE OF INFORMATION

Here's an example using the previous passage about solubility. Don't forget to refer back to the graph on page 312.

2. How many grams of NH_4Cl can be dissolved in 200 mls of water at 70°C?

   F. 70 grams
   G. 90 grams
   H. 140 grams
   J. 180 grams

Here's how to crack it:

The passage tests your ability to interpret the graph. What are the units? Temperature is measured in degrees Celsius and solubility is measured in grams of solute per 100 milliliters of water. You need to identify which line represents NH_4Cl on the graph. Then, follow the curve until you see where it crosses 70°C. You can then look at the *y*-axis to see how many grams of NH_4Cl can dissolve in water. The answer is 70 grams. But hold it! The question is asking you to determine how many grams of NH_4Cl dissolve in *200* mls of water at 70°C. (This is what makes it an analysis question.) This question requires that you *double* the number of grams of solute since you're dissolving the solute in *double* the amount of water. Therefore the correct answer choice is **H**.

Generalization

In this type of question, you need to go beyond the information given. You may be presented with a new situation and asked to apply the concepts provided in the passage. So for generalization questions:

STEP BACK AND LOOK AT THE BIG PICTURE

Here's an example using the same passage about solubility.

3. Based on the passage, what can you conclude about the relationship between solubility and temperature?

   A. The solubility of a substance has little to do with the concentration of the solvent or the temperature.

   B. Temperature is a dependent variable in the study.

   C. For any given solution, a temperature increase allows for more solute to be dissolved in a solvent.

   D. An increase in temperature will always lead to a decrease in solubility.

Here's how to crack it:

This is a generalization question, which means you're supposed to look at the "big picture." The ACT test writers want you to make a generalization not just about the six solids on the graph, but about solids *in general*. What are some of the trends you notice among all the solutes? As the temperature increases, the number of grams that can be dissolved in water increases (more stuff can be added). This means that higher temperatures allow for more solute to be dissolved in water. Therefore **C** is the correct answer. Answer choice A is clearly wrong since solubility and temperature are related (just look at the graph). Is temperature an independent variable or a dependent variable? The *x*-axis displays the independent variable and the *y*-axis displays the dependent variable. Therefore, temperature is the independent variable, so answer choice B is wrong. Answer choice D presents just the opposite and is incorrect—an increase in temperature leads to an *increase* rather than a decrease in solubility.

STEP 3. GUESSTIMATING

INTERPOLATION

Sometimes the ACT writers will give you a graph and ask you to predict the outcome of a new, independent variable. This means that you may have to make a guess about where a point will lie on the graph based on the data you already have. The fancy word for this is "**interpolation**," and it's a skill you'll need for analyzing graphs. The values that they want you to guess are *within* the range of points on the graph. Let's look at the graph below.

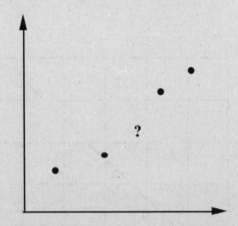

What if the test writers asked you to predict the value of *y* if you were given a value *x* on the graph. Based on the position of the other points (the trend) you would predict the point would be located where the question mark is.

Let's try an example.

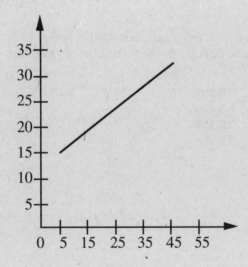

If *x* is 10, what is the value of *y*?

We're not sure! The ACT test writers didn't give you a value of 10 on the *x*-axis. What should you do? First determine where 10 would lie on the *x*-axis. This is the first step in **guesstimating**. Remember, guesstimating will help you approximate an answer. Since 10 falls between 5 and 15, you can guesstimate where *x* and its corresponding *y*-value lie on the graph. Can you make a guess as to the value of *y* on the graph? Move across the *x*-axis to the approximate position of 10, then move up from the *x*-axis until you reach the line. What is the value of *y*? It's about 18.

LET'S DO IT AGAIN

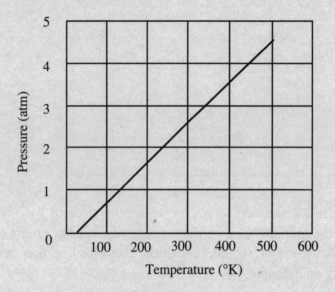

1. Based on the graph above, what is the atmospheric pressure when the temperature is 350°K?

    A. 2.0 atm
    B. 2.5 atm
    C. 3.0 atm
    D. 3.5 atm

Here's how to crack it:

Once again, the test writers didn't give a value of 350°K for *x*. But, you do know that 350°K falls somewhere between 300°K and 400°K. In fact, it's exactly halfway between the two numbers. So, what do you do next? Guesstimate. Move across the *x*-axis until you reach the midpoint between 300°K and 400°K. Then move up until you reach the line. What is the approximate value of *y*? The answer is 3.0 atm, answer choice **C**.

EXTRAPOLATION

The ACT writers want to test another skill. Sometimes, they want you to *extend* the line on a graph.

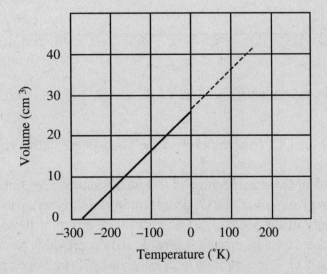

See the dashed line on the picture above? This shows that if you continued the experiment and picked values of *x* that were outside of the range given, by the solid line you would get the dashed line shown above. This is called **"extrapolation."** Let's look at an example:

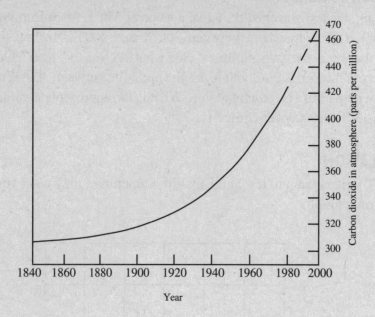

Fig 3. Estimated CO_2 concentration in the atmosphere up to the 2000.

What will be the CO_2 concentration in the atmosphere in the year 2000?

This is a graph of the concentration of CO_2 in the atmosphere since 1840. Notice that the graph gives values of CO_2 concentration all the way up to the year 2000. But we're only in the 1990's! So how did they arrive at these values? They "projected" the CO_2 concentration level based on previous trends in the data. Therefore the CO_2 concentration will be about 470 parts per million. That's extrapolation. You'll probably need this skill to answer several analysis or generalization questions.

STEP 4. USE PROCESS OF ELIMINATION

Often the ACT test writers will give you several answer choices that look a lot alike. Why's that? They are attempting to disguise the correct answer choice. Test writers usually write the question first, then the correct answer, and finally the incorrect answers. Since they don't want the correct answer to be too obvious, they often surround it with several similar (but wrong) answers.

SO HOW DOES THIS INFORMATION HELP YOU?

It means that if you're given a couple of answer choices that look alike, you should always consider them first. This technique works particularly well with answer choices that present opposite trends—one of them is usually correct. Let's look back at question 1, which refers to the solubility passage on page 312.

1. Which of the following factors affect(s) the degree to which KCl is soluble in water?

   A. Only the quantity of KCl added to 100 grams of water
   B. The quantity of KCl added to 100 grams of water and the temperature of the solution
   C. Only the amount of solvent present in the solution
   D. The weight of KCl

Did you notice that answer choices A, B, and C all started the same way? So which *answer* choices should you consider first—answer choices A, B, and C.

PUTTING THE STRATEGY TO WORK

Let's try this strategy on the sample data representation passages. For practice, write down what type of question it is *before* you work out the answer.

Passage I

The kinetic molecular theory provides new insights into the movement of molecules in liquids. It states that molecules are in constant motion and collide with one another. When the temperature of a liquid increases there will be an increase in the movement of molecules and in the average kinetic energy. The figure below depicts the distribution of the kinetic energy of two samples of water at different temperatures (T).

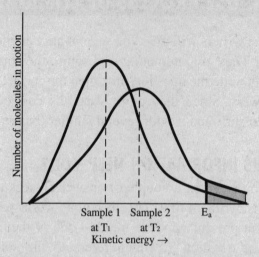

Distribution of Kinetic Energy for Two Samples of Water

Figure 1

Water has attractive intermolecular forces that keep the molecules together. When enough heat is added to water, it will weaken these forces and allow some molecules to escape the liquid and change to a gas. The activation energy (E_a) is the minimum energy necessary for molecules to escape the liquid and undergo a phase change.

1. Which of the following statements best describes the changes observed in the graph?

   A. The molecules in Sample 2 have, on average, less kinetic energy than those in Sample 1.

   B. The molecules in Sample 1 have, on average, less kinetic energy than those in Sample 2.

   C. An increase in temperature leads to a decrease in kinetic energy.

   D. Water never undergoes a phase change.

QUESTION TYPE: _____

2. Assume that water undergoes a phase change to a gas. Which of the following statements would be true?

F. The attractive forces of the liquid on the escaping molecule(s) are weak.
G. The average kinetic energy of the water remains the same.
H. The rate of movement of the gas molecules decreases.
J. The gas will undergo no further phase changes.

QUESTION TYPE: _____

3. Suppose a third sample of water is heated to a higher temperature than Sample 2. It is then found that a greater number of molecules escaped the liquid in Sample 3 than in Sample 2. Would these results be consistent with the results depicted in Figure 1?

A. Yes, an increase in temperature leads to a decrease in the number of escaping molecules in the liquid.
B. Yes, as the temperature increases it leads to more molecules escaping the attractive forces of the liquid phase.
C. No, the temperature reading of Sample 2 would be five times as high as that of the third sample.
D. No, the average kinetic energy of the water will decrease.

QUESTION TYPE: _____

4. It can be inferred from Figure 1 that when a substance undergoes a phase change from a liquid to a gas it will:

F. boil.
G. condense.
H. disintegrate.
J. remain the same.

QUESTION TYPE: _____

Here's how to crack them:

Question 1: This is an understanding question on which you can use POE. As you were reading the question, did you notice that answer choices A and B were the same except that the words "Sample 1" and "Sample 2" were switched? The answer choices are opposites, and one of them will probably be correct. Let's try A and B first. We need to compare the average kinetic energies of Sample 1 and Sample 2 at the peaks of their line graphs, or where, for each, the number of molecules in motion is the greatest. Look at the *x*-axis and follow the dotted line of each peak down to the *x*-axis. Sample 1 clearly has a lower kinetic energy. So the answer is B. Even though Sample 1's peak is higher than Sample 2's peak, this reinforces our original observation that Sample 1 has a lower average kinetic energy. Now let's check the other two choices. Does an increase in temperature lead to a decrease in kinetic energy? No. So we can eliminate choice C. The passage states that an increase in temperature leads to an increase in kinetic energy. Now, let's look at answer choice D. Is it true that water never undergoes a phase change? No, in fact the text accompanying the graph says just the opposite. So we can eliminate answer choice D. The correct answer is **B**, as suspected.

Question 2: This is an analysis question since it requires a greater understanding of the passage than does question 1. The question refers to the second paragraph, which mentions phase changes. What happens during a phase change? Two things happen: (1) Increased kinetic energy weakens the attractive intermolecular forces of the water and (2) some molecules escape the liquid and change to a gas. Now that we have reviewed this information, it's pretty easy to eliminate answer choices G and H. Now, let's look at answer choice J. Did we read anything in the passage that told us about other phase changes? No. This answer choice is beyond the realm of the passage and can be eliminated. So the correct answer choice is **F**, and again we've reached it by using POE.

Question 3: This is a generalization question. The ACT writers want to see if you can predict what will happen if you raise the temperature of water higher than that of Sample 2. What answer choices should you eliminate? Decide whether the correct answer should begin with a yes or a no. How do we do that? Just check the graph with the results for Samples 1 and 2. When you increase the temperature will the sample have more or less kinetic energy? It will have more. That means we can rule out answer choice D. We can eliminate C because the temperature reading of Sample 2 is lower than the third sample. Now compare answer choices A and B to see which one is correct. Does an increase in temperature lead to greater or fewer numbers of molecules escaping the liquid? Greater. Thus, the correct answer is choice **B**.

Question 4: This is an analysis question. The passage states that when a substance goes from the liquid to the gas phase, it will evaporate. When a substance has reached the temperature at which it undergoes the phase change, it will boil. That's how molecules will escape. Therefore, the answer is **F**.

Passage II

Amphibians are unique organisms that undergo developmental changes during the transformation from an immature organism into an adult form. This process, called metamorphosis, begins with the determination of cells at the tadpole stage. A study was conducted using tadpoles to determine the influence of thyroxine (a hormone) on metamorphosis.

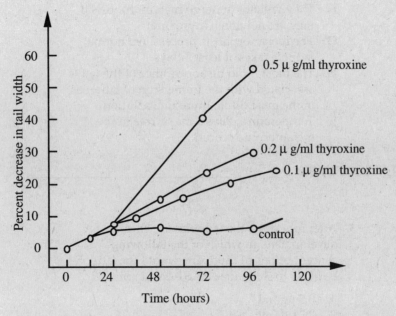

Decrease in tail width in relation to varying levels of thyroxine solutions.

Figure 2

As shown in the graph above, tadpoles were placed in solutions containing various concentrations of thyroxine. Increased levels of thyroxine correlated with increased rates of tail reabsorption and the appearance of adult characteristics such as lungs and hind legs.

1. Suppose that a tadpole were immersed in a 0.3 µg/ml solution for 72 hours. What would be the expected approximate decrease in tail width?

   A. 22%
   B. 30%
   C. 41%
   D. 50%

QUESTION TYPE: _____

2. Which of the following generalizations about tadpoles is supported by the results of the study?

   F. They will not undergo metamorphosis if they are not given thyroxine.
   G. The metamorphosis process in a normal tadpole takes at least 5 days.
   H. The most rapid disappearance of the tail is associated with the immersion of tadpoles in the most dilute thyroxine solution.
   J. Temperature plays a major role in the metamorphic process.

QUESTION TYPE: _____

3. After four days, the tadpoles are checked for development. In which of the following concentrations of thyroxine would the tadpoles be likely to show the LEAST development?

   A. 0.5 µg/ml
   B. 0.2 µg/ml
   C. 0.1 µg/ml
   D. All of the tadpoles would show the same development.

QUESTION TYPE: _____

4. Based on the information in the passage, which of the following would be a correct order of the stages of tadpole development?

F. Tadpole → adult → reabsorption of tail → cell determination

G. Tadpole → cell determination → reabsorption of tail → adult

H. Tadpole → reabsorption of tail → adult → cell determination

J. Cell determination → tadpole → adult → reabsorption of tail

QUESTION TYPE: _____

Here's how to crack them:

Question 1: This is an analysis question. Do we see a solution of thyroxine that is 0.3 μg/ml? No. The ACT test writers want you to "guesstimate" where 0.3 μg/ml would fall on the table. This value would have to lie somewhere between 0.2 μg/ml and 0.5 μg/ml. The question requires that you make a guess within the values given. What do we call this type of skill? Interpolation! Now, if we move across the *x*-axis to the values of 72 hours, and we move up to the range of values between 0.2 μg/ml and 0.5 μg/ml, we see that the *y*-values range from about 23 percent to 37 percent. The only answer choice that falls in that range is answer choice **B**—30 percent.

Question 2: This is a generalization question. Notice that they want to know what is true for tadpoles in general. Let's start with answer choice F. This is a ridiculous answer choice. We know that all normal tadpoles undergo metamorphosis. If you're not sure, take a look at the graph. The control group in the graph represents normal tadpoles. They do have some decrease in tail width, although not a lot, in 120 hours or 5 days. (Notice that you needed to know that 5 days is the same as 120 hours.) Thus, answer choice F is incorrect. You can also rule out answer choice H since the figure clearly shows that high concentrations of thyroxine solutions lead to the greatest decrease in tail width. Nor does the passage mention anything about temperature. Thus answer choice J is out. The correct answer choice is **G**. We see that the control sample shows some reduction in tail size in 120 hours, so it must take longer for the process to be complete.

Question 3: This is an understanding question. You must realize that as the tadpole develops, his tail is reabsorbed, or it shrinks. The graph compares percent decrease in tail width to hours. At 96 hours (4 days), the tadpoles showing the lowest percent decrease in tail width would be the least developed. Therefore, the answer must be choice **C**, the tadpoles in 0.1 μg/ml.

Question 4: This is also an understanding question. Thyroxine affects the metamorphosis of the tadpole by influencing the process of cell determination from tadpole cells into mature adult cells. You don't have to understand this process—just realize that it occurs between tadpole and adult stages. Begin with answer choices F, G and H since you need a tadpole to start the process. Using POE, the correct answer choice can only be **G**.

Passage III

Elements are arranged in the periodic table according to their atomic number which represents the number of protons in the nucleus. In every neutrally charged atom, the number of electrons outside the nucleus equals the number of protons. The table below lists some of the properties of row 2 elements in the periodic table. *Electronegativity* is a measure of the relative strength with which the atoms attract outer electrons. Within a row of the periodic table, the electronegativity tends to increase with increasing atomic number, due to the tighter bonding between protons and electrons. The highest value for electronegativity is 4.0.

Element	Atomic number	Atomic radius	Electro–negativity	Characteristic
Li	3	1.52	1.0	metal
Be	4	1.13	1.5	metal
B	5	0.88	2.0	non-metal
C	6	0.77	2.5	non-metal
N	7	0.70	3.0	non-metal
O	8	0.66	3.5	non-metal
F	9	0.64	4.0	non-metal

Table 1

1. Which of the following graphs best represents the relationship between atomic number and atomic radius for row 2 elements?

A.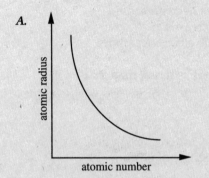

B.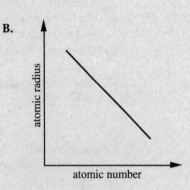

C.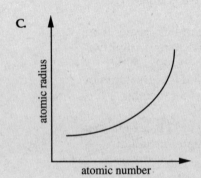

D.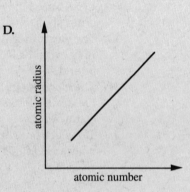

2. What conclusion could be appropriately drawn from the data regarding electronegativity in Table 1?

F. An element with high electronegativity has an even atomic number.

G. An element with high electronegativity will be a metal.

H. An element with high electronegativity will have little tendency to attract outer electrons.

J. An element with high electronegativity will be a non-metal.

3. What generalization can one make concerning the relationship between two properties of elements?

   A. As the atomic radius decreases, the electronegativity decreases.
   B. As the atomic radius decreases, the electronegativity increases.
   C. All metals have large electronegativity values.
   D. The atomic radius of F is larger than that of N.

4. Which of the following is true regarding the comparative electronegativity of flourine (F) and lithium (Li)?

   F. The electronegativity of F is greater than Li because F has more electrons in its outer shell.
   G. The electronegativity of F is greater than Li because F electrons are more tightly bound.
   H. The electronegativity of F is greater than Li because F has a greater metallic character.
   J. The electronegativity of Li is greater than F because Li has a greater metallic character.

5. Generally speaking, ionization energy follows the same trends as does electronegativity. Elements with a high electronegativity also have a high ionization energy. Which of the following is a correct order of elements with INCREASING ionization energies?

   A. Li, N, F
   B. F, N, Li
   C. O, N, F
   D. F, N, O

Here's how to crack them:

Question 1: Finally, a question about drawing a graph! This question was easy because you only needed to look at the *x*- and *y*-axes (a typical understanding question). The atomic number of the elements was the independent variable, and the atomic radius was the dependent variable. What happens to the atomic radius as you increase the atomic number? It gets smaller. That means we can eliminate answer choices C and D. Now we have to decide if it's a linear relationship or an exponential one. Just check the numbers. Notice that the numbers are decreasing gradually—so it's probably a curve. Thus, the correct answer is **A**.

Question 2: This question requires that you integrate information from two parts of the table—so it's an analysis question. You should look at relationships between electronegativity and one of the other properties of elements. Let's start with answer choices G and J. Why? They are opposites (the switch again) so they can't both be true. If an element has a high electronegativity, is it a metal or a non-metal? It's a non-metal, so eliminate answer choice G. Now we can check the other answer choices. Must an element with a high electronegativity have an even or an odd atomic number? Let's check. If you look at the two highest electronegative elements, O and F, one is even and one is odd. So, is it true that elements with high electronegativity values have even atomic numbers? No. As for answer choice H, we know that elements with high electronegativity pull their outer electrons (the passage defines electronegativity as a measure of that strength). Therefore, we can eliminate answer choice H. The correct answer is **J**.

Question 3: This question asks you to make a generalization about trends in the chart, with regard to the bigger picture. Let's take a moment to think about the answer choices. If we want to make generalizations about elements, would an answer choice that refers to specific elements be the correct answer? Probably not. So we can probably scratch answer choice D. But, let's look at answer choice D more closely to be sure. Is the atomic radius of flourine larger than nitrogen? No. Do all metals have high electronegativity values? No. Now notice that choices A and B state opposite trends. Use the chart to determines which answer choice is correct. As the atomic radius decreases, electronegativity increases. Thus, the correct answer choice is **B**.

Question 4: This is an analysis question, since you have to integrate the information on the chart and information in the passage. The first part is easy. Look at the chart to tell you which has a greater electronegativity, Li or F? F, of course! So, we can get rid of J. Now, why is the electronegativity of F greater than that of Li? Well, certainly *not* because it has a greater metallic character, because the chart tells us it's a non-metal. So, cross out H. Now we have to choose between F and G. The passage says specifically that within a row of the periodic table, the electronegativity tends to increase with increasing atomic number, due to the tighter bonding between protons and electrons. F has a higher atomic number than Li and more electrons than Li, so, F's electrons are more tightly bound than Li's. Therefore, the best answer is **G**.

Question 5: This is an analysis question. You must take new information given in the question and apply it to the chart given in the passage. Fortunately, this is very easy. Be careful, the question asks for *increasing* order of ionization energies. Since it follows the same trend as electronegativity, just find the answer choice that lists elements with increasing electronegativities. The answer can only be choice **A**.

CHAPTER 17

Experimental Reasoning

Experimental reasoning passages are easy to spot. They usually contain an introductory paragraph followed by a number of experiments. Like the data representation passages, they may include graphs, tables, illustrations, or charts.

STEP 1. SCAN THE PASSAGE

IDENTIFY THE RESEARCH OBJECTIVE

Have you ever heard of the *scientific method*? That's a fancy name for the steps an investigator takes in conducting a study. One of the key steps is to state the objective. An objective is a statement that tells you the purpose of the study. For every experiment described on the ACT, there will always be an objective. Let's look at an example:

An investigator was interested in observing whether a chemical reaction occurs when compounds are mixed with water. Chemical reactions are known to produce heat. Three compounds were selected to be observed whether, based on the release of heat, a reaction took place. A thermometer was placed in each test tube to record any change in temperature.

Test tubes	$\triangle$ Heat	
	Yes	No
1. Powdered bleach +H_2O	X	
2. Salt + H_2O		X
3. Sugar + H_2O		X

How Do You Spot The Objective?

It's easy. The objective is to determine whether a catalyst was involved in any of the reactions listed on the table. Notice that the objective tells you exactly what the investigator wants to know: which of the reactions involved a catalyst?

Where do you usually find the objective of the study? The objective is usually found in the beginning or at the end of the introductory paragraph. Once you find the objective of the study, *underline* it. Knowing the objective of the study will keep you focused throughout your reading of the passage.

Your Underlined Passage Should Look Like This

An investigator was interested in observing whether a chemical reaction occurs when compounds are mixed with water. Chemical reactions are known to produce heat. <u>Three compounds were selected to be observed whether, based on the release of heat, a reaction took place. A thermometer was placed in each test tube to record any change in temperature</u>.

Let's Do It Again

A laboratory experiment was conducted to determine whether the lack of sunlight influences photosynthesis (production of glucose). Eight potted *Salvia* flowers were randomly selected and divided into two groups and labeled Group A and Group B. The plants were then placed under differing light conditions and examined 1 week later.

Group A

These plants were exposed to sunlight for the duration of the study. At the end of the study these plants were green in appearance and produced glucose.

Group B

These plants were kept in the dark. At the end of the study they were yellow in appearance and did not produce glucose.

What is the objective of the study?

Here's how to crack it:

The objective of the study is to determine whether the lack of sunlight influences photosynthesis in plants. This time, the objective is found in the *first* line of the introductory paragraph.

<u>A laboratory experiment was conducted to determine whether the lack of sunlight influences photosynthesis (production of glucose).</u> Eight potted *Salvia* flowers were randomly selected and divided into two groups and labeled Group A and Group B. The plants were then placed under differing light conditions and examined 1 week later.

So, what should you do once you realize you've been given an experimental reasoning passage? Identify the objective and don't answer the questions until you're sure you understand it. Test takers often make careless mistakes when they read the passage too quickly and lose sight of the objective.

Follow the procedure
and identify the variables

It's a good idea to make notes on each experiment. These notes should highlight the *differences* between each experiment in a passage. (Why else would the ACT test writers design two or more experiments if they weren't different?) Often times these notes will refer to the procedure in the experiment.

The ACT test writers also want to see whether you can identify the variables in the experiments. Generally, there will be two or more variables that are important in the passage, and you're supposed to identify the relationship between them.

So whenever you read an experimental reasoning passage, you should do two things:

(1) Follow the procedure and

(2) Identify the variables.

Let's take some notes using the experiment about photosynthesis.

A laboratory experiment was conducted to determine whether the lack of sunlight influences photosynthesis (production of glucose). Eight potted *Salvia* flowers were randomly selected and divided into two groups and labeled Group A and Group B. The plants were then placed under differing conditions and examined 1 week later.

Group A

These plants were exposed to sunlight for the duration of the study. At the end of the study these plants were green in appearance and produced glucose.

Group B

These plants were kept in the dark. At the end of the study they were yellow in appearance and did not produce glucose.

Look at each of the study groups and follow the procedure. What happened in Group A? What happened in Group B?

Just refer back to the appropriate sections of the passage. Group A plants were green and made glucose. Group B plants turned yellow and didn't undergo photosynthesis (or make glucose). For experimental reasoning passages on the test, you should scribble a few key words next to each study. That way, you'll come away with not only a better understanding of the key points in the paragraph, but you'll also leave out extraneous information.

Here's What The Scribbles Should Look Like

A laboratory experiment was conducted to determine whether the lack of sunlight influences photosynthesis (production of glucose). Eight potted *Salvia* flowers were randomly selected and divided into two groups and labeled Group A and Group B. The plants were then placed under differing light conditions and examined 1 week later.

Group A

These plants were exposed to sunlight for the duration of the study. At the end of the study these plants were green in appearance and produced glucose.

Group A = sunlight = glucose

Group B

These plants were kept in the dark. At the end of the study they were yellow in appearance and did not produce glucose.

Group B ≠ sunlight ≠ glucose

Study the results

The results are the conclusion of the study. When you examine the results, make sure that you underline them or scribble some notes in the margin. Once you've completed this step, try to identify any similarities or differences between the results. Do you notice any trends in the data?

For example, let's look at a passage about the effects of gibberellins (a plant hormone) on plants.

Dr. Keller examined the influence of gibberellins (a plant hormone) on a crop of dwarf tomato plants for 180 days.

	Amount of gibberellins (ml)	Average height of tomato plants (cm)
Sample 1	0	10.0
Sample 2	2	13.5
Sample 3	4	15.7
Sample 4	6	16.0
Sample 5	8	16.0

What was the trend in the experiment?

The average plant height increased with the addition of the hormone until the plants reached a certain height, at which point they grew no further.

Here's what the scribbles should look like

Plant height ≠ with more gibberellins, then leveled off.

What are the variables?

Look at the chart. The variables are the amount of gibberellins and the height of the tomato plants.

Let's read the passage about catalysts and apply the same technique.

An investigator was interested in observing whether a chemical reaction occurs when compounds are mixed with water. Chemical reactions are known to produce heat. Three compounds were selected to be observed whether, based on the release of heat, a reaction took place. A thermometer was placed in each test tube to record any change in temperature.

Test tubes	△ Heat	
	Yes	No
1. Powdered bleach +H_2O	X	
2. Salt + H_2O		X
3. Sugar + H_2O		X

What was the procedure in this experiment?

The investigator took a bunch of test tubes and filled them with different mixtures to see if a chemical reaction took place.

Here's what the scribbles should look like

Powdered bleach + H_2O =Reaction

Salt + H_2O =No reaction

Sugar + H_2O =No reaction

What are the variables?

In this case, all you have to do is to look at the chart. The variables are the reactants and the presence or absence of reaction. Did you need to take a lot of notes for this experiment? Nope. Why not? The key information was already laid out for you in a simple table.

So How Do You Scan Experimental Reasoning Passages?

(1) Look for the objective,

(2) Follow the procedure and identify the variables, and

(3) Study the results.

STEP 2. IDENTIFY THE QUESTION TYPE

You'll see the same categories of questions as those for data representation.

UNDERSTANDING

The ACT test writers want to know whether you understand the experiment. For instance, do you know the variables? (We now know how to tackle those questions.) If you removed one of the variables in the study, would it change the results? Does the data in the experiment support the original hypothesis? Can you identify the control group in the experiment?

Let's look at an example using the study about gibberellins on page 340.

1. Which of the following graphs would best represent the effect of gibberellins on dwarf tomato plants in the study?

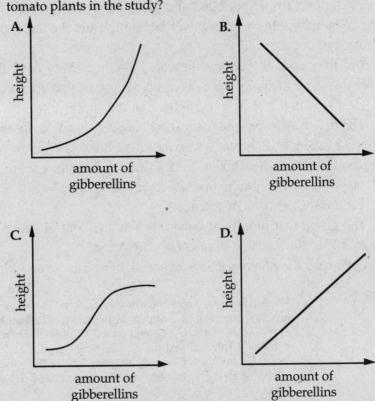

Here's how to crack it:

Remember our technique on how to translate charts into graphs? Well, we can also use it in this section of the test. Let's go back to our notes on the trend we found in the study. We said:

"Plant height ↑ with more gibberellins, then leveled off."

We can use this information to find the correct graph. The answer choice that illustrates the same trend as our notes is **C**. Look at the numbers in the chart and notice that the height increases up to sample 4 and then it remains constant.

KNOW HOW TO IDENTIFY CONTROLS

The ACT test writers will sometimes ask you to identify the control of the study. Almost every experiment will have at least one variable that remains constant throughout the study. A control is simply a standard of comparison. What does a control do? It enables the investigator to be certain that the outcome of the study is due to changes in the independent variable and nothing else. This constant variable is called the control.

Let's look at an example.

Say the principal of your school thinks that students who eat breakfast do better on standardized tests than those who don't eat breakfast. He takes a group of ten students from your class and gives them free breakfast every day for a year. When the school year is over he administers the ACT and they all score brilliantly!

Did they do well because they ate breakfast every day? But, how do you know that the principal's theory is right? Maybe he just got lucky and picked the smartest kids in the class to participate in the study.

The best way to be sure that eating breakfast made a difference in this case is to pick students in the class who *never* eat breakfast and to follow them for a year as well. Have *them* take the ACT and see how they score. What if they do just as well as the group that ate breakfast? Then we'll know that eating breakfast didn't make a difference.

The group that didn't eat breakfast was the control group. They were not "exposed" to the variable of interest—breakfast.

Let's read the photosynthesis experiment again.

A laboratory experiment was conducted to determine whether the lack of sunlight influences photosynthesis (production of glucose). Eight potted *Salvia* flowers were randomly selected and divided into two groups and labeled Group A and Group B. The plants were then placed under differing light conditions and examined 1 week later.

Group A

These plants were exposed to sunlight for the duration of the study. At the end of the study these plants were green in appearance and produced glucose.

Group B

These plants were kept in the dark. At the end of the study they were yellow in appearance and did not produce glucose.

Which of the following plants served as the control(s) in this study?

The plants in group A served as controls. Why? Because these plants were exposed to sunlight throughout the study. The experimental group was subjected to the factor being investigated—no sunlight. Here's another example using the gibberellin experiment.

Dr. Keller examined the influence of gibberellins (a plant hormone) on a crop of dwarf tomato plants for 180 days.

	Amount of gibberellins (ml)	Average height of tomato plants (cm)
Sample 1	0	10.0
Sample 2	2	13.5
Sample 3	4	15.7
Sample 4	6	16.0
Sample 5	8	16.0

1. Which of the following samples served as the control(s) in the study?

   A. Sample 1
   B. Sample 2
   C. Sample 4
   D. Sample 1 and 2

Here's how to crack it:

Let's find out the control in this study. A control in this case is something that is *not* exposed to the hormone. In this case, the control is the first sample. The first measure of the sample was collected *before* the hormone was added to the crop (the chart tells you that the amount of gibberellins found in sample 1 plants is 0). Basically, this measure is a standard against which to compare the other measures. So the correct answer is **A**.

ASSUMPTIONS

Another common understanding question on the science reasoning test asks you to identify the assumption in the argument.

What is an assumption? An assumption is a sort of simple logic that everyone takes for granted. Suppose I say,

> *Brenda's car is in the driveway; now I can stop by and see her.*

What is the assumption in this statement? The assumption is:

> *Brenda is home when her car is in the driveway.*

Yet, Brenda could be at a neighbor's house or out of town. For the ACT, an assumption is a unwritten belief that, if *false*, would make the conclusion of the study invalid.

Here's an ACT-like assumption question that refers to the passage on photosynthesis.

2. Which of the following can be assumed about the design of the experiment?

    F. Each plant requires the same amount of water.
    G. The plants are genetically identical.
    H. The plants are naturally green all season.
    J. The plants will be exposed to sunlight.

Here's how to crack it:

Think about it for a moment. What are some of the things you would have to assume about the study in order for the results to be acceptable? A major assumption is that the plants are genetically identical. If they weren't, then the findings could be invalid. For example, if a bunch of different plants were used, the experimenter couldn't be sure if the differences in the results were due to the lack of sunlight or to the variety of the plants themselves. So, the answer to this question is **G**.

ANALYSIS

Remember the *analysis* questions that came with data representation passages? They required you to integrate two or more pieces of information. Well, it's usually true for experimental reasoning questions as well. The only difference is that they may also ask you to compare the results of the data with the ideas presented in the passage. Here are some of the types of questions they may ask:

Can you think of another way to test the same relationship between the independent and dependent variables? If the experiment were repeated many times and gave different results, what would that mean in terms of the conclusion of the study?

Let's look at an example that refers to the passage on photosynthesis.

3. Suppose the Group B plants were placed in the dark for only 2 days and continued to produce glucose. What do these results mean in terms of the objective of the study?

   A. Plants require sunlight to produce glucose.
   B. Plants are able to make glucose under any conditions.
   C. Photosynthesis occurs in all plants.
   D. Photosynthesis is not completely inhibited by the lack of sunlight for 2 days.

Here's how to crack it:

The ACT test writers want to see if you can relate these new results to the original ones. The Group B plants did not undergo photosynthesis if they were placed in the dark for 96 hours. However, the plants did undergo photosynthesis if they were put in the dark for 2 days. This must mean that 2 days wasn't enough time to halt photosynthesis. The correct answer choice is therefore **D**.

GENERALIZATION

Sometimes you'll be asked how the knowledge gained from the experiment might be applied to new situations. As usual, we're supposed to look at the "bigger picture." Here are some sample questions:

Given the results of the study, can we predict the outcome of some future experiments? How do these results influence our understanding of the world?

Let's look at a generalization question that refers to the passage about gibberellins.

4. Suppose 20 mls of the plant hormone was given to a similar crop of tomato plants for 180 days. What would happen to the height of these plants relative to the height of the plants in the initial experiment?

F. The new plants would be taller than the plants in the experiment.
G. The new plants would be shorter than the plants in the experiment.
H. The new plants would die.
J. The new plants would have the same height as Samples 4 and 5 in the experiment.

Here's how to crack it:

Let's look back at the experiment and review the results. The tomato plants grew when the hormone was added, but eventually leveled off. What would happen if we added even more hormone to the plants? Based on the results of the experiment, their height should remain the same. The correct answer is **J**.

PUTTING THE STRATEGY TO WORK

Let's try this strategy on some sample experimental reasoning passages. For practice, write down the objective and the type of question before you work out the answer.

Passage I

It has been observed that plants exhibit phototropism (bending toward light) when placed in the presence of a light source. The actual part of the plant that bends toward the light source is not the tip of the plant but rather a region farther down the stem. Four flowering plants were exposed to sunlight in order to determine the site of light detection and the response of these plants.

Experiment 1

When light struck Plant 1 from the side, a region a few millimeters down from the tip bent as it grew until the tip pointed directly toward the light source.

Experiment 2

Plant 2 was also placed in the presence of sunlight, but the tip of the plant was covered with a dark cap. The plant failed to bend toward the light source.

Experiment 3

Plant 3 was exposed to the same conditions as Plant 2 except that a clear cap replaced the dark cap. This plant bent toward the light source.

Experiment 4

When a flexible dark collar was placed around the bending region of Plant 4, the plant still bent in toward the light source.

OBJECTIVE: _____

1. The results of Experiments 1 and 2 indicate that:

   A. the plant requires both sunlight and nutrition in order to bend.
   B. the tip of the plant detects the light source.
   C. the light-proof cap assists the plant in its bending action.
   D. it is the amount of sunlight that causes the bending of the plant.

QUESTION TYPE: _____

2. Which of the following plant(s) served as the control(s) in the experiment?

    F. Plant 1 only
    H. Plant 3 only
    J. Plants 1 and 3 only
    K. Plants 2 and 3 only

QUESTION TYPE: _____

3. Based on the results of the Experiments 1–4, it can be concluded that:

    A. the strength of the sun's rays correlated with the bending of the plant.
    B. flowering plants are unaffected by sunlight.
    C. the tip of the plant must transmit information about light direction to the lower bending region.
    D. flowering plants respond to light quite differently than non-flowering plants.

QUESTION TYPE: _____

4. Suppose the tip of the flowering plant is cut off in the presence of a light source, and a new tip does not grow. What will be the response of the plant?

    F. The plant will not bend toward the light.
    G. The plant will exhibit phototropism.
    H. The plant will die.
    J. The plant will produce flowers.

QUESTION TYPE: _____

Here's how to crack them:

Question 1: This is an understanding question and it directs your attention to Experiments 1 and 2. In Experiment 1, the plant bends when exposed to sunlight. In Experiment 2, the light-proof cap inhibits the influence of sunlight in such a way that prevents the bending of the plant. Clearly, the cap prevented sunlight from having any effect. So we can eliminate C. The passage doesn't give any information on the amount of sunlight (D) or the influence of nutrition (A). The only answer that correctly addresses the effect of the cap on the plant tip is answer choice **B**. It was the tip of the plant that was covered by the cap and therefore the tip of the plant must somehow perceive sunlight.

Question 2: Here is a typical question about the control of the study. The control sample is Plant 1. This plant is used as a source of comparison. Plants 2, 3, and 4 were all *manipulated* to some degree to determine the influence of sunlight on phototropism. Plant 1 is left *as is* in the sunlight. Therefore the answer is **F**.

Question 3: This is an analysis question that requires more than one piece of information. So you need to look at the results of all of the experiments. Did you notice that when the tip was covered, the plant didn't bend? Actually, it's not the tip that bends but a region farther down from the tip. That means there must be some sort of communication between the tip of the plant and that region in order for this response to take place. Therefore the answer is **C**. Answer choice B is incorrect because plants do respond to sunlight—they bend. The passage does not give any information about differences between flowering plants and non-flowering plants (D) or the strength of the sun's rays (A).

Question 4: This is a generalization question. Did you notice that the question begins with the word "suppose"? That's a hint that you're *supposed* to predict the outcome of a similar study. You already know that the initial communication for phototropism occurs in the tip of the plant. If the tip is cut off, the most likely reaction would be that the plant will no longer be able to send information to the lower bending region and therefore the plant will not bend. If you followed all the results of the study, then this should have been a logical follow-up based on the results. The answer to this question is choice **F**.

Passage II

Stratification (the horizontal layering of particles) causes the settling of sediments to form distinct rock formations that contain different types of fossils. Breaks in the sequence of layers may be due to erosion by wind or water. A geologist studied the bedding of different rock formations in an area in order to establish the stratigraphic succession of rock formations and their fossil assemblage.

Study 1

On her expedition the geologist found rock formations with the order and content shown below.

Rock	Fossil assemblage
1. Limestone	all kinds of marine animal fossils
2. Black shale	small marine animal fossils only
3. Coal	plant fossils

Study 2

The geologist examined the rock formation in another location 10 miles away and discovered rock formations with the order and content shown below.

Rock	Fossil assemblage
1. Black shale	small marine animal fossils only
2. Coal	plant fossils
3. Sandstone	rare vertebrate bones

Study 3

At a third site 20 miles away the geologist discovered another rock sequence.

Rock	Fossil assemblage
1. Limestone	all kinds of marine animal fossils
2. Coal	plant fossils
3. Sandstone	rare vertebrate bones

The following table gives the types of organisms normally found in a variety of rock formations.

Rock	Types of organisms
1. Sandstone	ancient fish skeletons and shark teeth
2. Coal	tree stumps, ferns, twigs, green algae
3. Black shale	snails, clams, oysters, and periwinkles
4. Limestone	annelids, sponges, clams and radiolarians

1. Which of the following findings would NOT be consistent with the types of fossils normally found in the black shale formation?

   A. Periwinkles
   B. Clams
   C. Oysters
   D. Sponges

2. Based on the information presented in the studies, it could be inferred that the remains of ancient pine needle would be found in which of the following types of rocks?

   F. Limestone
   G. Black shale
   H. Coal
   J. Sandstone

3. Given the sequence of rock formation in Studies 1 and 2, what might have been the ordered sequence of rock formations in the area at one time?

   A. Limestone, coal, black shale, and sandstone
   B. Limestone, black shale, coal, and sandstone
   C. Coal, sandstone, black shale, and limestone
   D. Black shale, limestone, black shale, and coal

4. The sequence of rock formations in study 3 is similar but not identical to the sequence of rock formations in Studies 1 and 2. Which of the following factors could be responsible for differences among the three sites?

    F. Weathering
    G. Extreme heat
    H. A mild rainstorm
    J. Cohesion

Here's how to crack them:

Question 1: This is an understanding question. You need to find the types of organisms that are found in the black shale layer. You should therefore look at the table. What types of organisms are found in the black shale layer? They are snails, clams, oysters, and periwinkles. You can eliminate any of these answer choices since you're looking for the *wrong* answer choice. The only one that is not found in this layer is sponges. So the answer is **D**.

Question 2: This is an analysis question. Pine needles are not mentioned in any of the studies, but if you look at the data in each study, you might notice that plant fossils occur in only one kind of rock: Coal. Thus the correct answer is **H**.

Question 3: This is an analysis question. You're supposed to observe the results of Studies 1 and 2 and figure out the correct sequence of the rock formations. Did you notice that the layers of Studies 1 and 2 overlap? The ordering of the layers must have been limestone, black shale, coal, and sandstone. The only answer choice with the correct sequence is **B**.

Question 4: This is an understanding question. The test writers want you to read the passage which mentions that the rock formations can be altered by various types of erosions. Which of the answer choices is an example of erosion? The correct answer is the term "weathering," which refers to the break-up of rock formations by physical or chemical means. Answer choice J is ridiculous in that it has nothing to do with the passage. In addition, a mild rainstorm or extreme heat would not be sufficient to wear away rock formations. So the correct answer is choice **F**.

Passage III

Consider a massless spring hanging vertically from a stationary wooden block. When a mass is attached to the spring it causes the spring to vibrate. This is an example of simple harmonic motion in which a force leads to the displacement of the spring.

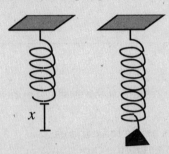

The equation for Hooke's spring law is $F = -kx$. The force (F) is proportional to the displacement (x) where k is called the proportionality constant pertaining to a given spring. The negative sign signifies that the force exerted by the spring is in the opposite direction of the displacement. Several trials were done to observe the relationship between force and the displacement of an object. The results are tabulated in the chart below.

Trial	Mass (gm)	k	x (cm)	F (lb)
1	2	2.0	4	8
2	3	2.0	6	12
3	4	2.0	8	16
4	5	2.0	10	20

Table 1

OBJECTIVE: _____

1. From the trials above, it can be concluded that the displacement of an object depends on the:

   A. length of the spring.
   B. force according to Hooke's Law.
   C. density of air.
   D. height of the wooden block.

QUESTION TYPE: _____

2. If a force of 9 lbs. were placed on the mass, the approximate displacement would be:

   F. 2.5 cm.
   G. 3.0 cm.
   H. 4.5 cm.
   J. 18.0 cm.

QUESTION TYPE: _____

3. Based on the results of the study, it appears that k:

   A. increases as the force increases.
   B. is a constant in the experiment.
   C. leads to a decrease in force.
   D. leads to an increase in force.

QUESTION TYPE: _____

Here's how to crack them:

Question 1: This is an understanding question. You can use the table to help you answer this question. Displacement changes according to what other variable? Force. As force changes, the displacement also changes. You could have looked at the formula $F=-kx$, which shows that force is related to (x) displacement. None of the other factors listed will affect the displacement. So, the answer to this question is **B**.

Question 2: This analysis question requires you to predict the displacement that would result from a hypothesized value of force. This is an example of interpolation. We're looking for a value that is going to fall within the range of values provided. What do we do? Guesstimate using the chart. The displacement from a force of 8 lbs. is 4 and from 10 lbs. would be 5. The only answer choice in that range is H, 4.5, and **H** is the correct answer.

Question 3: This is an analysis question. What function does k serve in this study? Look at the table. It's a constant. How can you tell? Because the value of k remains the *same* throughout the trials. So, the correct answer is **B**.

CHAPTER 18

Alternative Viewpoints

The third type of passage is called "alternative viewpoints." Each of these passages presents two conflicting views on a scientific phenomenon.

Think of it as a debate. Each debater proposes a hypothesis and then supports that hypothesis with facts, opinions, and assumptions. The ACT test writers want you to evaluate and compare the arguments made by each debater. As far as they're concerned, it doesn't matter which hypothesis is correct. (They don't care who wins the debate.) They only want you to understand each of the viewpoints.

So don't choose sides. Your goal is to analyze the arguments based on the information provided in the passage. Even if you know something about the topic, your answers should come from the passage and nothing else.

STEP 1. IDENTIFY THE DISAGREEMENT

Your first task when you see an alternative viewpoint passage is to identify the disagreement. You will be given two paragraphs, each one expressing a particular point of view.

Because the arguments are going to conflict with each other, you're going to have to learn how to pick out the points in each argument that make it different from the other. So as you read each argument, look for its main point. This is particularly important because it helps make the argument less confusing. Let's look at an example:

Passage A

Is the Earth the center of the solar system? Here are two conflicting views.

Hypothesis 1

The Earth is the center of our solar system and all celestial bodies revolve around it. When we look up at the sky, we see that the sun rises from the East and sets in the West. The idea of a moving Earth is absurd. If the Earth is a revolving planet, why don't we feel its motion? These phenomena, which are obvious to even a child, must prove that the Earth is a stationary body.

Hypothesis 2

The sun is the center of our solar system. The only reason we perceive the sun as moving is because of the Earth's rotation on its axis. Mathematical calculations by astronomers have shown that the Earth is not a stationary body and that it makes a complete revolution around the sun every 365 days. In addition, it is the Earth's gravitational force that does not allow us to perceive the Earth's motion.

What are the two opinions in this passage?

The main point of each argument appeared in the first sentence of each paragraph, and in this case each was clearly stated. The best way to remember the main point of the argument is to underline the sentence that states it.

YOUR UNDERLINE VERSION SHOULD LOOK LIKE THIS

Hypothesis 1

<u>The Earth is the center of our solar system and all celestial bodies revolve around it.</u> When we look up at the sky, we see that the sun rises from the East and sets in the West. The idea of a moving Earth is absurd. If the Earth is a revolving planet, why don't we feel its motion? These phenomena, which are obvious to even a child, must prove that the Earth is a stationary body.

Hypothesis 2

<u>The sun is the center of our solar system.</u> The only reason we perceive the sun as moving is because of the Earth's rotation on its axis. Mathematical calculations by astronomers have shown that the Earth is not a stationary body and that it makes a complete revolution around the sun every 365 days. In addition, it is the Earth's gravitational force that does not allow us to perceive the Earth's motion.

Some of the scientific theories you'll read about on this section of the ACT are antiquated and were disproved a long time ago. That doesn't matter. For the ACT, it's the *arguments* that count. You may already know that the Earth isn't the center of solar system. But it's still possible to evaluate, scientifically, the *argument*.

Now that we know how an ACT alternative viewpoints passage is set up, let's look at another example and try to find the main point of each argument:

Passage B

Why did dinosaurs become extinct? Here are two opinions.

Hypothesis 1

About 65 million years ago the dinosaurs, the largest land animals, became extinct. Although no prevailing theory exists that explains their disappearance, the most logical explanation is that dramatic changes in sea level and climate destroyed their habitat. About the same time that dinosaurs died off, many other life forms, both on land and in the sea, became extinct. The shallow seas dried up and were suddenly empty. Since dinosaurs were quite heavy, it is believed that the only way they could have supported their weight was by using the buoyancy of water in swamps and lakes. Thus, the lack of water limited their mobility and their ability to acquire food. These enormous creatures therefore became extinct as a result of their inability to adapt to the harsh conditions that limited their natural habitat.

Hypothesis 2

For many years scientists have speculated about the cause of the extinction of the dinosaurs. Fossil records confirm that dinosaurs as well as other life forms were suddenly wiped out. The most natural cause of extinction is the inability of an organism to adapt to environmental changes. Yet, the extinction of all life forms is unlikely. Chemical analysis of clay found from this era attributes the sweeping extinction of dinosaurs to the collision of a huge meteorite with the Earth. These fossil records confirm the presence of a high concentration of iridium, a rare heavy metal, which is abundant in meteorites. It is believed that a meteorite hit the Earth, and created a huge crater which threw up dust that clouded the sun for several months. This event first led to the destruction of plant life and eventually all other life forms, including the dinosaurs.

Can you identify the disagreement in the passage?
What is the main point of Hypothesis 1?
What is the main point of Hypothesis 2?

According to Hypothesis 1, the extinction of dinosaurs was caused by changes in sea level and climate. According to Hypothesis 2, the extinction of dinosaurs was caused by dust from a meteorite collision.

If you didn't come up with the right answer, look at the underlined portions of the passages below.

Hypothesis 1

About 65 million years ago the dinosaurs, the largest land animals, became extinct. <u>Although no prevailing theory exists that explains their disappearance, the most logical explanation is that dramatic changes in sea level and climate destroyed their habitat.</u> About the same time that dinosaurs died off, many other life forms, both on land and in the sea, became extinct. The shallow seas dried up and were suddenly empty. Since dinosaurs were quite heavy, it is believed that the only way they could have supported their weight was by using the buoyancy of water in swamps and lakes. Thus, the lack of water limited their mobility and their ability to acquire food. <u>These enormous creatures therefore became extinct as a result of their inability to adapt to the harsh conditions that limited their natural habitat.</u>

Hypothesis 2

For many years scientists have speculated about the cause of the extinction of the dinosaurs. Fossil records confirm that dinosaurs as well as other life forms were suddenly wiped out. The most natural cause of extinction is the inability of an organism to adapt to environmental changes. Yet, the extinction of all life forms is unlikely. <u>Chemical analysis of clay found from this era attributes the sweeping extinction of dinosaurs to the collision of a huge meteorite with the Earth.</u> These fossil records confirm the presence of a high concentration of iridium, a rare heavy metal, which is abundant in meteorites. It is believed that a meteorite hit the Earth, and created a huge crater which threw up dust that clouded the sun for several months. This event first led to the destruction of plant life and eventually all other life forms, including the dinosaurs.

Did you notice that the main point of Hypothesis 1 could be found in two places? That's because in that case the last sentence was a *summary* of the main point.

IDENTIFY THE QUESTION TYPE

Now that you understand how to evaluate arguments, you need to know which kinds of questions follow them.

Understanding

The ACT test writers are looking to see if you're able to understand and explain the arguments as well as the scientific concepts behind them. These types of questions test your ability to draw conclusions based on each of the arguments. Whenever you see an understanding question, stick to our general rule: the answer is contained in one portion of the passage.

Let's try an example using the passage about the dinosaurs on page 358.

1. The two hypotheses are alike in that they both suggest that dinosaurs:

   I. were hit by meteorites.
   II. became extinct due to the limitations on their habitat.
   III. became extinct due to some external force other than predation.

   A. I only
   B. II only
   C. III only
   D. I and III only

Here's how to crack it:

We're looking for a statement that agrees with *both* theories. The best way to tackle this question is to eliminate answer choices that only support *one* of the theories. Let's start with statement I. Does the statement that dinosaurs were hit by meteorites support both theories? No. In fact, it doesn't support either of them! The passage didn't state that the meteorite hit the dinosaurs, it stated that a meteorite hit the Earth and threw up a cloud of dust. So we can cancel choices A and D. (Both contain statement I.) Statement II says that dinosaurs became extinct because they were limited by their habitat. Hypothesis 1 agrees with this statement but not Hypothesis 2. So, we can get rid of answer choice B. Now let's check statement III. Do both hypotheses state that dinosaurs become extinct because of some external force? Yes. So the correct answer choice is **C**.

HOW TO TACKLE ASSUMPTION QUESTIONS

Another question that comes up a lot concerns the *assumption* of the argument. Remember what assumptions are? We just covered them under the experimental reasoning section. Let's look back at the example we used under experimental reasoning.

> *Brenda's car is in the driveway; now I can stop by and see her.*

What's the *assumption* in this sentence again? The assumption is:

> *Brenda is home when her car is in the driveway.*

That's right. An assumption is a unwritten belief that, if *false,* would make the conclusion invalid. Remember, *assumptions* are those points we take for granted. When it comes to alternative viewpoints passages, the underlying assumption is used to *support* the argument. If the assumption is proved false, then the argument will be weakened.

Here's an example concerning the dinosaur passage:

2. To accept Hypothesis 1, one must assume that:

    F. dinosaurs were primarily plant-eaters.
    G. all dinosaurs were large and thus depended on water for movement.
    H. the dinosaurs died because they were unable to drink the sea water.
    J. a meteor hit the Earth approximately 65 million years ago.

Here is how to crack it:

First, let's review what Hypothesis 1 stated. It said that the dinosaurs died off because they were unable to thrive in their natural habitat. We need an answer choice that states something we take for granted about this theory. If dinosaurs were limited because of their size, then we must assume that *all* dinosaurs were huge. Only if all dinosaurs became extinct because they were huge would the lack of water in the swamps and seas limit their movement. That's the *assumption.* The correct answer is therefore **G**. Answer choice J supports Hypothesis 2 so it should be eliminated immediately. Do dinosaurs have to eat plants? No. So get rid of F. Was the problem that dinosaurs were unable to drink the sea water? No, the passage said they needed water for movement, not for drinking, so H is out. Remember, stick to the scope of the passage.

ANALYSIS

These questions involve the *integration* of information from both arguments. For instance, they may ask you to identify a strength or weakness in the argument of one of the debaters. How do you do that? You want to find a statement or an assumption that, if invalid, would make the theory wrong.

There are two ways to weaken an argument. One way is to find a shaky point in the argument of the debater. Let's go back to the passage about the Earth being the center of the solar system. One shaky point might be that just because the sun looks like it revolves around the Earth doesn't mean it actually does. The other way to weaken this argument is to use information from the "opposing camp," the other debater. For instance, let's go back to the passage about the Earth being the center of the solar system. You could say that there is mathematical evidence to prove that the Earth does revolve around the sun. Where did we get this point? From the other debater.

Here's an example using the dinosaur passage.

3. Which of the following discoveries would best support Hypothesis 2?

   A. The existence of radioactive substances in the soil.
   B. The presence of other rare metals common to meteorites in the clay beds of the ocean from that period.
   C. Fossil records of land-dwelling reptiles that roamed the Earth for an additional 10 million years.
   D. Evidence of dramatic changes in sea level 65 million years ago.

Here's how to crack it:

This question tests your ability to recognize trends in the argument. What type of evidence would support Hypothesis 2? Any evidence that shows that dinosaurs were wiped out as a result of the impact of a meteorite. Would the presence of radioactive substances in the soil support Hypothesis 2? It could only support the passage if the radioactive elements were from meteorites (like iridium). Answer choice A did not specify that. Would the fact that some land-dwelling reptiles survived past this period support Hypothesis 2? No, so answer choice C doesn't give us additional information to support Hypothesis 2. We can also get rid of answer choice D because it supports Hypothesis 1. What about answer choice B? What if other rare metals that are known to be found in meteorites were discovered? Would this support Hypothesis 2? Yes. The correct answer choice is **B**.

Now let's answer the same question, this time with different answer choices.

4. Which of the following discoveries would best support Hypothesis 2?

   F. Dinosaurs were warm-blooded animals.
   G. The bones of dinosaurs were massive but fragile.
   H. The dinosaurs' original habitat was primarily arid.
   J. Dinosaurs were not reptiles.

Here's how to crack it:

We already know the main point of Hypothesis 2. Now, how could we support that argument? We can disprove the main point of Hypothesis 1. One way to do that is to weaken the argument made by Hypothesis 1. Hypothesis 1 states that the extinction of the dinosaurs was due to the destruction of their habitat. What if it were shown that the habitat was different than that stated in Hypothesis 1? Let's look at the answer choices. Answer choice H indicates that the dinosaurs *never* had much water. If that were true, is it likely that dinosaurs ever needed water for movement? No. Therefore this evidence would weaken the first argument and strengthen the second one. So the correct answer is **H**.

GENERALIZATION

This type of question requires that you make predictions based on the information provided. This time, the test writers may give you new information such as the discovery of a fossil, or the results of a new experiment, and ask how this information influences the conclusions of the two hypotheses. Here again they are asking you to look at the "big picture."

Let's look at an example using the dinosaur passage again:

5. Suppose a geologist discovered that the bones of dinosaurs contained traces of radioactive iridium. How would this evidence influence the two hypotheses?

    A. It would support both hypotheses.
    B. It would support Hypothesis 1 and weaken Hypothesis 2.
    C. It would support Hypothesis 2 and weaken Hypothesis 1.
    D. It would not support Hypothesis 1 or Hypothesis 2.

Here's how to crack it:

Did you notice that this question starts with the word "suppose"? This tells you that this is probably a generalization question. Now, which of the hypotheses would be supported if a geologist found fossil bones that contained traces of radioactive iridium? Hypothesis 2 of course! The passage states that radioactive iridium is abundant in meteorites. If dinosaurs were exposed to the dust of meteorites, their bones would contain this metal. The correct answer is **C**. Which answer choices were you supposed to begin with? Answer choices B and C. Why? Because both answer choices began with the same words and present opposite trends.

PUTTING THE STRATEGY TO WORK

Let's try this strategy on these sample alternative viewpoints passages. For practice, write down what type of question it is *before* you work out the answer.

Passage I

How did the continents take on their current shape? Two differing views are presented below:

Scientist 1

According to a theory based on plate tectonics, the land surface of the Earth once comprised a single continent, termed *Pangaea,* which was surrounded by a single vast ocean. Pangaea broke apart because the surfaces of the Earth floated on massive plates above the deeper mantle of the ocean's basin. Horizontal movement of the plates began to split up the land about 137 million years ago during the Jurassic period. The continents and the ocean basins moved along convection currents in the mantle resulting in a continuous degeneration of the Earth's physical features. The movement of these rigid plates produced zones of tectonic activity along their margins such as earthquakes, volcanoes, and mountain formations. Fossil records as well as geological evidence show similarities between widely displaced continents. For instance, the coastlines of South America and Africa contain similar rock formations and appear to fit together like a jigsaw puzzle.

Scientist 2

The continents and the ocean basins of the Earth are permanent, fixed features of the planet. The hypothesis of plate tectonics is flawed because there is insufficient evidence to support it. The force of gravity is stronger than any known tangential force that can act on the Earth's crust. The layers of crust that support the continents and ocean basins are strong enough to preserve the earth's physical features and are too strong to permit horizontal drift. Tectonic activity has always been present but the hypothesis of plate tectonics only explains such activity in one late period of ancient history. In addition, it is not clear what kind of force could allow the continents, composed largely of granite, to move through areas of dense iron-rich rock that comprise the ocean basins. Any geological evidence that supports such a theory may be due to the existence of similar conditions on different continents.

1. Which of the following statements is the most inconsistent with the beliefs of Scientist 1?

    A. Continents were once part of a large land mass.
    B. Continents split up and drifted apart.
    C. Ocean basins have not changed for millions of years.
    D. When land masses ruptured they formed mid-ocean ridges.

QUESTION TYPE: _____

2. Scientist 1 studied the fossils along the coast of South America and Africa and found identical fern-like plants on rocks of the same age. What claim could Scientist 2 make to refute the findings of Scientist 1?

    F. The dating and comparison of plant fossils is an exact science.
    G. The ferns floated from the shore of one continent to the other.
    H. The ferns were extremely large.
    J. The ferns thrive in tropical regions.

QUESTION TYPE: _____

3. A new zone of tectonic activity has been discovered in the large land mass of Eurasia. This zone shows geological evidence of having been active for several thousand years. Which scientist is supported by this finding and why?

    A. Scientist 1, because it proves that tectonic activity occurs on the planet.
    B. Scientist 1, because it shows that Pangaea and Eurasia are the same land mass.
    C. Scientist 2, because it proves that tectonic activity occurs in land masses and not solely in the ocean basin and along coastlines.
    D. Scientist 2, because it shows that the continents are made out of granite.

QUESTION TYPE: _____

4. Both Scientist 1 and Scientist 2 are experts in plate tectonics. To what discipline of science do these scientists belong?

F. Physics
G. Geology
H. Biology
J. Chemistry

QUESTION TYPE: _____

5. Which of the following claims would be supported by both scientists?

   I. Tectonic activity has always been a factor in the geology of land masses.
  II. The continents and the ocean basins are fixed features of the planet.
 III. Continental drift occurred in the Jurassic period.

A. I only
B. II only
C. I and II only
D. II and III only

QUESTION TYPE: _____

Here's how to crack them:

Question 1: This is an understanding question. What are the beliefs of Scientist 1? His main point is that Pangaea (one continent) existed 137 million years ago. Now, let's start by looking at each of the answer choices. Were the continents once part of one large land mass? Yes. We read that in the passage. What about choice B? Did the continents break up and drift apart? Definitely. Does the statement that the ocean basins remained fixed agree with the theory? No. If so, how would the continents drift apart? So answer choice C is inconsistent. Answer choice D is also consistent with the theory of Scientist 1. So the correct answer choice is **C**.

Question 2: This is an analysis question. Scientist 2 needs to come up with a statement that would disprove the other scientist's argument. How can he do that? By stating a point that weakens the argument. Let's look at which answer choice does that best. Answer choice F states that the techniques used to date and compare fossils are accurate. This statement supports the opinion of Scientist 1. What about the statement that ferns floated from one continent to the other. Would that weaken the argument? Most definitely! Then the rock would contain the same plants! Answer choice **H** supports Scientist 1 because extremely large ferns would have a hard time floating thousands of miles across the ocean. You can eliminate answer choice J, because it doesn't support either scientist. You can only infer that these ferns grow well in Africa and South America.

Question 3: This is an analysis question and it's kind of tricky. Either scientist could use this information to support his theory if he could come up with a valid reason. Answer choice A says that Scientist 1 is supported because the finding shows tectonic activity. But we already knew about that and besides, that's a point on which the scientists agree. So eliminate choice A. Answer choice D also gives us information that was already stated in Scientist 2's statement, so this choice is weak. Choice B is ridiculous because neither scientist believes that Pangaea exists today, so cross it out. At this point, answer choice C is looking pretty good. Scientist 2 could soundly reason that tectonic activity in a solid land mass demonstrates that this geological phenomenon does not lead to continental drift. The best answer choice is **B**.

Question 4: This is an understanding question. The passage tells us about the formation of land masses, tectonic plates, and other geological evidence, namely fossils. You must be able to add this together and determine that the scientists know something about geology. So, only answer **G** can be the correct answer.

Question 5: This is an understanding question. You must know what each scientist supports. Let's go through the choices one by one. Statement I is supported by both scientists because both believe that tectonic activity exists and changes geological formations. (Scientist 1 thinks it's more important than does Scientist 2, but that doesn't matter here.) So, statement I is correct and we're down to choices A and C. Let's keep checking. Only Scientist 2 supports statement II and only Scientist 1 supports statement III. Therefore, **A** must be the correct answer choice.

Passage II

How did life on Earth originate? Two differing views are presented.

Hypothesis 1

In 1953 a graduate student attempted to recreate the conditions of primeval Earth in a sealed glass apparatus that he filled with methane, ammonia, hydrogen, and water. Sparks were released into the glass to simulate lightning, and heat was applied to the water. The result was the formation of organic compounds, known as amino acids which are the building blocks of proteins. Since that time, others have shown how DNA may have been synthesized under various conditions as well. RNA, which is

DNA's partner in the translation of genetic information into protein products, has been found to have the ability to reproduce itself under certain conditions. Thus, the origins of life are to be found in the "primordial soup" of the ancient Earth that provided conditions for the simplest forms of organic matter to form and develop increasingly sophisticated means of organization. With the ability of compounds to make copies of themselves comes the opportunity for evolution by the mechanisms of heredity and mutation.

Hypothesis 2

Previous assumptions about the makeup of the "primordial soup" are inaccurate. It is not at all clear that methane and ammonia were present on the primeval Earth or that conditions were as favorable as in the graduate student's experiment. The ability of RNA to reproduce itself is also limited to particular conditions that the primeval Earth is unlikely to have provided. There is a possibility that, given enough time, random events could alone have resulted in the development of entire single-celled organisms, but some have likened that possibility to the chance that a tornado whirling through a junkyard could result in the formation of a 747 jetliner. During much of the time when the "primordial soup" was to have existed, the Earth was a regular target of meteors that kept oceans boiling and the atmosphere inhospitable to organic development. Clearly much more research is needed before this theory can be widely accepted.

1. Which of the following statements about the conditions on primeval Earth could be used to support Hypothesis 2?

   A. Atmospheric conditions were too unstable to support the gases essential to the theories of the "primordial soup"
   B. Organic molecules were able to thrive under primeval Earth conditions.
   C. The origin of life began in the "primordial soup."
   D. The atmosphere contained methane, ammonia, hydrogen, and water.

QUESTION TYPE: _____

2. To accept Hypothesis 1, one must assume that:

    F. the Earth was bombarded by meteors during that time period.

    G. the conditions in the glass were analogous to the conditions on primeval Earth.

    H. proteins are the building blocks of amino acids.

    J. the Earth lacked hydrogen in the atmosphere.

QUESTION TYPE: _____

3. Which of the following word equations shows how, according to Hypothesis 1, the building blocks of life were formed?

    A. Methane + Ammonia + Hydrogen + Water → Primordial Soup → Amino Acids.

    B. Meteors → Primordial Soup → Amino Acids.

    C. Amino Acids → Primordial Soup → DNA → Methane + Ammonia + Hydrogen + Water

    D. Primordial Soup → proteins → Amino Acids.

QUESTION TYPE: _____

Here's how to crack them:

Question 1: This is an analysis question because we're asked to find an answer that supports the argument. What's the main point of Hypothesis 2? The debater believes that the chance of RNA reproducing as the graduate student described is extremely small. Look for an answer choice that supports this argument. Answer choice A states that conditions in the atmosphere were too unstable to support the necessary gases. Does this statement support Hypothesis 2? Yes. How? Because it weakens Hypothesis 1. So answer choice **A** is correct. Answer choices B, C, and D are wrong because they support Hypothesis 1.

Question 2: This is an understanding question and we're looking for an assumption in the argument. What does Scientist 1 believe? That his experiment shows how the first organic compounds were made. Is answer choice F an assumption in this argument? No, it refers to Hypothesis 2. What about answer choice G? Yes. The scientist assumed that his experiment mimicked the conditions of primeval Earth. So, **G** is correct. Answer choice H states that proteins are the building blocks of amino acids. That's wrong, as stated in Hypothesis #1. Amino acids are the building blocks of *proteins*. So get rid of H. Answer choice J is incorrect because the Earth had to have hydrogen in order to form organic compounds.

Question 3: This is an understanding question. What does Hypothesis 1 say about amino acids? The passage tells us that amino acids are the building blocks of life, so let's start with the answer choices that list amino acids last. We can quickly eliminate C. We can also eliminate B, because the meteor theory was part of Hypothesis 2, not 1. And we're down to choices A and D. We can also find in the passage that amino acids are the building blocks of proteins, so amino acids should be before protein in the list. So, by POE and understanding the passage, we arrive at the correct answer, **A**.

Passage III

Will the Earth experience another ice age?

Hypothesis 1

Scientists have long speculated whether glaciation will ever take place again. Given that glaciation is an unusual event, it is highly unlikely that such a phenomenon will ever repeat itself. Glaciation usually takes place under periods of extremely cool temperatures. However, it appears that the temperature on the Earth has been milder and more stable than at any other period. In fact, it would take a 5°C drop in the average surface temperature in order for glaciation to occur. In addition, there would have to be a significant increase in precipitation.

Hypothesis 2

Although the Earth has not experienced glaciation in a long time, the event, no matter how rare, can occur if the right conditions are met. Two factors that are critical to the growth of glaciers are precipitation and temperature. There are a number of areas, specifically land masses in the polar regions, that are presently cold enough to produce glaciers but do not have sufficient snowfall to develop glacier systems. However, if enough events occur simultaneously, they can bring on an ice age. For instance, if there is an increase in the level of snowfall in the winter in these polar regions, this could eventually lead to glaciation. On the other hand, the level of pollution in the atmosphere is also sufficient to gradually cool the earth. Under these conditions it is quite clear that glaciation is only a matter of the right combination of events at the right time.

1. Which of the following discoveries would most clearly favor Hypothesis 2?

   A. Canada has more snowfall this year than any other year.
   B. When snow falls, it sticks to the ground.
   C. The more pollution in the air, the more the temperature drops.
   D. The Earth's bodies of waters are becoming more polluted.

QUESTION TYPE: _____

2. Which of the following statements is the strongest argument a supporter of Hypothesis 2 would use to counter Hypothesis 1?

   F. The temperature around polar regions fluctuates.
   G. The precipitation rate has been increasing in the Swiss Alps.
   H. Just because ideal conditions are rare does not mean they will not occur in the future.
   J. The temperature in the North pole has gone up 2°C.

QUESTION TYPE: _____

3. If Hypothesis 2 is correct and glaciation can take place in the future, what regions would be most affected?

   I. Heavily polluted regions
   II. Polar regions
   III. Humid regions

   A. I only
   B. II only
   C. I and II only
   D. II and III only

QUESTION TYPE: _____

4. According to Hypothesis 2, what conditions could cause glaciation?

    A. Low levels of pollution leading to high precipitation

    B. High levels of pollution leading to a blanketing effect that blocks out the sun and decreases the temperature dramatically

    C. High levels of pollution leading to low precipitation

    D. A major snowstorm for three days in Chicago

QUESTION TYPE: _____

Here's how to crack them:

Question 1: We are looking for an answer choice that supports Hypothesis 2. Hypothesis 2 states that an increase in precipitation or an increase in pollution would lead to a significant drop in temperature. Answer choice A says that there is more snow in Canada this year but we don't know if that's enough snow for glaciation. So we can eliminate it. Let's look at B. If snow didn't stick to the ground, would there be an ice age? Answer choice B is silly; eliminate it. What about answer choice C? If there is a drop in temperature for every increase in the pollution rate, could that lead to glaciation? Yes. Let's look at answer choice D. If the water became more polluted would that necessarily lead to the next ice age? We're not sure. The passage states that pollution in the *air*, not necessarily water, leads to a decrease in temperature. So the correct answer is **C**.

Question 2: For this question we're looking for an answer choice that could disprove Hypothesis 1. What is the main point of Hypothesis 1? The debater says that it is highly unlikely that the Earth will experience another ice age. Why? Because he believes that the necessary conditions will not be met in the future. What is the best way to disprove this point? Just indicate that the conditions could change in the future and then the chance for glaciation could increase. Which answer choice states that? Answer choice H. Now let's look at answer choice F. A fluctuation in temperature would not necessarily mean that the temperature was low enough for glaciation to occur. We therefore can eliminate this choice. Even if there was more snowfall in the Swiss Alps, we are not given an indication of how long it lasted. So you can get rid of answer choice G. Now, if the temperature went up 5°C in the North pole it would be warmer, not colder so answer choise J is out. So the correct answer choice is **H**.

Question 3: What type of question is this? It's an understanding question because you are being asked to identify the regions in which glaciation would take place. Let's start with statement II, since it appears in the most answer choices. Based on the passage, would glaciation take place in polar regions? The passage tells us that polar regions would be one of the first locations in which glaciation would take place. Now that you can eliminate answer choices that don't include statement II, you can eliminate answer choice A. What about heavily polluted regions? Yes, the passage refers to the other possible cause of a temperature drop—pollution. Now, according to the passage, does humidity have anything to do with glaciation? No. So answer choice is **C** is correct.

Question 4: This is also an understanding question. There are two conditions that are critical to glaciation: a *heavily* polluted atmosphere or a *major* snowfall. Answer choice A is incorrect because pollution doesn't *cause* precipitation. Answer choice **B** sounds good since it states that pollution leads to a *major* drop in temperature (it has both conditions). What about answer choice C? You can eliminate C since it states that pollution leads to low precipitation levels. Answer choice D is ridiculous: as unpleasant as it may be, a Chicago snowstorm would not cause glaciation!

SCIENCE REASONING SUMMARY

1. There are three types of passages on the ACT science reasoning test. They are data representation, experimental reasoning, and alternative viewpoints.

2. For the science reasoning section of the test you should always scan the passage first.

3. If you're given a data representation passage, you should emphasize the graphs, tables, and charts. If you're given an experimental reasoning passage, you should look for the objective, identify the variables, and study the results. If you're given an alternative viewpoints passage, identify the disagreement.

4. Once you have read the passage, go directly to the questions.

5. Your next task is to identify the question type. If it is an understanding question, the answer is supposed to be in a specific portion of the passage. If it is an analysis question, you'll need to draw upon larger portions of the passage and integrate them. If it is a generalization question, you're supposed to look at the big picture and relate the results to the real world.

6. An understanding question may ask you to find the *control* of the study. Look for the variable (the thing) that has *not* been manipulated or exposed: that's the control!

7. An understanding question may also ask you to find the *assumption* of an argument. The assumption is an underlying point in the experiment or argument. Look for an answer choice with a statement that is taken for granted in the study.

8. Guesstimate to help you approximate values on a graph or figure. This will save you a lot of time that could be better spent on other questions.

9. Use Process of Elimination (POE) to eliminate ridiculous answer choices.

PART VI

The Princeton Review Assessment (PRA)

Most colleges require that you submit either an ACT or SAT score with your transcript. However, you may find it difficult to determine which test will best represent your abilities. The Princeton Review Assessment (PRA) is a single three-and-a-half-hour test that will give you an idea of how you will perform on *both* exams so that you can make an educated decision about which test to take.

It is important that you take the PRA as if it were a real ACT or SAT.

> - Find a quiet spot to take the exam, preferably at a desk or table where you can sit up straight.
> - Tell your family that you have important business to attend to and should not be interrupted.
> - Disconnect any phones within earshot. You can talk with your friends after the test.
> - Use a timer. Do not give yourself more than the indicated amount of time on any section. Extra time will invalidate your scores.

The best results will be obtained if you take the entire exam in one sitting with a five-minute break between the third and fourth section. The answers and a guide for scoring are printed on the pages following the exam. Take some time after you finish to read about what your score means.

Good luck!

LANGUAGE SKILLS
45 Minutes—75 Questions

DIRECTIONS: In the five passages that follow, certain words and phrases are underlined and numbered. In the right-hand column, you will find alternatives for each underlined part. You are to choose the one that best expresses the idea, makes the statement appropriate for standard written English, or is worded most consistently with the style and tone of the passage as a whole. If you think the original version is best, choose "NO CHANGE."

You will also find questions about a section of the passage, or the passage as a whole. These questions do not refer to

an underlined portion of the passage, but rather are identified by a number or numbers in a box.

For each question, choose the alternative you consider best and blacken the corresponding oval on your answer sheet. Read each passage through once before you begin to answer the questions that accompany it. You cannot determine most answers without first reading several sentences beyond the question. Be sure that you have read far enough ahead each time you choose an alternative.

Passage I

It seems inconceivable to us <u>when</u> some animals
                                    1
travel thousands of miles during their life cycles.

For understanding why they do it, we need only look at
‾‾‾‾‾‾‾‾‾‾‾‾‾
        2
the changing seasons in the North. As summer fades into

fall, which in turn fades into winter, we turn on our

furnaces and take our warm coats out of storage

<u>because it is cold</u>. We eat less fresh food. If our winter
    3

food is <u>fresh, it has</u> probably been shipped from a
          4
warmer climate.

Wild animals, <u>nevertheless</u>, have not developed the
                    5
sophisticated technologies necessary for the

<u>adaptations and adjustments that we employ and utilize.</u>
‾‾
                            6
In order to endure the harsher seasons, some change their

coats like us. Others, though, are not able to adapt to the

fluctuating temperatures. They follow the warm weather

south (or north, if they live south of the Equator). These

1. **A.** NO CHANGE
   B. whereby
   C. that
   D. if

2. **F.** NO CHANGE
   G. To understand
   H. As understanding
   J. If we understand

3. **A.** NO CHANGE
   B. as if it was cold
   C. because it was cold
   D. OMIT the underlined portion.

4. **F.** NO CHANGE
   G. fresh. They have
   H. fresh; it has
   J. fresh. It has

5. **A.** NO CHANGE
   B. however
   C. although
   D. despite this

6. **F.** NO CHANGE
   G. adaptations and adjustments that we employed and utilized.
   H. adaptations and adjustments that we are employing.
   J. adaptations we employ.

GO ON TO THE NEXT PAGE

migratory creatures, a group which encompasses birds,
                                    ‾‾‾‾‾‾‾‾‾‾‾‾‾‾‾‾‾‾
                                           7
whales, fish, insects, and quadrupedal mammals, have

bodies adapted to the demands of long seasonal

journeys.

    Why do they travel so very far? This is something

of a mystery, especially since some creatures must

traverse inhospitable areas during the trip to they're
                                                ‾‾‾‾‾‾
                                                  8
seasonal homes. For example, certain sea birds must

cross oceans to get to their winter nesting grounds.

During its migration from equatorial Africa to northern

Europe, the white stork crossed the Sahara Dessert and
                        ‾‾‾‾‾‾‾
                           9
the Mediterranean Sea. Although the exact cause for

such journeys is impossible to determine. Scientists
                               ‾‾‾‾‾‾‾‾‾‾‾‾‾‾‾‾‾‾‾‾
                                      10
speculate that continental drift has pulled traditional

seasonal grounds far apart and that instinct
                    ‾‾‾‾‾‾‾‾‾
                       11

having precluded a change in territorial preference.
‾‾‾‾‾‾‾‾‾‾‾‾‾‾‾
      12

7. A. NO CHANGE
   B. encompasses: birds
   C. encompasses, birds
   D. encompass birds

8. F. NO CHANGE
   G. their
   H. it's
   J. its

9. A. NO CHANGE
   B. having crossed
   C. crosses
   D. had crossed

10. F. NO CHANGE
    G. determine—scientists
    H. determine; scientists
    J. determine, scientists

11. A. NO CHANGE
    B. apart and,
    C. apart: and
    D. apart; and

12. F. NO CHANGE
    G. had precluded
    H. was precluding
    J. has precluded

┌─────────────────────────────────────┐
│ Item 13 poses a question about Passage I │
│ as a whole.   │
└─────────────────────────────────────┘

13. Which of the following best describes the tone and
    purpose of this essay?

    A. The tone is ironic; the purpose is to point out
       the similarities between people and animals.
    B. The tone is objective; the purpose is to discuss
       some possible reasons for migration in animals.
    C. The tone is critical; the purpose is to condemn
       animals for being unable to adapt to the
       seasons.
    D. The tone is humorous; the purpose is to present
       an amusing anecdote.

GO ON TO THE NEXT PAGE →

Passage II

[1]

Max Ernst, in the Dada movement, was a German
                                                    14
artist and a leading figure.

However, Ernst cut up photographs, engravings, and
          15
illustrations, and recombined the images in collage form.

The featured objects thereby assumed new, sometimes

multiple, identities.

[2]

Horrified by trench warfare, a lasting imprint was
                                              16
left on the generation of European intellectuals who

came of age during World War I. Painters, sculptors,

and people who wrote turned their expressions of protest
        17
into works of art and gave their movement the

nonsensical and meaningless name Dada. Dada
      18
condemned the existing cultural institutions and

advocated the liberation of artistic form.

14. **F.** NO CHANGE
    G. In the Dada movement, a leading figure and a German artist, was Max Ernst.
    H. Max Ernst was a German artist and a leading figure in the Dada movement.
    J. A German artist and a leading figure in the Dada movement was Max Ernst.

15. **A.** NO CHANGE
    B. As a consequence,
    C. Despite the fact,
    D. OMIT the underlined portion and begin the sentence with Ernst.

16. **F.** NO CHANGE
    G. Horrified, trench warfare left a lasting imprint
    H. The horror of trench warfare left a lasting imprint
    J. A lasting imprint left by trench warfare

17. **A.** NO CHANGE
    B. writers
    C. writing people
    D. OMIT the underlined portion.

18. **F.** NO CHANGE
    G. nonsensical, and meaningless
    H. nonsensical and absurd
    J. nonsensical

GO ON TO THE NEXT PAGE →

[3]

Max Ernst is best known for contributing to this
                                                    19
period was the development of the frottage technique.

Ernst lay down paper over raised surfaces, rubbed a
          20
pencil over the paper, then isolated images in the

haphazard design that resulted. These images were then

to be translated into paintings. The desolate landscapes
        21

portrayed in many of Ernsts' later works suggest the
                                        22
destruction of a depraved society.

[4]

The Dada movement had lost much of their impetus
                                            23
by the early 1920s. At that time, Ernst moved to Paris

where another artistic movement, surrealism, was in its

formative stages. Surrealists sought to capture the

images produced by free association of the unconscious

mind. They combined these images in incongruous

ways, creating effects that were sometimes humorous,

although sometimes frightening.

19. A. NO CHANGE
    B. Max Ernst's best-known contribution
    C. Max Ernsts' best-known contribution
    D. Max Ernst is best known for his contribution

20. F. NO CHANGE
    G. placed down
    H. placed
    J. placed and lay

21. A. NO CHANGE
    B. translated into paintings.
    C. translated into becoming paintings.
    D. being translated into paintings.

22. F. NO CHANGE
    G. Ernsts' later work
    H. The later work of Ernst's
    J. Ernst's later works

23. A. NO CHANGE
    B. its
    C. the movement's
    D. the movements'

Item 24 poses a question about Passage II
as a whole.

24. Which of the following sequences of paragraphs
    will make the essay most logical?

    F. NO CHANGE
    G. 4, 2, 1, 3
    H. 2, 1, 3, 4
    J. 2, 3, 4, 1

GO ON TO THE NEXT PAGE

Passage III

Jazz singer, Ella Fitzgerald, was born in 1918 in
                    25

Newport News, Virginia. She took part in a performance
                                              26
on amateur night at the Apollo Theatre in New York

when she caught the eye and ear of band leader Chick

Webb, who hired her immediately. Fitzgerald performed

with Webb's band until his death in 1935, at which time

she took over the group. Two years later, she left

to pursue a career as a soloist.
    27

[1] She has flawlessly interpreted the works of such

musical legends as Jerome Kern, Cole Porter, and

George Gershwin, who are very famous. [2] She has
                   28
sung a broad spectrum of music, ranging from slow and

sultry to upbeat and swinging. [3] Nicknamed "The

First Lady of Song," Ella Fitzgerald has had a long and

illustrious career. [4] Her contribution to the world of
                          29
music, and indeed to society as a whole, has

been great. 30

25. **A.** NO CHANGE
    B. singer: Ella Fitzgerald,
    C. singer Ella Fitzgerald
    D. singer Ella Fitzgerald,

26. **F.** NO CHANGE
    G. was performing
    H. has been performing
    J. is performing

27. **A.** NO CHANGE
    B. having pursued
    C. only to pursue
    D. and pursuing

28. **F.** NO CHANGE
    G. all of who are famous
    H. all famous
    J. OMIT the underlined portion.

29. **A.** NO CHANGE
    B. contributions
    C. contributing
    D. having contributed

30. For the sake of unity and coherence, Sentence 3
    should be placed

    F. where it is now
    G. after Sentence 1
    H. it should be omitted
    J. before Sentence 1

GO ON TO THE NEXT PAGE

Fitzgerald helped pave the way for other black
31

singers and brought jazz to a larger audience. Her
32
singing facilitated the integration of blacks and whites, at

least within the confines of the music hall. Either blacks
33
or whites flocked to hear her sing,

united under a brief time by the magic of her sound.
34

31. A. NO CHANGE
    B. the paving of
    C. paving
    D. OMIT the underlined portion.

32. F. NO CHANGE
    G. Since her singing
    H. Since Fitzgerald's singing
    J. That her singing

33. A. NO CHANGE
    B. All blacks and whites
    C. Both blacks and whites
    D. Because blacks and whites

34. F. NO CHANGE
    G. united for a brief time
    H. united—for a brief time
    J. united, for a brief time

Item 35 poses a question about Passage III
as a whole.

35. Suppose that a newspaper editor had assigned the
writer to describe an instance of racial unity in the
arts. Does the essay successfully fulfill the assignment?

    A. No, because its main focus is on the career of
       Ella Fitzgerald.
    B. Yes, because Fitzgerald sang works by white
       composers.
    C. Yes, because blacks and whites alike went to
       see Fitzgerald sing.
    D. No, because very few people listen to jazz.

GO ON TO THE NEXT PAGE

Passage IV

Approximately ten thousand years ago, a radical change took place in the way people lived, <u>significantly</u> <u>altering their lives</u>. They abandoned the traditional methods of hunting and gathering their food, which required an arduous migration to seasonal grounds. <u>Instead,</u> they domesticated the plants and animals they

37

needed <u>to survive.</u>

38

The shift <u>to</u> domestication and a sedentary lifestyle

39
wrought great change. A given area of land could now support more people <u>than were</u> ever before possible.

40
Moreover, agriculture necessitated the storage of seed stock, the division of labor, and <u>allocating land.</u>

41

[3]
As each region became more specialized in <u>what</u> <u>they produced, the need</u> for greater trade and

42
communication intensified. The population in each area became situated around natural, centrally located <u>points, which</u> developed

43
into the first cities. It became necessary to organize the

36. F. NO CHANGE
    G. to alter their lives
    H. which significantly altered their lives
    J. OMIT the underlined words and end the sentence with lived.

37. A. NO CHANGE
    B. Nevertheless,
    C. However,
    D. Even so,

38. F. NO CHANGE
    G. surviving.
    H. for surviving.
    J. to have survived.

39. A. NO CHANGE
    B. from
    C. of
    D. for

40. F. NO CHANGE
    G. than was
    H. than they were
    J. than it were

41. A. NO CHANGE
    B. to allocate
    C. allocated
    D. the allocation of

42. F. NO CHANGE
    G. it produced. The need
    H. they produced. The need
    J. it produced, the need

43. A. NO CHANGE
    B. points: which
    C. points: which,
    D. points; which

increasingly complex and complicated economic
                44

relationships and develop a structure capable to deal with
                                                45
the many societal changes. Thus, centrally located

authority developed, giving rise to the first real

governments.

44. F. NO CHANGE
    G. complex, and complicated
    H. complex but complicated
    J. complex

45. A. NO CHANGE
    B. of dealing
    C. to have dealt
    D. OMIT the underlined portion.

Passage V

[1] Many legends, such as those of Bluebeard and

King Arthur, are based on real people and events. [2]

One of the most striking examples of a legendary

character who is based on real people is Count Dracula.
                                  46
[3] Many people believe that Dracula is a fictional

character invented by Bram Stoker, the nineteenth

century writer, and that tales of vampires in turn derive
                                                    47
from from Stoker's popular story. [4] In actuality,

though, Stoker based his character on Prince Vlad IV, a

Transylvanian resistance fighter also known as "Vlad the

Impaler." [5] Vlad had been living in the fifteenth
                48
century, when Transylvania was under constant attack.

[6] He united armies to fight the invaders, who were

notorious for their cruelty and barbarity, for which they
                                                    49
were famous. [7] Vlad earned his nickname by outdoing

his enemies at their own game; when he captured them

alive, he would impale them on stakes and watch them

die slow, excruciating deaths. [8] The Prince's cruelty

was not limited to foes, however. [9] When

soldiers who deserted his army or failed to meet his

military standards received the same treatment.
               50
[10] Hundreds of thousands of people died while Vlad

46. F. NO CHANGE
    G. on real people was
    H. on a real person was
    J. on a real person is

47. A. NO CHANGE
    B. were deriving
    C. are deriving from
    D. being derived from

48. F. NO CHANGE
    G. Vlad, living
    H. Vlad lived
    J. Vlad, who lived

49. A. NO CHANGE
    B. and which made them famous
    C. which they were famous for
    D. OMIT underlined portion.

50. F. NO CHANGE
    G. standards receiving the same treatment.
    H. standards, they received the same treatment.
    J. standards, received the same treatment.

GO ON TO THE NEXT PAGE

calmly went about his everyday business. [51]

It is neither surprising that Vlad's legend lived long after his death. Nor is it surprising that in the retelling, 52 several details were changed and exaggerated. For example, the stakes upon which Vlad impaled his victims became, in popular legend, the only weapon that could kill a vampire. Similarly, Vlad's bloodthirsty nature was also likewise transformed into a central 53 feature of vampire lore—by the vampire's grisly habit of 54 sucking his victim's blood. The enduring legend of Dracula is one of countless examples of the merging of fact and fiction.

51. The writer has been told that the first paragraph needs to be broken into two. Where would the best place be to split the paragraph?

   A. between Sentences 3 and 4
   B. between Sentences 4 and 5
   C. between Sentences 5 and 6
   D. between Sentences 8 and 9

52. F. NO CHANGE
   G. death. Or is it surprising
   H. death, nor is it surprising
   J. death, or is it surprising

53. A. NO CHANGE
   B. also
   C. likewise
   D. OMIT the underlined words.

54. F. NO CHANGE
   G. lore: the vampire's
   H. lore as evidenced by the vampire's
   J. lore: as evidenced by the vampire's

> Item 55 poses a question about Passage V as a whole.

55. Which of the following sentences most effectively summarizes the conclusion drawn by the essay as a whole?
   A. Vlad the Impaler was very famous.
   B. Dracula is an example of a fictional character who is based on an actual historical figure.
   C. Vlad the Impaler was also known as Count Dracula.
   D. History often repeats itself.

S T O P

IF YOU FINISH BEFORE TIME IS CALLED, YOU MAY CHECK YOUR WORK ON THIS SECTION ONLY. DO NOT WORK ON ANY OTHER SECTION IN THE TEST.

NO TEST MATERIAL ON THIS PAGE.

Section 2 2 2 2 2 2

Reference Information

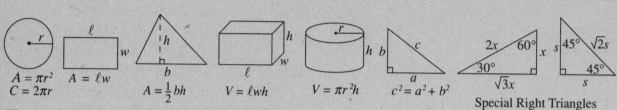

$A = \pi r^2$
$C = 2\pi r$

$A = \ell w$

$A = \frac{1}{2} bh$

$V = \ell w h$

$V = \pi r^2 h$

$c^2 = a^2 + b^2$

Special Right Triangles

The number of degrees of arc in a circle is 360.
The measure in degrees of a straight angle is 180.
The sum of the measures in degrees of the angles of a triangle is 180.

Directions for Quantitative Comparison Questions

Questions 1-15 each consist of two quantities in boxes, one in Column A and one in Column B. You are to compare the two quantities and on the answer sheet fill in oval

A if the quantity in Column A is greater;
B if the quantity in Column B is greater;
C if the two quantities are equal;
D if the relationship cannot be determined from the information given.

AN E RESPONSE WILL NOT BE SCORED.

Notes:

1. In some questions, information is given about one or both of the quantities to be compared. In such cases, the given information is centered above the two columns and is not boxed.
2. In a given question, a symbol that appears in both columns represents the same thing in Column A as it does in Column B.
3. Letters such as x, n, and k stand for real numbers.

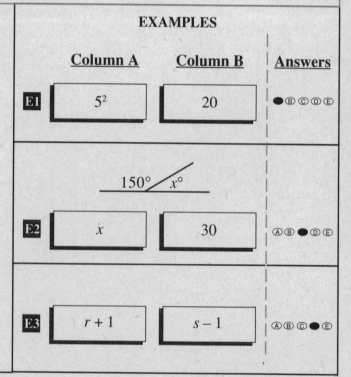

Column A	Column B

$$61x = 743$$
$$62y = 743$$

1 | x | y |

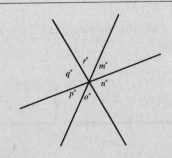

Three lines intersect at a point.

2 | $m + o + q$ | $n + p + r$ |

3 | $(2a + 3b) - (3a + 2b)$ | $(a - b)$ |

Column A	Column B

T is the set of integers from 1 to 80, inclusive.

4 | The number of integers in T that are closer to 25 than to 35 | The number of integers in T that are closer to 35 than to 25 |

5 | $4\sqrt{3}$ | $\sqrt{50}$ |

GO ON TO THE NEXT PAGE

Column A	**Column B**

Car 1 costs p dollars and Car 2 costs q dollars more than Car 1.

6 | $p - q$ | $q - p$ |

$ab = 20$ and $bc = 15$

7 | $\dfrac{12}{a}$ | $\dfrac{9}{c}$ |

Column A	**Column B**

In DABC, side $\overline{AB}$ has length 3 and side $\overline{AC}$ has length 4.

8 | Perimeter of $\triangle ABC$ | 12 |

$x + y = 10$
$x - y = 11$

9 | y | -1 |

---

10 | $2^{19} - 2^{18}$ | 2^{18} |

GO ON TO THE NEXT PAGE

Directions for Student-Produced Response Questions

Each of the remaining 10 questions (16–25) requires you to solve the problem and enter your answer by marking the ovals in the special grid, as shown in the examples below.

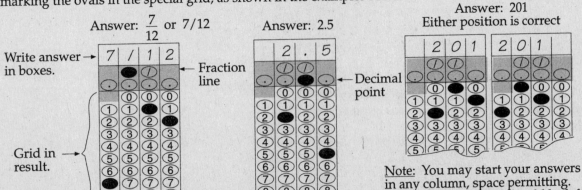

Answer: $\frac{7}{12}$ or 7/12

Write answer → in boxes.

← Fraction line

Grid in → result.

Answer: 2.5

← Decimal point

Answer: 201
Either position is correct

Note: You may start your answers in any column, space permitting. Columns not needed should be left blank.

- Mark no more than one oval in any column.

- Because the answer sheet will be machine-scored, **you will receive credit only if the ovals are filled in correctly.**

- Although not required, it is suggested that you write your answer in the boxes at the top of the columns to help you fill in the ovals accurately.

- Some problems may have more than one correct answer. In such cases, grid only one answer.

- No question has a negative answer.

- **Mixed numbers** such as $2\frac{1}{2}$ must be gridded as 2.5 or 5/2. (If [2 1 / 2] is gridded, it will be interpreted as $\frac{21}{2}$, not $2\frac{1}{2}$.)

- **Decimal Accuracy:** If you obtain a decimal answer, **enter the most accurate value the grid will accommodate.** For example, if you obtain an answer such as 0.6666 . . . , you should record the result as .666 or .667. **Less accurate values such as .66 or .67 are not acceptable.**

Acceptable ways to grid $\frac{2}{3}$ = .6666 . . .

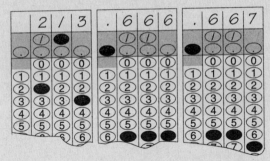

---

11 If $\dfrac{x + 2x + 3x}{2} = 6$, then $x =$

12 There are 24 fish in an aquarium. If $\frac{1}{8}$ of them are tetras and $\frac{2}{3}$ of the remaining fish are guppies, how many guppies are in the aquarium?

GO ON TO THE NEXT PAGE →

13 When n is divided by 5, the remainder is 4. When n is divided by 4, the remainder is 3.
If $0 < n < 100$, what is one possible value of n?

14 If $x^2 = 16$ and $y^2 = 4$, what is the greatest possible value of $(x - y)^2$?

15 Segment AB is perpendicular to segment CD. Segment AB and segment CD bisect each other at point x. If $AB = 6$ and $CD = 8$, what is the length of BD?

16 At a certain high school, 30 students study French, 40 study Spanish, and 25 study neither. If there are 80 students in the school, how many study both French and Spanish.

17 In the figure above, if $AE = 1$, what is the sum of the area of $\triangle ABC$ and the area of $\triangle CDE$?

GO ON TO THE NEXT PAGE

For questions 18-35 solve each problem, using any available space on the page for scratchwork. Then decide which is the best of the choices given and fill in the corresponding oval on the answer sheet.

Notes:
(1)   The use of a calculator is permitted. All numbers used are real numbers.

(2)   Figures that accompany problems in this test are intended to provide information useful in solving the problems. They are drawn as accurately as possible EXCEPT when it is stated in a specific problem that the figure is not drawn to scale. All figures lie in a plane unless otherwise indicated.

---

18   If $8 + x = 12$, then $4 - x =$

(A) -8
(B) -4
(C) 0
(D) 4
(E) 8

---

19 $\dfrac{1}{5} + \dfrac{2}{25} + \dfrac{3}{50} =$

(A) 0.170
(B) 0.240
(C) 0.320
(D) 0.340
(E) 0.463

---

20   What number is exactly in the middle of the set of consecutive whole numbers from 20 to 100, inclusive?

(A) 40
(B) 50
(C) 55
(D) 60
(E) 80

---

21   What are the coordinates of B if $\overline{A\,OB}$ is a straight line and the measure of $\overline{BO}$ is equal to the measure of $\overline{A\,O}$?

(A) $(-x, -y)$
(B) $(-x, y)$
(C) $(x, -y)$
(D) (x, y)
(E) $(y, -x)$

---

22   An hour long call to Smithtown from Jonestown at the normal day rate costs $12.50. If Bill calls at night and talks for one hour, how much does he pay if the company gives a 40% discount for night calls?

(A) $5.00
(B) $7.50
(C) $12.10
(D) $12.90
(E) $17.50

GO ON TO THE NEXT PAGE

–375–

23 Ann scored 82, 85, 92, and 95 on her first 4 tests. What grade must she get on her other test to earn an average (arithmetic mean) of 90 for all 5 tests.

(A) 88
(B) 89
(C) 92
(D) 95
(E) 96

24 Jill has twice as many sand dollars as Carla. After Jill gives Carla 8 sand dollars, Jill still has 6 more sand dollars than Carla. How many sand dollars did Carla have originally?

(A) 14
(B) 16
(C) 18
(D) 20
(E) 22

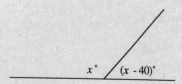

Note: Figure not drawn to scale

25 In the figure above, $x =$

(A) 70
(B) 110
(C) 130
(D) 135
(E) 140

26 A 30-inch by 40-inch rectangular kitchen counter is to be competely covered with 1-inch square tiles, which cannot overlap one another and cannot overhang the counter. If white tiles are to cover the center of the counter, and red tiles are to form a 1-inch wide border along the edges of the counter, how many red tiles will be used?

(A) 70
(B) 136
(C) 140
(D) 142
(E) 144

27 At Clinton College, 50% of the students have radios. Of the students who have radios, 30% have televisions. What percentage of the students at Clinton College have both a radio and a television?

(A) 15
(B) 20
(C) 25
(D) 40
(E) 80

GO ON TO THE NEXT PAGE

28 If a car's odometer reads 73,333 miles, what is the LEAST number of miles the car must travel before four digits on the odometer are identical again?

(A)　　99
(B)　　444
(C)　　666
(D)　1,111
(E)　4,444

29 $\dfrac{1}{10^{100}} - \dfrac{1}{10^{99}}$

(A) $\dfrac{-9}{10^{100}}$　(B) $\dfrac{-1}{10^{100}}$　(C) $\dfrac{1}{10^{100}}$

(D) $\dfrac{1}{10}$　(E) $\dfrac{9}{10}$

30 The figure above is made of 3 concentric semi-circles. What is the area of the shaded region?

(A) 3π

(B) $\dfrac{9}{2}\pi$

(C) 6π

(D) 7π

(E) 9π

31 If, for all real numbers p and q,

$p \oslash q = 3pq - (p + 2q)$, which of the following must be true?

I. $q \oslash q = 3q(q-1)$
II. $0 \oslash q = 0$
III. $q \oslash q = 2q$

(A) I only
(B) II only
(C) II and III only
(D) I and III only
(E) I, II, and III

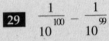

32 In the figure above, what is the sum of the degree measures of the marked angles?

(A) 180
(B) 270
(C) 360
(D) 540
(E) It cannot be determined from
　　　the information given.

GO ON TO THE NEXT PAGE

33 If twice the length of the shortest leg of a right triangle is equal to $\frac{3}{2}$ the length of the other leg, what is the ratio of the length of the longer leg to the length of the hypotenuse of the triangle?

(A) $\frac{1}{3}$

(B) $\frac{2}{3}$

(C) $\frac{4}{5}$

(D) 1

(E) $\frac{3}{2}$

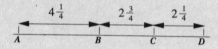

Note: Figure not drawn to scale

34 On the straight line in the figure above, if P is the midpoint of $\overline{BC}$ and Q is the midpoint of $\overline{AD}$, what is the length of $\overline{PQ}$?

(A) $5\frac{5}{8}$ (B) $2\frac{1}{2}$ (C) 2   (D) 1   (E) $\frac{1}{2}$

35 Jim's recipe for cranberry-grape juice calls for 4 cups of grape juice for every 7 cups of cranberry juice. He wants to make 132 ounces of cranberry-grape juice, but realizes that he is short by exactly 4 cups of cranberry juice. How many ounces of cranberry juice does he have? (1 cup = 8 ounces)

(A) 32
(B) 52
(C) 56
(D) 84
(E) 132

IF YOU FINISH BEFORE TIME IS CALLED, YOU MAY CHECK YOUR WORK ON THIS SECTION ONLY. DO NOT TURN TO ANY OTHER SECTION IN THE TEST. **STOP**

NO TEST MATERIAL ON THIS PAGE

MATHEMATICS TEST

30 Minutes—27 Questions

DIRECTIONS: Solve each problem, choose the correct answer and then darken the corresponding oval on your answer sheet.

Do not linger over problems that take too much time. Solve as many as you can; then return to the others in the time you have left fot this test.

Note: Unless otherwise stated, all of the following should be assumed.

1. Illustrative figures are NOT necessarily drawn to scale.
2. Geometric figures lie in a plane.
3. The word *line* indicates a straight line.
4. The word *average* indicates arithmetic mean.

DO YOUR FIGURING HERE.

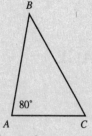

1. In the figure above, the measure of ∠A is 80°. If the measure of ∠B is half the measure of ∠A, what is the measure of ∠C?

 A. 40°
 B. 60°
 C. 80°
 D. 100°
 E. 120°

2. A plumber charges $75 for the first thirty minutes of each house call plus $2 for each additional minute that she works. The plumber charges Adam $113 for her time. For what amount of time, in minutes, did the plumber work?

 F. 38
 G. 44
 H. 49
 J. 59
 K. 64

GO ON TO THE NEXT PAGE.

3. $\sqrt{64 + 36}$ = ?

   A.   10
   B.   14
   C.   28
   D.   48
   E.   100

4. $4.326 \div 0.2$ = ?

   F.   0.2163
   G.   2.163
   H.   21.63
   J.   216.3
   K. 2,163.0

5. If $x = -2$, then $3x^2 - 5x - 6$ = ?

   A. -30
   B. -8
   C. -4
   D.   10
   E.   16

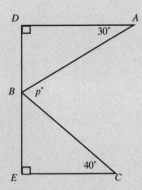

6. In the figure above, D, B, and E are colinear. What is the measure of $\angle p$?

   F. 20°
   G. 35°
   H. 50°
   J. 60°
   K. 70°

GO ON TO THE NEXT PAGE.

7. A rectangular garden is surrounded by a 60 foot long fence. One side of the garden is 6 feet longer than the other. Which of the following equations could be used to find s, the shorter side, of the garden?

    A. $8s + s = 60$
    B. $4s = 60 + 12$
    C. $s(s + 6) = 60$
    D. $2(s - 6) + 2s = 60$
    E. $2(s + 6) + 2s = 60$

8. Property tax is 8% of the assessed value of a house. How much would the property tax be on a house with an assessed value of $80,000?

    F. $100
    G. $640
    H. $1,000
    J. $6,400
    K. $10,000

9. For all x, $(10x^4 - x^2 + 2x - 8) - (3x^4 + 3x^3 + 2x + 8) = ?$

    A. $7x^4 - 3x^3 - x^2 - 16$
    B. $7x^4 - 4x^2 - 16$
    C. $7x^4 + 3x^3 - x^2 + 4x$
    D. $7x^4 + 2x^2 + 4x$
    E. $13x^4 - 3x^3 - x^2 + 4x$

10. If $\sqrt[N]{48} = 2\sqrt[N]{3}$, then $N = ?$

    F. 1
    G. 2
    H. 3
    J. 4
    K. 5

DO YOUR FIGURING HERE.

GO ON TO THE NEXT PAGE.

11. Which of the following is the sum of both solutions to the equation $x^2 - 2x - 8 = 0$?

    A. -6
    B. -4
    C. -2
    D. 2
    E. 6

12. After N chocolate bars are divided equally among 6 children, 3 bars remain. How many would remain if $(N + 4)$ chocolate bars were divided equally among the 6 children?

    F. 0
    G. 1
    H. 2
    J. 3
    K. 4

13. For all $y \neq 3$, $\dfrac{y^2 - 9}{3y - 9} = ?$

    A. y

    B. $\dfrac{y + 1}{8}$

    C. $y + 1$

    D. $\dfrac{y}{3}$

    E. $\dfrac{y + 3}{3}$

DO YOUR FIGURING HERE.

GO ON TO THE NEXT PAGE.

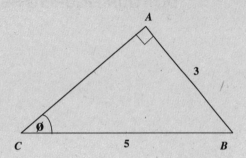

14. In the figure above, $\angle A$ is a right angle. $\overline{AB}$ is 3 units long and $\overline{BC}$ is 5 units long. If the measure of $\angle C$ is Ø, what is the value of cosØ?

    F. $\dfrac{3}{5}$

    G. $\dfrac{3}{4}$

    H. $\dfrac{4}{5}$

    J. $\dfrac{5}{4}$

    K. $\dfrac{5}{3}$

15. The hypotenuse of an isosceles right triangle has a length of 20 units. What is the length of one of the legs of the triangle?

    A.   10
    B. $10\sqrt{2}$
    C. $10\sqrt{3}$
    D.   20
    E. $20\sqrt{2}$

16. What is the y-intercept of the line determined by the equation $5x + 2 = 7y - 3$?

    F. -1

    G. $-\dfrac{1}{7}$

    H. $\dfrac{1}{7}$

    J. $\dfrac{5}{7}$

    K.   5

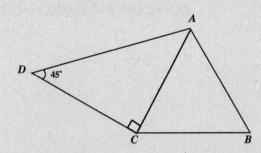

17. In the figure above, $\triangle ABC$ is an equilateral triangle with $\overline{BC}$ 7 units long. If $\angle DCA$ is a right angle and $\angle D$ measures 45°, what is the length of $\overline{AD}$, in units?

    A. 7
    B. $7\sqrt{2}$
    C. 14
    D. $14\sqrt{2}$
    E. It cannot be determined from the information given.

18. What graph would be created if the equation $x^2 + y^2 = 12$ were graphed in the standard (x, y) coordinate plane?

    F. Circle
    G. Ellipse
    H. Parabola
    J. Straight line
    K. 2 rays forming a "V"

19. The formula for calculating sales tax is $S = Ar$, where S is the sales tax, A is the cost of the product, and r is the local sales-tax rate. If the cost of a television was $400 and the sales tax was $24, what was the local sales-tax rate?

    A.   .60%
    B. 1.67%
    C. 6.00%
    D. 16.67%
    E. 60.00%

GO ON TO THE NEXT PAGE.

20. Grace tried to compute the average of her 5 test scores. She mistakenly divided the correct total (T) of her scores by 6 and her result was 14 less than what it should have been. Which of the following equations would determine the value of T?

DO YOUR FIGURING HERE.

F. $5T + 14 = 6T$

G. $\dfrac{T}{6} = \dfrac{(T-14)}{5}$

H. $\dfrac{T}{6} - 14 = \dfrac{T}{5}$

J. $\dfrac{(T-14)}{6} = \dfrac{T}{5}$

K. $\dfrac{T}{6} + 14 = \dfrac{T}{5}$

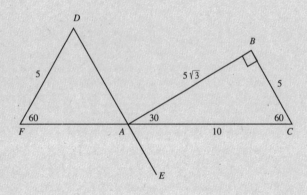

21. In the figure above, $\angle B$ is a right angle, $\overline{BC}$ is parallel to $\overline{DE}$, and $\angle C$ and $\angle F$ both measure 60°. If $\overline{BC}$ and $\overline{DF}$ both measure 5 units, what is the sine of $\angle C$?

A. $\dfrac{1}{2}$

B. $\dfrac{\sqrt{3}}{2}$

C. 5

D. 30°

E. 60°

GO ON TO THE NEXT PAGE.

22. Which of the following represents the solution to the inequality $x^2 - 9x + 8 < 0$?

DO YOUR FIGURING HERE.

F. $-8 < x < -1$

G. $\dfrac{-1}{8} < x < 1$

H. $1 < x < 8$

J. $x < 8$ or $x > 1$

K. $x < -1$ or $x > 8$

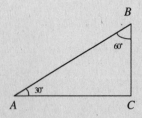

23. In the figure above, the measure of $\angle A$ is 30° and the measure of $\angle B$ is 60°. If $\overline{AC}$ is 6 units long, what is the measure of $\overline{BC}$, in units?

A. 3
B. $2\sqrt{3}$
C. $3\sqrt{3}$
D. 6
E. $6\sqrt{3}$

24. A line in the standard (x, y) coordinate plane has the same slope as the line $12 = 3y - 7x$. If the line passes through the point $(3, 6)$, what is its y-intercept?

F. -3

G. $-\dfrac{7}{3}$

H. -1

J. 1

K. $\dfrac{7}{3}$

GO ON TO THE NEXT PAGE.

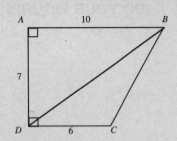

25. In the figure above, $\angle A$ and $\angle ADC$ are right angles, the length of $\overline{AD}$ is 7 units, the length of $\overline{AB}$ is 10 units, and the length of $\overline{DC}$ is 6 units. What is the area, in square units, of $\triangle DCB$?

    A.   21
    B.   24
    C. $3\sqrt{149}$
    D.   42
    E.   210

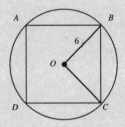

26. In the figure above, $ABCD$ is a square inscribed in the circle centered at O. If $\overline{OB}$ is 6 units long, how many units long is minor arc BC?

    F. $\dfrac{3}{2}\pi$

    G. 3π

    H. 6π

    J. 12π

    K. 36π

GO ON TO THE NEXT PAGE.

27. At what point (x, y) do the two lines with equations
$y = 2x - 2$ and $7x - 3y = 11$ intersect?

DO YOUR FIGURING HERE.

   A. $(5, 8)$

   B. $(8, 5)$

   C. $\left(\dfrac{5}{8}, -1 \right)$

   D. $\left(\dfrac{5}{8}, 1 \right)$

   E. $\left(\dfrac{25}{16}, \dfrac{9}{8} \right)$

END OF TEST 3
STOP! DO NOT TURN THE PAGE UNTIL TOLD TO DO SO.

Time — 30 Minutes
35 Questions

For each question in this section, select the best answer from among the choices given and fill in the corresponding oval on the answer sheet.

Each sentence below has one or two blanks, each blank indicating that something has been omitted. Beneath the sentence are five words or sets of words labeled A through E. Choose the word or set of words that, when inserted in the sentence, <u>best</u> fits the meaning of the sentence as a whole.

Example:

Medieval kingdoms did not become constitutional republics overnight; on the contrary, the change was ----.

(A) unpopular
(B) unexpected
(C) advantageous
(D) sufficient
(E) gradual

1. There is no place in today's active society for idle and dependent ---- who would like nothing more than to sit back and leave all the tasks and responsibilities to more energetic souls.

   (A) introverts
   (B) athletes
   (C) sluggards
   (D) vertebrates
   (E) cowards

2. Although our excuses for arriving late to the party seemed ---- enough, it was obvious to everyone that our disappointed hostess did not believe us.

   (A) rigid
   (B) far-fetched
   (C) plausible
   (D) mature
   (E) obtuse

3. Despite the efforts of family and friends to enliven him, Wilson remained ---- in his ----.

   (A) vulnerable. .unease
   (B) content. .anger
   (C) mired. .depression
   (D) obdurate. .zest
   (E) steadfast. .enjoyment

4. Certain animal behaviors, such as mating rituals, seem to be ----, and therefore ---- external factors such as climate changes, food supply, or the presence of other animals of the same species.

   (A) learned. .immune to
   (B) innate. .unaffected by
   (C) intricate. .belong to
   (D) specific. .confused with
   (E) memorized. .controlled by

5. While many of today's critics busy themselves ---- the death of classical music, composers the world over are producing exciting, often brilliant work that due to its lack of ---- appeal, goes unnoticed by the established critical community.

   (A) ignoring. .popular
   (B) proclaiming. .mainstream
   (C) enjoying. .borderline
   (D) mourning. .cryptic
   (E) avoiding. .musical

6. The new nation is attempting to ---- its present and its past, to mix age-old traditions with ---- political realities.

   (A) compare. .unknown
   (B) reconcile. .contemporary
   (C) understand. .fundamental
   (D) denounce. .modern
   (E) dislodge. .uncertain

7. Paradoxically, much social etiquette involves inverting traditional virtues and vices: tact, for instance, inevitably entails ----, whereas what is commonly condemned as a lack of tact is nothing more than ----.

   (A) politeness. .curiosity
   (B) humility. .humor
   (C) generosity. .beneficence
   (D) lying. .honesty
   (E) ingenuity. .prying

GO ON TO THE NEXT PAGE

8 Despite a marked increase in efforts to stem the tide of unwanted domestic animals that are born every day, and despite ---- evidence of a slower birth-rate, the sheer number of animals has risen so sharply in recent years that even the most committed of animal advocates is ---- of ever solving the problem.

(A) depressing. .hopeful
(B) disheartening. .lessening
(C) overwhelming. .confident
(D) encouraging. .despairing
(E) ambiguous. .unsure

9 A truly ---- writer, Shakespeare has something to say to all people of whatever time, culture, or race.

(A) celebrated
(B) catholic
(C) soporific
(D) experienced
(E) artful

10 Modern evolutionary biologists have shifted from ---- mirroring Darwin's ideas to actually ---- elaborate innovative theories that call into question the very foundations of Darwinian evolution.

(A) knowingly. .inscribing
(B) utterly. .defoliating
(C) overtly. .implementing
(D) naturally. .selecting
(E) merely. .formulating

11 Only when one actually visits the ancient ruins of marvelous bygone civilizations does one truly appreciate the sad ---- of human greatness.

(A) perspicacity
(B) magnitude
(C) artistry
(D) transience
(E) quiescence

GO ON TO THE NEXT PAGE

Each question below consists of a related pair of words or phrases, followed by five pairs of words or phrases labeled A through E. Select the pair that best expresses a relationship similar to that expressed in the original pair.

Example:

CRUMB : BREAD ::
(A) ounce : unit
(B) splinter : wood
(C) water : bucket
(D) twine : rope
(E) cream : butter

12 LABORATORY : SCIENTIST ::
(A) hospital : patient
(B) desktop : writer
(C) apartment : tenant
(D) ladder : painter
(E) classroom : teacher

13 CLIMAX : DRAMA ::
(A) plateau : land
(B) tension : scene
(C) peak : mountain
(D) suspense : movie
(E) tragedy : theatre

14 THERMOMETER : TEMPERATURE ::
(A) radio : news
(B) fahrenheit : degrees
(C) scale : weight
(D) hourglass : sand
(E) barometer : rain

15 ALLOY : METALS ::
(A) carat : gold
(B) compound : elements
(C) atom : chemicals
(D) germ : disease
(E) tree : blossom

16 PHARMACIST : PRESCRIPTION ::
(A) chef : order
(B) seamstress : stocking
(C) juror : defense
(D) driver : auto
(E) disciplinarian : prohibition

17 IRASCIBLE : PROVOKE ::
(A) angry : violate
(B) desirable : tempt
(C) sad : fury
(D) intolerant : initiate
(E) docile : lead

18 INVALUABLE : ASSESS ::
(A) incorrigible : lie
(B) important : enjoy
(C) insatiable : satisfy
(D) innovative : change
(E) indescribable : appreciate

19 VOLATILE : VAPORIZED ::
(A) oily : dried
(B) combustible : smoked
(C) concave : curved
(D) diverse : concentrated
(E) malleable : molded

20 FOMENT : AGITATION ::
(A) ossify : fission
(B) contain : division
(C) cohere : remission
(D) disperse : separation
(E) view : magnification

20 ORDER : CHAOS ::
(A) anarchy : power
(B) distaste : enmity
(C) sadness : fury
(D) diffidence : confidence
(E) dilemma : confusion

22 APOCRYPHAL : AUTHENTICITY ::
(A) casual : attire
(B) unique : precedent
(C) destruction : bomb
(D) lucid : truth
(E) catastrophic : power

23 PERSPICACITY : DISCERNING ::
(A) ravishing : attractive
(B) infatuation : distasteful
(C) perspiration : moist
(D) pursuing : desisting
(E) graceful : dancing

GO ON TO THE NEXT PAGE →

NO TEST MATERIAL ON THIS PAGE.

GO ON TO THE NEXT PAGE →

Each passage below is followed by questions based on its content. Answer the questions on the basis of what is <u>stated</u> or <u>implied</u> in the passage and in any introductory material that may be provided.

Questions 24-28 are based on the following passage.

The following passage describes a conversation between a young student and his private tutor.

What Morgan said at last was said suddenly, irrelevantly, when the moment came, in the middle of a lesson, and consisted of the apparently unfeeling words: "You ought to *filer*, you know—you really ought."

Line
(5)　Pemberton stared. He had learnt enough French slang from Morgan to know that to *filer* meant to go away. "Why should I do that?"

Morgan pulled a Greek dictionary toward him, to look up a word, instead of asking it of Pemberton. "You can't
(10)　go on like this, you know."

"Like what, my boy?"

"You know they don't pay you up," said Morgan, blushing and turning his leaves.

"Don't pay me?" Pemberton stared again and feigned
(15)　amazement. "What on earth put that into your head?"

"It has been there a long time," the boy replied, continuing his search.

Pemberton was silent, then he went on: "I say, what are you hunting for? Your parents pay me beautifully."

(20)　"I'm hunting for the Greek for transparent fiction," Morgan dropped.

"Find that rather for gross impertinence, and disabuse your mind. What do I want of money?"

"Oh, that's another question!"

(25)　Pemberton hesitated—he was drawn in different ways. The severely correct thing would have been to tell the boy that such a matter was none of his business and bid him go on with his lines. But they were really too intimate for that; it was not the way he was in the habit
(30)　of treating him; there had been no reason it should be. On the other hand Morgan had quite lighted on the truth—he really shouldn't be able to keep it up much longer; therefore why not let him know one's real motive for forsaking him? At the same time it wasn't
(35)　decent to abuse to one's pupil the family of one's pupil; it was better to misrepresent than to do that. So in reply to Morgan's last exclamation he just declared, to dismiss the subject, that he had received several payments.

24　Morgan tells Pemberton to *filer* (line 4) because he:

(A) doesn't think Pemberton will understand him.
(B) seeks a better tutor.
(C) wishes to be left alone.
(D) is concerned with Pemberton's interests.
(E) plans to abandon his parents also.

25　When Morgan says, "I'm hunting for the Greek for transparent fiction," (line 20) his attitude is most likely one of:

(A) pointed sarcasm.
(B) probing intelligence.
(C) supreme indifference.
(D) benign negligence.
(E) casual regard.

GO ON TO THE NEXT PAGE

26 According to the passage Pemberton may be forced to forsake Morgan because he:

(A) fears an unpleasant confrontation with Morgan's parents.

(B) can no longer tolerate Morgan's gross impertinences.

(C) refuses to apologize for verbally abusing his employers.

(D) is not receiving due payments for his tutoring.

(E) disapproves of Morgan's incessant use of slang.

27 According to the passage, Pemberton chooses "to misrepresent" (lines 35–36) because he:

(A) believes it is discourteous to criticize Morgan's parents.

(B) is obligated to protect Morgan from painful discoveries.

(C) intends to demonstrate his authority over Morgan.

(D) wishes to conceal his duplicity from Morgan and his parents.

(E) hopes it will successfully instruct Morgan in the ways of the world.

28 It can be inferred from the passage that Pemberton is least likely to be which of the following?

(A) respectful

(B) erudite

(C) selfish

(D) anxious

(E) evasive

GO ON TO THE NEXT PAGE

Questions 29-33 are based on the following passage.

This passage discusses a number of theories on the subject of dreaming, many of which challenge established notions of the scientific community.

The phenomenon of dreaming has long fascinated philosophers and scientists. The ancients believed that dreams were messages from the gods or portents of
Line one's future. Nineteenth and twentieth century
(5) scientists have sought rational explanations—the first such effort to receive wide acceptance was Sigmund Freud's psychoanalytic theory. Freud called dreams "the royal road to the unconscious," by which he meant that dreams lead the way to a realm of mental
(10) functioning where our fantasies, emotional conflicts, repressed memories, and infantile impulses find expression. Through condensation, displacement, and symbol formation, troubling and fantastic thoughts evade the vigilant censor that keeps us largely unaware
(15) of them in our waking moments.

Recently, however, cognitive psychologists have challenged Freud's ideas. They point out that cats in laboratory experiments have been repeatedly shown to dream. So, in fact, have all other mammals except one:
(20) the anteater, which has a tiny brain. In addition, newborn infants spend half the day dreaming. These organisms do not have unconscious conflicts of the type Freud described, but during sleep they show obvious signs of dreaming. For example, when humans dream,
(25) their eyes dart around. This period of sleep, called Rapid Eye Movement (REM) sleep, is one of the most reliable signs that a person is dreaming and also is part of the sleeping pattern of almost all mammals. It happens at regular intervals: every hour and a half for a
(30) human, for instance, or every twelve minutes for a rat. Some researchers have even linked acetylcholine, a neurotransmitter in the brain, to dreaming. All of this research suggests that the cause of dreaming is physiological, rather than emotional.

(35) Others have proposed different alternatives. They suggest that the brain functions in some ways like an enormous computer, and that REM sleep is a way of "dumping" unwanted data that could otherwise overload the system. With 50 billion neurons and ten times that
(40) many glial cells wiring them all together, the brain is capable of taking on huge amounts of information. But like a computer, it has a finite capacity for storing information, and REM sleep may be a way that the brain "clears out" unusable data in order to free itself to attend
(45) new tasks during waking hours.

29 The passage primarily concerns:

(A) Sigmund Freud's psychoanalytic theories.
(B) the effect of dreams on the personality.
(C) the attempts of psychologists to explain dreaming.
(D) the role of REM sleep in dreaming.
(E) the similarities of computers to the brain.

30 "Condensation, displacement, and symbol formation" (lines 12–13) are probably:

(A) an attempt by Freud to make his theories sound more scientific than they in fact were.
(B) terms that Freud used to explain the process by which feelings find expression in dreams.
(C) universally accepted explanations for the fantastic images that occur during dreaming.
(D) simplistic attempts to account for a complex process.
(E) repressed material that is found in the unconscious.

31 The two new theories outlined in the passage challenge Freud's belief that:

(A) dreams must be primarily understood as an attempt to come to terms with unconscious material.
(B) we dream in order to find out about ourselves.
(C) dreams originate in a specific area of the brain.
(D) researchers have discovered the place in the brain where repressed memories are stored.
(E) the conscious mind represses unpleasant thoughts.

GO ON TO THE NEXT PAGE

32 The author would most likely argue that the reason an anteater does not dream is that:

(A) it lacks the type of unconscious conflict Freud describes.

(B) neurotransmitters other than acetylcholine have been found in anteaters' brains.

(C) its brain is not complex enough to support the mechanisms that cause dreams.

(D) anteaters' REM sleep differs from that of humans or rats.

(E) its glial cells outnumber its neurons ten to one.

33 The author's attitude toward Sigmund Freud's theories could best be described as:

(A) skeptical

(B) emotional

(C) envious

(D) indifferent

(E) admiration

GO ON TO THE NEXT PAGE

Each passage below is followed by questions based on its content. Answer the questions on the basis of what is <u>stated</u> or <u>implied</u> in the passage and in any introductory material that may be provided.

Questions 34-46 are based on the following passages.

In passage 1, the author presents his view of the early years of the silent film industry. In passage 2, the author draws on her experiences as a mime to generalize about her art. (A mime is a performer who, without speaking, entertains through gesture, facial expression, and movement.)

Passage 1

Talk to those people who first saw films when they were silent, and they will tell you the experience was magic. The silent film had extraordinary powers to draw
Line members of an audience into the story, and an equally
(5) potent capacity to make their imaginations work. It required the audience to become engaged—to supply voices and sound effects. The audience was the final, creative contributor to the process of making a film.

The finest films of the silent era depended on two
(10) elements that we can seldom provide today—a large and receptive audience and a well-orchestrated score. For the audience, the fusion of picture and live music added up to more than the sum of the respective parts.

The one word that sums up the attitude of the silent
(15) filmmakers is *enthusiasm*, conveyed most strongly before formulas took shape and when there was more room for experimentation. This enthusiastic uncertainty often resulted in such accidental discoveries as new camera or editing techniques. Some films experimented
(20) with players; the 1915 film *Regeneration*, for example, by using real gangsters and streetwalkers, provided startling local color. Other films, particularly those of Thomas Ince, provided tragic endings as often as films by other companies supplied happy ones.

(25) Unfortunately, the vast majority of silent films survive today in inferior prints that no longer reflect the care that the original technicians put into them. The modern versions of silent films may appear jerky and flickery, but the vast picture palaces did not attract four
(30) to six thousand people a night by giving them eyestrain. A silent film depended on its visuals; as soon as you degrade those, you lose elements that go far beyond the image on the surface. The acting in silents was often very subtle, very restrained, despite legends to the
(35) contrary.

Passage 2

Mime opens up a new world to the beholder, but it does so insidiously, not by purposely injecting points of interest in the manner of a tour guide. Audiences are not unlike visitors to a foreign land who discover that the
(40) modes, manners, and thoughts of its inhabitants are not meaningless oddities, but are sensible in context.

I remember once when an audience seemed perplexed at what I was doing. At first, I tried to gain a more immediate response by using slight exaggerations. I
(45) soon realized that these actions had nothing to do with the audience's understanding of the character. What I had believed to be a failure of the audience to respond in the manner I expected was, in fact, only their concentration on what I was doing; they were enjoying
(50) a gradual awakening—a slow transference of their understanding from their own time and place to one that appeared so unexpectedly before their eyes. This was evidenced by their growing response to succeeding numbers.

(55) Mime is an elusive art, as its expression is entirely dependent on the ability of the performer to imagine a character and to re-create that character for each performance. As a mime, I am a physical medium, the instrument upon which the figures of my imagination
(60) play their dance of life. The individuals in my audience also have responsibilities—they must be alert collaborators. They cannot sit back, mindlessly complacent, and wait to have their emotions titillated by mesmeric musical sounds or visual rhythms or acrobatic
(70) feats, or by words that tell them what to think. Mime is an art that, paradoxically, appeals both to those who respond instinctively to entertainment and to those whose appreciation is more analytical and complex. Between these extremes lie those audiences conditioned
(75) to resist any collaboration with what is played before them; and these the mime must seduce despite themselves. There is only one way to attack those reluctant minds—take them unaware! They will be delighted at an unexpected pleasure.

GO ON TO THE NEXT PAGE

34 Lines 12-15 of passage 1 indicate that:

   (A) music was the most important element of silent films.

   (B) silent films rely on a combination of music and image in affecting an audience.

   (C) the importance of music in silent film has been overestimated.

   (D) live music compensated for the poor quality of silent film images.

   (E) no film can succeed without a receptive audience.

35 The "formulas" mentioned in line 16 of the passage most probably refer to:

   (A) movie theaters.

   (B) use of real characters.

   (C) standardized film techniques.

   (D) the fusion of disparate elements.

   (E) contemporary events.

36 The author uses the phrase *enthusiastic uncertainty* in line 17 to suggest that the filmmakers were:

   (A) excited to be experimenting in an undefined area.

   (B) delighted at the opportunity to study new acting formulas.

   (C) optimistic in spite of the obstacles that faced them.

   (D) eager to challenge existing conventions.

   (E) eager to please but unsure of what the public wanted.

37 The author uses the phrase *but the . . . eyestrain* (lines 29–30) in order to:

   (A) indicate his disgust with the incompetence of early film technicians.

   (B) suggest that audiences today perceive silent films incorrectly.

   (C) convey his regret about the decline of the old picture palaces.

   (D) highlight the pitfalls of the silent movie era.

   (E) argue for the superiority of modern film technology over that of silent movies.

38 The word *legends* in line 34 most nearly means:

   (A) arguments

   (B) symbolism

   (C) propaganda

   (D) movie stars

   (E) misconceptions

39 The last sentence of passage 1 implies that:

   (A) the stars of silent movies have been criticized for overacting.

   (B) many silent film actors became legends in their own time.

   (C) silent film techniques should be studied by filmmakers today.

   (D) visual effects defined the silent film.

   (E) many silent films that exist today are of poor quality.

40 The word *restrained* (line 34) most nearly means:

   (A) sincere

   (B) dramatic

   (C) understated

   (D) inexpressive

   (E) consistent

41 The author mentions the incident in lines 42–54 in order to imply that:

   (A) the audience's lack of response was a positive sign and reflected their captivated interest in the performance.

   (B) she was forced to resort to stereotypes in order to reach an audience that was otherwise unattainable.

   (C) exaggeration is an essential part of mime because it allows the forums used to be fully expressed.

   (D) her audience, though not initially appearing knowledgeable, had a good understanding of the subtlety of mime.

   (E) although vocalization is not necessary in mime, it is sometimes helpful for slower audiences.

GO ON TO THE NEXT PAGE

42 Lines 42–54 indicate that the author of passage 2 and the silent filmmakers of passage 1 were similar because:

(A) neither used many props.

(B) both conveyed universal truths by using sophisticated technology.

(C) for both, trial and error was a part of the learning process.

(D) both used visual effects and dialogue.

(E) both had a loyal following.

43 The sentence *As a . . . life* (lines 58–60) suggests that the author of passage 2 feels mimes:

(A) cannot control the way audiences interpret their characters.

(B) must suspend their own identities in order to successfully portray their characters.

(C) have to resist outside attempts to define their acting style.

(D) should focus on important events in the lives of specific characters.

(E) know the limitations of performances that do not incorporate either music or speech.

44 Which of the following pieces of information makes mime and silent film seem less similar?

(A) Vaudeville and theatrical presentations were also popular forms of entertainment during the silent film era.

(B) Silent films presented both fictional drama and factual information.

(C) Silent film sometimes relied on captions to convey dialogue to the audience.

(D) Musicians working in movie theaters were usually employed for long periods of time.

(E) Many of the characters in silent films gained wide popularity among moviegoers.

45 Passages 1 and 2 are similar in that both are mainly concerned with:

(A) the use of special effects.

(B) differences among dramatic styles.

(C) the visual aspects of performance.

(D) the suspension of disbelief in audiences.

(E) nostalgia for a bygone era.

46 Which of the following is an element that figures in the success of the dramatic arts described in both passages?

(A) A successful combination of different dramatic styles

(B) The exaggeration of certain aspects of a character

(C) The incorporation of current events in the narrative

(D) High audience attendance

(E) The active participation of the audience

IF YOU FINISH BEFORE TIME IS CALLED, YOU MAY CHECK YOUR WORK ON THIS SECTION ONLY. DO NOT TURN TO ANY OTHER SECTION IN THE TEST. STOP

NO TEST MATERIAL ON THIS PAGE.

SCIENTIFIC REASONING TEST
30 Minutes—34 Questions

DIRECTIONS: There are six passages in the following section. Each passage is followed by several questions. After reading a passage, choose the best answer to each question and blacken the corresponding oval on your answer sheet. You may refer to the passages as often as necessary.

Passage I

Four different strains of bacteria were raised in petri dishes at different temperatures (10°, 20°, 30°, & 40° C). Four sets of experiments were conducted. At each temperature, each strain was placed in a separate petri dish in a lighted chamber. They were each taken out of the chamber after one hour and the number of living organisms in each dish was counted, using approximation techniques. The results are shown in Figure 1.

A researcher also used these data to approximate the growth rates of these bacteria strains within each tested temperature. *Growth rate* represents the percentage increase in the total number of organisms in the experimental dish. Table 1 shows the growth rates, during the test period of one hour, for each strain at 40° C.

During this experiment, the only *limiting factor* was food supply. So, the total growth of these bacteria populations was limited by the available food supply. If a population uses up its food supply, the growth rate declines and the organisms die. In this experiment some test strains used up all of the petri dish medium (their food supply) within the test period of 1 hour.

Note: Each petri dish began with approximately 1,000 organisms.

Table 1

Strain 1	Strain 2	Strain 3	Strain 4
400%	650%	800%	0%

Growth rate at 40° C

Figure 1

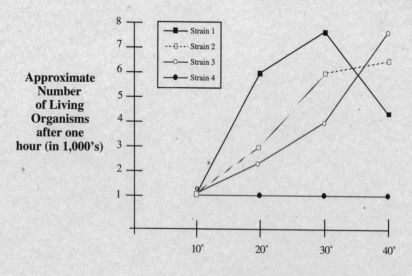

Temperature in ° C

GO ON TO THE NEXT PAGE.

1. Given the test conditions of the experiment, which temperature produces the maximum growth in Strain 1?

   A. 30° C
   B. 35° C
   C. 40° C
   D. It cannot be determined from the information given.

2. If Strain 1 was kept at 40° C for a period of time longer than one hour and all other test conditions remained constant, what would you expect to find?

   F. More organisms than the total in the initial trial at 40° C
   G. Fewer organisms than the total in the initial trial at 40° C
   H. Approximately the same total number of organisms as in the initial trial at 40° C
   J. Approximately the same total number of organisms as in the initial trial at 10° C

3. At which temperatures do Stains 2 and 3 exhibit the same <u>growth</u> <u>rate</u>?

   A. 10° C
   B. Between 10° C and 20° C
   C. 20° C
   D. Between 20° and 30° C

4. Some bacteria are sensitive to light and will not grow in a lighted environment. Of the strains used in this experiment, which types of bacteria are NOT light-sensitive?

   F. Strain 3 only
   G. Strain 4 only
   H. Strains 1, 2, and 3 only
   J. Strains 2, 3, and 4 only

5. Which test strains show signs of being affected by a limiting factor present in this experiment?

   A. Strain 1 only
   B. Strain 4 only
   C. Strains 1 and 2 only
   D. Strains 1, 2, 3, and 4

6. To clarify the bacteria's dependence on food supply, the researcher continued these experiments using petri dishes large enough to contain an unlimited supply of food. Given these conditions, how many organisms of Strain 3 bacteria would exist after one hour at 40° C?

   F. 4,000
   G. 8,000
   H. 10,000
   J. 16,000

GO ON TO THE NEXT PAGE.

Passage II

In the full electromagnetic spectrum, waves vary greatly in length and frequency. Radio waves, which can measure up to many miles, are approximately 10 million times longer than visible light rays, which are 10 million times longer than gamma rays. How we use waves are indicative of these characteristics. For instance, television, AM/FM broadcasts, and short-wave signals are types of radio waves which can travel long distances.

Visible light rays are composed of several waves at different wavelengths. White light can be refracted through a prism to display the different color components of the light. Each color band represents a distinct wavelength. Figure 1 below depicts the wavelengths (cm) and frequencies (cycles/second) of some common waves.

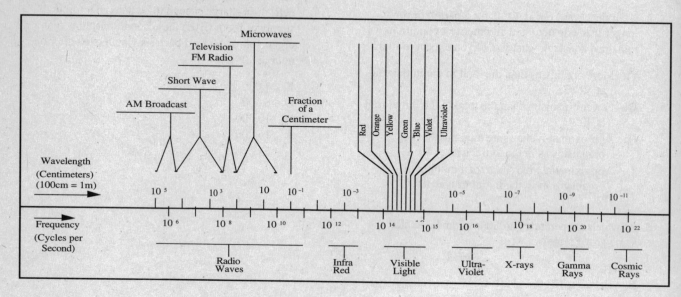

Figure 1

7. Vitamin D can be collected from rays with a wavelength of 1×10^{-6} cm. These rays could be:

   A. radio waves
   B. visible light rays
   C. ultraviolet rays
   D. gamma rays

8. A short-wave radio emits waves of a wavelength 5×10^4 cm. Express this term in meters.

   F. 400 m
   G. 500 m
   H. 40,000 m
   J. 50,000 m

9. Which of the following is a correct sequence of waves in order of increasing frequency?

   A. cosmic rays, gamma rays, infra-red
   B. infra-red, ultraviolet, visible light
   C. yellow, orange, and red light
   D. radio waves, visible light, x-rays

10. Wavelength, frequency, and velocity are interrelated characteristics of an electromagnetic wave. According to Figure 1, as wavelength increases, at a constant velocity, the frequency of a wave would:

    F. decrease
    G. increase
    H. increase by a factor of 2
    J. be unchanged

11. When a prism refracts white light, the longest component rays are refracted the least, while the rays with the shortest wavelengths are refracted the most. In the visible light spectrum, which color is refracted the LEAST?

    A. ultraviolet
    B. blue
    C. red
    D. white

GO ON TO THE NEXT PAGE.

Passage III

The complex behavior of the poor-sighted, three-spined male stickleback fish has been studied extensively as a model of species behavior in courtship and mating. After a male has migrated to a suitable spot, he builds a spawning nest of sand and sediment. In courting, he performs a special "zig zag" dance. The female then follows the male to the nest where she spawns and he fertilizes the spawned eggs. Also, male sticklebacks have been shown to exhibit territorial behaviors. A biologist performed three experiments to learn more about the behavior of the stickleback.

Experiment 1

Tank 1 and Tank 2 are set up with identical conditions and one male stickleback is placed in each tank. Both fish build nests in their respective tanks. The male from Tank 1 is removed from his tank and is replaced with an egg-laden female; the male from Tank 2 is removed from his tank and is introduced into Tank 1. In Tank 1, the male does not perform the zig zag dance and no spawning occurs. The male retreats to a corner of the tank.

Experiment 2

A male stickleback in an aquarium builds his nest. A fat, round male is introduced into the environment. The original male performs the zig zag dance and attempts to lead the round male to the nest. The round male refuses and begins to flap his fins and swim in circles. The first male then begins to flap his fins, circle his nest, and occasionally prod the other fish to a far corner of the tank.

Experiment 3

A small, flat-shaped female is introduced into a tank where a male has built a nest. The male circles the female a few times, then retreats to a corner of the tank.

12. The experimental data would support the hypothesis that the purpose of the male stickleback's mating dance is to:

    F. keep away other male sticklebacks.
    G. lure and entice the female to the nest.
    H. fertilize the eggs.
    J. establish territorial rights.

13. Based on observations from the above experiments, which factor initially stimulates the male to do the zig zag dance?

    A. The physical environment
    B. The number of fish in the tank
    C. The sex of the fish
    D. The shape of the fish

14. Which experiment supports the hypothesis that the male exhibits territorial behavior?

    F. 2 only
    G. 3 only
    H. 2 and 3 only
    J. 1, 2, and 3

15. To further investigate the territorial behavior of the stickleback, the biologist should vary which of the following factors in Experiment 2?

    A. The temperature of the water
    B. The sediment and sand in the tank
    C. The fatness of the male fish
    D. The size of the tank

16. To clarify the results of Experiment 1, the biologist should set up which of the following test situations?

    F. Return the original male stickleback to Tank 1 and observe its behavior with the female fish.
    G. Maintain the positions of the male sticklebacks and add another egg-laden female to Tank 1.
    H. Place both male sticklebacks in Tank 2.
    J. Repeat the experiment using a different species of fish.

17. A male stickleback has been established in an aquarium and has built a nest. If one egg-laden female and several flat-shaped male sticklebacks are placed in the tank, one would most likely observe:

    A. all the males performing the zig zag dance.
    B. only the male that was originally in the tank performing the zig zag dance.
    C. all the males circling the female.
    D. the female retreating to a corner.

GO ON TO THE NEXT PAGE.

Passage IV

Photosynthesis is a biological process in which light energy is converted to chemical bond energy. This essential process takes place on the primary level of the food chain and provides most of the food energy available to living organisms. Also, photosynthesis is the source for most of the oxygen in the Earth's atmosphere. Photosynthesis takes place in two distinctive stages called the "light" reactions and the "dark" reactions.

Light reactions:

These reactions are also known as the photochemical reactions. Plants and some types of microorganisms contain specialized organelles called chloroplasts. In the chloroplasts, light energy is absorbed by the pigment chlorophyll. Some of this energy is used to convert water molecules into hydrogen ions and oxygen gas. The oxygen gas is released into the atmosphere through specialized openings on the plant's leaves. Some of the light energy is used to produce molecules of ATP.

Dark reactions:

These reactions, also called "carbon-fixing" reactions, are not dependent on light. During the dark reactions, the hydrogen ions produced in the light reactions and carbon dioxide from the atmosphere pass through a series of chemical changes to form the simple sugar glucose and other compounds, including water. This glucose can be either consumed immediately or stored for later use. To test the effect of various environmental factors on the process of photosynthesis, a student observed the growth of plants over a period of time. The conditions and the results are described in Table 1. All plants were watered on a regular basis.

Table 1

Plant	Conditions	Results
1	Sunlight	Normal Growth Green
2	Darkness	PLant sickly Yellow
3	Sunlight Cut off all the flowers, but left the leaves intact.	Plant dead Brown
4	Sunlight Cut off all the flowers, but left the leaves intact.	Normal Growth Green
5	Sunlight Entire plant covered with plastic wrap	Normal Growth Green Condensed water on the plastic wrap.

18. Which word equation represents the process of photosynthesis?

   F. Sunlight + Carbon Dioxide + Water → Glucose + Oxygen + Water

   G. Glucose + Sunlight → Alcohol + Carbon Dioxide

   H. Oxygen + Sunlight + Water → Sugar + Carbon Dioxide + Water

   J. Glucose + Sunlight + Oxygen → Carbon Dioxide + Water

19. According to the passage, oxygen gas is produced in which of the following processes?

   A. Carbon-fixing reactions only
   B. Photochemical reactions only
   C. Chlorophyll-fixing reactions
   D. Both the photochemical and carbon-fixing reactions

20. Which of the following substances undergoes a transformation during the dark reactions of photosynthesis?

   I. Chlorophyll
   II. Hydrogen Ions
   III. Carbon Dioxide

   F. I only
   G. III only
   H. I and III only
   J. II and III only

21. Which of the plants represents the control for the experiments?

   A. 1 only
   B. 1 and 2 only
   C. All of the plants
   D. None of the plants

GO ON TO THE NEXT PAGE.

22. What hypothesis is supported by a comparison of the changes in Plant 1 and Plant 2?

    F. Darkness is a necessary factor in photosynthesis.

    G. The researcher neglected to water Plant 2.

    H. Plant respiration occurs only in sunlight.

    J. Chloroplasts can function only in sunlight.

23. Which of the following hypotheses is supported by the comparison of changes in Plant 3 and Plant 4?

    A. Chloroplasts are found in leaves, not flowers.

    B. Chloroplasts are found in flowers, not leaves.

    C. Oxygen is an essential requirement for photosyn thesis.

    D. No chemical reactions occur in the stems.

24. Based on the information in the passage, what caused the condensation of water to occur inside the plastic wrap in Plant 5?

    F. Temperature differences between the environ ment inside the plastic wrap and outside the plastic wrap

    G. Trapped water vapor in the air surrounding the plant

    H. Water given off by the plant not used as a byproduct of photosynthesis

    J. Excess water not used in the synthesis of glucose n the carbon fixation reactions

GO ON TO THE NEXT PAGE.

Passage V

Social insects live in colonies and the survival of the colony is dependent on each of its members working together to obtain food, to secure safe home sites, and to continue the reproductive cycle of the species. All species of termites exhibit this social behavior. Biologists have observed that certain members of a termite colony, called soldiers, patrol the area surrounding a colony and, if alarmed, they alert other soldier termites of the danger. At this time, the soldier termite exhibits synchronous, convulsive movements and it may strike its head against wood or other nest materials. Though the convulsive movements are inaudible to human ears, the head-striking can be heard by man as a rustling or cracking sound. Two divergent theories exist concerning what kind of information is exchanged by these motions.

Hypothesis 1

Termites have highly specialized appendages which enable them to receive vibrations sent through the air. The convulsive movements of an alarmed soldier termite create "sound waves" which are perceivable to other termites, but not to humans. This method is used to communicate with nearby termites. When a soldier termite strikes its head against wood, it creates a louder sound message which provides a warning to distant termites. The rate of these movements indicate how near the danger is to the colony— the closer the source, the more convulsions or head-strikes occur within a certain time period.

Hypothesis 2

Termites are known to have highly developed sensory organs for smell. This theory supposes that the convulsive motions of a soldier termite do not emit sound messages, but instead accompany the release of pheromones, or scent. The characteristic scent of the soldier termite serves as a warning to members of the colony. Head-striking is a ritual that does not, by itself, carry any information about the danger or its distance from the colony.

25. In order to support Hypothesis 2, what must be assumed?

   A. Termites do not have well-developed sensory organs for sight.
   B. All termites can release different types of scents in order to send the colony different messages.
   C. Termites cannot perceive sources of danger which are more than 500 feet from the colony.
   D. The soldier termite scent is sufficient to alert the colony that a danger is present.

26. These hypotheses are similar because they both suggest that termites:

   I. use a symbolic language to communicate information to the other members of the colony.
   II. require exact information about a danger source in order to respond to a warning.
   III. are social insects that work together within a colony.

   F. I only
   G. II only
   H. III only
   J. II and III only

27. Which of the following observations would support Hypothesis 2?

   A. Soldier termites strike their heads against wood or other nest materials when food is found, but no danger is present.
   B. All types of termites, not just soldier termites, convulse and strike their heads when a danger source is present.
   C. Termites respond more quickly to danger signals when no wind is present.
   D. Termites respond more quickly to danger signals during the daylight hours.

GO ON TO THE NEXT PAGE.

28. Using a device which emits a high-pitched sound, a biologist determined the frequency of sound that triggers the soldier termites' danger mechanisms. These devices were placed at different distances from the colony. Data were collected to compare the rate of a soldier termite's convulsions to the distance the danger was from the colony. All experiments were performed on calm days and the sound devices were placed on flat land in a straight line from the colony. A significant variation in convulsion rates was reported in different soldiers reacting to a sound source at an equal distance. Furthermore, each soldier seemed to exhibit a uniform number of convulsions, regardless of the distance the sound source was placed from the colony. Which of the following explanations for this behavior was NOT investigated in this study?

I. Wind may affect a soldier termite's perception of the distance of a danger source.

II. The convulsion rate does not convey information about the distance of a danger source.

III. Experienced soldiers can more accurately determine the distance of a danger source than can a novice soldier.

F. I only
G. II only
H. I and II only
J. I and III only

29. Which of these discoveries would NOT support Hypothesis 1?

A. When a soldier termite's scent has been re moved, it can still effectively warn a colony of danger.

B. Termites have a range of hearing that is exactly the same as humans.

C. If a termite loses its specialized appendages, it is forced out of the soldier position by other members of the colony.

D. On a windy day, a soldier termite cannot as accurately warn the colony of danger as it can on a calm day.

GO ON TO THE NEXT PAGE.

Passage VI

Ionization energy is the amount of energy needed to take one electron from the outer shell of an elemental atom. Ionization energies are measured by removing successive electrons from the shells of an atom. The energy needed to withdraw the first electron is termed the first ionization energy, and each successive stage of electron withdrawal—named the second or third ionization energy, accordingly—requires more energy than the stage preceding it. Yet, an atom just beginning a new shell or subshell will have a smaller first ionization energy than the atom preceding it.

Figure 1 shows the first ionization energies (Kcal/mole of atoms) of the first fifty-three elements on the periodic table. Each of the first five periods is represented by a line connecting the elements of that period. The first period, containing only hydrogen, is represented by a dot. The noble gases are excluded.

If an element has a low first ionization energy, the atom is likely to form a positive cation, while an element with a high first ionization energy is less likely to lose an electron and more likely to form a negative anion. Also, metals tend to have lower first ionization energies and tend to give away electrons, forming positive cations. Figure 2 shows an expanded graph of Group IA to give a clearer representation of the trend down a group on the periodic table.

30. Some cations and anions will form ionic bonds with each other. Which of the following pairs of atoms could form a cation and an anion pair, respectively?

   F. Na and Mg
   G. Na and
   H. Br and I
   J. Li and F

31. As a general trend, the lower the first ionization energy, the more metallic character the element exhibits. According to Figure 1, which three elements are the MOST metallic?

   A. Na, K, Rb
   B. Li, Na, Al
   C. Ca, Ga, Sr
   D. F, Cl, O

32. Comparing the first ionization energies of Mg and Al, what is a possible explanation for their different values?

   F. Mg > Al because Mg contains more electrons than Al.
   G. Mg > Al because Mg is more metallic and more energy is required to remove its outermost electron.
   H. Mg > Al because Al represents a new subshell and less energy is required to remove its outermost electron.
   J. Al > Mg because each successive ionization stage requires more energy.

GO ON TO THE NEXT PAGE.

33. Using Figure 2, predict the approximate first ionization energy for Cesium (Cs), element #55 (Group IA, Period 6)?

A. 55
B. 90
C. 160
D. 280

34. Hydrogen (H), element #1, has a high first ionization energy compared to Lithium (Li), element #3, though they both have only one electron in their outermost shell. What is a possible explanation for this phenomenon?

F. Hydrogen is heavier than lithium.
G. Hydrogen has fewer shells than lithium and its nucleus exerts a greater comparative force on its one electron.
H. In a vacuum, hydrogen and lithium would have the same first ionization energy.
J. Hydrogen is an anomaly and it is usually not included in first ionization energy charts.

END OF TEST 5
STOP! DO NOT TURN THE PAGE UNTIL TOLD TO DO SO.

READING

30 Minutes—36 Questions

DIRECTIONS: There are four passages in this test. Each passage is followed by several questions. After reading a passage, choose the best answer to each question and blacken the corresponding oval on your answer sheet. You may refer to the passages as often as necessary.

Passage I

Karenin was not overjoyed by the move to Switzerland. Karenin hated change. Dog time cannot be plottezzzzd along a straight line; it does not move on and on, from one thing to the next. It moves in a circle
5 like the hands of a clock, which they too, unwilling to dash madly ahead — turn round and round the face, day in and day out following the same path. In Prague, when Tomas and Tereza brought a new chair or moved a flower pot, Karenin would look on in displeasure. It
10 disturbed his sense of time. It was as though they were trying to dupe the hands of the clock by changing the numbers on its face.

Nonetheless, he soon managed to reestablish the old order and old rituals in the Zurich flat. As in
15 Prague, he would jump up on the bed and welcome them to the day, accompany Tereza on her morning shopping jaunt, and make certain he got the other walks coming to him as well.

He was the timepiece of their lives. In periods of
20 despair, she would remind herself she had to hold on because of him, because he was weaker than she, weaker perhaps even than Dubcek and their abandoned homeland.

One day when they came back from a walk, the
25 phone was ringing. She picked up the receiver and asked who it was.

It was a woman's voice, and Tereza felt there was a hint of derision in it. When she said that Tomas wasn't there and she didn't know when he'd be back,
30 the woman on the other end of the line started laughing and, without saying good-bye, hung up.

Tereza knew it did not mean a thing. It could have been a nurse from the hospital, a patient, a secretary, anyone. But still she was upset and unable to
35 concentrate on anything. It was then that she realized she had lost the last bit of strength she had had at home; she was absolutely incapable of tolerating this absolutely insignificant incident.

Being in a foreign country means walking a
40 tightrope high above the ground without the net afforded a person by the country where he has his family, colleagues, and friends, and where he can easily say what he has to say in a language he has known from childhood. In Prague she was dependent
45 on Tomas only when it came to the heart; here she was dependent on him for everything. What would happen to her here if he abandoned her? Would she have to live her whole life in fear of losing him?

She told herself: Their acquaintance had been
50 based on an error from the start. The copy of *Anna Karenina* under her arm amounted to false papers; it had given Tomas the wrong idea. In spite of their love, they had made each other's life a hell. The fact that they loved each other was merely proof that the fault
55 lay not in themselves, in their behavior or inconstancy of feeling, but rather in their incompatibility; he was strong and she was weak. She was like Dubcek, who made a thirty-second pause in the middle of a sentence; she was like her country, which stuttered, gasped for
60 breath, could not speak.

But when the strong were too weak to hurt the weak, the weak had to be strong enough to leave.

And having told herself all this, she pressed her face against Karenin's furry head and said, "Sorry,
65 Karenin. It looks as though you're going to have to move again."

1. From the information in the passage, it can be inferred that:

A. Tomas now lives in Prague.
B. Tomas and Tereza want to move to Zurich.
C. Tomas wants to move to Prague.
D. Tomas and Tereza used to live in Prague.

GO ON TO THE NEXT PAGE.

2. According to the passage, it can be inferred that Karenin jumps in Tereza's bed (line 15) in order to:

   F. let Tereza know it is time to go shopping.
   G. let Tereza know he is hungry.
   H. reestablish his old routines.
   J. express his happiness.

3. Tereza believed that her copy of *Anna Karenina:*

   A. made her see she had to move from Switzer-land.
   B. gave Tomas a false impression of her.
   C. indicated her weakness.
   D. symbolized her love.

4. Karenin is displeased about the move because:

   F. it disturbed his sense of time.
   G. he doesn't like the new place.
   H. he is unable to understand the change.
   J. he prefers to move in a circle.

5. In lines 39–44, an analogy is drawn between being in a foreign country and walking a tightrope in order to:

   A. show how difficult it is for Tereza.
   B. emphasize that Tereza's love for Tomas was in danger.
   C. show the precarious political situation.
   D. show how important it is to have friends.

6. In the passage, Tereza's state of mind can best be described as:

   F. despairing
   G. calm
   H. frantic
   J. jealous

7. Dubcek (line 57) is mentioned as an example of:

   A. a powerful ruler.
   B. an enemy of the state.
   C. a weak figure.
   D. a political refugee.

8. Tereza believed that the difficulty with her relationship with Tomas was that:

   F. they did not truly love each other.
   G. Tomas was too dependent.
   H. her feelings were constantly changing.
   J. he was strong while she was weak.

9. The author probably uses Karenin to symbolize:

   A. Tomas's love for Tereza.
   B. the recent move to Zurich.
   C. feelings of strength.
   D. continuity amidst change.

GO ON TO THE NEXT PAGE.

Passage II

In the 1740's, gold mines were discovered in what was then eastern Hungary, and is now northwestern Rumania. The usual avid search uncovered more veins of gold elsewhere in Hungary, but sometimes the quantity of gold obtained from such veins was disappointingly small. Hungarian mineralogists naturally got to work in order to find out what was wrong.

One of them, Anton von Rupprecht, analyzed ore from a gold mine in 1782 and found that a non-gold impurity accounted for the gold that was not obtained. Studying this impurity, Rupprecht found it had some properties that resembled those of antimony, an element well known to the chemists of the day. Judging from its appearance, therefore, he concluded that antimony was what he had.

In 1784, another Hungarian mineralogist, Franz Joseph Muller (1740–1825), studied Rupprecht's ore and decided that the metal impurity was not antimony because it did not have some of that metal's properties. He began to wonder if he had a completely new element, but didn't dare commit himself to that. In 1796, he sent samples to the German chemist Martin Heinrich Klaproth (1743–1817), a leading authority, telling him of his suspicions that he had a new element and asking him to check the matter.

Klaproth gave it all the necessary tests and, by 1798, was able to report it as a new element. He carefully, as was proper, gave Muller credit for the discovery, and supplied it with a name. He called it "tellurium," from the Latin word for "earth."

Tellurium is a very rare element, less than half as common in the earth's crust as gold is. However, it is commonly associated with gold in ores, and since few things are as assiduously searched for as gold, tellurium is found more often than one would expect from its rareness.

Tellurium is (as was eventually understood) one of the sulfur family of elements, and the Swedish chemist Jons Jakob Berzelius (1779–1848) was not surprised, therefore, when, in 1817, he found tellurium in the sulfuric acid being prepared in a certain factory. At least he found an impurity that looked like tellurium so that he took it for granted that that was what it was.

Working with the supposed tellurium, he found that some of its properties were not like those of tellurium. By February, 1818, he realized that he had still another new element on his hands, one that strongly resembled tellurium... he called it "selenium."

In the periodic table, selenium falls between sulfur and tellurium. Selenium is not exactly a common element, but it is more common than either tellurium or gold. Selenium is, in fact, nearly as common as silver.

Selenium and tellurium were not particularly important elements for nearly a century after their discovery. Then, in 1873, there came a peculiar and completely unexpected finding. Willoughby Smith found that selenium would conduct an electric current with much greater ease when it is exposed to light than when it is in the dark. This was the first discovery ever made of something that was eventually called "the photoelectric effect"; that is, the effect of light upon electrical phenomena.

10. Rupprecht found that:

F. gold is impure.
G. a non-gold impurity accounted for the little gold obtained.
H. antimony is an element just like gold.
J. the impurity was not antimony.

11. The credited discoverer of tellurium is:

A. Klaproth
B. Rupprecht
C. Berzelius
D. Muller

12. Based on the information in the passage, which of the following is a hypothesis rather than a fact?

F. Selenium falls between sulfur and tellurium in the periodic table.
G. Tellurium's being found with gold is due to the special bonding between them.
H. Selenium conducts an electric current.
J. Tellurium is often found because of its closeness to gold.

13. It can be inferred that silver is:

A. slightly more common than selenium.
B. slightly less common than gold.
C. as common as sulfur.
D. as common as tellurium.

GO ON TO THE NEXT PAGE.

14. Based on the information in the passage, the periodic table (line 51) is most likely:

F. a list of new elements.
G. a listing of all elements.
H. a description of selenium, sulfur, and tellurium.
J. a list of the properties of common elements.

15. Selenium and tellurium:

A. have no important applications.
B. were ignored until 1873.
C. were not utilized practically until well after their discovery.
D. are equally important in terms of practical applications.

16. In can be inferred from the passage that all of the following are elements EXCEPT:

F. sulfuric acid
G. antimony
H. selenium
J. gold

17. Which event most contributed to the discovery of selenium?

A. The discovery of tellurium in gold ore
B. The analysis of sulfuric acid
C. The discovery of the photoelectric effect
D. The discovery that tellurium is similar to sulfur

18. Given the information on the photoelectric effect (lines 59–65), which of the following can be inferred?

F. Electricity and light are the same thing.
G. Electricity is usually the result of light.
H. Electricity and light are related phenomena.
J. Electricity has little effect on light.

GO ON TO THE NEXT PAGE.

Passage III

Every school child is taught that Robert Fulton was the first American to build and operate a steamboat on New York waters. When his *Clermont* sauntered four miles per hour upstream on the Hudson
5 River in 1807, Fulton opened up new possibilities in transportation, marketing, and city building. What is not often taught about Fulton is that he had a monopoly enforced by the state. The New York legislature gave Fulton the privilege of carrying *all* steamboat traffic in
10 New York for thirty years. It was this monopoly that Thomas Gibbons, a New Jersey steamboat man, tried to crack when he hired young Cornelius Vanderbilt in 1817 to run steamboats in New York by charging less than the monopoly rates.

15 Vanderbilt was a classic market entrepreneur, and he was intrigued by the challenge of breaking the Fulton monopoly. On the mast of Gibbon's ship Vanderbilt hoisted a flag that read: "New Jersey must be free." For sixty days in 1817, Vanderbilt defied
20 capture as he raced passengers cheaply from Elizabeth, New Jersey, to New York City. He became a popular figure on the Atlantic as he lowered the fares and eluded the law. Finally, in 1824, in the landmark case of *Gibbons* vs. *Ogden,* the Supreme Court struck
25 down the Fulton monopoly. Chief Justice John Marshall ruled that only the federal government, not the states, could regulate interstate commerce. This extremely popular decision opened the waters of America to complete competition. A jubilant
30 Vanderbilt was greeted in New Brunswick, New Jersey, by cannon salutes fired by "citizens desirous of testifying in a public manner their good will." Ecstatic New Yorkers immediately launched two steamboats named for John Marshall. On the Ohio River,
35 steamboat traffic doubled in the first year after *Gibbons* vs. *Ogden* and quadrupled after the second year.

The triumph of market entrepreneurs in steamboating led to improvements in technology. As
40 one man observed, "The boat builders, freed from the domination of the Fulton-Livingston interests, were quick to develop new ideas that before had no encouragement from capital." These new ideas included tubular boilers to replace the heavy and
45 expensive copper boilers Fulton used. Cordwood for fuel was also a major cost for Fulton, but innovators soon found that anthracite coal worked well under the new tubular boilers, so "the expense of fuel was down one-half."

50 The real value of removing the Fulton monopoly was that the costs of steamboating dropped. Passenger traffic, for example, from New York City to Albany immediately dropped from seven to three dollars after *Gibbons* vs. *Ogden.* Fulton's group couldn't meet the
55 new rates and soon went bankrupt. Gibbons and Vanderbilt, meanwhile, adopted the new technology, cut their costs, and earned $40,000 profit each year during the late 1820's.

With such an open environment for market
60 entrepreneurs, Vanderbilt decided to quit his pleasant association with Gibbons, buy the two steamboats, and go into business for himself. During the 1830's, Vanderbilt would establish trade routes all over the Northeast. He offered fast and reliable service at low
65 rates. He first tried the New York to Philadelphia route and forced the "standard" three-dollar fare down to one dollar. On the New Brunswick to New York City run, Vanderbilt charged six cents a trip and provided free meals. As *Niles' Register* said, the "times must be
70 hard indeed when a traveller who wishes to save money cannot afford to walk."

19. According to the passage, Vanderbilt was a "market entrepreneur" (line 15) because he:

   A. broke the Fulton monopoly.
   B. ran a successful steamship company.
   C. operated the cheapest steamship line on the Hudson.
   D. believed in the free market as opposed to a state enforced monopoly.

20. The phrase "New Jersey must be free" (lines 18–19) meant that:

   F. there should be no fares on the Hudson line.
   G. the New Jersey market should be open to competition.
   H. Fulton's line should be dismantled.
   J. the government should regulate the steamship industry.

21. The Supreme Court's decision in *Gibbons* vs. *Ogden* had all of the following effects EXCEPT:

   A. it struck down the Fulton monopoly.
   B. it led to cheaper fares.
   C. it enabled Fulton to expand.
   D. it opened America's waterways to competition.

GO ON TO THE NEXT PAGE.

22. It can be inferred that Fulton's business faltered while Gibbons's and Vanderbilt's business flourished because:

    F. Fulton didn't adopt the new technology.
    G. Gibbons and Vanderbilt took over Fulton's state-enforced monopoly.
    H. Fulton was less popular than Vanderbilt.
    J. steamship travel on the Hudson, Fulton's primary route, decreased.

23. After *Gibbons* vs. *Ogden,* steamboat travel most probably increased because of:

    A. larger steamships
    B. more efficient technology
    C. reduced fares
    D. a population explosion

24. Gibbons and Vanderbilt were:

    F. competitors
    G. employer and employee
    H. equal partners
    J. legal experts

25. According to the passage, Vanderbilt was able to expand all over the Northeast because:

    A. demand was very high there for steamship transportation.
    B. Gibbons's monopoly was broken.
    C. there were very few rival steamship lines.
    D. he offered cheap and efficient service.

26. It can be inferred from the passage that:

    F. Fulton was essentially dishonest.
    G. Everything that children are usually taught about Fulton is wrong.
    H. School children learn only part of Fulton's story.
    J. Fulton does not deserve to be honored.

27. The author's tone towards Vanderbilt is one of:

    A. admiration
    B. glorification
    C. understanding
    D. empathy

GO ON TO THE NEXT PAGE.

Passage IV

We know today that the traditions of tribal art are more complex and less "primitive" than its discoverers believed; we have even seen that the imitation of nature is by no means excluded from its aims. But the style of these ritualistic objects could still serve as a common focus for that search for expressiveness, structure, and simplicity that the new movements had inherited from the experiments of the three lonely rebels; Van Gogh, Cezanne, and Gauguin.

The experiments of Expressionism are, perhaps, the easiest to explain in words. The term itself may not be happily chosen, for we know that we are all expressing ourselves in everything we do or leave undone, but the word became a convenient label because of its easily remembered contrast to Impressionism, and as a label it is quite useful. In one of his letters, Van Gogh had explained how he set about painting the portrait of a friend who was very dear to him. The conventional likeness was only the first stage. Having painted a "correct" portrait, he proceeded to change the colors and the setting: "I exaggerate the fair color of the hair, I take orange, chrome, lemon color, and behind the head I do not paint the trivial wall of the room but the Infinite. I make a simple background out of the most intense and richest blue the palette will yield. The blond luminous head stands out against this strong blue background mysteriously like a star in the azure. Alas, my dear friend, the public will see nothing but caricature in this exaggeration, but what does that matter to us?"

Van Gogh was right in saying that the method he had chosen could be compared to that of the caricaturist. Caricature had always been "expressionist," for the caricaturist plays with the likeness of his victim, and distorts it to express just what he feels about his fellow man. As long as these distortions of nature sailed under the flag of humor nobody seemed to find them difficult to understand. Humorous art was a field in which everything was permitted, because people did not approach it with the prejudices they reserved for "Art with a capital A." But the idea of a serious caricature, of an art which deliberately changed the appearance of things not to express a sense of superiority, but maybe love, or admiration, or fear, proved indeed a stumbling block as Van Gogh had predicted. Yet there is nothing inconsistent about it. It is the sober truth that our feelings about things do color the way in which we see them and, even more, the forms which we remember. Everyone must have experienced how different the same place may look when we are happy and when we are sad.

What upset the public about the Expressionist art was, perhaps, not so much the fact that nature had been distorted as that the result led away from beauty. That the caricaturist may show up the ugliness of man was granted — it was his job. But that men who claimed to be serious artists should forget that if they must change the appearance of things they should idealize them, rather than make them ugly, was strongly resented. But an Expressionist might have retorted that a shout of anguish is not beautiful, and that it would be insincere to look only at the pleasing side of life. For the Expressionists felt so strongly about human suffering, poverty, violence and passion, that they were inclined to think that the insistence on harmony and beauty were only born out of a refusal to be honest. The art of the classical masters, of a Raphael or Correggio, seemed to them insincere and hypocritical. They wanted to face the stark facts of our existence, and to express their compassion for the disinherited and the ugly. It became almost a point of honor with them to avoid anything which smelt of pettiness and polish, and to shock the "bourgeois" out of his real or imagined complacency.

28. The term "correct" in line 20 means:

F. critically acclaimed
G. traditionally accepted
H. objectively beautiful
J. simple and trivial

29. Van Gogh, Cezanne, and Gauguin all:

A. used the same methods of distortion.
B. began their careers as caricicturists.
C. experimented with new styles of expression.
D. were concerned with educating people about the "new" art.

30. It can be inferred from the passage that people found it easier to accept distortions in humorous art for all of the following reasons EXCEPT:

F. people had fewer preconceptions towards it.
G. people didn't take it seriously.
H. they thought of the distortions as deliberate attempts at humor.
J. they accepted the distortions as expressions of love, admiration, and fear.

GO ON TO THE NEXT PAGE.

31. What was the Expressionist position regarding beauty in art?

    A. There was essentially no such thing as true beauty.

    B. It resulted from conformity and fear of change.

    C. It was totally unnecessary.

    D. It stemmed from dishonesty.

32. Expressionism was essentially a(n):

    F. close association of radical artists.

    G. new style whose sole purpose was to shock people.

    H. artistic movement founded on a more expressive style.

    J. fundamental revolution in art.

33. The author quotes Van Gogh's description of his painting (lines 21–30) in order to:

    A. show how the Expressionist style differed from conventional painting.

    B. show that Van Gogh was essentially a caricaturist.

    C. give the reader a feel for a typical Expressionist work.

    D. demonstrate Van Gogh's importance to the new movement.

34. The author implies that the art of Raphael and Correggio:

    F. was similiar to that of the Expressionists.

    G. used caricature to show the darker side of the human condition.

    H. was characterized by an insistence on harmony and beauty.

    J. expressed compassion for the disinherited and the ugly.

35. It can be inferred that the Expressionists:

    A. were lonely people.

    B. were motivated by a desire to change for the sake of changing.

    C. were not immediately accepted by the public.

    D. were appreciative of the influence of caricatures on their work.

36. The author believes that:

    F. Expressionism is a more advanced style of art than conventional painting.

    G. caricatures are not serious art.

    H. Expressionism was responsible for an eventual decrease in the importance of beauty in twentieth-century art.

    J. Expressionism shares characteristics with the art of caricature.

END OF TEST 6
STOP! DO NOT TURN THE PAGE UNTIL TOLD TO DO SO.

How to Score the PRA

STEP A

Count the number of correct answers for Section 1 and record the number in the space provided for your raw score on the Score Conversion Worksheet on the next page. Repeat for each section of the test.

STEP B

On Section 2, questions 1-10, subtract a third of a point from your raw score for every question that you answered incorrectly. Do not deduct points for those questions you left blank. On Section 2, questions 18-35, deduct a quarter of a point for every wrong answer. Again, do not deduct points for those questions you left blank. On Section 4, deduct a quarter of a point for any question you answered incorrectly. And, you guessed it: Do not deduct points for those questions you left blank.

STEP C

Some questions count toward both of your scores. We call these Crossover Points. You'll notice that on your answer key, sections 2, 3, 4, and 6 have two columns, and selected questions in each have two lines for marking a point. If you get one of those right, give yourself an ACT point and an SAT point. Then add those points to their respective raw scores. Crossover Points on Section 2 count toward Section 3 and Crossover Points on Section 6 count toward your score on Section 4. (Don't bother deducting anything for wrong answers.)

STEP D

Using the score conversion charts on page 435, convert your raw scores on each section to scaled scores. Then compute your composite ACT score by averaging the four subject scores: add them up and divide by four. To calculate the range of your SAT scores, add the lowest number from math to the lowest number from verbal and the highest number from math to the highest number from verbal.

Let's see how Joe B. did on his PRA:

ACT:		SAT:	
English:	20-26	Math:	390-450
Math:	23-29	Verbal:	520-580
Science:	14-20		
Reading:	25-31		

So, by adding 20 + 23 + 14 + 25 and dividing the sum (82) by four and rounding up, he gets a low score of 21. When he adds 26 + 29 + 20 + 31, he gets 106, which averages out to 27. So, his ACT range is 21 – 27. By adding 390 + 520 and 450 + 580, he gets an SAT range of 910 – 1,030.

Estimated ACT Score

PRA SECTION	RAW SCORE		ACT SCORE
SECTION 1	_____ / (55)	converts to	_____ - _____
SECTION 3	_____ / (27)	converts to	_____ - _____
CROSSOVER POINTS	+ _____ / (8)	converts to	_____ - _____
TOTAL	_____ / (35)	converts to	_____ - _____
SECTION 5	_____ / (34)	converts to	_____ - _____
SECTION 6	_____ / (36)	converts to	_____ - _____

TOTAL (add ACT scores):

Composite ACT score (divide total by 4): _____ - _____

Estimated SAT Score

PRA SECTION	RAW SCORE	SAT SCORE
SECTION 2: Math		
NUMBER RIGHT	_____ / (35)	
NUMBER WRONG:		
Questions 1–10 divided by 3	– _____	
Questions 18–35 divided by 4	– _____	
CROSSOVER POINTS	+ _____ / (12)	
TOTAL	_____ / (47) converts to	_____ - _____
SECTION 4: Verbal		
NUMBER RIGHT	_____ / (46)	
NUMBER WRONG divided by 4	– _____	
CROSSOVER POINTS	+ _____ / (7)	
TOTAL	_____ / (53) converts to	_____ - _____

COMBINED SAT SCORE (add scores): _____ - _____

CORRECT ANSWERS FOR PRINCETON REVIEW ASSESSMENT

Section 1 ACT Lang. Skills	Section 2 SAT Math (SAT ACT)	Section 3 ACT Math (ACT SAT)	Section 4 SAT Verbal	Section 5 ACT Science	Section 6 ACT Reading (ACT SAT)
1. C	1. A ___	1. B ___ *	1. C	1. A	1. D ___
2. G	2. C ___	2. H ___	2. C	2. G	2. H ___
3. D	3. D ___	3. A ___	3. C	3. A	3. B ___
4. F	4. B ___	4. H ___	4. B	4. H	4. F ___
5. B	5. B ___	5. E ___ *	5. B	5. C	5. A ___ *
6. J	6. D ___	6. K ___ *	6. B	6. G	6. F ___
7. A	7. C ___	7. E ___	7. D	7. C	7. C ___
8. G	8. D ___	8. J ___ *	8. D	8. G	8. J ___
9. C	9. A ___	9. A ___	9. B	9. D	9. D ___
10. J	10. C ___	10. J ___	10. E	10. F	10. G ___ *
11. A	11. 2 ___	11. D ___	11. D	11. C	11. D ___
12. J	12. 14 ___	12. G ___ *	12. E	12. G	12. G ___
13. B	13. 19, 39, 59, 79 or 99 ___	13. E ___ *	13. C	13. D	13. A ___
14. H	14. 36 ___	14. H ___	14. C	14. J	14. G ___
15. D	15. 5 ___	15. B ___	15. B	15. C	15. C ___
16. H	16. 15 ___	16. J ___	16. A	16. F	16. F ___
17. B	17. .5 ___	17. B ___	17. E	17. B	17. B ___
18. J	18. C ___ *	18. F ___	18. C	18. F	18. H ___
19. B	19. D ___ *	19. C ___ *	19. E	19. B	19. D ___ *
20. H	20. D ___	20. K ___ *	20. D	20. J	20. G ___
21. B	21. A ___ *	21. B ___	21. D	21. A	21. D ___ *
22. J	22. B ___ *	22. H ___ *	22. B	22. J	22. F ___
23. B	23. E ___ *	23. B ___ *	23. A	23. A	23. C ___ *
24. H	24. E ___	24. H ___	24. D	24. H	24. G ___
25. C	25. A ___	25. A ___ *	25. A	25. D	25. D ___
26. G	26. B ___	26. G ___ *	26. D	26. H	26. H ___
27. A	27. A ___ *	27. A ___	27. A	27. A	27. A ___
28. J	28. B ___		28. C	28. J	28. G ___
29. A	29. A ___		29. C	29. B	29. C ___
30. J	30. A ___ *		30. B	30. J	30. J ___ *
31. A	31. A ___		31. A	31. A	31. D ___
32. F	32. C ___		32. C	32. H	32. H ___
33. C	33. C ___		33. A	33. B	33. A ___ *
34. G	34. D ___ *		34. B	34. G	34. H ___
35. A	35. B ___		35. C		35. C ___
36. J			36. A		36. J ___
37. A			37. B		
38. F			38. E		
39. A			39. A		
40. G			40. C		
41. D			41. A		
42. J			42. C		
43. A			43. B		
44. J			44. C		
45. B			45. C		
46. J			46. E		
47. A					
48. H					
49. D					
50. H					
51. B					
52. H					
53. D					
54. G					
55. B					

Section 2: *If you got this question right, add a crossover point to your raw score on Section 3 of the PRA.

Section 3: *If you got this question right, add a crossover point to your raw score on Section 2 of the PRA.

Section 6: *If you got this question right, add a crossover point to your raw score on Section 4 of the PRA.

Number Correct	Number Correct	Number Correct	Number Correct	Number Correct	Number Correct
_____ /(55)	_____ /(47)	_____ /(35)	_____ /(53)	_____ /(34)	_____ /(36)

ESTIMATED ACT SCALE SCORE

Section 1 — ACT Language Skills

Raw Score	ACT Score
55	30 – 36
54	30 – 36
53	30 – 36
52	29 – 35
51	28 – 34
50	27 – 33
49	26 – 32
48	25 – 31
47	24 – 30
46	23 – 29
45	23 – 29
44	22 – 28
43	21 – 27
42	21 – 27
41	20 – 26
40	20 – 26
39	19 – 25
38	19 – 25
37	18 – 24
36	18 – 24
35	17 – 23
34	16 – 22
33	16 – 22
32	16 – 22
31	15 – 21
30	15 – 21
29	14 – 20
28	14 – 20
27	13 – 19
26	13 – 19
25	12 – 18
24	12 – 18
23	11 – 17
22	11 – 17
21	11 – 17
20	10 – 16
19	10 – 16
18	10 – 16
17	9 – 15
16	9 – 15
15	8 – 14
14	7 – 13
13	7 – 13
12	6 – 12
11	6 – 12
10	6 – 12
9	5 – 11
8	4 – 10
7	4 – 10
6	3 – 9
5	2 – 8
4	2 – 8
3	1 – 7
2	0 – 6
1	0 – 6
0	0 – 6

Section 3 (and 2) — ACT Math

Raw Score	ACT Score
35	30 – 36
34	30 – 36
33	30 – 36
32	29 – 34
31	27 – 33
30	26 – 32
29	26 – 32
28	25 – 31
27	24 – 30
26	24 – 30
25	23 – 29
24	22 – 28
23	21 – 27
22	20 – 26
21	19 – 25
20	18 – 24
19	17 – 23
18	17 – 23
17	16 – 22
16	16 – 22
15	15 – 21
14	14 – 20
13	14 – 20
12	13 – 19
11	13 – 19
10	12 – 18
9	11 – 17
8	10 – 16
7	9 – 15
6	8 – 14
5	7 – 13
4	6 – 12
3	5 – 11
2	2 – 8
1	1 – 7
0	0 – 6

Section 5 — ACT Science

Raw Score	ACT Score
34	30 – 36
33	30 – 36
32	30 – 36
31	29 – 35
30	27 – 33
29	26 – 33
28	24 – 30
27	23 – 29
26	23 – 29
25	22 – 28
24	21 – 27
23	20 – 26
22	19 – 25
21	18 – 24
20	17 – 23
19	17 – 23
18	16 – 22
17	16 – 22
16	15 – 21
15	14 – 20
14	13 – 19
13	12 – 18
12	12 – 18
11	11 – 17
10	11 – 17
9	10 – 16
8	9 – 15
7	8 – 14
6	7 – 13
5	6 – 12
4	5 – 11
3	4 – 10
2	3 – 9
1	0 – 6
0	0 – 6

Section 6 — ACT Reading Comp

Raw Score	ACT Score
36	30 – 36
35	30 – 36
34	30 – 36
33	30 – 36
32	29 – 35
31	28 – 34
30	27 – 33
29	26 – 32
28	25 – 31
27	24 – 30
26	23 – 29
25	22 – 28
24	21 – 27
23	20 – 26
22	19 – 25
21	18 – 24
20	17 – 23
19	16 – 22
18	15 – 21
17	14 – 20
16	13 – 19
15	12 – 18
14	11 – 17
13	11 – 17
12	10 – 16
11	9 – 15
10	8 – 14
9	7 – 13
8	6 – 12
7	5 – 11
6	4 – 10
5	3 – 9
4	2 – 8
3	1 – 7
2	0 – 6
1	0 – 6
0	0 – 6

ESTIMATED SAT SCALE SCORE

Section 2 (and 3) — SAT Math

Raw Score	SAT Score
47	740 – 800
46	740 – 800
45	730 – 790
44	730 – 790
43	730 – 790
42	720 – 780
41	710 – 770
40	690 – 750
39	690 – 750
38	680 – 740
37	670 – 730
36	650 – 710
35	630 – 690
34	610 – 670
33	600 – 660
32	590 – 650
31	580 – 640
30	550 – 610
29	530 – 590
28	520 – 580
27	500 – 560
26	480 – 540
25	460 – 520
24	440 – 500
23	430 – 490
22	410 – 470
21	400 – 460
20	390 – 450
19	380 – 440
18	370 – 430
17	360 – 420
16	340 – 400
15	330 – 390
14	310 – 370
13	300 – 360
12	270 – 330
11	260 – 320
10	250 – 310
9	240 – 300
8	230 – 290
7	210 – 270
6	200 – 260
5	200 – 260
4	200 – 260
3	200 – 260
2	200 – 260
1	200 – 260
0	200 – 260

Section 4 (and 6) — SAT Verbal

Raw Score	SAT Score
53	740 – 800
52	740 – 800
51	730 – 790
50	730 – 790
49	720 – 780
48	710 – 770
47	690 – 750
46	680 – 740
45	650 – 710
44	640 – 700
43	620 – 680
42	620 – 670
41	600 – 660
40	590 – 650
39	580 – 640
38	570 – 630
37	550 – 610
36	540 – 600
35	520 – 580
34	510 – 570
33	500 – 560
32	490 – 550
31	480 – 540
30	470 – 530
29	460 – 520
28	450 – 510
27	440 – 500
26	430 – 490
25	420 – 480
24	410 – 470
23	390 – 450
22	380 – 440
21	370 – 430
20	360 – 420
19	350 – 410
18	340 – 400
17	330 – 390
16	320 – 380
15	310 – 370
14	290 – 350
13	280 – 340
12	270 – 330
11	240 – 300
10	200 – 260
9	200 – 260
8	200 – 260
7	200 – 260
6	200 – 260
5	200 – 260
4	200 – 260
3	200 – 260
2	200 – 260
1	200 – 260
0	200 – 260

CHAPTER 20

Using the PRA

Take some time before deciding which admissions test is right for you. The chart on the next page will help you compare your scores on the ACT and the SAT.

Most schools will accept either score; others accept only one or the other. The best way to determine which schools take which scores is to look at an up-to-date college guide like The Princeton Review's *Student Access Guide to the Best Colleges*. What is the average score on each test of incoming freshmen at the schools you are considering? How do your scores stack up against their scores?

A warning: While this is a good way to decide which test to take, it is a lousy way to pick a school. Colleges print average test scores: many of their students scored lower. Colleges consider your grades and your extracurricular record along with your scores (as a rule of thumb, the smaller the school, the more time they spend reading your application). Don't drop a school from your list simply because your SAT score was 100 points below its average.

Your scores will change in fits and starts. Good preparation should increase your scores on either test, but in different ways. The ACT is more straightforward and relies a little more on actual knowledge of subject matter. The SAT, on the other hand, is pretty much a test of how well you take the SAT. The best way to prepare is to practice on real tests, available from the Educational Testing Service (for the SAT) and the American College Testing Program (for the ACT).

As you might have guessed, we at The Princeton Review believe that there is no better way to prepare for these tests than by taking a good course. But you already have all the tools you need at your disposal. Get copies of old tests and practice, practice, practice. Review concepts that you haven't used for a while. Use the information in this book to brush up on what you need to know to do well on the ACT. The Question-by-Question Breakdown at the end of this chapter will help you home in on your weaknesses (what to learn) and your strengths (what to practice).

If you decide that the SAT is the test for you, get ready to beef up your vocabulary. About half of your SAT Verbal score is based entirely on your knowledge of words. So, start looking up words that you don't know. Make flash cards. Keep lists of unfamiliar words. Most important of all: read more! By the way, we also publish *Cracking the System* for the New SAT.

The New SAT? Yes, in March of 1994, the SAT changed forever. You may have heard some wild rumors about this ("There's an essay!" "It stays crispy in milk.") but it really isn't that dramatic. Here's the scoop: antonyms have been dropped from the verbal section, and more problems are devoted to reading comprehension, including a thirteen-question dual passage. The math section is pretty much the same, except for the ten Student-Generated Response (Grid In) questions they've added. And they've dumped the Test of Standard Written English (TSWE). Otherwise, the changes are pretty cosmetic. By the way, the PRA you just took was designed to take into account all these changes to the SAT.

Time and again, we hear from former students who laugh at how anxious they once were about the college admissions process. Take it seriously, do your homework, but relax. Wherever you go to school, you'll find kids getting a great education and kids goofing off, kids enjoying themselves and kids hating every minute of the day. Do your best, but don't let any person (or any standardized test) make you crazy.

Good luck!

THE PRA CHART

Directions: Follow these steps to help you decide which admissions test (ACT or SAT) better represents you.

I. Add your SAT math and verbal scores. Since they are estimates, you should estimate. For example, if your SAT math score is in the 480–640 range and your SAT verbal score is in the 450–510 range, your total would be about 520 + 480 = 1,000

II. Find your combined SAT score on the bottom line of the chart. Draw a vertical line up from that point.

III. Find your ACT score on the left side of the chart (e.g., go to 25 if your projected score is between 22 and 27). Draw a horizontal line across from that point.

IV. Look at the point where the two lines intersect. If it's in the white area, your scores on the two tests are about the same. If it's in the light grey area, your SAT score is stronger. If it's in the dark grey area, your ACT score is stronger.

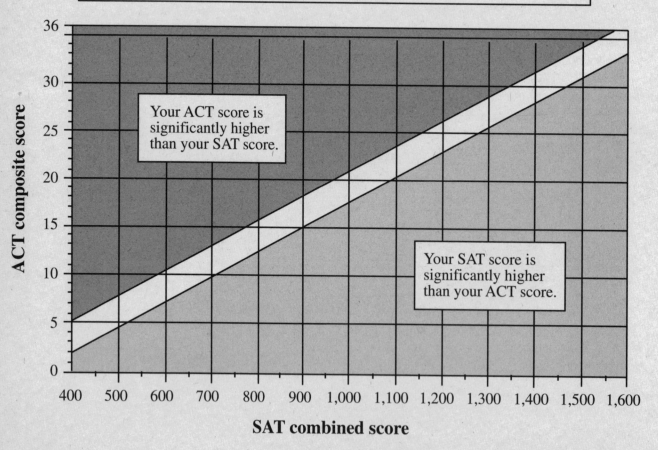

ACT composite score

Your ACT score is significantly higher than your SAT score.

Your SAT score is significantly higher than your ACT score.

SAT combined score

Each category refers to certain questions on the test. This breakdown helps you analyze your weak areas. Take a close look at each question in the category where you feel you need improvement. Try to identify the problem. Difficult vocabulary? Look up the words you don't know. Too tough a concept? Have a friend or teacher help, or refer back to the appropriate chapter in this book. Carelessness? The final analysis you have to do yourself.

ACT English   **Section 1 Questions**
Punctuation   4, 7, 8, 10, 11, 19, 22, 23, 25, 34, 43, 44, 48, 52, 54
Grammar   9, 12, 20, 21, 26, 27, 38, 40, 41, 47
Sentence Structure   2, 3, 6, 14, 18, 28, 32, 33, 36, 45, 46, 49, 50
Diction/Style   1, 5, 15, 17, 29, 31, 37, 39, 53
Logic/Organization   13, 24, 30, 35, 42, 51, 55

SAT Math   **Section 2 Questions**
Fractions/Ratios   12, 19, 35
Percent/Decimals   22, 27
Averages   23
Arithmetic Operations   4, 5, 10, 14, 16, 20, 29
Algebra Basics   1, 18
Algebra Manipulation   3, 6, 7, 9, 11, 24, 31
Angles/Lengths   2, 15, 21, 25, 32, 33, 34
Area/Perimeter/Volume   8, 17, 26, 30
Abstract Math   13, 28

ACT MATH   **Section 3 Questions**
Fractions/Ratios
Percent/Decimals   4, 8
Averages
Arithmetic Operation   2, 3
Algebra Basics   5, 12, 19
Algebra Manipulation   7, 9, 10, 11, 13, 20
Intermediate Algebra   22
Angles/Lengths   1, 6, 15, 17, 23
Area/Perimeter/Volume   25, 26
Graphs and Trig   14, 16, 18, 21, 24, 27

SAT VERBAL   **Section 4 Questions**
Sentence Completion: 1–11   Analogies: 12–23
Reading Comprehension: ■ Line reference 24, 27, 30, 34, 35, 36, 37
                                     ■ Tone 25, 28, 33, 43
                                     ■ Specifics 26, 32, 39, 46
                                     ■ General Idea 29, 31, 41, 42, 44, 45
                                     ■ Vocabulary in Context 38, 40

ACT SCIENCE
Biology

Physics
Chemistry

ACT READING
Fiction
Science
Social Science
Humanities

Section 5 Questions
1, 2, 3, 4, 5, 6, 13, 14, 15, 16, 17, 18, 19, 20
21, 22, 23, 24, 25, 26, 27, 28, 29
7, 8, 9, 10, 11
30, 31, 32, 33, 34

Section 6 Questions
1, 2, 3, 4, 5, 6, 7, 8, 9
10, 11, 12, 13, 14, 15, 16, 17, 18
19, 20, 21, 22, 23, 24, 25, 26, 27
28, 29, 30, 31, 32, 33, 34, 35, 36

ABOUT THE AUTHORS

Geoff Martz attended Dartmouth College and Columbia University, joining The Princeton Review in 1985 as a teacher and writer. His first book for The Princeton Review was *Cracking the GMAT*, published in 1989.

Ted Silver is a graduate of Yale University, the Yale University School of Medicine, and the law school at the University of Connecticut. He has been intensely involved in the fields of education and testing since 1976, and has written several books and computer tutorials pertaining to those fields. He became affiliated with The Princeton Review in 1988 as the chief architect of The Princeton Review's MCAT course. Dr. Silver's fulltime profession is as Associate Professor of Law at Touro College Jacob D. Fuchsberg Law Center.

Kim Magloire is a graduate of Princeton University. She joined The Princeton Review in 1984 as an SAT teacher, and has since taught The Princeton Review's SAT II, LSAT, GMAT, GRE, and MCAT programs. Magloire is currently attending graduate school at Columbia University.

PRINCETON REVIEW ASSESSMENT
ANSWER SHEET

Start with number 1 for each new section. If a section has fewer questions than answer spaces, leave the extra answer spaces blank.

SECTION 1

1 cAɔ cBɔ cCɔ cDɔ cEɔ
2 cFɔ cGɔ cHɔ cJɔ cKɔ
3 cAɔ cBɔ cCɔ cDɔ cEɔ
4 cFɔ cGɔ cHɔ cJɔ cKɔ
5 cAɔ cBɔ cCɔ cDɔ cEɔ
6 cFɔ cGɔ cHɔ cJɔ cKɔ
7 cAɔ cBɔ cCɔ cDɔ cEɔ
8 cFɔ cGɔ cHɔ cJɔ cKɔ
9 cAɔ cBɔ cCɔ cDɔ cEɔ
10 cFɔ cGɔ cHɔ cJɔ cKɔ
11 cAɔ cBɔ cCɔ cDɔ cEɔ
12 cFɔ cGɔ cHɔ cJɔ cKɔ
13 cAɔ cBɔ cCɔ cDɔ cEɔ
14 cFɔ cGɔ cHɔ cJɔ cKɔ
15 cAɔ cBɔ cCɔ cDɔ cEɔ

16 cFɔ cGɔ cHɔ cJɔ cKɔ
17 cAɔ cBɔ cCɔ cDɔ cEɔ
18 cFɔ cGɔ cHɔ cJɔ cKɔ
19 cAɔ cBɔ cCɔ cDɔ cEɔ
20 cFɔ cGɔ cHɔ cJɔ cKɔ
21 cAɔ cBɔ cCɔ cDɔ cEɔ
22 cFɔ cGɔ cHɔ cJɔ cKɔ
23 cAɔ cBɔ cCɔ cDɔ cEɔ
24 cFɔ cGɔ cHɔ cJɔ cKɔ
25 cAɔ cBɔ cCɔ cDɔ cEɔ
26 cFɔ cGɔ cHɔ cJɔ cKɔ
27 cAɔ cBɔ cCɔ cDɔ cEɔ
28 cFɔ cGɔ cHɔ cJɔ cKɔ
29 cAɔ cBɔ cCɔ cDɔ cEɔ
30 cFɔ cGɔ cHɔ cJɔ cKɔ

31 cAɔ cBɔ cCɔ cDɔ cEɔ
32 cFɔ cGɔ cHɔ cJɔ cKɔ
33 cAɔ cBɔ cCɔ cDɔ cEɔ
34 cFɔ cGɔ cHɔ cJɔ cKɔ
35 cAɔ cBɔ cCɔ cDɔ cEɔ
36 cFɔ cGɔ cHɔ cJɔ cKɔ
37 cAɔ cBɔ cCɔ cDɔ cEɔ
38 cFɔ cGɔ cHɔ cJɔ cKɔ
39 cAɔ cBɔ cCɔ cDɔ cEɔ
40 cFɔ cGɔ cHɔ cJɔ cKɔ
41 cAɔ cBɔ cCɔ cDɔ cEɔ
42 cFɔ cGɔ cHɔ cJɔ cKɔ
43 cAɔ cBɔ cCɔ cDɔ cEɔ
44 cFɔ cGɔ cHɔ cJɔ cKɔ
45 cAɔ cBɔ cCɔ cDɔ cEɔ

46 cFɔ cGɔ cHɔ cJɔ cKɔ
47 cAɔ cBɔ cCɔ cDɔ cEɔ
48 cFɔ cGɔ cHɔ cJɔ cKɔ
49 cAɔ cBɔ cCɔ cDɔ cEɔ
50 cFɔ cGɔ cHɔ cJɔ cKɔ
51 cAɔ cBɔ cCɔ cDɔ cEɔ
52 cFɔ cGɔ cHɔ cJɔ cKɔ
53 cAɔ cBɔ cCɔ cDɔ cEɔ
54 cFɔ cGɔ cHɔ cJɔ cKɔ
55 cAɔ cBɔ cCɔ cDɔ cEɔ
56 cFɔ cGɔ cHɔ cJɔ cKɔ
57 cAɔ cBɔ cCɔ cDɔ cEɔ
58 cFɔ cGɔ cHɔ cJɔ cKɔ
59 cAɔ cBɔ cCɔ cDɔ cEɔ
60 cFɔ cGɔ cHɔ cJɔ cKɔ

SECTION 2

1 cAɔ cBɔ cCɔ cDɔ cEɔ
2 cAɔ cBɔ cCɔ cDɔ cEɔ
3 cAɔ cBɔ cCɔ cDɔ cEɔ
4 cAɔ cBɔ cCɔ cDɔ cEɔ
5 cAɔ cBɔ cCɔ cDɔ cEɔ
6 cAɔ cBɔ cCɔ cDɔ cEɔ
7 cAɔ cBɔ cCɔ cDɔ cEɔ
8 cAɔ cBɔ cCɔ cDɔ cEɔ
9 cAɔ cBɔ cCɔ cDɔ cEɔ
10 cAɔ cBɔ cCɔ cDɔ cEɔ

Grid-in questions 11, 12, 13, 14, 15, 16, 17 (bubble grids 0–9 with fraction/decimal marks)

18 cAɔ cBɔ cCɔ cDɔ cEɔ
19 cAɔ cBɔ cCɔ cDɔ cEɔ
20 cAɔ cBɔ cCɔ cDɔ cEɔ
21 cAɔ cBɔ cCɔ cDɔ cEɔ
22 cAɔ cBɔ cCɔ cDɔ cEɔ

23 cAɔ cBɔ cCɔ cDɔ cEɔ
24 cAɔ cBɔ cCɔ cDɔ cEɔ
25 cAɔ cBɔ cCɔ cDɔ cEɔ
26 cAɔ cBɔ cCɔ cDɔ cEɔ
27 cAɔ cBɔ cCɔ cDɔ cEɔ

28 cAɔ cBɔ cCɔ cDɔ cEɔ
29 cAɔ cBɔ cCɔ cDɔ cEɔ
30 cAɔ cBɔ cCɔ cDɔ cEɔ
31 cAɔ cBɔ cCɔ cDɔ cEɔ
32 cAɔ cBɔ cCɔ cDɔ cEɔ

33 cAɔ cBɔ cCɔ cDɔ cEɔ
34 cAɔ cBɔ cCɔ cDɔ cEɔ
35 cAɔ cBɔ cCɔ cDɔ cEɔ
36 cAɔ cBɔ cCɔ cDɔ cEɔ
37 cAɔ cBɔ cCɔ cDɔ cEɔ

BE SURE TO ERASE ANY ERRORS OR STRAY MARKS COMPLETELY.

Start with number 1 for each new section. If a section has fewer questions than answer spaces, leave the extra answer spaces blank.

SECTION 3

1 ⊂A⊃ ⊂B⊃ ⊂C⊃ ⊂D⊃ ⊂E⊃	8 ⊂F⊃ ⊂G⊃ ⊂H⊃ ⊂J⊃ ⊂K⊃	15 ⊂A⊃ ⊂B⊃ ⊂C⊃ ⊂D⊃ ⊂E⊃	22 ⊂F⊃ ⊂G⊃ ⊂H⊃ ⊂J⊃ ⊂K⊃
2 ⊂F⊃ ⊂G⊃ ⊂H⊃ ⊂J⊃ ⊂K⊃	9 ⊂A⊃ ⊂B⊃ ⊂C⊃ ⊂D⊃ ⊂E⊃	16 ⊂F⊃ ⊂G⊃ ⊂H⊃ ⊂J⊃ ⊂K⊃	23 ⊂A⊃ ⊂B⊃ ⊂C⊃ ⊂D⊃ ⊂E⊃
3 ⊂A⊃ ⊂B⊃ ⊂C⊃ ⊂D⊃ ⊂E⊃	10 ⊂F⊃ ⊂G⊃ ⊂H⊃ ⊂J⊃ ⊂K⊃	17 ⊂A⊃ ⊂B⊃ ⊂C⊃ ⊂D⊃ ⊂E⊃	24 ⊂F⊃ ⊂G⊃ ⊂H⊃ ⊂J⊃ ⊂K⊃
4 ⊂F⊃ ⊂G⊃ ⊂H⊃ ⊂J⊃ ⊂K⊃	11 ⊂A⊃ ⊂B⊃ ⊂C⊃ ⊂D⊃ ⊂E⊃	18 ⊂F⊃ ⊂G⊃ ⊂H⊃ ⊂J⊃ ⊂K⊃	25 ⊂A⊃ ⊂B⊃ ⊂C⊃ ⊂D⊃ ⊂E⊃
5 ⊂A⊃ ⊂B⊃ ⊂C⊃ ⊂D⊃ ⊂E⊃	12 ⊂F⊃ ⊂G⊃ ⊂H⊃ ⊂J⊃ ⊂K⊃	19 ⊂A⊃ ⊂B⊃ ⊂C⊃ ⊂D⊃ ⊂E⊃	26 ⊂F⊃ ⊂G⊃ ⊂H⊃ ⊂J⊃ ⊂K⊃
6 ⊂F⊃ ⊂G⊃ ⊂H⊃ ⊂J⊃ ⊂K⊃	13 ⊂A⊃ ⊂B⊃ ⊂C⊃ ⊂D⊃ ⊂E⊃	20 ⊂F⊃ ⊂G⊃ ⊂H⊃ ⊂J⊃ ⊂K⊃	27 ⊂A⊃ ⊂B⊃ ⊂C⊃ ⊂D⊃ ⊂E⊃
7 ⊂A⊃ ⊂B⊃ ⊂C⊃ ⊂D⊃ ⊂E⊃	14 ⊂F⊃ ⊂G⊃ ⊂H⊃ ⊂J⊃ ⊂K⊃	21 ⊂A⊃ ⊂B⊃ ⊂C⊃ ⊂D⊃ ⊂E⊃	28 ⊂F⊃ ⊂G⊃ ⊂H⊃ ⊂J⊃ ⊂K⊃

SECTION 4

1 ⊂A⊃ ⊂B⊃ ⊂C⊃ ⊂D⊃ ⊂E⊃	16 ⊂A⊃ ⊂B⊃ ⊂C⊃ ⊂D⊃ ⊂E⊃	31 ⊂A⊃ ⊂B⊃ ⊂C⊃ ⊂D⊃ ⊂E⊃	46 ⊂A⊃ ⊂B⊃ ⊂C⊃ ⊂D⊃ ⊂E⊃
2 ⊂A⊃ ⊂B⊃ ⊂C⊃ ⊂D⊃ ⊂E⊃	17 ⊂A⊃ ⊂B⊃ ⊂C⊃ ⊂D⊃ ⊂E⊃	32 ⊂A⊃ ⊂B⊃ ⊂C⊃ ⊂D⊃ ⊂E⊃	47 ⊂A⊃ ⊂B⊃ ⊂C⊃ ⊂D⊃ ⊂E⊃
3 ⊂A⊃ ⊂B⊃ ⊂C⊃ ⊂D⊃ ⊂E⊃	18 ⊂A⊃ ⊂B⊃ ⊂C⊃ ⊂D⊃ ⊂E⊃	33 ⊂A⊃ ⊂B⊃ ⊂C⊃ ⊂D⊃ ⊂E⊃	48 ⊂A⊃ ⊂B⊃ ⊂C⊃ ⊂D⊃ ⊂E⊃
4 ⊂A⊃ ⊂B⊃ ⊂C⊃ ⊂D⊃ ⊂E⊃	19 ⊂A⊃ ⊂B⊃ ⊂C⊃ ⊂D⊃ ⊂E⊃	34 ⊂A⊃ ⊂B⊃ ⊂C⊃ ⊂D⊃ ⊂E⊃	49 ⊂A⊃ ⊂B⊃ ⊂C⊃ ⊂D⊃ ⊂E⊃
5 ⊂A⊃ ⊂B⊃ ⊂C⊃ ⊂D⊃ ⊂E⊃	20 ⊂A⊃ ⊂B⊃ ⊂C⊃ ⊂D⊃ ⊂E⊃	35 ⊂A⊃ ⊂B⊃ ⊂C⊃ ⊂D⊃ ⊂E⊃	50 ⊂A⊃ ⊂B⊃ ⊂C⊃ ⊂D⊃ ⊂E⊃
6 ⊂A⊃ ⊂B⊃ ⊂C⊃ ⊂D⊃ ⊂E⊃	21 ⊂A⊃ ⊂B⊃ ⊂C⊃ ⊂D⊃ ⊂E⊃	36 ⊂A⊃ ⊂B⊃ ⊂C⊃ ⊂D⊃ ⊂E⊃	51 ⊂A⊃ ⊂B⊃ ⊂C⊃ ⊂D⊃ ⊂E⊃
7 ⊂A⊃ ⊂B⊃ ⊂C⊃ ⊂D⊃ ⊂E⊃	22 ⊂A⊃ ⊂B⊃ ⊂C⊃ ⊂D⊃ ⊂E⊃	37 ⊂A⊃ ⊂B⊃ ⊂C⊃ ⊂D⊃ ⊂E⊃	52 ⊂A⊃ ⊂B⊃ ⊂C⊃ ⊂D⊃ ⊂E⊃
8 ⊂A⊃ ⊂B⊃ ⊂C⊃ ⊂D⊃ ⊂E⊃	23 ⊂A⊃ ⊂B⊃ ⊂C⊃ ⊂D⊃ ⊂E⊃	38 ⊂A⊃ ⊂B⊃ ⊂C⊃ ⊂D⊃ ⊂E⊃	53 ⊂A⊃ ⊂B⊃ ⊂C⊃ ⊂D⊃ ⊂E⊃
9 ⊂A⊃ ⊂B⊃ ⊂C⊃ ⊂D⊃ ⊂E⊃	24 ⊂A⊃ ⊂B⊃ ⊂C⊃ ⊂D⊃ ⊂E⊃	39 ⊂A⊃ ⊂B⊃ ⊂C⊃ ⊂D⊃ ⊂E⊃	54 ⊂A⊃ ⊂B⊃ ⊂C⊃ ⊂D⊃ ⊂E⊃
10 ⊂A⊃ ⊂B⊃ ⊂C⊃ ⊂D⊃ ⊂E⊃	25 ⊂A⊃ ⊂B⊃ ⊂C⊃ ⊂D⊃ ⊂E⊃	40 ⊂A⊃ ⊂B⊃ ⊂C⊃ ⊂D⊃ ⊂E⊃	55 ⊂A⊃ ⊂B⊃ ⊂C⊃ ⊂D⊃ ⊂E⊃
11 ⊂A⊃ ⊂B⊃ ⊂C⊃ ⊂D⊃ ⊂E⊃	26 ⊂A⊃ ⊂B⊃ ⊂C⊃ ⊂D⊃ ⊂E⊃	41 ⊂A⊃ ⊂B⊃ ⊂C⊃ ⊂D⊃ ⊂E⊃	56 ⊂A⊃ ⊂B⊃ ⊂C⊃ ⊂D⊃ ⊂E⊃
12 ⊂A⊃ ⊂B⊃ ⊂C⊃ ⊂D⊃ ⊂E⊃	27 ⊂A⊃ ⊂B⊃ ⊂C⊃ ⊂D⊃ ⊂E⊃	42 ⊂A⊃ ⊂B⊃ ⊂C⊃ ⊂D⊃ ⊂E⊃	57 ⊂A⊃ ⊂B⊃ ⊂C⊃ ⊂D⊃ ⊂E⊃
13 ⊂A⊃ ⊂B⊃ ⊂C⊃ ⊂D⊃ ⊂E⊃	28 ⊂A⊃ ⊂B⊃ ⊂C⊃ ⊂D⊃ ⊂E⊃	43 ⊂A⊃ ⊂B⊃ ⊂C⊃ ⊂D⊃ ⊂E⊃	58 ⊂A⊃ ⊂B⊃ ⊂C⊃ ⊂D⊃ ⊂E⊃
14 ⊂A⊃ ⊂B⊃ ⊂C⊃ ⊂D⊃ ⊂E⊃	29 ⊂A⊃ ⊂B⊃ ⊂C⊃ ⊂D⊃ ⊂E⊃	44 ⊂A⊃ ⊂B⊃ ⊂C⊃ ⊂D⊃ ⊂E⊃	59 ⊂A⊃ ⊂B⊃ ⊂C⊃ ⊂D⊃ ⊂E⊃
15 ⊂A⊃ ⊂B⊃ ⊂C⊃ ⊂D⊃ ⊂E⊃	30 ⊂A⊃ ⊂B⊃ ⊂C⊃ ⊂D⊃ ⊂E⊃	45 ⊂A⊃ ⊂B⊃ ⊂C⊃ ⊂D⊃ ⊂E⊃	60 ⊂A⊃ ⊂B⊃ ⊂C⊃ ⊂D⊃ ⊂E⊃

SECTION 5

1 ⊂A⊃ ⊂B⊃ ⊂C⊃ ⊂D⊃ ⊂E⊃	16 ⊂F⊃ ⊂G⊃ ⊂H⊃ ⊂J⊃ ⊂K⊃	31 ⊂A⊃ ⊂B⊃ ⊂C⊃ ⊂D⊃ ⊂E⊃	46 ⊂F⊃ ⊂G⊃ ⊂H⊃ ⊂J⊃ ⊂K⊃
2 ⊂F⊃ ⊂G⊃ ⊂H⊃ ⊂J⊃ ⊂K⊃	17 ⊂A⊃ ⊂B⊃ ⊂C⊃ ⊂D⊃ ⊂E⊃	32 ⊂F⊃ ⊂G⊃ ⊂H⊃ ⊂J⊃ ⊂K⊃	47 ⊂A⊃ ⊂B⊃ ⊂C⊃ ⊂D⊃ ⊂E⊃
3 ⊂A⊃ ⊂B⊃ ⊂C⊃ ⊂D⊃ ⊂E⊃	18 ⊂F⊃ ⊂G⊃ ⊂H⊃ ⊂J⊃ ⊂K⊃	33 ⊂A⊃ ⊂B⊃ ⊂C⊃ ⊂D⊃ ⊂E⊃	48 ⊂F⊃ ⊂G⊃ ⊂H⊃ ⊂J⊃ ⊂K⊃
4 ⊂F⊃ ⊂G⊃ ⊂H⊃ ⊂J⊃ ⊂K⊃	19 ⊂A⊃ ⊂B⊃ ⊂C⊃ ⊂D⊃ ⊂E⊃	34 ⊂F⊃ ⊂G⊃ ⊂H⊃ ⊂J⊃ ⊂K⊃	49 ⊂A⊃ ⊂B⊃ ⊂C⊃ ⊂D⊃ ⊂E⊃
5 ⊂A⊃ ⊂B⊃ ⊂C⊃ ⊂D⊃ ⊂E⊃	20 ⊂F⊃ ⊂G⊃ ⊂H⊃ ⊂J⊃ ⊂K⊃	35 ⊂A⊃ ⊂B⊃ ⊂C⊃ ⊂D⊃ ⊂E⊃	50 ⊂F⊃ ⊂G⊃ ⊂H⊃ ⊂J⊃ ⊂K⊃
6 ⊂F⊃ ⊂G⊃ ⊂H⊃ ⊂J⊃ ⊂K⊃	21 ⊂A⊃ ⊂B⊃ ⊂C⊃ ⊂D⊃ ⊂E⊃	36 ⊂F⊃ ⊂G⊃ ⊂H⊃ ⊂J⊃ ⊂K⊃	51 ⊂A⊃ ⊂B⊃ ⊂C⊃ ⊂D⊃ ⊂E⊃
7 ⊂A⊃ ⊂B⊃ ⊂C⊃ ⊂D⊃ ⊂E⊃	22 ⊂F⊃ ⊂G⊃ ⊂H⊃ ⊂J⊃ ⊂K⊃	37 ⊂A⊃ ⊂B⊃ ⊂C⊃ ⊂D⊃ ⊂E⊃	52 ⊂F⊃ ⊂G⊃ ⊂H⊃ ⊂J⊃ ⊂K⊃
8 ⊂F⊃ ⊂G⊃ ⊂H⊃ ⊂J⊃ ⊂K⊃	23 ⊂A⊃ ⊂B⊃ ⊂C⊃ ⊂D⊃ ⊂E⊃	38 ⊂F⊃ ⊂G⊃ ⊂H⊃ ⊂J⊃ ⊂K⊃	53 ⊂A⊃ ⊂B⊃ ⊂C⊃ ⊂D⊃ ⊂E⊃
9 ⊂A⊃ ⊂B⊃ ⊂C⊃ ⊂D⊃ ⊂E⊃	24 ⊂F⊃ ⊂G⊃ ⊂H⊃ ⊂J⊃ ⊂K⊃	39 ⊂A⊃ ⊂B⊃ ⊂C⊃ ⊂D⊃ ⊂E⊃	54 ⊂F⊃ ⊂G⊃ ⊂H⊃ ⊂J⊃ ⊂K⊃
10 ⊂F⊃ ⊂G⊃ ⊂H⊃ ⊂J⊃ ⊂K⊃	25 ⊂A⊃ ⊂B⊃ ⊂C⊃ ⊂D⊃ ⊂E⊃	40 ⊂F⊃ ⊂G⊃ ⊂H⊃ ⊂J⊃ ⊂K⊃	55 ⊂A⊃ ⊂B⊃ ⊂C⊃ ⊂D⊃ ⊂E⊃
11 ⊂A⊃ ⊂B⊃ ⊂C⊃ ⊂D⊃ ⊂E⊃	26 ⊂F⊃ ⊂G⊃ ⊂H⊃ ⊂J⊃ ⊂K⊃	41 ⊂A⊃ ⊂B⊃ ⊂C⊃ ⊂D⊃ ⊂E⊃	56 ⊂F⊃ ⊂G⊃ ⊂H⊃ ⊂J⊃ ⊂K⊃
12 ⊂F⊃ ⊂G⊃ ⊂H⊃ ⊂J⊃ ⊂K⊃	27 ⊂A⊃ ⊂B⊃ ⊂C⊃ ⊂D⊃ ⊂E⊃	42 ⊂F⊃ ⊂G⊃ ⊂H⊃ ⊂J⊃ ⊂K⊃	57 ⊂A⊃ ⊂B⊃ ⊂C⊃ ⊂D⊃ ⊂E⊃
13 ⊂A⊃ ⊂B⊃ ⊂C⊃ ⊂D⊃ ⊂E⊃	28 ⊂F⊃ ⊂G⊃ ⊂H⊃ ⊂J⊃ ⊂K⊃	43 ⊂A⊃ ⊂B⊃ ⊂C⊃ ⊂D⊃ ⊂E⊃	58 ⊂F⊃ ⊂G⊃ ⊂H⊃ ⊂J⊃ ⊂K⊃
14 ⊂F⊃ ⊂G⊃ ⊂H⊃ ⊂J⊃ ⊂K⊃	29 ⊂A⊃ ⊂B⊃ ⊂C⊃ ⊂D⊃ ⊂E⊃	44 ⊂F⊃ ⊂G⊃ ⊂H⊃ ⊂J⊃ ⊂K⊃	59 ⊂A⊃ ⊂B⊃ ⊂C⊃ ⊂D⊃ ⊂E⊃
15 ⊂A⊃ ⊂B⊃ ⊂C⊃ ⊂D⊃ ⊂E⊃	30 ⊂F⊃ ⊂G⊃ ⊂H⊃ ⊂J⊃ ⊂K⊃	45 ⊂A⊃ ⊂B⊃ ⊂C⊃ ⊂D⊃ ⊂E⊃	60 ⊂F⊃ ⊂G⊃ ⊂H⊃ ⊂J⊃ ⊂K⊃

SECTION 6

1 ⊂A⊃ ⊂B⊃ ⊂C⊃ ⊂D⊃ ⊂E⊃	16 ⊂F⊃ ⊂G⊃ ⊂H⊃ ⊂J⊃ ⊂K⊃	31 ⊂A⊃ ⊂B⊃ ⊂C⊃ ⊂D⊃ ⊂E⊃	46 ⊂F⊃ ⊂G⊃ ⊂H⊃ ⊂J⊃ ⊂K⊃
2 ⊂F⊃ ⊂G⊃ ⊂H⊃ ⊂J⊃ ⊂K⊃	17 ⊂A⊃ ⊂B⊃ ⊂C⊃ ⊂D⊃ ⊂E⊃	32 ⊂F⊃ ⊂G⊃ ⊂H⊃ ⊂J⊃ ⊂K⊃	47 ⊂A⊃ ⊂B⊃ ⊂C⊃ ⊂D⊃ ⊂E⊃
3 ⊂A⊃ ⊂B⊃ ⊂C⊃ ⊂D⊃ ⊂E⊃	18 ⊂F⊃ ⊂G⊃ ⊂H⊃ ⊂J⊃ ⊂K⊃	33 ⊂A⊃ ⊂B⊃ ⊂C⊃ ⊂D⊃ ⊂E⊃	48 ⊂F⊃ ⊂G⊃ ⊂H⊃ ⊂J⊃ ⊂K⊃
4 ⊂F⊃ ⊂G⊃ ⊂H⊃ ⊂J⊃ ⊂K⊃	19 ⊂A⊃ ⊂B⊃ ⊂C⊃ ⊂D⊃ ⊂E⊃	34 ⊂F⊃ ⊂G⊃ ⊂H⊃ ⊂J⊃ ⊂K⊃	49 ⊂A⊃ ⊂B⊃ ⊂C⊃ ⊂D⊃ ⊂E⊃
5 ⊂A⊃ ⊂B⊃ ⊂C⊃ ⊂D⊃ ⊂E⊃	20 ⊂F⊃ ⊂G⊃ ⊂H⊃ ⊂J⊃ ⊂K⊃	35 ⊂A⊃ ⊂B⊃ ⊂C⊃ ⊂D⊃ ⊂E⊃	50 ⊂F⊃ ⊂G⊃ ⊂H⊃ ⊂J⊃ ⊂K⊃
6 ⊂F⊃ ⊂G⊃ ⊂H⊃ ⊂J⊃ ⊂K⊃	21 ⊂A⊃ ⊂B⊃ ⊂C⊃ ⊂D⊃ ⊂E⊃	36 ⊂F⊃ ⊂G⊃ ⊂H⊃ ⊂J⊃ ⊂K⊃	51 ⊂A⊃ ⊂B⊃ ⊂C⊃ ⊂D⊃ ⊂E⊃
7 ⊂A⊃ ⊂B⊃ ⊂C⊃ ⊂D⊃ ⊂E⊃	22 ⊂F⊃ ⊂G⊃ ⊂H⊃ ⊂J⊃ ⊂K⊃	37 ⊂A⊃ ⊂B⊃ ⊂C⊃ ⊂D⊃ ⊂E⊃	52 ⊂F⊃ ⊂G⊃ ⊂H⊃ ⊂J⊃ ⊂K⊃
8 ⊂F⊃ ⊂G⊃ ⊂H⊃ ⊂J⊃ ⊂K⊃	23 ⊂A⊃ ⊂B⊃ ⊂C⊃ ⊂D⊃ ⊂E⊃	38 ⊂F⊃ ⊂G⊃ ⊂H⊃ ⊂J⊃ ⊂K⊃	53 ⊂A⊃ ⊂B⊃ ⊂C⊃ ⊂D⊃ ⊂E⊃
9 ⊂A⊃ ⊂B⊃ ⊂C⊃ ⊂D⊃ ⊂E⊃	24 ⊂F⊃ ⊂G⊃ ⊂H⊃ ⊂J⊃ ⊂K⊃	39 ⊂A⊃ ⊂B⊃ ⊂C⊃ ⊂D⊃ ⊂E⊃	54 ⊂F⊃ ⊂G⊃ ⊂H⊃ ⊂J⊃ ⊂K⊃
10 ⊂F⊃ ⊂G⊃ ⊂H⊃ ⊂J⊃ ⊂K⊃	25 ⊂A⊃ ⊂B⊃ ⊂C⊃ ⊂D⊃ ⊂E⊃	40 ⊂F⊃ ⊂G⊃ ⊂H⊃ ⊂J⊃ ⊂K⊃	55 ⊂A⊃ ⊂B⊃ ⊂C⊃ ⊂D⊃ ⊂E⊃
11 ⊂A⊃ ⊂B⊃ ⊂C⊃ ⊂D⊃ ⊂E⊃	26 ⊂F⊃ ⊂G⊃ ⊂H⊃ ⊂J⊃ ⊂K⊃	41 ⊂A⊃ ⊂B⊃ ⊂C⊃ ⊂D⊃ ⊂E⊃	56 ⊂F⊃ ⊂G⊃ ⊂H⊃ ⊂J⊃ ⊂K⊃
12 ⊂F⊃ ⊂G⊃ ⊂H⊃ ⊂J⊃ ⊂K⊃	27 ⊂A⊃ ⊂B⊃ ⊂C⊃ ⊂D⊃ ⊂E⊃	42 ⊂F⊃ ⊂G⊃ ⊂H⊃ ⊂J⊃ ⊂K⊃	57 ⊂A⊃ ⊂B⊃ ⊂C⊃ ⊂D⊃ ⊂E⊃
13 ⊂A⊃ ⊂B⊃ ⊂C⊃ ⊂D⊃ ⊂E⊃	28 ⊂F⊃ ⊂G⊃ ⊂H⊃ ⊂J⊃ ⊂K⊃	43 ⊂A⊃ ⊂B⊃ ⊂C⊃ ⊂D⊃ ⊂E⊃	58 ⊂F⊃ ⊂G⊃ ⊂H⊃ ⊂J⊃ ⊂K⊃
14 ⊂F⊃ ⊂G⊃ ⊂H⊃ ⊂J⊃ ⊂K⊃	29 ⊂A⊃ ⊂B⊃ ⊂C⊃ ⊂D⊃ ⊂E⊃	44 ⊂F⊃ ⊂G⊃ ⊂H⊃ ⊂J⊃ ⊂K⊃	59 ⊂A⊃ ⊂B⊃ ⊂C⊃ ⊂D⊃ ⊂E⊃
15 ⊂A⊃ ⊂B⊃ ⊂C⊃ ⊂D⊃ ⊂E⊃	30 ⊂F⊃ ⊂G⊃ ⊂H⊃ ⊂J⊃ ⊂K⊃	45 ⊂A⊃ ⊂B⊃ ⊂C⊃ ⊂D⊃ ⊂E⊃	60 ⊂F⊃ ⊂G⊃ ⊂H⊃ ⊂J⊃ ⊂K⊃

BE SURE TO ERASE ANY ERRORS OR STRAY MARKS COMPLETELY.